NEWMAN THE THEOLOGIAN

NEWMAN
THE THEOLOGIAN

The Nature of Belief and Doctrine as
Exemplified in His Life and Works

by

J.-H. WALGRAVE, O.P.

Translated by A. V. LITTLEDALE

SHEED & WARD - NEW YORK

This book is a translation of *Newman, le Developpement du Dogme* by J.-H. Walgrave, O.P., which was first published by Casterman, Tournai and Paris, in 1957.

Nihil obstat: Carolus Davis, S.T.L., *Censor Deputatus*
Imprimatur: E. Morrogh Bernard, *Vic. Gen.*
Westmonasterii, die 8a Septembris, 1960.

Acknowledgement
The quotations on pp. 365-367 are taken from *The Victorian Sage* by J. Holloway, by kind permission of Macmillan & Co.

Library of Congress Catalog Card Number 60-16895

Made and printed in Great Britain.

Contents

v

PART II

THE GROWTH OF FAITH AND DOGMA. THE PROBLEM OF DEVELOPMENT

PART III

THE IMMUTABILITY OF FAITH AND DOCTRINE
THE PROBLEM OF TRADITION AND ITS CONTINUITY

PART IV

MERITS AND DEFECTS OF NEWMAN'S DOCTRINE
A CRITICAL ASSESSMENT

APPENDICES

ABBREVIATIONS*

Apologia	*Apologia pro Vita Sua* (Everyman's Library)
Arians	*The Arians of the Fourth Century*
Diff. Angl.	*Certain Difficulties felt by Anglicans in Catholic Teaching*
Disc. Arg.	*Discussions and Arguments*
Disc. M. Cong.	*Discourses addressed to Mixed Congregations*
Essay	*An Essay on the Development of Christian Doctrine*
Ess. Crit. Hist.	*Essays Critical and Historical*
Grammar	*Essay in Aid of a Grammar of Assent*
Idea	*The Idea of a University*
Newman-Perrone	*The Newman-Perrone Paper on Development*, ed. Rev. T. Lynch in *Gregorianum*, XVI (1935), 403-444.
Occ. Ser.	*Sermons Preached on Various Occasions*
O.U.S.	*Fifteen Sermons Preached before the University of Oxford*
P.P.S.	*Parochial and Plain Sermons* (Rivington London 1882)
Present Position	*Lectures on the Present Position of Catholics in England* (J. Duffy, Dublin, 1857)
Ser. Subj.	*Sermons on Subjects of the Day*

* Where the edition used is not stated, the reference is to the edition of Longmans, Green & Co.

PREFACE

SINCE the middle of the last century, the various techniques of science have been pressed into the service of the historian of Christian dogma. The facts brought to light by this microscopic scrutiny bring the Catholic apologist sharply up against the problem of the development of doctrine, one of the most difficult he has ever had to confront.[1] Newman, however, at the time of the Oxford Movement, long before this problem was generally recognised, had seen it as concerning him vitally and ineluctably in his journey "ex umbris et imaginibus in veritatem". He attacked it with all the force of his intellect, and the victory he gained revealed to him a "Blessed Vision of Peace"[2] : the living Church of Christ. It is due to him that the idea of development has found a permanent place in Anglican theology.[3] In the Catholic field, his *Essay* opened up new problems in the history of dogma, broadened its scope, and rendered more fruitful its

[1] Cf. R. Draguet, "Évolution des dogmes", in *Apologétique*, ed. by M. Brillant and M. Nédoncelle (Paris), p.1167; A. Janssens, *Inleiding tot de Theologie* (Brussels, 1934), pp.120-121.

[2] So Newman describes the Church at the close of his unfinished work, *Essay on the Development of Christian Doctrine*, which he left off as a result of his "vision of the Catholic Church" on the night of his conversion. Cf. *Essay*, p.445.

[3] Cf. A. M. Fairbairn, *The Place of Christ in Modern Theology* (London, New York, 1893), p.23. Typical of the High Church attitude is Gore, who admits evolution in the early centuries, but denies its application to recent Roman dogmas. Cf. C. Gore, *The Holy Spirit and the Church* (London, 1924), p.212.

pursuit.[1] If only for its historic significance, Newman's work merits close study.

But, in addition, Newman's own personality, in the eyes of a Catholic, has all the marks of the guidance of Providence. We have only to view his entry into the Church as he would have done—that is, in the light of the action of Divine Providence—to be strongly convinced that he was entrusted with a special mission. His wonderful genius, so concordant with the modern outlook; his holiness, in its high dignity so deeply touching the heart of men to-day; his life and conversion, still a living apologia of the Church for many in our time—all this must, surely, have a special purpose in the designs of God. This idea is reinforced by the actions of Popes Leo XIII and Pius X : the former publicly ratifying his work by creating him a cardinal, the latter publishing a special Brief to clear him of any taint of modernism.[2] These acts give us strong encouragement to examine objectively his views on the evolution of doctrine, in order to throw as much light as possible on this difficult problem.

A whole literature has grown up round Newman's theory. It has given rise to commentaries and opinions of the most varied kinds, and this only increases the difficulty of the subject. The most important works are unquestionably those of Jean Guitton[3] and James J. Byrne.[4] Both of them trace the idea of doctrinal evolution in Newman's Anglican writings up to the *Essay*. Guitton gives particular attention to the analysis of some of his principal works : *The Arians of the Fourth Century, The Prophetical Office of the Church, An Essay on the Development of Christian Doctrine*. Guitton succeeds admirably in viewing Newman's thought in the light of his very distinctive personality and in the setting of his life; but he is mainly concerned with his theory in its philosophical aspect, and the work concludes with a criticism from this standpoint. Byrne's little work is a perfect complement to Guitton. It deals with three distinct questions, whose successive occurrence to Newman's mind sowed and brought to fruition the

[1] Cf. Draguet, *op. cit.*, pp.1175-1176.

[2] See his letter to Mgr. O'Dwyer, "Tum Illud Opusculum" (March 10, 1908) *Revue Théologique*, XL (1908), 419-420.

[3] J. Guitton, *La philosophie de Newman: Essai sur l'Idée de développement* (Paris, 1933).

[4] James J. Byrne, "The Notion of Doctrinal Development in the Anglican Writings of J. H. Newman", *Ephem. Theol. Lov.*, XIV (1937), pp.230-287.

idea of evolution; these were the development of scriptural knowledge, of the *credo*, and of the idea. These two writers, however,
hardly touch upon Newman's Catholic writings. Moreover,
neither of them tried to assemble all Newman's observations on
evolution dispersed among his various works, in order to compare
and evaluate them and work out a synthesis. That work yet remains to be done, and it is to that task that our own efforts are
directed.

We began by reading through, and carefully analysing, all the
works of Newman; but it soon became evident that we should
have to work out a complete synthesis of his thought with his
Essay of 1845 as the nucleus. For all the main arteries of his
thought, during the Anglican period, converge on this book, at
once so characteristic and so definite a turning-point in his life.
From that time, the essential lines of his theory of development
are firmly established. The future Cardinal returned to it explicitly on only one occasion, when, in 1847, he submitted his theory
to the judgment of Perrone[1] at Rome.

This, however, does not mean that he had lost interest in the
subject, or that he thought the *Essay* difficult to reconcile with a
purely Catholic view of theology. Quite the contrary, for he held
that the criticisms of Perrone did not affect in the least the essence
of his theory[2] and, right up to his death, he held it to be consistent
with Catholic doctrine.[3] This is amply proved by the new
edition of this essay in 1878. For, about the same time, Newman
published anew his principal works as an Anglican, with the
addition of corrective notes. His purpose was to set right even the
slightest inaccuracy, and he is almost pedantically meticulous. In
the *Via Media*, the notes pile up monotonously. But, when he
comes to the theories of the *Essay*, there is nothing to retract. In
his final preface, he emphasises that his argument ranges wider
than he had first intended; it provides not merely a hypothesis
to surmount a particular difficulty, but a positive proof of the
divine origin of the Church. He concedes only one point and, in
this, shows himself too indulgent to the Protestants in taking

---

[1] T. Lynch, "The Newman-Perrone Paper on Development", *Gregorianum*,
XVL (1935), pp.402-445.

[2] Wilfrid Ward, *The Life of John Henry Cardinal Newman* (London, 1912),
I, p.185.

[3] *Ibid.* II, p.419.

certain facts as historically established; but he asks his readers to consider this merely as an *argumentum ad hominem*, a hypothetical admission of the premise of his opponents' objections.

Not only did Newman retain his allegiance to the theory expounded in the *Essay*, but its principal idea underwent continuous expansion in his mind. In his various writings he returns to it, whether in several pages or in a few sentences only. Here and there we come across observations of great interest, even fresh ideas, which throw new light on the theory, imparting to it a profound and novel meaning. They occur, at times, in his studies of new subjects, which may be looked upon as new chapters in the theory of development. In his later works, especially in the *Grammar of Assent*, he explores and vindicates the psychological and methodological grounds of the *Essay*. All this goes to show that a synthetic study, based on an exhaustive analysis of his complete works, must be of extreme interest.

Such an enterprise, however, has its own pitfalls. When all is said and done, Newman's intellectual activity stretched over some sixty years, and resulted in fifty volumes of the most varied kind. It may well be doubted whether work of such diversity could be homogeneous or endowed with any degree of interior unity. Moreover, it is absolutely essential to bear in mind the course of development undergone by the author's own ideas. Our own research, however, has convinced us beyond any doubt of the internal unity and the consistency of Newman's fundamental views through the whole course of his work. His conversion to Catholicism may appear to disrupt the course of his life, yet the current of his religious and philosophical thought followed uninterruptedly the one channel throughout his works, a stream ever gaining in breadth because continually fed from the same hidden springs of his intimate personal convictions. Everywhere we come upon the same fundamental ideas, the same orientation, the same mode of treatment. Reflection, unremitting and exacting, sharpens their outlines and gives them more definitive form; their fecundity is enriched by fresh instances of their application; essentially, however, the ideas remain unchanged. In the variety of Newman's work we see the manifold expression—over a long period and in differing, often pressing, circumstances—of a single, prolific, integral concept of man. Dealing primarily with religious problems, he was drawn to elaborate, over the years, a philosophy of human nature. His early obscure, mysterious experiences and vague intuitions gave place to firm and clear conceptions, with every detail finely drawn. His exploration of the mind of man was directed by a concern, religious in origin, for the destiny of Christianity and the Church, involved in the vicissitudes of an unstable world.

Newman's innate sense of the spiritual made him alive to the first stirrings, troubled and troubling, of a new, anti-religious paganism soon to appear.[1] He regarded it as his special vocation to raise an embankment against the flood which threatened.[2] The greater part of his works makes up one vast apologetic. The unity and the continuity of his intellectual life are the guarantee that it is possible to form, out of his entire work, a synthesis of his philosophy and of his theology of development. In fact, such a synthesis is obligatory. For, with Newman, the psychology of development is but one aspect of a comprehensive view of human nature in its entirety, and his use of the idea of evolution, in defending the faith, is a part of a sweeping plan of apologetic, with its characteristic method. It is clear, then, that the theory of dogmatic development can be thoroughly grasped only in its psychological and apologetic context. The reason why so many studies of Newman are unbalanced or even totally misleading is that insufficient attention has been paid to the structure of his thought as a whole. To proceed aright it is imperative, we think, not to confine attention to a partial and circumscribed study of the theory of doctrinal evolution, but to set out the entire psychological and apologetic context. It is not enough to bring together the elements of a theory of development dispersed, in the course of years, throughout a work of steady and homogeneous growth. The synthesis must comprise relevant factors of general psychology and of method, which make up the context that accounts for the theory.

The need for a synthetic study is seen more clearly still when we take into consideration the originality and special character of Newman's thought and writings. For he is far from being systematic himself; he is, primarily, a man of intuitive vision, but capable, through strict mental discipline, of analysing his intuition from various standpoints and, by a detailed elaboration of

[1] P. Sobry, *Newman en zijn Idea of a University* (Brussels, 1934), p.23.
[2] Ward, *op. cit.*, I, p.58.

some of its aspects, of furnishing a strict, though partial and abstract, description of the reality perceived. What he invariably does is to "take a view", but his intuition always reminds him that these abstract considerations are only of relative value, "as far as it goes". His attention is continually—and painfully—divided between the inexhaustible, many-sided reality, and the abstract view required by the task in question. His mind is always on the move between its intuition of the total reality and the degree of abstraction relative to a particular standpoint. He finds it quite impossible to think otherwise than in continual reference to the whole.

This accounts for certain peculiarities of his work and of his style. He is, primarily, a master of the essay. An essay is not a close-knit systematisation of all that can be said on a given subject, but the working-out of a personal point of view. Newman's mind was pre-eminently fitted to discover the manifold aspects of a problem, and to open up new approaches. His was, in the highest possible degree, the philosophic spirit he extolled in his *Idea of a University*.

This spirit, in fact, was what he considered the real fruit of a university education. It consists, precisely, in an exact sense of all the different aspects in which reality is presented to the mind, and of their relative value and significance. His acute feeling for the fathomless richness of the real impelled him invariably to define, with the utmost care, the exact standpoint of his approach to the subject. He was fully aware that he could never deal exhaustively with the problem. We must constantly bear in mind that he never approached any subject for purely speculative purposes, but because he was moved thereto by particular circumstances.[1] Whatever he wrote was prompted by the occasion. Moreover, he was a born orator. The rhetorical drive never left him. He always wrote for a specific public, against certain given opponents. Consequently, he never broached a subject without specifying his exact purpose and strictly defining the standpoint adopted. He took the greatest pains to confine the structure of his books and discourses within the zone prescribed by these considerations. Each sequence

---

[1] "I scarcely ever have written without an argument or compulsive force applied to me." Quoted in G. Huntington Harper, *Cardinal Newman and William Froude, A Correspondence* (Baltimore, 1933), p.178. See also one of Newman's last discourses in W. P. Neville, *Addresses to Cardinal Newman and his Replies (1879-1881)* (London, 1905), p.189.

of ideas is an *economy*, that part only of his thought called forth by the occasion. His light is focused on certain features; the rest are left in shadow, and these may be of greater interest, and more important, too, for a complete system. Once again it follows that his complete thought can be grasped only if we assemble its various constituents that lie separately on many converging routes, each leading to a partial view.

None the less, Newman's skill in the exposition of his personal points of view never confined his consideration entirely to his chosen field of vision. At each instant he is aware of the partial character of his standpoint. He is possessed by a longing for the concrete "whole" that eludes expression. He cannot prevent his intuition disturbing the course of his abstract disquisition. All at once, he brings in balancing factors; he uses ideas drawn from other perspectives to modify what he has just asserted. So, in reading his works, we often come across, right in the middle of a logical development, principles and considerations belonging to a totally different set of ideas. Hence his well-known complexity of style, his fine shades of meaning, his sentences full of subordinate clauses, reservations, parentheses, incidental reflections; it needed the magic of his style to give these the appearance of a classical limpidity. This combination of clearness and complexity explains the sharpness and suppleness of his writing. At times, however, it gives an impression of excessive subtlety, of hesitant and confused thought, to those, at any rate, who, unfamiliar with the working of his mind, are unable to distinguish and follow the many concentric routes it pursues.

What Father Tristram says on the subject of Newman's greater works can now be readily understood. "Their author," he says, "scattered his principles broadcast through his works, and passages essential for the synthetic view are to be found in the most unlikely places."[1] This applies throughout his works. They embody, in their entirety, a vast synthetic intuition; but, as occasion demands, the foreground is occupied by one aspect or other of the organic whole, an aspect powerfully conceived, it is true, but restricted in scope and expressed in a style perfect but highly subtle. The various groups of ideas are supported and completed by principles, complements and conclusions to be found in pas-

[1] H. Tristram, "A Newman Synthesis", *The Clergy Review, vol. I* (1931), pp.131-132.

sages dealing with other matters. A letter or a sermon may provide us with the most valuable elucidation.

Newmans' style is the counterpart of the visionary quality of his thought. It is lucid and fluent, the tool of his intuition. A wide knowledge of his works is needed to place each sentence in the context of his intuition. In the fifteenth of his *University Sermons,* in which he describes the course of theological development, Newman states that each sentence is the outcome of a concrete intuition.[1] In so saying, he makes a generalisation of his own experience and reveals, unawares, the secret of his style. It is deceptive in its transparent simplicity; how much so can be seen only if we try to analyse baldly the latent thought and express it in another tongue.

It is necessary to insist once more on the *literary nature of Newman's works.* Both in style and in method they are literary rather than scientific. He himself expressed, with great subtlety and refinement, the difference between the language of science and that of letters. Science, he says, uses words to represent *things,* literature to express *thoughts.* The scientist merely substitutes a determinate verbal symbol for a given object (hence comes a scientific terminology), but the man of letters uses language in all its full compass, as including phraseology, idiom, style, composition, rhythm, eloquence, and whatever other properties included in it.[2] Newman's style is peculiarly fitted to express the concrete, his language to cause the reader to "realise" it. He does not substitute words for things but, beyond the words, his look penetrates to the reality, and it is this that he continually aims to grasp and express in its native richness. He is never content with his efforts; invariably he is painfully conscious of the gulf which separates the words from the things.[3] This literary approach of his gives rise to serious difficulties in a scientific study of Newman. There is little in the way of exact terminology and it is the context that determines the precise shade of meaning. For example, in the fifteenth of the *University Sermons,* he makes use of a dozen different words and expressions to bring home to us the object of intuition, and the same applies to the knowledge of the abstract. Words that repeatedly flow from his pen, like idea, object, faith,

[1] *O.U.S.,* p.334.
[2] *Idea,* p.275.
[3] On Newman's style, cf. Sobry, *op. cit.,* pp.55-56.

reason, undergo so many shades of meaning that a comparative study of the context is essential if we are to attempt any kind of scientific appraisal of the terms he uses.

Our purpose should now be clear enough, and the need evident; it is the working out of a synthesis of Newman's theory of the development of doctrine, by collating all the elements contained in his works. We shall try to see them in their organic unity and cohesion. That will involve setting the theory of development in its proper framework, viewing it as a section of a complete psychology and apologetic.

However, that does not mean ignoring the way the theory took gradual shape in his mind. We begin, therefore, with a brief account of its growth. First of all, we shall set out the sequence of Newman's spiritual and intellectual attitudes, in so far as they influenced or determined his views on doctrinal development; next, we shall take his principal works in chronological order, explain the scope and significance of each, and their contribution to the understanding of his doctrine. This will take up the first part of the book.

The second and third parts will be devoted to the synthesis properly so called. It will consist of two parts, one treating the psychological aspect of the development of doctrine, the other the apologetical. In the latter aspect, Newman shows that development within the Church's tradition brought no change of substance, and he sees therein a positive proof of the divine origin of the Catholic Church. In each of these sections we shall devote a chapter to the general structure : the fundamental ideas and the method of Newman's psychology, and the principles governing the whole apologetic.

In the psychology of development, a clear distinction must be drawn between the individual and the collective aspect. As will be seen later on, to understand the growth of the idea in its social aspect a preliminary survey of the whole psychology of knowledge will be needed. At each of these stages of the enquiry, we shall have to distinguish the general theory and its application to religious belief.

The apologetic aspect of the problem of doctrinal development will be chiefly dealt with in connection with the *Essay on Development*. It will comprise a twofold demonstration corresponding to the two parts into which the book itself is divided, where the author adopts, first a strictly religious standpoint, and then one purely rational and philosophical.

In fact, the three parts of the book deal with the same corpus of ideas, but in different aspects. The repetition of certain central ideas is thus unavoidable. This is not necessarily a drawback, since ideas which are charged with life need to be illumined from many sides to stand out in sharp relief.

With reference to the footnotes, in the chapters that deal directly with the theory of development we have, as far as possible, reinforced our main contentions with quotations in footnotes, to give the reader at least some ground for our assertions. But where the latter are of less importance or the quotations, if made, would be too disconnected or lengthy, we have merely given the reference. It goes without saying that the synthesis we have made is, in great part, a personal interpretation. At times, we have assembled elements of very varying kinds under the aegis of the one central idea, with the unavoidable risk of forcing Newman's own thought. We can but hope that, in so doing, we have not entirely lost our own "illative sense".

PART I

Newman's personality.

Origin and development of his thought.

Chapter I

LIFE AND CHARACTER
FOUNDATIONS OF THE IDEA OF DEVELOPMENT

NO part of the history of ideas can be studied in complete isolation; it must be reinstated in the period and environment in which the idea came to birth and developed. In other words, the idea in question has to be reset within those movements which constituted its actual framework.

Newman belongs to no school. In the history of philosophy and theology, he appears as a great "outsider"; he is to be seen as one of those creative personalities whose place is not in the line of tradition, but who are the inspiration of new departures. He had certain personal qualities of a high order: an intimate sense of ideas in their living, experienced, incarnate, concrete reality,[1] joined to a very rare power of analysis and deduction.[2] The pressing needs of his life impelled him to have recourse to these powers; he was driven by the force of his circumstances to commit himself to lands still unexplored.[3] His greater works are, as it were, voyages of pre-scientific exploration. He compared them himself

[1] P. Sobry, *op. cit.*, p.46: "His speciality was to divine the *ethos*, either in a person, a society, a movement, an institution, or, not least, in himself. By *ethos* he understood a disposition, attitude, essential propensity, mentality, tendency, atmosphere."

[2] Newman himself was aware of this: "I have a vivid perception of the consequences of certain admitted principles, have a considerable intellectual capacity for drawing them out." *Letters and Correspondence*, ed. 1891, p.416; ed. 1901, p.366.

[3] Towards the end of his life, Newman declared he had never written unless urgently impelled by circumstances. See Neville, *op. cit.*, p.189.

to maps provisionally drawn.[1] The *Essay*, too, is a reconnaissance of hitherto unexplored territory.[2] It's originality is almost universally admitted.[3]

This originality, however, by no means rules out any profound influence on Newman's thought. His nature particularly predis-

[1] In the *Grammar of Assent*. See Ward, *op. cit.*, p.271. In a letter of June 12, 1853, Newman states that his works are merely approaches to their subjects, both in the case of development of doctrine and of university education.

[2] See Note 1, *supra*. See also the "Advertisement" to the *Essay*, p.x.

[3] In the *Essay*, Newman refers the reader to De Maistre and Moehler, but in vague, uncertain terms: "Its basic idea has, perhaps, been always adopted, implicitly, by theologians; it has been lately illumined, I believe, by various distinguished continental writers, among others De Maistre and Moehler," (p.29). Some writers—for example, E. Vermeil, *Jean-Adam Moehler et l'École catholique de Tubingue* (Paris, 1913), p.457—considered Newman closely dependent upon Moehler; but Tristram and Minon have discounted this influence. See H. Tristram, "J. A. Moehler et J. H. Newman", *Rev. des Sc. Phil. et Theol.*, XXVII (1938), pp.184-204, and A. Minon," L'Attitude de J. A. Moehler (1798-1838) dans la question du Développement du Dogme", *Eph. Theol. Lovan*, XVI (1939), pp.357-377. Neither is it possible to establish a connection between Newman's theory of doctrinal development and those general philosophies of evolution deriving from the natural sciences. The works of Darwin and Spencer did not appear until long after the publication of the *Essay*. Newman's idea is, essentially, alien to the "evolutionism" of the nineteenth century. J. V. De Groot, O.P., expresses himself to this effect with a certain tartness: "The origin and progress of the evolutionary process, its profound causes and explanatory principles, not to mention the narrow range of the application in practice of the main principle: all is to be found in the catholic and doctrinal notion of *development*, a reality *sui generis*, unaffected by anything outside it"—*Denkers van onzen Tijd* (2nd ed.; Bussum, 1918), p.285. Nor can Hegel and the German philosophy of evolution be adduced in this connection, though L. de Grandmaison alleges a strong resemblance in his "Le Développement du Dogme chrétien", *Rev. Prac. d'Apol.*, VI (1908), pp.23, 30, 32, 33. Newman, in fact, had no knowledge of German, and philosophies of the Hegelian type were at the furthest remove from his cast of mind. Besides, Hegel began to interest an English public round about 1840 only, at the time of the scandal caused by Strauss and his *Life of Jesus*. At that period, the idea of evolution had long matured in Newman's mind. In any case, Anglican theology was a complete stranger to doctrinal development; it owes the idea to Newman, who was the first to bring it to light and systematize it (Draguet, *op. cit.*, pp.1175-1176). Fairbairn (p.27) asserts that Newman is indebted for his theory to his own personal history and experience; V. F. Storr, in *The Development of English Theology in the Nineteenth Century* (London, 1913), writes (p.295): "The originality of Newman's work is astonishing". These two detractors of Newman are in accord with his most enthusiastic admirers, for example, H. Tristram: "We can affirm without hesitation that Newman derived the idea of development from no other source than his own mind" (*op. cit.*, p.196). See also A. Janssens, *op. cit.*, pp.123-124.

posed him to such influences, but the strongest of them, for the most part, escape the notice of the historian : for Newman's mind found its chief nourishment less in books than in the living contact between man and man and in the mental climate of Oxford, whose influence he was later to exalt so enthusiastically in the *Idea of a University*. A striking characteristic of Newman's was his use of personal intercourse to elucidate and form his own judgments.[1]

He was, however, not the passive subject of these various influences. They were filtered through his own powerful personality, following out its elective affinities. What he retained he transformed and assimilated and, perhaps without knowing it, submitted to the test of his own early experience. They helped to enrich the inner springs of his being at its deepest and most authentic level. In reading the *Essay* for the first time, we undergo a strange impression in face of Newman's complete and confident assurance of the identity of the idea persisting through the varying influences upon it : the stronger the pressure brought to bear by outside forces, the more persistently it asserts itself and reveals its true nature; the more vigorous it is in its original constitution, the freer are its powers of movement, of progress on all fronts.[2] The source of this confidence, so surprising to the historian, is doubtless to be found in Newman's own very personal reactions to outside influences.[3] Consequently, the first and chief analogy used by this self-analyst in working out his psychology of development is the pattern of growth followed by his own mind.[4] That is where he could detect, most directly and clearly, that unconscious growth to maturity, the innumerable, scarcely perceptible stages of advance, above all that immanent and living unity, that unerring finality, characteristic of the living idea. Always faithful

---

[1] J. Guitton, *op. cit.*, p.xx.

[2] *Essay*, pp.39-40, 188-189.

[3] A forceful account of his extremely personal way of reacting to his milieu is to be found in his two novels, *Loss and Gain* and *Callista*. On this point, J. Ellis Barker (*The Novel and the Oxford Movement* (Princeton, 1932)), observes: "The novel of Hardy and Zola, under the sway of 'scientific' determinism, was to become a study of the influence of environment upon character. Newman in each of his novels gives us a plot based on the opposite assumption, a picture of a character acting in a certain way *in spite of* heredity, environment and self-interest" (p.62).

[4] *Grammar*, pp.384-385: "In these provinces of inquiry, egotism is true modesty. In religious inquiry each of us can speak only for himself, and for himself he has a right to speak."

to the psychological method he was to set out in the *Grammar of Assent*, he submitted the evidence of his own experience to the test of an objective study of the intellectual life of others; but, even in this, his own experience is what invariably provides the key to his interpretation.[1]

The problem of the development of doctrine forced itself on Newman's attention, because, as everyone knows, it was so intimately bound up with his intellectual life. The *Essay*, in fact, opened to him the gates of the Catholic Church. The exact moment in which the idea took shape even he could not tell.[2] It ripened slowly and by degrees from unconscious beginnings. Real convictions, he often remarked, have a pre-history wrapped in obscurity. Hence the difficulty, he concludes, of "dating", after the event, their exact origin. No sooner do they become fully conscious than we are convinced they were always so.[3]

Hence, we may fairly conclude that to set Newman's theory of development in its historical context amounts to perceiving its relation to the personality of its author. For this reason, we propose to sketch briefly the life of Newman, the early beginnings and subsequent flowering of his personality.[4] (See Appendix A, *Biographies of Newman.*)

SECTION A
THE ROOTS OF NEWMAN'S RELIGIOUS PERSONALITY

John Henry Newman was born in London, the 21st of February 1801. His father was English, his mother half French. He was

[1] *Grammar*, p.409: "Everyone who thinks on these subjects takes a course of his own, though it will also happen to be the course that others take besides himself. The minds of many separately bear them forward in the same direction, and they are confirmed by it in each other. This I consider to be my own case."

[2] In the *Apologia*, Newman states that he accepted the principle of development from 1842 onwards, and began to study it closely in 1843. But he had already spoken of it in 1836 in *Home Thoughts Abroad*, and it was one of his favourite subjects of meditation (*Apologia*, pp.184-185). In a letter of July, 1844, he writes: "Since I wrote the *Arians*, or at least since 1836, my mind has been haunted by the idea" (Harper, *op. cit.*, p.58). As to the first steps his mind took in that direction, he admits he is unable to date them exactly (*Difficulties of Anglicans*, I, p.395).

[3] *O.U.S.*, p.326.

[4] The dates and facts of this sketch are borrowed mainly from the excellent article of H. Tristram and F. Bacchus in *D.T.C.*, *XI*, pp.327-353.

brought up mainly on "Bible religion", the most usual form of piety in England at that time. Later he wrote that the only doctrine to which Bible reading brings about "real assent" is that of Divine Providence.[1] This statement is autobiographical. For his view of Providence was, in fact, to govern uninterruptedly his studies and his thought, to hearten and fortify his spirit plunged in its "encircling gloom", and to emerge, at the end of his researches, as the final seal of his convictions.[2] Later on, we shall see how the idea of Providence is the basis of his whole apologetic.

The Bible had its influence on his poetic imagination, on the unfolding in his mind of a sort of impression of unreality in its contact with the physical world : as if the world were but a dream, he himself an angel, and the material universe an illusion, a mirage where other angels, his companions, hid from him in play.[3]

These imaginings of his are a kind of childish version of an experience of the external world which, later in life, when various influences have moulded it into a definite form, will be called Christian Platonism.[4] These influences issue directly from certain traditional forms of English thought, whose traces are seen in thinkers like Berkeley and Butler, poets like Wordsworth, and contemporary novelists like Charles Morgan. Newman, however, was never fully conscious of their action on him. On the other hand, he was clearly cognisant of the influence of the Greek Fathers, especially the Alexandrians, Clement and Origen, whose religious philosophy seemed to him the exact formulation of his own metaphysican intuition of the world.[5] This may be called Platonic in so far as it holds the visible world to be a veil, more or less unreal

[1] *Grammar*, p.57.

[2] *O.U.S.*, pp.348-349; *Essay*, pp.111-112; *Grammar*, pp.351-352.

[3] *Apologia*, p.2.

[4] L. Bouyer, "Newman et le Platonisme de l'Âme anglaise", *Rev. de Phil.*, XXXVI (1936), pp.285-305; J. Willebrands, "Het Christelijk Platonisme van Kardinaal Newman", *Studia Cathol.*, XVI (1941), pp.373-378.

[5] *Apologia*: "The broad philosophy of Clement and Origen carried me away ... some portions of their teaching, magnificent in themselves, came like music to my inward ear, as if the response to ideas which, with little external to encourage them, I had cherished for so long. They were based on the mystical or sacramental principle, and spoke of the various Economies or Dispensations of the External. I understood these passages to mean that the exterior world, physical and historical, was but the manifestation to our senses of realities greater than itself. Nature was a parable."

in itself, disguising and hiding from our spiritual view an invisible world, which alone is real and unchanging, yet calling us to its hidden presence as would a pale reflection or an image in a mirror. But it is, too, a Christian conception, since the world to which it draws our minds consists of immortal beings : God, the angels, souls. Finally, and in characteristically English fashion, it refuses to insulate these two worlds, to disjoin the visible and the invisible, like the dualistic philosophies of Asia. On the contrary, it discerns and contemplates, by its interior vision, the spiritual universe at the very heart of concrete reality, of objects perceptible to sense—a mystical presence shining through the visible form and perceived by a sensibility at once poetical and religious.[1]

This Platonism deeply affected Newman's spiritual outlook in his Anglican days. It inspired many of his sublimest sermons at Oxford, sermons penetrated with poetic feeling.[2] It was never to be absent from either his sensibility or his thought, but it became increasingly tempered, balanced by another typically English trait : the taste for the "given", a clear sense of empirical reality. There we have, as it were, the obverse, the counterpoise, of his Platonism.[3] In fact, an extreme tension pervades Newman's thought, drawn as it was by two opposing tendencies of the English mind, namely, a Platonic longing for immaterial ideas and invisible realities, and the need for facts precisely perceived, recorded and verified. This latter tendency holds in check the possible extravagance of the other. Aided by a similar influence— his study of Aristotle, the "great master" he venerated as "the oracle of nature and of truth", and the Aristotelianism traditional for seven centuries in Catholic philosophy—it succeeded in gradually detaching Newman from certain extreme conclusions drawn from the Platonist, or rather Platonising, standpoint so congenial to him. For example, for many years he held it not impossible that the physical qualities we perceive by our senses are not genuine

---

[1] "A region which was the haunt of all the great English poets; a spiritual world to be attained at the very heart of that tangible life to which the English are said to be so greatly attached" (Bouyer, *op. cit.*, p.289). Bouyer contrasts with this outlook the habit, peculiar to the French poets, of separating the idea from the thing.

[2] See for example, *The Powers of Nature* and *The Invisible World* (in *P.P.S.*, II, pp.358-367; IV, pp.200-203). Lewis May considers Newman a greater poet in his sermons than in his verse.

P. Sobry, *op. cit.*, pp.34-37, gives a good resumé of the contrast between facts and fancy in the young Newman.

properties of the real world, but purely subjective impressions, relative to the structure of our bodies and corresponding to a divine "economy" which uses them as signs giving us a hint of a higher, invisible world. The most forcible expression of this is to be found in the famous Oxford sermon on the development of religious doctrine. Later, Newman added a note to tone down its exaggerations.[1]

Newman's Platonism is significant for the understanding of his theory of development; his conception of the idea "growing", as it were, in its given surroundings is, without any doubt, redolent of Platonism : and, in addition, the principle of analogy, fundamental to his method of apologetics, is closely allied to it.

The passage just quoted from the *Apologia* shows that, in the case of Newman, Platonism harmonised with a very early tendency of his, characteristic of him from childhood. The Greek Fathers simply aided him to clarify it, to raise it to the level of a distinct idea. How are we to account for its presence at all? It might be of interest to study Newman in the light of modern characterology, were it not that its findings are still so tentative and provisional.[2] None the less, it is very tempting to see in Newman one of Jung's introverted types.[3]

Newman, in fact, exhibits strikingly the characteristics of this type : the Platonic tendency to substitute for the realist, common-sense view of the world, an introverted conception, adapted to the needs of the interior life; a vivid sense of the strangeness of the world, in which the soul feels itself an alien; finally, in his reactions to the external world, a constant hesitancy, a perpetual uncertainty. Consider his ambiguous attitude towards the beauties of nature. When he encounters them directly by the contact of sense, he invariably feels ill at ease, unresponsive; but no sooner are they presented indirectly, interiorly, in memory, than they move him to ecstacy.[4] Consider, too, his seeming "egocentricity", because of which his heart, so sensitive and hungry for friendship, could never give itself completely; whence his continual, painful

---

[1] *O.U.S.*, pp.347-349.

[2] See the acute but somewhat superficial and drastic criticism by C. Spearman, *Psychology down the Ages*, II, pp.189-205.

[3] Cf. C. G. Jung's *Psychological Types*. Jung's division into extroverts and introverts is not definite. In his later work, he shows the need for further differentiation.

[4] P. Sobry, *op. cit.*, pp.41-42.

sense of isolation.[1] All this is characteristic of the introverted type described by Jung.

Still, the sense of disengagement, of alienation, from the outside world is not to be accounted for, principally, by temperamental factors of any kind. Innate dispositions may have their influence, but the psychologist of Zurich himself acknowledges the decisive nature of other factors, arising out of the history of the individual, in determining the fundamental orientation of his mind. The key to Newman's introversion—if the technical term may be applied to him—is to be found in a later, definite experience which was to settle the direction of his life, and to enclose him, as Pascal would say, "within the four walls" of his soul. An interior experience, felt wholly in the most intimate depths of his being, but no less real and objective for all that, it guides us into the hidden recesses of Newman's personality and reveals the springs of his intellectual activity. It is of this that he speaks in his *Apologia*; and its unmistakable echo is to be heard in the description he gives, in the *Grammar of Assent*, of the conscience of the child.[2] After his first conversion, the young Newman knew only two beings whose existence was immediately evident to him : God and himself.[3] So exceptional a degree of religious introversion, fortified with the passage of years, has necessarily a tendency to isolate a man from the world. The main factor in it must have been the profound awe characteristic of Newman's piety. For him, God was the Judge to come, whom he awaited with anxious foreboding. His own greatest concern was to prepare himself for the judgment by a rigorous obedience and a continuous moral purification. Only the absolutely pure could sustain the presence of the God of sanctity. At the destined moment, it is not so much God who will banish the soul to Purgatory as the soul itself which will flee from the sight of God to take refuge in the place of purification. This is the theme of *The Dream of Gerontius*, that poem so original and compelling, where Newman has left perhaps his most authentic self-revelation. In his *Parochial and Plain Sermons*, he suggests that hell may not be an *extrinsic* punishment of mortal

---

[1] F. Hermans, "Portrait de Newman", *Rev. Gen.*, CXL (1938), pp. 453-471. This slight article, in its just balance, corrects Bremond's imaginary and egocentric portrait of Newman.

[2] *Grammar*, pp. 112-115.

[3] *Apologia*, pp. 31, 183, 186, 271.

sin, but that the soul, seeing itself but for a moment stained by mortal sin in the divine presence, kindles its own hell in itself.[1]

What, then, should be the state of the soul, what should it do, to be capable of appearing before God? This question dominates the eight volumes of the immortal sermons preached at St. Mary's. Not a single tare, however "insignificant" or imperceptible, escapes Newman's scrutiny. The slightest transgression, even semi-deliberate, even practically involuntary, is the subject of investigation. He examines closely its subtle influence on the character. He discloses and inveighs against the immense ruin it can work in the soul—yes, very gradually and barely consciously. He lays bare every trace of egoism and pride, brings to light all the sophistries in which they shelter, unmasks the seeming virtues which disguise them. All this, however, takes place in an atmosphere where the presence of God is felt, almost tangibly. It is under the eye of God that the soul, overwhelmed by the majesty of its Lord, examines itself "with fear and trembling", as the Apostle says, "dismantles" itself, so to speak, even in its most hidden movements, to purify itself, by grace, of all that hinders the divine Will and to confide itself, by humbly acknowledging its own impotence and sinful state, to his mercy. This conjunction of high religious inspiration and acute psychological penetration gives a unique grandeur and beauty to these slight, completely unpretentious sermons. In the whole history of spirituality, they form one of the most striking documents of self-knowledge in the sight of God.

A man whose interior life is ruled by this fear and foreboding is bound to feel himself solitary and alien in this life. The world may present an idyllic aspect, but, in its visible "figure", it seems to him unreal and deceptive. He can have no attachments in it, he is incapable of giving himself completely to another. Everything he meets may, he believes, hide a menace to his eternal destiny. The fear of danger keeps him always cautious and alert. To use the words of Newman's greatest sermons, he is ever "waiting and watching". He can never engage himself totally in any worldly task or in the pursuit of a merely human perfection. True, he is obliged to discharge all the duties incidental to life in the world, to our human condition, but in a spirit of absolute interior detachment: that is one of the principle themes of Newman's preach-

[1] *P.P.S.*, IV, p.246.

3

ing. A characteristic example is to be seen in the later discourses in his *Idea of a University*, where he indicts that rational culture so much extolled. In delivering them, he was alive to the dangers inherent in purely human and worldly values; he emphasises, therefore, the necessity of interior detachment, even as to the highest culture, if it be no more than human. His sense of awe influences even that love of truth to which his religious Odyssey is indebted for its high intellectual integrity and moral greatness. Under its dominance, he moves only step by step; and each of these steps is maturely weighed yet inevitable, obliging him to sever his tenderest bonds to gain the truth.

The fear of God forms, then, the inmost spring of his life. He could have written, like St. Jerome, that he paid no heed to the tumult of the world—"for my sole concern is fear of the impending judgment of God"[1]—had not the world itself inspired such a feeling of wonder and fascination that he could never sever his attention from it.

Newman does not view the world with the calm detachment of a traveller in an unknown land; rather, the world confronts him forcibly, in an experience that afflicts him sorely. If he views the panorama of its happenings, the silence of God astounds, bewilders and tortures him. The world flatly opposes the evidence of the spiritual realities so deeply rooted in his being; it appears, at first sight, as a kind of beguiling illusion, a maddening, oppressive temptation. Yet of this strange, inhospitable world he finds himself in his physical being an integral part. The impression this makes on him is poignant. Between his interior gaze and the God who, formerly, shed his clear and shining light in his conscience, the visible world interposes a thick mist.[2] Doubtless, in the event, this applies not so much to the physical world, as to the world of men, as seen in its present conduct and historical course, the world of bustle and business, ceaselessly agitated by formidable impulses of possession, power and pleasure. These are the real enemies of conscience, ever threatening to stifle, even to annihilate it. None the less, the visible creation, too, is something of an accomplice, for it provides the setting where the powerful, absurd tragedy of man is played out, that pompous futility. Nature, admirable though it be, is no path for Newman to reach the God of his

---

[1] *Prol. in libr. XIV Isaiae*, P.L., XXIII, col. 477.
[2] This painful impression is described in *O.U.S.*, p.131.

conscience. His journey has to start from within himself and only thus will he be able, and even then with serious difficulty, to endow the visible world with any religious significance. Platonism, for him, means the projection of conscience onto the world of nature.

To gain some idea of this painful experience of his, its profound meaning for his life, and the acute sense of foreboding it caused in him, we cite the passage from the last chapter of the *Apologia* which prefaces his account of Catholicism. Its spasmodic style reflects the pain he was undergoing; it is charged with sighs and groans and abounds in parentheses; it is weighty with its load of ideas; yet it is one of the finest pieces in the literature of the world. Here, if anywhere, the style reflects the very being of the author, the deepest levels of his personality. For that reason, we give the passage in full, in spite of its length :

Starting then with the being of a God, (which, as I have said, is as certain to me as the certainty of my own existence, though when I try to put the grounds of that certainty into logical shape I find a difficulty in doing so in mood and figure to my satisfaction,) I look out of myself into the world of men, and there I see a sight which fills me with unspeakable distress. The world seems simply to give the lie to that great truth, of which my whole being is so full; and the effect upon me is, in consequence, as a matter of necessity, as confusing as if it denied that I am in existence myself. If I looked into a mirror and did not see my face, I should have the sort of feeling which actually comes upon me, when I look into this living busy world, and see no reflexion of its Creator. This is, to me, one of those great difficulties of this absolute primary truth, to which I referred just now. Were it not for this voice, speaking so clearly in my conscience and my heart, I should be an atheist, or a pantheist, or a polytheist when I looked into the world. I am speaking for myself only; and I am far from denying the real force of the arguments in proof of a God, drawn from the general facts of human society and the course of history, but these do not warm me or enlighten me; they do not take away the winter of my desolation, or make the buds unfold or the leaves grow within me, and my moral being rejoice. The sight of the world is nothing else than the prophet's scroll, full of "lamentations, and mourning, and woe".

To consider the world in its length and breadth, its various history, the many races of man, their starts, their fortunes, their mutual alienation, their conflicts; and then their ways, habits, governments, forms of worship; their enterprises, their aimless courses, their random achievements and acquirements, the impotent conclusion of long-standing facts, the tokens so faint and broken of a superintending design, the blind evolution of what turn out to be great powers or truths, the progress of things as if from unreasoning elements, not towards final causes, the greatness and littleness of man, his far-reaching aims, his short duration, the curtain hung over his futurity, the disappointments of life, the defeat of good, the success of evil, physical pain, mental anguish, the prevalence and intensity of sin, the pervading idolatries, the corruptions, the dreary, hopeless irreligion, that condition of the whole race so fearfully yet exactly described in the Apostle's words, "having no hope and without God in the world"—all this is a vision to dizzy and appal; and inflicts upon the mind the sense of a profound mystery, which is absolutely beyond human solution.

What shall be said to this heart-piercing, reason-bewildering fact?[1]

This contrast between conscience and the alien, hostile world is Newman's starting-point, in the *Apologia*, for an argument from concrete existence for the unfolding of his Catholic view of the universe. Further on, when we come to consider how he justifies his beliefs, we shall give an account of that argument. G. Soehngen rightly counts this contrast as one of Newman's basic ideas.[2] But its significance is wider than that; for we can see it as the origin of that tension in his mind which impelled it on its quest. We are here concerned, not so much with an "idea", an abstract concept, as with a concrete, living experience, which set before him a crucial choice. On the attitude adopted by his conscience depended the whole structure of his life, whether it was to remain erect or fall into ruins.

Now, Newman found it impossible to accept the situation confronting his conscience at first sight. It affirmed, as a supremely

[1] *Apologia*, pp.217-218.

[2] G. Soehngen, "Kardinal Newman, ein Neugestalter Augustinischer Religionsphilosophie", *Wissenschaft und Weisheit*, (1937), pp.23-24.

evident truth, the existence of God, which the vast, alluring spectacle of the world seemed to deny. The reality of God presented itself to his mind with overwhelming force; but, no sooner did he try to plumb the depths of that idea, to harmonise it with the undeniable realities of life, than it seemed beset with every kind of difficulty.[1] The pain this antinomy caused in his mind, agitating it and disturbing its equilibrium, forced him to attempt to resolve it, to work out by thought the reconciliation of its interior needs with the facts of the external world. His general line of thought was determined by his continual wrestling with all the problems arising from the opposition between two kinds of knowledge—that which came to him from within, and that given by his experience of the world and his immediate surroundings. These are the two poles between which his mind pursued its inquiries.

In Newman's thought, the primary factor is always conscience. It is his starting-point in throwing a bridge across to the external world, in "situating" it in the perspective of Divine Providence, which is itself the first and supreme truth of religious experience. Here lies the fundamental principle of his method of apologetics, the one which governs every one of his proofs; all the other principles he uses we shall see to be correlative to this. It may not provide a complete solution to every difficulty; he is content with an answer that is, on the whole, satisfactory, one enabling him, supported by the clear voice of conscience, to bear up against the manifold difficulties that yet remain—"Ten thousand difficulties do not make one doubt."[2] He courageously sustains the burden they lay on that intelligence of his, so sensitive to the demands of logic. Whether they take the form of involuntary doubts to harass him, or flutter as "vague suspicions", *muscae volitantes*, in the luminous rays of his conscience, they never reach the point of impairing the active certitude of his assent.[3] He knows there exists, must exist, a solution to these difficulties. He confronts them

---

[1] *Apologia*, p.216; this is, also, the fundamental idea of the admirable sermon, "Mysteries of Nature and Grace", in *Disc. M. Cong.*, pp.260-283.

[2] *Apolgia*, p.215.

[3] *Grammar*, pp.184, 217. The more or less autobiographical nature of these descriptions is shown in several of his letters; cf. *Letters and Correspondence*, II, pp.459-461; Harper, *op. cit.* pp.62-63; Ward, *op. cit.*, I, pp.616-617, regarding his conversion: "It was a mere conviction, however flickered with doubts, which were no part of it any more than motes are part of the sunbeam."

squarely on their own ground, no matter where they arise, but his victory is not made to depend on their total defeat. He has no need of premature solutions, or the consolations of a pseudo-science; he is ready to wait in patience.

This attitude to intellectual difficulties he achieved only by degrees; it did not come easily or spontaneously. By his very nature, he was unusually sensitive to them[1], and they disturbed him; that was why he was able to see into them so clearly. He could not put them away lightheartedly. He was anything but a romantic, calmly disdaining reason with all its pretensions. Both by nature and upbringing, he was a man of intellect; it was in mathematics that he achieved greatest brilliance at the university. He had a spontaneous admiration for intellectual talents and their outcome. He was, more than anyone, alive to the inexorable demands of reason; if the difficulties they occasioned struck home to his intellect, they also touched, and wounded, his heart.

His acute awareness of intellectual difficulties had a great influence on his way of thinking; it made him ever critical of himself and of his grounds for certainty, and necessitated a constant self-control. The circumspection with which his mind worked suggests, at times, soundings taken from a ship voyaging among sandbanks and reefs. His way to God never lay open to his sight, like a road stretching straight ahead. He went forward in fear and in darkness; and the fitful light of Providence, however kindly, seemed as cold and distant as the Pole star, or the one which guided the Magi to Bethlehem.[2]

Later, we shall see how much these factors contribute to an understanding of his theory of development. In fact, the first part of the *Essay* consists of a search for the right route, a search guided by principles derived from conscience. In the second, more elaborate part he confronts objections from the standpoint of reason and surmounts them by his theory of the seven criteria of true development. His chief purpose in writing the *Essay* was to allay those "vague misgivings"[3] that troubled his mind, and to attain

---

[1] *Apologia*, p.215: "Many persons are very sensitive of the difficulties of religion; I am as sensitive as anyone." Hence his gentleness with the doubting and lukewarm.

[2] Cf. his hymn, "Lead, kindly Light".

[3] *Apologia*, p.208.

to the contemplation of the "Blessed Vision of Peace" which took shape on the conclusion of the work.[1]

His preliminary investigations in psychology were also directed by the contrast between conscience and the knowledge gained from external experience. What, for instance, is the source of the impiety of the world, so baffling to his mind? Newman discovers that man has two ways of thinking, one valid, the other not. The first is practised by those who start from the inner experience of conscience in constructing their view of the world and remain faithful to that "kindly light" illumining within us those first principles of religion whose consequences gradually emerge with reflection on the experience of life. Others lack the living, animating inspiration of conscience, which is the only source of true personality. Their philosophy is determined by the body of impersonal opinions which prevail in what is vaguely termed the "world". Newman's principal aim in his psychological study is to understand the nature and development of these two types.

Finally, his Platonism is no less at work in his attempt to solve the antinomy indicated above. He interiorized the material world, gathering it into the interior one of conscience, and interpreting it as an appearance, a veil, an "economy", a kind of provisional, ambiguous revelation—darkened, still, by original sin—of those same sublime realities which, through conscience, become "sensible to the heart".

We have ventured, perhaps rashly, to reduce the main features of Newman's thought to the fundamental trait of his engaging personality. From his childhood, this trait took on clear and precise form, the sense of a conflict between two worlds—that of the soul, wholly interior, and that of the environment, the world outside. We are well aware that our attempt is, of necessity, one-sided and imperfect. It is only one view, and so an inadequate one, of a highly complex subject. There are other ways of approach to Newman's personality, serving the same end, and rectifying ours. Professor Sobry has attempted to explain his way of thinking by an interior "rending apart" or discord, due to some temperamental unbalance. This idea is very suggestive, and we are greatly indebted to it. Our own view is not opposed to it; in fact, our two views seem rather to converge. Every human personality is a more

[1] *Essay*, p.445.

or less coherent complex of tendencies, which may be called dynamic ideas or, in Newman's terminology, principles (quite apart from those principles of which one may be conscious). Sometimes these are innate, sometimes acquired by effort, education, or habit; others are, so to speak, inoculated by particular experiences, especially in childhood. As a rule, they are of many different kinds and, though differing in origin, modify and supplement one another. In spite of their diversity, they act together as a single living, organic whole. They are either in alliance or opposition, in varying degree, and to them the individual owes his particular character and capabilities. They become organised in groups, more or less independent, even antagonistic; the character derives from these its variety of hidden qualities, and its various possibilities of choice in the range of experience.[1]

The chief function of the personality is to integrate these tendencies and bring them under the dominance of a single one in the moral order, moulding them to work in harmony. It is, therefore, quite permissible for us to view the central tendency governing Newman's characteristic way of thinking as a complex one attributable partly to a particular experience, partly to innate endowment. As to the dualist and dialectical nature of his thought, there is no reason why it should not be ascribed both to the opposition he felt between his religious experience and his experience of the world and, at the same time, to a congenial unbalance. Were it not for the special character of his experience, the conflict of his innate tendencies would not have worked itself out so fully in the religious sphere. Without his peculiar temperament, he would not have felt so acutely the contrast between his conscience and the world. Nor would this antinomy have become both the centre of gravity and the basis of his personality and thought. (See appendix B, *Newman's Personality*.)

---

[1] This is the idea of personality indicated by much modern research, along various lines, in psychology and anthropology. Cf. the slight, but significant work of C. Baudouin, *Découverte de la personne*, (Paris, 1940). A similar view is taken in *Psychologie der Weltanschauungen*, where Jaspers attempts a synthesis of the life of the mind. Burloud's great work, *Principes d'une psychologie des tendances*, (Paris, 1938), sees the whole psychic life as an ordered complex of tendencies, in which the psychosomatic personality plays the principal part. This is all the more significant in that Burloud is rather averse to current "subjective" psychology (p.70).

Section B
Newman's Spiritual Growth and the Idea of Development

In all truly great men we perceive one basic tendency enabling us to unify, and so to understand, the different elements which make up their mental life and their view of the world. This tendency achieves expression only in a context determined by the empirical facts of their life and personal history. A strong personality, it is true, may give the impression that all that outside influences and circumstances effect is to actuate forces already latent in the mind, and to stimulate a set of reactions already specified. Yet this predisposition applies only to the general nature of these reactions, not to their individual form and the way they are applied. Every tendency is manifold; it has any number of possible modes and spheres of application. The form it happens to take depends on circumstances. We must, therefore, describe briefly the external facts of Newman's life and the turning-points of his spiritual development, especially those which confronted him with the problem of the development of doctrine, and indicated the direction of his solution.

Ealing, his first conversion

From May, 1808 to 1816, Newman was at school in Ealing. There it was that, towards the end of 1816, he experienced his first conversion, which, in 1885, he still held to have been a radical turning-point.[1] In the *Apologia*, he declares himself more certain of that interior change than of his own hands and feet.[2] He describes it thus: "When I was fifteen, a great change of thought took place in me. I fell under the influence of a definite Creed, and received into my intellect impressions of dogma which, through God's mercy, have never been effaced or obscured."[3] It is highly significant that Newman emphasises the intellectual aspect of this conversion. We may distinguish two "moments" in this experience, his contact with the living God, and its specifically Christian character. In his early youth, when his personality was beginning to form, he had passed through a characteristic stage:

[1] H. Tristram and F. Bacchus, *op. cit.*, cols. 328-329.
[2] *Apologia*, p.31.
[3] *Ibid.*

he aspired to a moral rather than a religious life.[1] To love God meant nothing to him; it even seemed to have no sense.[2] He found a certain satisfaction in some books hostile to religion.[3] His conversion was primarily a transition from a purely moralistic outlook to one that was both ethical and religious. Previously, he had only an implicit experience of what, in religious terminology, is known as conscience; but now its transcendent significance appears to him quite clearly. He is fully aware of it and apprehends it, once and for all, by a "real assent", by his entire submission to a living reality, a presence.[4] The second factor in his experience is important for its emphasis on the principle of dogma, without which, he considered, religion could not subsist. This principle is the root of his opposition to liberalism.[5] Later, in the *Essay*, the existence of an objective, exactly defined revelation will form one of the first, indisputable principles of his demonstration. Newman was never disposed to grant that the doctrinal creed could ever be, in its essence, relative or subject to change. Right from the start his bent was anti-liberal and antimodernist.

This first conversion took place under evangelical influence. Newman was deeply influenced by certain writers of evangelical opinions, particularly Thomas Scott.[6] "Growth is the only evidence of life", was one of the sayings which summed up for him

---

[1] "I recollect, in 1815 I believe, thinking that I should like to be virtuous but not religious", *Letters and Correspondence*, I, p.22.

[2] "Nor did I see the meaning of loving God", *Ibid*.

[3] *Apologia*, p.30.

[4] A meeting, not simply a conclusion from premises. Like Charles Reading, the hero of his novel *Loss and Gain*, Newman's personality from that moment was conditioned by his habitual sense of the divine presence. All his later, and increasingly clear, analyses of the religious conscience are based on this experience, which finds its definite explanation in the first part of the *Grammar*.

[5] According to *Apologia* (p.57), the first of the three fundamental principles of the Oxford Movement was "the dogmatic principle, my enemy was liberalism, and by liberalism I understood the anti-dogmatic principle with all its corollaries". The best description of the dogmatic principle is to be found in the *Essay*, pages 357-358. The liberalism combated by Newman is, in fact, identical with rationalism, which denies the absolute, immutable truth of religion.

[6] Thomas Scott (1741-1821), "the author to whom, humanly speaking, I practically owe my soul" (*Apologia*, p.32). He was especially drawn by the practical scope of Scott's books, which insisted upon the necessity of good works and personal holiness.

the whole of Scott's work.[1] Later, it was to bring its own contribution to Newman's reflections on the development of doctrine.

The first Oxford period, 1817-1833

Newman arrived at Oxford in June, 1817. Three years later, he gained, in undistinguished fashion, his degree of Bachelor of Arts. In 1822, he was elected Fellow of Oriel with general acclaim. In 1824 and 1825, he took Orders in the Church of England and acted during the next two years as assistant preacher at St. Clement's. In 1828, he became vicar of St. Mary's and began his celebrated sermons which take up ten volumes.[2] Meanwhile, in 1826, he was appointed tutor at Oriel, but was obliged to resign in 1832 on account of a dispute with Hawkins, the Provost. The same year, he finished his history of Arianism, but his health suffered from overwork and he embarked on a tour abroad, visiting Malta, Italy, Corfù and Sicily in company with Hurrell Froude and Froude's father. After returning by himself to Sicily, he fell seriously ill and when he got back to England, became convinced that, if God had kept him alive, it was for the sake of a particular mission : "I have a work to do in England."[3] It was then that his second, and principal, period in Oxford began. We shall speak of it later.

His intellectual formation took place in the first period at Oxford. The *Apologia* describes at length what he owed to the Oriel common room, and particularly to Hawkins and Whately.[4] Under Whately's influence, he soon came to accept the idea of the Church as an independent society and this is of particular importance. Whately's anti-erastian views (opposing the subordination of the Church to the State) deeply coloured his thought. They found expression later in the Oxford movement.[5] Through the influence of Keble, whom Georges Goyau called an "Anglican

---

[1] *Apologia*, p.32.

[2] *Parochial and Plain Sermons*, 8 vols.; *Sermons on Subjects of the Day* ; *Oxford University Sermons*.

[3] *Apologia*, p.55.

[4] *Ibid.*, pp.34-39.

[5] *Ibid.*, p.37. R. H. Froude (1803-1836) was mainly responsible for the spread of Whately's ideas in the Oxford Movement. Cf. R. W. Church, *The Oxford Movement* (3rd ed.; London, 1892), pp.51-52.

saint",[1] and of Butler's *Analogy of Religion*, a classic of Anglican apologetics,[2] he discovered another fundamental of Christianity,[3] the sacramental principle, and, in addition, was drawn to consider the problem of the grounds of belief and the foundations of religious certitude. This problem was to be the main concern of his whole life.[4] His final break with Anglicanism took place in this period.[5]

The first Oxford period was marked by a profound and decisive experience which made Newman, for the rest of his life, an irreconcilable and far-seeing opponent of liberalism.[6] It explains the part he played later in the Oxford Movement. It was at this time that he became acquainted with the outlook, the *ethos*,[7] of the "Noetics"—the name given, at a later date, to his Oriel contemporaries; this experience, and his opposition to them, clarified his own religious and philosophical views. He detected, at once, the deep psychological and historical roots of nascent liberalism. At Oriel was to be found the cream of the Oxford intelligentsia, men who had reformed the curriculum and restored the ideal of university education. They were well aware of their eminence. With full confidence in their intellectual prowess, they set out boldly to solve all problems solely by the light of a trained intellect. They delighted in criticising and questioning and freely examined,

---

[1] Newman himself reveals Keble's influence on him; in his account of his illness in Sicily, he says: "I compared myself with Keble, and realized that I was content to develop his convictions rather than my own." *Letters and Correspondence* (I, p.416). Cf. W. Lock, *John Keble* ("Leaders of Religion"; London, 1896).

[2] On Joseph Butler (1692-1752), see W. A. Spooner, *Bishop Butler* ("Leaders of Religion"; London, 1901). His *Analogy*, a work of great originality, was very influential on Newman's philosophical and religious thinking (*Apologia*, p.36).

[3] *Apologia*, p.42. Under the influence of Butler, Keble, and Whately, the second principle of Newman's teaching in the Oxford Movement was "There is a visible Church, whose sacraments and rites are the channels of invisible grace " (*Apologia*, p.67).
For the place of the Church in Newman's life and writings, cf. H. W. van de Pol, *De Kerk in het leven en denken van Newman*, (Nijkerk, 1936).

[4] *Apologia*, p.42. "My own peculiar subject," he wrote to the celebrated barrister, E. Bellasis, to whom he dedicated the *Grammar* (Cf. *Memorials of Mr. Serjeant Bellasis*, note to p.172).

[5] *Apologia.*, p.35; cf. also "Autobiographical Memoir" in *Letters and Correspondence*, p.120.

[6] On this experience, cf. Sobry, *op. cit.*, pp.71-84.

[7] For the meaning of *ethos* cf. note 1 p.13. It signifies the general tendency, moral atmosphere, of an individual or society.

in language invariably moderate and lucid, every religious and ecclesiastical problem. They attached greater importance to breadth of view and logical consistency than to the authority of the Church and doctrinal orthodoxy. Their standpoint was wholly rationalistic and superficial, and they detached such notions as sin and virtue from their religious context and their connection with conscience, to treat them in terms of autonomous reason and in a purely humanistic setting. All, in fact, that originated from the hidden action of God they accounted for in human terms.[1] In spite of this, the Noetics were Anglicans loyal to their Church and were motivated by the best intentions; but they failed to discern the impasse to which their movement was inevitably leading. It was Newman's psychological genius that was to expose them, to penetrate the recesses of their thought hidden even from them and to foresee the conclusions liberalism was later to draw and which lay already in germ, unperceived, in the principles of his friends. This was his task and he was to discharge it, not as a disinterested observer, but as one personally and intensely involved; for he had himself, only a short time before, experienced the seduction of rationalism and recognised his true direction only after passing through a critical phase. Newman recognised that reason had laid her spell on him : "I was beginning to prefer intellectual excellence to moral; I was drifting in the direction of the Liberalism of the day."[2] But Scott's rule of "holiness first" was too firmly anchored in his heart, together with his fear of the impending judgment of God, for him to wander far in that labyrinth. The dream was finally dissipated by his illness in 1827 and the death of his sister Mary in the following year.[3]

It is hardly possible to exaggerate the importance of Newman's experience at Oriel. In the development of his personality, it was both critical and highly productive. The same world which had previously seemed to his conscience a peril at once formidable and fascinating, seduced him for a moment at Oriel in the form of an arrogant intellectual culture, and threatened to set him at vari-

---

[1] Cf. Sobry, op. cit., p.83. The author rightly emphasizes that the Noetics were the origin of Oxford liberalism (p.75). Evans (Tract 90 (London, 1933), p.x) comments: "They were, in fact, the forerunners of present-day Modernism".

[2] Apologia, p.39; "Autobiographical Memoir", p.126.

[3] Apologia, p.39.

ance with his conscience. A brief conflict arose between his worldly experience and his conscience, each striving to fix the direction his personality was to take. Now he was to choose deliberately between two orientations of life, two conceptions of the world; his was the grave responsibility of deciding which was to be victorious. This crisis brought home to him strongly the opposition between the liberal and the religious "ethos". Newman was never likely to decide in favour of reason divorced from the findings of conscience. His religious experience and fear of divine judgment were too deeply rooted. But if he had ventured on such a decision, he would undoubtedly in view of his sensitivity and his mental subtlety and caution, have had to undergo, "with fear and trembling," the counter-attacks of conscience for the rest of his life. In all probability, his life would have followed a quite different course but with a similar tension between its two poles. Fortunately his conscience carried the day. On the instant, he fixed, and for ever, the direction of his life and thought; he was committed to expose the real nature of liberalism and to wage war upon it.

The liberalism in question was a form of rationalism. Its first principle was the primacy of logical reason. It supposed that reason, cold, impartial, unbiased, impersonal—in other words, knowledge of things from outside and at a distance, without personal commitment—is the supreme, even the sole, motive force of life. For it alone has the means to declare what is true in every sphere and so to govern the whole of human conduct, as if the correctness of initial views and deductions from them were not relative to the accuracy and sensitivity of the instruments recording them. Now there is one sphere where the instrument is, in fact, conscience, which speaks to each of us in the depths of the heart. It is the sole instrument which enables us to perceive what pertains to religion and morals, and to judge those first principles which follow accordingly. It is an instrument of knowledge whose sensitivity, fineness and accuracy—and so whose value for the seeker after truth—are dependent on the moral life, its growth, and its purity.

Newman was to dedicate his life to the war against liberalism. Its *ethos*, he considered, derived from intellectual pride, a danger inherent in a high state of culture. Hence the apparent distrust of reason seen in all his writings which later left him open to the charge of scepticism.[1] The object of his scepticism, however, was neither reason nor culture in itself. All his writings display his brilliant use of reasoning; and so far as culture is concerned, he sang its praises in a work of singular excellence.[2] What he always vehemently opposed was the superficial application of purely rational means to a sphere where it did not belong, that of religion and morals; it meant judging from the outside matters which, for the attainment of truth, demand fidelity to the interior light. Moreover, he was well aware that a certain pride, the subtlest and most rooted vice of the human mind, aids and abets this shallow and self-satisfied reason, so that, as history shows, the temptation of rationalism becomes the gravest of all for sinful man.

Man's pride and natural rebelliousness against the severe de- mands of conscience come only too easily, in the course of life, to dim the remembrance of his early experiences and of the basic principles of right judgment in matters of religion. Consequently, by its bias towards scepticism, so natural to fallen man, reason becomes the most powerful of instruments for constructing a view of the world penetrated with irreligion.[3] That is why Newman always considered that reason, when applied to religion, acts as a solvent. In its actual working in history, reason has been warped in the direction of hostility towards that order of the heart where it should have struck its deepest roots. As Newman's intuition of this tragedy became more and more clear, he reached the con- viction that dogmatic religion requires an infallible authority.[4]

All through Newman's writings, this opposition between con- science and arrogant reason is to be discerned under a variety of forms. Orthodoxy and heresy in the *Arians* and in the *Essay*, faith and reason in the *University Sermons,* the Catholic and the

[1] An accusation made in his lifetime by A. M. Fairbairn in the *Contemporary Review* of May, 1885. Newman answered it in his last important article, "The Development of Religious Error", published in the same review. Fairbairn returned to the charge, and Newman's reply appeared only after his death in an opusculum, *Stray Essays.* Later, the same charge was often made and as often refuted (cf. Sobry, *op. cit.*, pp.30-32). What Newman meant by reason, when he opposed it, he made clear in his reply to Fairbairn, and in the 1871 introduction to the *O.U.S.:* "Reasoning about religion on secular principles intrinsically alien to religion" (p.xv).

[2] *The Idea of a University.*

[3] This process is wonderfully described in "The Development of Religious Error"; but it is also sketched out in all Newman's works, perhaps best in the *Idea,* pp.181 ff.

[4] *Essay,* pp.89-91. That is also the central idea of the *Apologia,* chap. 7.

rationalistic spirit in *Tract 73*, later on the *ethos* of the gentleman and the religious *ethos* in the *Idea*, the opposition of the real and the notional in the *Grammar of Assent*—all these antitheses serve to elucidate the same radical contrast.

The Second Oxford period : the Oxford Movement (1833-1845)

Newman returned from Italy impatient to open his attack on the liberals.[1] The first shot was fired on the following Sunday, four days later, when Keble preached his famous sermon on national apostasy.[2] At this time, the Church of England was at a serious crisis, due to its establishment as an organ of the State,[3] for, from 1688, it had been precisely that; its life depended on the secular power. Now the State was itself undergoing a rapid process of secularisation; one law after another granted to all, whether Anglican or not, an equal right to share in the government of the country, and consequently only disaster awaited the Church from its subjection to the State. In fact, from this time on, the State was to exercise its power over the Church for purely political ends. In 1833, for instance, Parliament suppressed ten Irish bishoprics because it judged them superfluous. It was, therefore, urgently necessary to establish a basis for the existence and authority of the Church independent of the State. A committee was set up at the end of July, 1833, to establish everywhere an "association of friends of the Church", and to send conciliatory manifestoes to the authorities. But Newman, urged on by the impetuous Froude, preferred more radical steps, and proposed to "reconstruct" the Church, separated from the State, on its only authentic foundation, the apostolic succession. On September 9, the first number of the *Tracts for the Times* trumpeted his plea throughout the country. In his own view, the struggle against political liberalism was only secondary; the main purpose of the movement was to counter liberalism in philosophy and religion, where it was generally undermining the foundations of the Christian life. In the following years, he devoted his enormous intellectual activity to two tasks : (1) the working-out of the *Via Media*,

---

[1] *Apologia*, pp.54-55.

[2] *Ibid.*

[3] The deep feeling and bewilderment in the Church are well described by A. W. Evans, *op. cit.*, pp.vii-xiv.

an apologetic and dogmatic theology of Anglicanism;[1] (2) the examination and defence, at Oxford, of religious belief.[2]

During the period 1833-1841, Newman is to be seen exerting the full force of his personality. He was the animating and driving spirit of the Oxford Movement. His was the mind, enthusiastic, fearless and confident, that guided its progress; more, even, than a party leader, he was the creator and propagator of new ideas. Not till 1839 did he begin to doubt, momentarily, the validity of the *Via Media*, as a consequence of his study of the Monophysites and of an article on the Donatists by Wiseman. For the first time, he had a suspicion that the *Via Media* was but a renewal of these old schisms.[3] In January, 1841, he published *Tract 90*, in which he explained in a Catholic sense the Thirty-nine Articles, to which every Anglican clergyman was obliged, officially, to subscribe. This caused an uproar. One by one, the Anglican bishops disavowed him.[4] He proceeded to examine anew the Arian heresy and the evidence in favour of his earlier impression became more and more compelling. The ethos of the semi-Arians was strictly identical with that of the Anglican Church of the day; that of the "great Catholic Church" persisted at Rome, whose position remained unchanged.[5] By degrees, the Anglican Church lost its hold on him; but, though drawn to Rome by his historical studies, he was held back by all that he thought it had added to the original deposit of faith. His hesitations lasted four years more. On April 9, 1842, he withdrew from Oxford to the solitude of Littlemore. There he gradually brought to fruition the hypothesis of the development of doctrine, which cleared the way. In 1843, he retracted some of his anti-Roman arguments and resigned the living of St. Mary's. From then on, he applied himself exclusively to the *Development of Christian Doctrine* in order to settle finally his opinions; but, before he had finished it, he yielded to the evidence and on October 9, 1845, he acceded to the Roman Catholic Church.

There are many reasons for which this whole period is of the

[1] The chief productions of this period were: *Lectures on the Prophetical Office of the Church* (1837), *Lectures on the Doctrine of Justification* (1838), and the fateful *Tract 90* (1841).

[2] Hence, the *Oxford University Sermons*.

[3] *Apologia*, pp.118-122.

[4] *Ibid.*, p.140.

[5] *Ibid.*, pp.139-140.

4

greatest importance to the problem which forms the subject of this book. First of all, his attack on liberalism at its root forced Newman to direct his attention to the psychology of faith, its origin and growth. The *University Sermons*, in particular, contain the outcome of his reflections on this subject and, in turn, they aided him to define his views on the birth and development of religious conviction in general.

Besides, Newman, as leader of the Oxford Movement, learned at first hand how ideas live and develop within a given society. The same careful scrutiny he continually gave to the motions of his own mind he now directed externally. A whole series of articles shows how he perceived more and more clearly that tradition, in the concrete, is not a static continuation, inert and lifeless, of the original ideas, but one that is living and dynamic. It adapts itself to, and assimilates, other ideas, takes new forms, extends its range, and, as circumstances alter, exhibits aspects hitherto unperceived. Though its development may seem to be ruled by chance occurrences, Newman senses that, underlying and governing these, is some deep-seated force. Some need, some impulse, takes hold of a group, takes possession of its members and impregnates them with a single spirit, with the result that both their thoughts and acts become, in a measure, functions in the life of an idea which unites and animates the whole.[1]

At the same time, Newman's study of the Fathers and of the great heresies and schisms of early Church history gradually presented to his view the ancient Church as it really was and the positions taken up by both sides in the controversies of the patristic era. He found these ideas, principles and standpoints analogous to those of the disputants of his own day. The *ethos* of the orthodox body he saw extant in the Roman Catholic Church, the position adopted by the semi-Arians, Monophysites and Donatists he found reproduced in the Anglican *Via Media*. The continuity of the

---

[1] We see the germination of these ideas in an article of the *British Critic* in 1839, entitled "Prospects of the Anglican Church". (Cf. *Essays Critical and Historical*, I, pp.262-306.) Guitton has ably described their genesis from a series of articles Newman wrote at this time (*op. cit.*, pp.45-63). Several passages from his articles in the *British Critic*, collected afterwards in the two volumes of his *Essays Critical and Historical*, may be looked upon as fragments of his future *Essay on Development*. Only after his conversion did Newman publish his full self-questioning as leader of the Oxford Movement; it forms the first part of his *Lectures on certain Difficulties felt by Anglicans* (1850).

ethos or character proper to Christian antiquity within the Roman Church would become for him the chief pledge and ground of her fidelity, throughout her history, to the original doctrine.[1]

Finally, in his attempt to provide the Church of England with a strict dogmatic theology, he came up against the problem of the development of doctrine.[2] In his *Prophetical Office of the Church*, he sets out, over against the Catholic position, the following thesis of the *Via Media* : all that pertains to the sphere of doctrine is to be judged by the famous text of Vincent of Lérins : *quod semper, quod ubique, quod ab omnibus* (what has been held always, everywhere, and by all). Applying this rule in good faith, he continues, for good faith is necessary, we consider that the Anglican Church has kept unaltered the doctrine handed down by the Apostles, as is shown by the history of the Church in the first five centuries; but, in recent times, the Church of Rome has falsified the deposit of faith by adding fresh articles to the original Creed. Soon, however, as a result of his patristic studies, Newman considered this position untenable; it was quite obvious that some development was already to be seen by the time of the first general councils. That of Nicaea saw the final stage of the most remarkable of the developments. The rule of Vincent of Lérins was, therefore, unacceptable. Its strict application would condemn the Council of Nicaea and hardly any of the actual Anglican doctrine would survive. Applied in a broad sense, it could well justify the Council of Trent. Another criterion would have to be found which would admit, at any rate, some development of doctrine; otherwise, one would have to jettison all the doctrines of the Anglican Church and the dogmatic principle as well. But any admissible hypothesis which allowed some kind of development would, while

[1] See the texts referred to above in *Apologia*, pp.118-122, 139-140. From April, 1944, onwards, Newman's letters show that he had modified his attitude to Rome; cf. Harper, *op. cit.*, pp. 43-50. In them occurs what was to constitute, in the *Essay*, the first criterion of true development: continuity of type, its persistence and preservation (pp.207-322). Newman continually returns to it. It is the subject of the last lecture in *Difficulties*. It is also, according to a letter of 1850, the main theme of the *Essay*: "It may be asked why the writer of this book went over to the Catholic Church. Answer: because it is the Church of St. Athanasius and St. Ambrose" (Ward, *Life*, I, p.237). See also a letter to H. Wilberforce (*Ibid.*, p.616), and especially one to Mozley published in the *Contemporary Review*, 1899 (cited in Sobry, *op. cit.*, p.47, and Guitton, *op. cit.*, pp.112-113).

[2] On this aspect of Newman's thought, see the Introduction to the *Essay*, pp.10-27, and *Diff. Angl.*, I, p.395.

saving the dogmatic principle, remove all objection to the doctrines of Rome. All of this shows that Newman's theory of development and his submission to Rome were the logical outcome of his defence of the dogmatic principle.

Newman in the Catholic Church (1845-1890)

On February 22, 1846, Newman left Littlemore and was sent by Cardinal Wiseman to Rome, where he arrived on October 28. Ordained priest on May 30, 1847, he entered the Oratory in the following month. He founded an Oratory in London and another at Edgbaston, Birmingham where, apart from a short period in Dublin, he spent the rest of his life. On the foundation of a Catholic University in Dublin, he was appointed its first Rector, on November 12, 1853; but his work collapsed and, seven years after, he resigned. In 1859 he was, from March to May, editor of the *Rambler*, a Catholic review founded in 1848. In the review a few laymen of progressive opinions, among whom was Acton, the great Cambridge historian, set out to air their views without restraint of any sort on all the questions of the day, including those bearing on religion and the Church on which no binding decision had yet been given by authority. The dissatisfaction of the bishops with the tone of some of these articles, which they considered too outspoken, compelled Newman to retire after the appearance of the first two numbers. His adventures in this sphere seriously compromised him; for, in spite of his resignation, he was for some time involved in the hostility in many Catholic circles to the review.[1] Without his knowledge, extracts from one of his articles were translated into Latin,[2] and submitted to the judgment of Rome. They aroused in the Vatican misunderstandings and suspicions which lasted till 1867, owing to the carelessness of Wiseman, who failed to communicate to Rome the explanations furnished by Newman.

Meanwhile, Newman had founded the Oratory School at Edgbaston, where Catholic boys could receive a public-school education in a Catholic setting. He devoted to it his best efforts, and remained more or less forgotten by the world till his controversy

---

[1] From this time dates the mistrust of Manning, cf. Tristram and Bacchus, *op. cit.*, col. 341.

[2] The celebrated *On Consulting the Faithful in Matters of Doctrine*.

with Kingsley[1] and his immortal *Apologia Pro Vita Sua* won him the lasting regard of the English people. From then on, he was the most conspicuous figure in English Catholicism. He deliberately assumed the position of leader of the moderate and conciliatory section of Catholic theologians in countering the Ultramontanism of the Manning-Ward group. In that way, he contributed more than anyone else to the intellectual prestige of Catholics, and to gaining for them the sympathy of the public.

In 1879, Leo XIII made him a cardinal; Newman chose for his motto, "Cor ad cor loquitur" (Heart speaks to heart). He went on living tranquilly at Edgbaston, revered by all, and died on August 11, 1890. He was buried at Rednal, where was set up a plaque with the inscription he had composed, *Joannes Henricus Newman, Ex umbris et imaginibus in veritatem* (From shadows and images to the truth).

The distrust and misunderstanding which cast their sad shadow over his Catholic life undoubtedly hindered the recognition of his genius, but could not prevent the ripening of his convictions and the expression of his ideas. In fact, it was on the occasion of his various ordeals that he wrote his masterpieces.

Throughout this period, his first concern remained the same : it was the conflict with liberalism; but he added to this a fresh one, the intellectual rebirth of Catholicism and the struggle against Ultramontanism. The latter were new tasks for his energies, and the study of these questions brought fresh insights to serve his theory of development. This occurred in several ways :

1. The war against liberalism in religion, which he carried on henceforth from a Catholic position, revolved round a new thesis, namely that "from a truly philosophical point of view, there is no middle term between atheism and Catholicism, so that,

---

[1] Charles Kingsley (1819-1875), professor of modern history at Cambridge, poet, and novelist. Reviewing Froude's *History of England* in *Macmillan's Magazine*, he asserted that "Truth for its own sake had never been a virtue with the Roman Clergy. Father Newman informs us that it need not be" (Ward, *op. cit.*, II, p.1). Kingsley was giving a malicious interpretation to Newman's idea of "economy". In reply to Newman's insistence, he published, in the same review, an obviously inadequate apology. Newman answered by publishing their correspondence with a shattering commentary. Kingsley, thereupon, published a pamphlet, "What, then, does Dr. Newman Mean?". He bolstered up his charges and defied Newman, whose reply appeared in weekly instalments, and, in book form, constitutes the *Apologia*. See *infra*, Chap. II.

given a strictly logical intelligence, it ought, in the circumstances it finds itself in, to adhere to either one or the other."[1] It is possible, in the face of reality, to adopt, as point of departure, a moral attitude whose counterpart in the mind would be a series of basic principles leading logically through liberalism to scepticism and irreligion. Or one could confront reality in an entirely different attitude, favourable to religious experience and giving birth to other first principles which would, of their own accord, clear the way to Christianity and, consequently, to Catholicism.[2] In this plan of apologetics, the theory of the development of doctrine is of capital importance since, through it, the truth of the Catholic Church is seen to follow strictly from that of the Christian revelation.[3]

2. While at Oxford, Newman was chiefly engaged in fostering a religious attitude in a highly cultured society. But, among his Catholic co-religionists, the same problem of harmonising religion and culture appeared with a different emphasis. They had to be persuaded that, if they were to influence public opinion at all strongly, they would have to rise to the level of the national culture and make contact with all the intellectual currents of the time.[4] This conviction of his was the mainspring of his actions as rector of the University of Dublin; it was, too, one of the chief reasons for his failure.[5] It inspired his foundation of the Oratory School

[1] *Apologia*, p. 186.

[2] See later chapter of Newman's apologetic.

[3] In the *Essay*, the only object, it seems, of the theory of development was to overcome a difficulty. In the edition of 1871, however, Newman inserted two passages to show the fact of development as an argument for Catholicism (in the new preface and the note added on p.326). He often returned to this idea (*Diff. Angl.*, I, pp.395-396; *Apologia*, pp.185-196; *Grammar*, p.498, note written in 1880). The two latter passages emphasize the relation between the development of doctrine and the position we have here outlined. The *Grammar* does not relate developments to apologetics, but argues that natural religion leads to Christianity. The *Grammar* and the *Essay* are thus complimentary.

[4] Newman's desire for this led to his *Idea of a University*, and it found forcible expression in his sermons at Dublin University (the first eight of *Sermons on various Occasions*), particularly the first, "Intellect, the Instrument of Religious Training".

[5] "While the Irish clergy feared the broadening of the mind as dangerous to faith, Newman's whole dread was of obscurantism, and he expected much profit, even for religion, from genuine culture," F. Tardivel, *La personnalité littéraire de Newman*, p.63. For the whole lamentable episode of the rectorate, see Ward, *op. cit.*, I, pp.305-389, and Fergal McGrath, *Newman's University*, (London, 1951).

and his plan for a Catholic college at Oxford. This latter he tried for years to effect, but his hopes were frustrated by the machinations of Manning and Mgr. Talbot at Rome. Newman found himself more isolated and misunderstood in this matter than in any other. This concern with education focused his attention on a fresh aspect of the problem, the relation between religion and culture, which led him to the very centre of the psychology of development.

3. In seeking after the Church, Newman had rediscovered in Catholicism the spirit and atmosphere of primitive Christianity. Now he was living in that Church and experiencing its nature and character. The solemn definition of the dogma of the Immaculate Conception and the meeting of the Vatican Council brought him into living contact with the laws governing the origin of dogmatic and theological propositions which, from the outset of his patristic studies, had aroused his keen interest.[1] He reacted against Ultramontanism, which carries to extremes the rôle of the central authority and "maximizes" the doctrinal significance of the pronouncements of the *magisterium*; but this attitude of his obliged him to express a more profound gratitude to that living institution which, in collaboration with various other factors, presents us with definitions of faith. His investigations on this subject led him to specify precisely the function, in the life of dogma, of the various elements in the Church, to assign to each its due importance and, finally, to distinguish the divergent tendencies and the relations between theology, Church government and devotional practice. This gave rise to a new chapter in the theory of the development of doctrine : the actual realization of this development in the living community of the Church.[2]

---

[1] *Diff. Angl.*, I. p.395.

[2] These new aspects are treated in a number of different writings: *On Consulting the Faithful, etc.* (1859); *Apologia* (1864); *Letter to Pusey* (1864); *Letter to the Duke of Norfolk* (1874); preface and Notes to the *Via Media* (re-published 1877). In the next chapter, we shall give a detailed account of the different aspects of Newman's thought, as expressed in each of his works.

Chapter 2

THE IDEA AND THEORY OF DEVELOPMENT IN NEWMAN'S WORKS

IN the biographical sketch just given, we examined the various experiences and influences which gave rise to Newman's views and inspired some of his convictions. His practical cares and the questionings of his mind led him to consider the idea of development under many of its aspects. We will now try to detect the birth and development of this idea as shown in his works.[1]

1. *The Arians of the Fourth Century* (1832)[2]

This is a historical analysis of great originality, in which Newman devotes close attention to the origin of doctrinal propositions regarding the Trinity.[3] These were called forth by a two-fold need, one external (the struggle against heresy), the other internal (the impulse, natural to an educated Christian, to give intellectual expression to his faith). Here, as later in the Oxford sermon, Newman looks on this process as the translation into abstract terms of an affective "vision", called into being and sustained by the concrete terms of Scripture. It is, then, a question of "translating" a kind of intuition into a system of concepts by discursive reasoning.

---

[1] In the Introduction we have already indicated the necessity, in regard to the greater part of Newman's works, of bearing in mind their literary character and circumstances of origin.

[2] For an analysis of this work, see Guitton, *op. cit.*, pp.2-22.

[3] This is the standpoint from which Newman approached the problem of development: "The study of its laws and of its exhibition, or, in other words, the science and history of the formation of theology, was a subject which had interested me more than anything else from the time I first began to read the Fathers" *Diff. Angl.*, I, p.393.

The Apostles, on their own account, had already reflected on the principal articles of belief, but their teaching gave rise to different interpretations in the age of the great heresies, and the Fathers of the Church saw themselves obliged to give stricter definitions, more careful distinctions, and so to create a new theological language. Newman was not yet occupied with the development of doctrine in its content. At this stage, he was aware only of an alternative mode of expressing the object of faith, itself always the same and unchanging.[1] Such a practice appeared to him, in this work, more as a necessary evil, and he emphasised the imperfection[2] and the danger[3] inherent in such "translation". So long as the light of faith shone brightly, the Church paid little heed to such formulas[4]; only the abuse of reason by heretics obliged her to refurbish and elaborate them.[5]

2. *Lectures on the Prophetical Office of the Church, viewed relatively to Romanism and Popular Protestantism* (1837)

This work forms the central element in Newman's theology of Anglicanism. In it he aims at setting out the doctrinal basis of his theology, and defending it both against Roman Catholicism and popular Protestantism.[6] He treats mainly the sources and rules of the faith.[7] He points out the necessity of an ecclesiastical tradition having equal authority with Scripture. The latter contains, it is true, the entire faith, but not in an explicit form; and the terms in which the divine message is, in fact, delivered do not always coincide with those used in the teaching of dogma.[8] How, then, are we to sift the fundamental tradition of the faith from

[1] The main thesis is stated on pp.143-145.

[2] See p. 145: "The shadow, projected for the contemplation of the intellect, of the object of scripturally-informed piety; a representation, economical, necessarily imperfect, as being exhibited in a foreign medium, and therefore involving apparent inconsistencies or mysteries."

[3] Danger of ambiguity, of which heretics take advantage (see pp.179-181).

[4] P.145.

[5] Pp.145, 163, 179-181.

[6] Basically, this popular Protestantism is allied with his principal enemy, liberalism; for, by the exercise of private judgment, it has practically eliminated the dogmatic principle entirely. See pp.1, ff.; also, p.333.

[7] The question at issue was, in fact, "Who was nearer to the original truth possessed by Ignatius and Polycarp, and which the nineteenth century has lost?" (p.6). Given his dogmatic position, Newman could not express the matter otherwise.

[8] P.192.

those non-dogmatic convictions and theological opinions which
have grown out of it? Newman answers by appealing to the rule
expressed by Vincent of Lérins : *Quod semper, quod ubique,
quod ab omnibus.*[1] This aphorism leads him to draw an important distinction between the episcopal and the prophetic tradition.
The first is a uniform and strictly doctrinal teaching, handed down
from bishop to bishop in creed and ceremonial; the second is the
product of those interpreters of revelation whom St. Paul calls
"prophets" and "doctors". This tradition is the outcome of a wide
proliferation of thought, a network and combination of explanations, conclusions, distinctions, spontaneous adaptations and systematic elaborations, variations due to local and temporal conditions; in short, all those elements which appear, with the passage
of time, under very diverse forms.

Each of these traditions has its characteristic obverse, its inherent danger. The first is exposed to a rigid conservatism, a worship of the letter to the exclusion of the spirit and life, a timorous
immobility. The second, under the influence of various forces,
among others the subtle, hidden tendencies in man weakened by
sin, is continually drawn to deviate from the faith of antiquity.
The two are divergent and complementary and serve to hold each
other in equipoise. The bishops have to keep continual watch over
the "prophets", but the latter have to prevent assent to doctrinal
propositions from degenerating into sterile conformity. The prophetic tradition exhibits the thought of the Church in its living
reality at each moment of her history together with the forms
actually taken by religious and devotional practice; it is less concerned with the content of faith.[2]

In this work, Newman sets out to plead the cause of a static
tradition, as opposed to the idea of doctrinal development, which
he stigmatizes as "papist".[3]

---

[1] Nevertheless, Newman was well aware of the practical difficulty of its
application: "The rule of Vincent is not of a mathematical or demonstrative
character, but moral; and requires practical judgment and good sense to
apply it . . . How many Fathers, how many places, how many instances
constitute a fulfilment of the test proposed? It is, then, from the nature of
the case, a condition which can never be satisfied as fully as it might have
been; it admits of various and unequal application in various instances"
(p.56).

[2] Pp.249-251.

[3] "The creed of Rome is ever subject to increase; ours is fixed once for
all" (p. 212).

3. *University Sermons*[1]

This work comprises fifteen sermons, the first nine of which date from the early Oxford period, and were delivered between 1825 and 1832. The last six belong to the time of the Oxford Movement, and were delivered between 1839 and 1843. Newman thought them the best of his Anglican works.[2] They embody the foundations of the intellectual structure he sought to rear against liberalism in religion and philosophy. His aim was to support the younger fellows and students in resisting the rationalistic influence of certain Oxford circles. Most of these sermons were directed against the Evidential School, which held faith to be the result of historical and rational investigation.[3] Newman shows that every person can, by his reason, reach the threshold of faith; even one of little education could do so, but through an "experiential" process of a kind of implicit and unconscious reasoning rather than by explicit examination. But this gradual approach to faith supposes personal fidelity to conscience, not a scientific attitude; the factors leading to conviction are the profound stirrings of conscience rather than the proofs furnished by history.[4] This is Newman's first formulation of the actual way in which religious conviction comes about.[5]

This collection of sermons on faith and reason concludes with the great sermon of 1843 on *The Theory of Development in Religious Doctrine*. The theory of development was taking shape in Newman's mind, and this is a first sketch. The standpoint he adopts here corresponds to the subject of the whole work, the relation of faith and reason.[6] The treatment is the same as in the *Arians*; first, the genesis of theology, then its rational working-out by reflection on the concrete intuitions of faith. As in the *Arians*,

---

[1] For a proper understanding of these sermons, see Newman's Preface to the third edition (1871), pp.ix-xvii, and the commentary of Bacchus in *The Month*, I (1922), pp.1-12. This article contains the essentials of the author's great article on Newman in the *D.T.C.*

[2] Cf. *Letters and Correspondence*, II, p.364.

[3] Cf. *D.T.C.*, *loc. cit.* Whately belonged to this school.

[4] In other words, the "evidences" of Christianity.

[5] In 1860, Newman described the purpose of the *University Sermons* as to show that, if religion is a conclusion of reason, there must be motives adequate for the conviction of any individual.

[6] This special element within the general problem is expressly noted by Newman on p.314.

the subject-matter is confined to the Trinitarian and Christological formulas.[1]

In this sermon the psychological standpoint, which, incidentally, prevails throughout the work, gives the atmosphere in which
Newman studied the problem of development, though we sense,
at the same time, his design of combating liberalism.

Newman, in the *Arians*, seems anxious to justify the existence
of theology, and takes up a defensive attitude; here, on the contrary, he exalts it over against the relativism of the liberals.[2] To
the liberal, dogma, the rational expression of the faith, is something wholly relative, a superficial garb of the interior life of the
faith. It is considered as having no substantial truth, and ever
liable to change. Newman's contention is that it expresses sub-

---

[1] P.319. Here Newman, using the technical terms of theology, speaks of
the Trinity and Incarnation as "objects of faith". Byrne says that this is his
earliest technical use of the word "object" to designate a reality external
to the mind, but giving rise in it to "impressions " and "ideas" (J. J. Byrne,
op. cit., pp. 282-283). In our opinion, the same use appears, though not so
clearly, in the *Arians*, where Newman speaks frequently of the Object
(generally with a capital letter because referring to something sacred). His
use of the word has four senses, the most usual being that of "end", and
objective. The second is that of "intentional" object, *objectum internum* or
subject-object (*Grammar*, p.81). The third makes it synonomous with
"thing", existing reality. The fourth, and for us the most important, sense
combines the second and third (e.g., *objects of faith*), where it is a question
of realities independent of the subject, but considered in relation to it, as
determining the content of the act of knowing. Newman held that certain
accompaniments of the act of knowing show that it refers to realities outside
the subject, and so objective (*O.U.S.*, pp.330-331; *Essay*, pp.34-35). That is
precisely what the term, "object", signifies; it bears a relation to consciousness, of which it is an immanent effect, but is viewed as, in itself, external
to it. Hence, he generally calls "vision" or "view" the act by which the
subject is aware of the object. Significantly, in the last Oxford sermon,
when treating of "objects of faith", Newman uses the words "vision" and
"view" instead of "idea", "judgment", "impression". This specific use of
"object" occurs throughout his works, particularly in the *Idea* and the
Grammar. He is not, however, to be confined to a strict terminology.

[2] In the Introduction, Newman presents Our Lady, who "kept all these
things in her heart", as the perfect model of the theologian: "first believing
without reasoning, next from love and reverence reasoning after believing".
The whole sermon is a panegyric of true theology. The words of the Gospel
"have a life in them which shows itself in progress; a truth which has the
token of consistency; a reality which is fruitful in resources; a depth which
extends into mystery". But heresy is barren: "it has no theology. Its
formulas end in themselves, without development, because they are words;
they are barren, because they are dead" (p. 318). He could not have applied more powerfully the saying of Scott: "Growth is the sole evidence
of life".

stantial and unchanging truth, and that between it and the living faith there is a real, though imperfect, correspondence.[1] Janssens rightly sees in this "one of the most striking expressions of his anti-modernism".[2]

We see here that Newman's way of looking at the history of dogma has changed; from the static conception of the *Arians* and the *Prophetical Office,* it has become dynamic. He no longer considers it the task of rational theology simply to find suitable formulas; still less is theology an unrestrained luxuriance of thought; he views it rather as functioning in the very interior of tradition, as one of its normal and legitimate agents of development. This change of view is shown in many details. For example, the principal motive force of theology is no longer the need for opposing heresy, but a "devout curiosity", an impulse inherent in the life of faith in the human mind : *fides quaerens intellectum.*

This advance is obviously due to his deepening insight into the psychology of knowledge, which he sketches in broad and vivid strokes, with a freshness and intuitive sweep in which his originality appears unmistakably. The relations between intuition and abstraction, the analogy of development of the faith with natural knowledge, are set out in a striking way. In the later part of the work, he studies the difficulties—already presaged in the *Arians* —which are obviously bound to arise from the abyss separating divine truths from the concepts and representations of it drawn from ordinary experience, as well as from the distance between the intuitive and the abstract idea.

4. *An Essay on the Development of Christian Doctrine* (1845)

This is a work of a very special kind. Newman had come, gradually, to realise that the theory of development was eliminating his remaining difficulties about Rome and impelling him to the decisive step. His reason was convinced, but he was still subject to that vague but profound doubt, so characteristic of his cast of mind, which we have already touched upon.[3] How was he to

---

[1] See pp.318-319, 327-329. The liberals claim that "there is, in truth, no necessary or proper connection between inward religious belief and scientific expositions" (p.319). Newman asserts that "there is a general, natural, and ordinary correspondence between the dogma and the inward idea" (p.328).

[2] A. Janssens, *op. cit.,* p.117.

[3] See above pp.24-27.

surmount this? He decided to follow out his thought to its ultimate conclusion, drawing out all its possible consequences, and to submit it, once and for all, to the strictest examination. He would commit himself to the judgment of reason and consider the outcome as the work of Providence. In this frame of mind he wrote the *Essay*.[1] This book, then, must be looked upon as an absolutely sincere attempt at his personal orientation. Its immediate aim was not to provide an apologia for Catholicism[2]; in fact, it was not even intended for publication, in its first form. Moreover, Newman reserved the right to change his mind after he had worked out his hypothesis.[3] But we are not to overlook his secondary motive; for if his thought, working objectively, should issue in Catholicism, the work would serve as an explanation to his friends of the Oxford Movement. In following the winding course of his mind, many of these were becoming inclined to scepticism, and Newman showed himself very concerned at this. Would his turning to Catholicism set them completely at sea? The *Essay* would prove that his conversion implied no substantial change of conviction, but was its logical consequence[4]; and so there was no reason why the same view could not be shared by his former companions. Still, he was aware that his idea was too novel and its form too provisional to be immediately successful. He wrote, deliberately, for the future.[5]

The sermon of 1843 had considered only one side of the problem of development, the psychological nature of the relations between faith and reason. The *Essay* of 1845 is not, in the main, a psychological description but a thesis, a demonstration, which, from the outset, envisages Christianity in its entirety, objectively. The author's mind ranges widely over the history of Christianity and its doctrine. The question before him is whether the historian

[1] *Apologia*, p.208.

[2] Cf. *Essay*, Preface to 1878 edition, p.vii.

[3] Cf. *Apologia*, p.176.

[4] This is shown in the correspondence with Froude. This highly interesting interchange of the years 1844-45 (cf. Harper, *op. cit.*, pp.33-38) was prompted by "William's chief distress, viz., that my changing opinion seemed to unsettle one's confidence in truth and falsehood as external things" (p.38). Newman describes at length the logical development of his thought and finishes by speaking of the *Essay:* "A book of some sort to advertise to people how things stood with me" (p.66).

[5] "It will be a sort of obscure philosophical work with little to interest and much to disappoint" (*Ibid.*, p.66).

is entitled to speak of Christianity as something clearly defined
and always unchanging. A difficulty at once appeared, for it
would seem that history witnesses a continual change; and, in
that case, does nineteenth-century Christianity represent the same
spiritual reality as that of previous centuries?[1] The *Essay* answers
in the affirmative. In a letter written subsequently, Newman describes the thesis of the work as follows: "The differences and
additions in doctrinal teaching observable in the history of the
Church are only apparent, being necessary for the development
of her ideas."[2] Here we have the problem of doctrinal development stated in its fullness and complexity; it is concerned with all
the possible ways of the total process, and all the influences which
furthered it. In the last resort, it is indistinguishable from the
problem of Christianity itself. Evidently, Newman's chief aim was
to reconcile the widest possible development with the requirements
of the apostolicity and invariability of the Catholic creed. [3]

It will be useful to say a few words about the two editions of the
work. The revised edition of 1878 was not, in Newman's opinion,
a recasting of his views, but continued to uphold strictly those of
thirty-three years earlier and to embody the same convictions.[4]
Still, he introduced some significant changes in the general
arrangement. The original appeared as a gradual elaboration, a
progressive unfolding, of a single argument. In the new edition, he
introduces a sharp distinction between two arguments—one, substantially religious; the other, strictly apologetic. The religious
discussion or, more exactly, historico-religious, aims at proving
the general identity of present Catholic doctrine with that of
primitive Christianity by the convergence of two lines of thought.
The first and principal one states *a priori* the judgments spontaneously formed by the mind when it reflects on the history of
Catholic doctrine; this method presupposes a religious standpoint
that already accepts the Christian revelation. The second confirms

[1] See *Essay*, pp.3-7.
[2] Letter to Mr. Joulkes, first published in Guitton, *op. cit.*, p.190.
[3] So he says in the *Apologia*, pp.91-92: "That work I believe I have not
read since I published it, and I do not doubt at all I have made many
mistakes in it; partly from my ignorance of the details of doctrine, as the
Church of Rome holds them, but partly from my impatience to clear as
large a range for the *principle* of doctrinal development (waiving the question
of *historical* fact) as was consistent with the strict apostolicity and identity
of the Catholic Creed".
[4] *Essay*, p. viii.

these judgments by "evidences", that is by taking a number of soundings in history. As to the second proof—the working out and application of the seven criteria—Newman intended it to be purely rational and defensive. Convinced by the first and principal argument, the intellect ventures into the neutral region of the mind in general to face the difficulties arising from reason. This second proof simply serves to refute objections.[1] The division introduced sets the whole argument in relief, and shows up better the real nature of Newman's thought.[2]

5. *De Catholici Dogmatis Evolutione* (1847)

This was written by Newman for Father Perrone to enable him to judge how far the author's views on development agreed with Catholic theology.[3] He divided the pages into two columns, in one of which he wrote his own opinions, and left the other for Perrone's comments. These were few and of slight interest, and show little understanding of Newman's ideas. Newman himself considered that Perrone's criticisms left his essential position unaffected.[4]

This study is, none the less, of the greatest interest. In it we find, once again, a frank and courageous expression of Newman's personal views; but whereas in the *Essay* he was concerned to prove that identity persisted throughout the changes wrought by development, here he reverses the order and introduces the idea of

[1] At the outset of the second part, Newman writes: "I have been engaged with a positive, direct argument to prove the intimate correspondence, nay the identity, of the teaching called Catholic today with that of apostolic times". Of the seven criteria, he says that they are of a scientific and polemic, rather than a practical, nature; and he adds, in 1878, that they are replies to objections against authoritative decisions rather than proofs of the rightness of these. It is difficult to understand how Guitton can say, of the second part of the *Essay*, that "without warning, the word has changed its meaning, and development comes to be used in a normative sense" (*op. cit.*, p.89). He appears to think that Newman, in the first part, dealt only with the psychology of development, and only in the second with its identity. But this would be to misunderstand both parts, for the chief proof of identity is to be found in the first.

[2] See above, p.24-27

[3] "This is the account sent by me to Father Perrone in 1874; I was eager to learn how far my idea of doctrinal development was admissible" (*Newman-Perrone Paper*, p.403).

[4] Ward, *op. cit.*, II, p.185. Perrone's chief objection was to the use of the expression "new doctrines" instead of "new definitions". In 1850, Newman adopted Perrone's terminology (*Diff. Angl.*, I, p.394).

development within that of "tradition" itself. Hence it is that the *Newman-Perrone Paper* is, mainly, an analysis of the process of development and is closer to the *Essay* than to the fifteenth Oxford sermon. The latter dealt especially with the passage from intuition to concept; whereas here Newman goes further and shows how revealed doctrine, in virtue of infallible definition, passes from subjective existence, latent in the mind of the Church, to objective, when it takes on absolute value as the unchanging norm of faith for all. The whole proof rests on a distinction between the *objective Word of God* and the *subjective Word of God*.[1] In this work, the impulse towards objectification is provided, once again, by the struggle against heresy, in contrast with the view taken in the Oxford sermon.

[1] The subject is treated in four chapters: *De Verbo Dei objectivo; De Verbo Dei subjectivo; De Verbo Dei in Ecclesia Catholica subjectivo; Theses quaedam de Verbo Dei per Ecclesiam manifestato.*
The distinction of subjective and objective seems to be far from clear. At first, it would appear that "objective" refers to the *Verbum Dei* as it is in itself, and "subjective" as it is in the human mind, that is, as subject to the laws governing abstract knowledge, to distinctions in its various aspects, and to progress in comprehension by discursive reason. Later, however, the Word of God present in the Church is said to be "objective" insofar as it is, or will be, transposed into dogma, and "subjective" inasmuch as it has not yet been defined. Now, the dogmatic formula is, *par excellence*—and Newman would agree—an expression dependent upon the nature of human knowledge, the outcome of analysis and abstraction, in constant growth through the centuries. At the moment, what we are really concerned with is its immutability. A dogma, once defined, is fixed for ever as unchangeable, of absolute validity. This is what is meant by the *Verbum Dei objectivum*. As to the *Verbum Dei subjectivum*, we are to understand by it revelation in its provisional form, before it has attained to definitive and universal validity (see the whole of the first chapter, pp.404-407).
The antithesis, subjective and objective, recurs continually in Newman, especially in the contrast of subjective and objective truth; but it seems to have more than one application. The following are some of its meanings:
(a) The principal one refers to the two-fold function of truth which, on the one hand, indicates things outside us and is thus called objective, and, on the other hand, has to be assimilated by us to become our personal possession, to become identical with the content of our minds, and in this way is called subjective. These two functions, or aspects, of truth prevail, respectively, in science and literature (cf. *Idea*, p.274): "Literature expresses not objective truth, as it is called, but subjective; not things, but thoughts". This distinction, as applied to that between faith and piety, refers above all to the practical effects of doctrinal knowledge, and its quickening of the emotional life and moral conduct of the believer. Cf. *Diff. Angl.*, II, pp.27-28.
(b) This antithesis also serves to draw attention to the presence or absence of personal assimilation, by the mind, of external truth. Here, the

This brief document is Newman's shortest work on our subject, and that gives it a particular interest. We find there his earlier views succinctly expressed, both the psychology of development outlined in the Oxford sermon (1843), and the sociology of the idea as expounded in the *Essay* (1845), but now they are applied to the Church. Besides, the old static notion of tradition is here replaced by a new conception which incorporates development.[1] Thus, the prophetic tradition—distinguished, in the *Prophetical Office*, from the episcopal, as not being doctrinal—is, in this work, formally integrated in the life of dogma; and so we have the culmination of that movement of Newman's mind that began with the *Via Media*. Finally, and by no means the least point of interest, Newman relates the ideas elaborated in the *University Sermons* and the future *Grammar of Assent* with the development of doc-

term "objective" takes on a slightly pejorative sense. For example: in the mass of Christians, the faith is only objective, whereas it is subjective in the Fathers, that is, with them it takes on various aspects according to their respective mentalities.

(c) But the standpoint may be reversed, and then it becomes a question, in the action of the mind, of the presence or absence of a corresponding external reality. Here, the contrast between objective and subjective is parallel and analogous to that between true and false. For example: "Judaism is an idea that was, at one time, objective, while Gnosticism is an idea that was never so, . . . a false and subjective aspect" (*Essay*, p.34).

(d) The same distinction is used to express the adequacy or inadequacy of knowledge in relation to the object. Here, truth is objective in an intelligence which conceives it in a stage of integral purity, for example, the divine intelligence; but it is subjective in the ordinary human mind, which is far removed from that state (*Newman-Perrone*, pp.405-406).

(e) Objective knowledge, in the sense just explained, must be held immutable and final. From this follows another meaning of the term "objective", which is attributable to human knowledge: the immutable and definitive possession of the truth. For, in the Church, dogma is objective *after* being defined; *before definition*, it is merely subjective (*Ibid.; Diff. Angl.*, I, p.215).

(f) In virtue of the inadequacy referred to, Newman affirms, against the Rationalists, that truth is itself objective, and not subjective; that is, it transcends our mode of knowledge, and cannot be grasped, in itself, by the human mind (*Essays Crit. Hist.*, I, pp.34-35).

(g) The antithesis, objective and subjective, acquires, in addition, a special meaning in its application to religion. Christianity is an objective religion, that is, one that has external motives of credibility (*Essay*, p.80), a religion endowed with an external authority (*Ibid.*, p.86). Natural religion has only an internal authority, that of conscience (*Ibid.*).

The length of this note will give the reader an appreciation of how elastic, subtle, and analogical is Newman's terminology.

[1] See Propositions 4 and 8, pp.430-432 and 436-439.

trine. For this takes place, in its first stage, by a process of implicit reasoning, more or less unconscious, by which the believing mind realises and gradually makes explicit what was, hitherto, but a confused intuition of faith.[1] The synthesis we have undertaken in this book accords well with the very spirit of Newman.

6. *Lectures on Certain Difficulties felt by Anglicans in Submitting to the Catholic Church* (1848)

These lectures are aimed at Anglicanism. In the first part, Newman shows that the Oxford Movement was, on its own principles, alien to the English State Church and that these principles led logically, not to the formation of a new party in the Anglican Church, nor to the setting up of a new "Branch Church" or sect,[2] but to the Catholic Church.[3] We have already seen that Newman, as leader of the Oxford Movement, had learnt from experience how the life of ideas within a society exhibits a unity of its own, which is rightly called a social unity. Now, this sociological experience is expressed in philosophic terms. These lectures bring out clearly the essentially transindividual aspect of the development of ideas, the almost autonomous character of the intellectual activity of a society, and the reality of collective thought. In this consists their contribution to the theory of development.

In the second part, Newman aims at resolving certain difficulties arising from the Catholicism of the day and likely to hinder the conversion of Anglicans. The last of these is, in fact, development: *Ecclesiastical History no Prejudice to the Apostolicity of the Church*. Newman argues that it was, precisely, his study of that history that led him to Catholicism, the rightful heir

---

[1] The second chapter studies this growth from the standpoint of the individual; the third applies the result to the Church: "The development of doctrines works in a similar way in the mind of the individual doctor and in that of the Catholic Church" (p.415). Doubtless, the *Essay* alludes to this characteristic of development, but it is submerged in a flood of incidental remarks. Here, however, it is brought out clearly.

[2] According to the "Branch Theory", the Catholic Church, one and indivisible in itself, consists of several "branches", locally distinct, e.g., the Roman, the Greek, and the Anglican "communions", which are equally, in their respective territories, the true Church. A schismatic, then, is not one who leaves the visible community, the "communion", but one who intrudes into the sphere of another "branch" (*Diff. Angl.*, I, pp.170-171). Newman, when an Anglican, had held this theory for some time.

[3] A lecture is devoted to each of these possibilities.

of the primitive Church. He gives particular emphasis to two facts which had impressed him strongly :

1. the resemblance in character between primitive Christianity and the Catholic Church, considered as a living religion on the stage of the world.[1]
2. the development of dogma, which is seen, *from the very beginning*, as a divine law, and which continues still, in its majestic course, within the Catholic Church alone.[2]

7. *The Idea of a University* (1852)[3]

This is Newman's principal work on education, written while he was rector of the University of Dublin. It is his masterpiece, seen from the literary point of view. We have seen that, throughout his tenure of office, he was chiefly preoccupied with raising the intellectual level of Catholics, so that they could take a respected place in English cultural life.[4] The *Idea* aims at describing the nature and ideal of a university and showing the proper effect of a university education.

The mind formed at a university should be stamped with the philosophic spirit, which implies the power to embrace, in a comprehensive view, the whole range of human knowledge and to distinguish the boundaries and mutual relations of its various domains and methods. The philosophic spirit keeps human reason balanced, for the latter, of its very nature, through knowledge by abstraction, tends to onesidedness and so to a distortion of reality. The authentic philosophic spirit can, therefore, be of service to religion, since by its very nature and its requirements it guards against the study of religion by inappropriate methods. Our nature, being unbalanced, tends to warp and distort our ideas of religion; this tendency may be rectified by the philosophic spirit. In itself, the cultivation of the mind offers no positive guarantee

---

[1] "No other form of Christianity but it has pretence to resemble, even in the faintest shadows, the Christianity of antiquity, viewed as a living religion on the stage of the world... To imbibe into the intellect the ancient Church as a fact, is either to be a Catholic or an infidel" (p.393).

[2] He concludes as follows: "The force of this, to me ineffably cogent, argument, I cannot hope to convey to another".

[3] P. Sobry's *Newman en zijn Idea of a University* forms an incomparable introduction to this work. It has the pure and authentic tone of Newman's personality. See also F. McGrath, *op. cit.* This copious work deals at length with all the problems raised by Newman's actions and thought in his time as rector.

[4] See above, p.42.

of religious growth; it goes naturally with pride of intellect. If he is wanting in a constant and scrupulous regard to his conscience, the educated man easily comes to strip his religious and moral experiences of their primitive significance as revelations of a living, personal God, and to interpret them from the standpoint of pure humanism. In that case, all the higher values inspired by a religious outlook on life become transposed on to the level of the refined, but superficial code of the "gentleman". Here we meet the fundamental theme of religious typology of which Newman was so fond.

In addition, *The Idea of a University* contributes to the theory of development by its acute analysis of the mental process of abstraction and of the *ethos* of narrow-mindedness. We shall meet this *ethos* again, in one of its forms, when we come to Newman's characterisation of heresy.

Two passages in the *Idea* define the method of theology in contrast with that followed in the natural sciences. In them, Newman brings out forcibly that Revelation may be made more explicit, but never added to; consequently, deduction, the method of analysis rather than of discovery, is the only one applicable in theology.[1]

To avoid misunderstanding, we must remember that, in this context, the author is studying the methods of the exact sciences; he does not, therefore, rule out that implicit and spontaneous growth which constitutes the development of doctrine. Further, he speaks, not as a private individual, but in his official capacity as rector of a Catholic university. It is, then, understandable— since he is not treating the development of doctrine *ex professo*, but only incidentally—that he approaches the question from the ordinary standpoint of Catholic theology.

8. *On Consulting the Faithful in Matters of Doctrine* (1859)

This celebrated article in the *Rambler*, whose consequences were so tragic for Newman, was not reprinted in his collected works. It is most easily accessible in the German translation, published in 1940, of selected works.[2] It was occasioned by a slight

---

[1] Pp.222-223 and 440-442: "Deduction only is the instrument of theology" (p.223); "As the conclusion is ever in its premises, such deductions are not, strictly speaking, an addition" (p.441).

[2] *Ausgewählte Werke* (ed. Matthias Laros), III, pp.198-239.

dispute caused by this statement which appeared in the *Rambler* :
"If even in the preparation of a dogmatic definition the Faithful
are consulted, as lately in the instance of the Immaculate Conception, it is at least as natural to anticipate such an act of kind
feeling in great practical questions."[1] The word "consult" was
interpreted by some as nothing more or less than a transcription of
the corresponding Latin term, which has a strict technical meaning in theology. Hence the alarm. Newman, however, underlines
the ordinary meaning of the word in English, and takes occasion
to remark on the interest furnished by the *sensus fidelium*, the
religious intuition of believers, as *locus theologicus* and a factor in
the development of doctrine.

The laity are not to be discouraged, he insists strongly, from
studying the truths of faith and examining them attentively for
the light they bring to bear on personal life, and for their principles
of practical conduct. They should not be content with that
"implicit faith" which leads to indifference in the educated and
to superstition in the simple.[2] What is brought out very clearly in
this article is a new aspect of the social life of dogma, the rôle of
the laity.

9.   *Apologia pro vita sua* (1864)

This unique work is widely known.[3] In it Newman goes back
over the history of his religious convictions, in which the theory
of development played such an important part. At the same time,
he sheds a vivid light on his method of thought and the origin of
the main principles guiding it. This odyssey leads up to its climax,
in the seventh and last part, in the most forceful and original expression of his Catholic faith he ever uttered. He exposes entirely
its secret sub-structure : the basic contrast between the experience
of God within his own conscience and the course of external events,
which are so apparently without meaning and devoid of God's
presence. Using this antinomy as a starting point, he attempts an
understanding of the human world and it is in reference to this
that he clarifies the position of the Church in the world and thus
discovers the necessity for an infallible *magisterium*. Finally, he
demonstrates that infallible authority is by no means a hindrance

[1] May, 1859, p.122.
[2] P.239.
[3] On the genesis of this book, see above, Chapter I, p.41.

to the free development of theology. On the contrary, he points out, it is a guide and stimulus. It is by this means that we are brought to consider the sociological structure of the Church and its significance so far as the life of dogma is concerned.

10.   *A Letter to the Rev. E. B. Pusey on his Recent Eirenicon* (1865)

Newman felt that his friend Pusey, far from proffering an olive branch to Catholics, as he intended, in 1865, had actually let fly a powerful bolt.[1] He felt compelled, therefore, to make a reply to the attack that the old "Tractarian" had made on Catholic mariology. His reply was quite deliberately based on his theory of development. Despite this fact, he took great pains to distinguish, with special reference to mariology, between the data of Faith and manifestations of piety, though the Ultramontanists did sometimes grant a dogmatic value to these expressions of religious feeling. Newman underlines the dangers that popular devotion can threaten orthodoxy with. In short, this little work is a perfect balance to the article which appeared in the *Rambler*.

11.   *An Essay in Aid of a Grammar of Assent* (1870)

Here we have Newman's chief philosophical work. To the uninitiated it is almost incomprehensible; it has, in fact, been frequently misunderstood.[2] We must bear in mind his aim; its

---

[1] "You will pardon me, but you present your olive branch with an archer's bow" (p.7).

[2] See F. Bacchus, "How to Read the Grammar of Assent", *The Month*, (1924), pp.108-115. What, he says, makes the work difficult for the reader is that it contains a completely original treatment of a subject already well known and discussed, so that, if he is not prepared, he approaches it with his ideas fixed in advance, which a superficial reading then rediscovers in the work (p.106). We may also recommend: Tristram and Bacchus, *op. cit.*; W. Ward, *Cardinal Newman on Constructive Religious Thought* ("Men and Matters"; London, 1914), pp.347-392; S. Juergens, *Newman on the Psychology of Faith in the Individual* (London, 1928); J. M. J. Willebrands, "Kardinal Newman: de persoonlijke aard van het denken", *Studia Cathol.*, XVIII (1941), pp.425-444; A. Karl, "Die Glaubensphilosophie Newman's", *Grenzfragen Theol. und Phil.*, XX (Bonn, 1941); P. Flanagan, *Newman, Faith, and the Believer*, (London, 1946); M. Nédoncelle, *La philosophie religieuse de J. H. Newman* (Strasbourg, 1946), pp.169-200; H. Fries, *Die Religionsphilosophie Newmans* (Stuttgart, 1948); A. J. Boekraad, *The Personal Conquest of Truth according to J. H. Newman* (Louvain, 1955). The best introduction to an understanding of the *Grammar* for those with a training in Scholasticism is the work of Father Zeno, O. F. M. Cap., *Newman's leer over het menselijk denken* (Utrecht-Nijmegen, 1943).

"prehistory" is most important. It was to be the realisation of what he considered his life's work;[1] whose plan he meditated incessantly, whose idea pursued him as an impelling duty.[2] In it we see the final outcome of his struggle against liberalism. All the great pre-occupations of his life form its background. In 1860, after his experience with the *Rambler*, at the time when he felt himself most deserted and misunderstood, he finally made up his mind to write the book.[3] Then it was, in all probability, that he embarked on the preliminaries; but the work itself was not ready till ten years later, after much mental travail.[4] The current did not flow smoothly. Only in 1866, by a sudden inspiration, did he hit upon a satisfactory plan,[5] and was enabled to set himself to the composition.[6] After finishing the book, he felt himself to have aged.[7] The work itself gave him no satisfaction.[8] None the less, he experienced a great peace; for, even if the work were of little value, he had, at any rate, employed all his powers to the execution

[1] "I have my own subject, one I have wished to do all my life . . . one which, if I did, I should, of course, think it the best thing I had done", (letter to E. Bellasis, in *Memorials of Mr. Serjeant Bellasis*).

[2] " It is one of various points which I have steadily set before me as requiring an answer, and an answer from me" (letter to W. Froude, in Harper, *op. cit.*, p.127). " As to the *Assent*, I had for years considered in my conscience that I could not leave the world without having written it. Right or wrong, I always thought that my duty lay there, as if I had been given a mission to write it" (Ward, *Life*, II, pp.400, 245).

[3] In his correspondence with W. Froude on the problem of the projected *Grammar*, Newman says: "If I ever come to attend in detail to the subject of this letter—which I would do in very slow degrees—I would permit myself to put to you several questions, as one sends samples of metal to the testing bench" (Harper, *op. cit.*, p.132). We have his notes from this period.

[4] The writing of his greater works always caused him intense physical and mental suffering (letter to Ward, cited in W. Ward, *W. G. Ward and the Catholic Revival*, p.198). Newman wrote of his *Grammar*: "Of all my works, it is the one that cost me most, tried me most" (Ward, *Life*, II, p.262).

[5] For this inspiration, on the shores of Lake Geneva, cf. *Ibid.*, pp. 245-246, 280.

[6] "My essay on Assent took four years, from 1866 to 1870" (*Ibid.*, p.399).

[7] "This will be my last work. I say 'work', for it is still possible for me to produce slight pieces, but a genuine work, fruit of a real effort, is now beyond my powers. That is what the old are incapable of; if they risk it, they kill themselves" (*Ibid.*, pp.268, 273).

[8] "I wrote and rewrote it more often than I can remember . . . I firmly believe that I could not do better if I spent a century on it. So perhaps it would be true to say that (now on, for me) the bad is the best I can give" (*Ibid.*, p.62). Newman held his work to be important but provisional, one that simply posed a problem, a first, partial sketch of a map (*Ibid.*, pp.270-271).

of what he held the supreme duty of his life. From now on, he could, in peace of mind, face the approach of death.[1]

What was his aim in writing this book, which is of surpassing interest to us? When he set himself to the task in 1860, it was in order to grapple with the problem touched on in the *Oxford University Sermons*, and to achieve its final solution. He considered he had barely touched its surface in those sermons and, since then, his ideas had matured.[2] What, exactly, was the problem? It was, in the first instance, that of the reasonable character of faith in uneducated persons.

The personal, spontaneous faith of the simple has to bring with it its own justification, valid on rational grounds; and the knowledge of its underlying motives, however implicit and unreflecting, is no less certain than that based on a scientific apologetic.[3] Newman, therefore, is drawn to contrast two modes of thought, the scientific and the personal.

He does not, however, view them with equal favour. In considering reality in the concrete, the only way of reaching truth is the personal. The only difference between scientific and spontaneous thought is the former's critical reflection on itself; their fundamental laws are identical. To confine valid knowledge to the products of technical, impersonal thought would be a conclusion of sophistry[4] and, besides, would lead to the destruction

---

[1] Cf. his letter to R. P. Coleridge (*Ibid.*, p.268) in which he gives expression to his very various feelings about his book. The dominant one, however, is the joy in his *Nunc dimittis*.

[2] Cf. H. Tristram "A Newman Synthesis", *The Clergy Review*, I (1931), p.138.

[3] In 1860, Newman expressed the problem before him thus: "If I wrote a new work, it would deal with the popular, practical, and personal proofs of Christianity, precisely inasmuch as they stand at the antipodes of scientific demonstration; it would aim at showing how any given person, educated or not, possesses as much right to certainty—has, therefore, motives as truly rational—as a learned theologian with his scientific arguments". The same point of view is expressed with great acuteness in the passage cited above, also dating from 1860, defining the object of the *Oxford University Sermons* as well as that of the *Grammar*. See above, p.47, note 5.

[4] Newman speaks of a "sophism" but adds: "A sophism may require an effort of almost genius to overset with its logical and luminous solution" (Harper, *op. cit.*, p.127).

of all certainty and so of all science.[1] All must agree that, apart from mere ascertainment and measurement of sensible phenomena, it is impossible to obtain certain knowledge of reality without previously satisfying two conditions: (1) certain principles have to be granted which cannot be proved themselves, though they admit of being justified to some extent; (2) we must accept as a sign and guarantee of truth, besides the technical procedure of reasoning, the synthesizing and personal intuition of the subject himself. It follows necessarily that the thought can never be viewed in complete isolation from the thinker. That is only natural, for it is the way we are made and, from the standpoint of a sound philosophy, it is futile to stigmatise as absurd the primary datum, that is, our human nature, the structure of our experience as vividly present in the consciousness of each of us. This is the specific point of view of the *Grammar*.[2] Newman, therefore, intends to confine himself to a description of the structure of thought, to discover its mechanism and movement, using thought itself as his starting-point, in the same way as grammar (hence the title, *Grammar of Assent*) derives the laws of language from current use. This is the only way, in his opinion, of obtaining a theory of knowledge at once exact and complete.

Newman's attitude to the problem is markedly polemical. His argument is directed not, as heretofore, at the "Evidential School", but at the post-Kantian "scientism" of his own era. Its upholders contended that absolute certainty was given only by explicit proofs of the type used in mathematical physics. W. Froude,[3] an old friend of Newman's, was an eminent represen-

---

[1] *Ibid.*, p.132: "I suspect that when all scientific proof . . . is examined microscopically there will be found hiatus(es) in the logical sequence so considerable as to tend to the question 'are there no broad, just principles of knowledge which will protect us from scepticism in all reasoning about things external to us, both scientific and popular?'" These "hiatuses" Newman analyzes in masterly fashion in the chapter of the *Grammar* which deals with logical inference.

[2] It is very clearly expounded in a paragraph on the "illative sense" and its trustworthiness. *Grammar*, pp.346-352.

[3] William Froude (1810-1879), younger brother of Hurrell and an inventor of genius. For his scientific career, cf. Harper, *op. cit.*, pp.4-6. The Newman-Froude correspondence published in Harper is of enormous importance in the study of the *Grammar*, both as bringing out Newman's ideas, and for the very detailed and stylistically "Oxford" letters where Froude puts the scientific point of view to Newman, and expresses his objections. Harper

tative of this school of thought. In 1859, this famous inventor and scholar wrote Newman a long letter expressing his intellectual attitude in detail and with perfect frankness. This was followed by a correspondence in which the *Grammar* is seen already in germ. So it was that many sincere persons, even close and lasting friends like Froude, abandoned their faith because of a theory of knowledge which Newman was firmly convinced was based on a sophism. This, finally, persuaded him of his moral obligation to write the *Grammar of Assent*.

There were, besides, personal reasons: he had to draw out and justify the principles and process of thought to which were due the direction of his life and his entry into the Catholic Church. He had long felt the need of a thorough inquiry into the workings of his mind[1] and now it became an imperative duty. Kingsley, as we know, impelled him to write the *Apologia* and to bring out clearly the principles and the stages of his intellectual growth. As might be expected, there was a reaction from the "spirit of the time". In September 1864, Fitzjames Stephen alleged that the method adopted by Newman had vitiated his thought. This method he interpreted as follows: for motives of an irrational nature, of purely personal feeling, Newman had arbitrarily imposed a particular convergence and direction on a whole collection of likelihoods which, interpreted differently, and under the influence of other sentiments, could have led him in quite another direction.[2] Among the numerous letters Newman[3] received on the subject, those of W. Froude, so moving in their sincerity and trust, taught him that the scientific world, though admiring his extraordinary intellectual power, were grieved and amazed to see how he had bridged the gap—so lightheartedly—between simple

---

fails completely, however, to understand the matter, and his commentary is beside the point. Cf. M. Olive, "Le problème de la *Grammaire de l'Assentiment* d'après la correspondance de Newman et Froude", *Bull. de Litt. eccl. de Toulouse*, (1936), pp.217-240.

[1] "I wish I had time and strength to write a work embodying the principles I have implied in my other books"—so Newman wrote, in 1853, in connection with an article of R. Simpson on "Dr. Newman's Style and Method" in *The Rambler* of June, 1853. Simpson alleged that Newman never proved anything (cited in Tardivel, *op. cit.*, p.67).

[2] Among the 70,000 letters preserved at the Birmingham Oratory, there are many, dealing with the problem of faith, which date from the years immediately after the *Apologia*. Cf. Harper, *op. cit.*, p.128.

[3] *Ibid.*, p. 180.

probability and firm certitude.[1] This reproach went to his heart. His *Apologia*, then, had to be reinforced with a substructure going much deeper. He would, to justify that work, bring to light the whole working of his mind, and this would give the key to his entire work. We can see from all this how important the *Grammar* is for the understanding of the theory of development.

Finally, the *Grammar of Assent* has a more special interest for the study of the development of doctrine. In its first part, it examines afresh the relations of two aspects of knowledge—intuitive perception and notional interpretation (here called "real" and "notional"). We are back on the same track as the Oxford Sermon, but the problem is now reversed. In 1843, he had to show how reflection on the "idea" gained by intuition leads to abstract formulations, which are then set in order by a reasoning process. Now, on the contrary, Newman shows how the abstract formulas of dogma bring forth intuitions of reality that bear fruit in genuine piety. This is another aspect of the relation between the doctrinal creed and living religion.

12. *A letter addressed to His Grace the Duke of Norfolk on the occasion of Mr. Gladstone's Recent Expostulation* (1874)

This work shows, once more, Newman's attitude of "prudent minimalism"[2] and recalls a famous controversy. Gladstone prided himself on his knowledge of theology (he claimed a part in the Oxford Movement). He affirmed it was impossible for anyone who accepted the dogma of papal infallibility, as defined by the Vatican Council, to combine obedience to the pope with loyalty to the State. In his reply, Newman asserted the primacy of conscience over external authority; and, at the same time, emphasised the limited scope of the definitions impugned by Gladstone. Incidentally, he makes his own position clear, contrasting it with that of Döllinger and his followers.[3] This part is of great interest. It serves to counterbalance those passages in the *Apologia* which so

---

[1] The interest of Newman's method is emphasised by Haecker, *Christentum und Kultur* (Munich, 1929), and E. Dublanchy, "Dogme", *D.T.C.*, IV, col. 1635.

[2] Newman's own description of his attitude, on p.339.

[3] Pp.311-315.

enthusiastically describe the role of free theological work in the elaboration of doctrine.[1]

The methods proper to theology, he now says, are, by themselves, nearly always inadequate to demonstrate conclusively any single article of faith. The only decisive factor is the Church's dogmatic use of the results attained in theology. The word of the Church itself, uttered by the *magisterium,* gives each doctrine the weight that demands the belief of the faithful.

13. *Preface to the third edition of the "Via Media"* (1877)

This closely-packed work is a refutation by Newman, the Catholic, of Newman the author of the *Via Media.* To the objection alleging a contradiction between the political, doctrinal and religious functions of the Church he replies that contrast, even tension, between the different functions of the Church is the natural consequence of the state of man in any large community. He goes on to analyse the influence exercised by the requirements of devotion and of the political life of the Church on the history of doctrine. In this way, he sheds light on a new aspect of the life of doctrine within the Church.

---

[1] Chiefly on pp.225-229 of the *Apologia.*

PART II

The growth of faith and dogma
The problem of development

INTRODUCTION

THE primary purpose of the theory of development is to furnish an answer to the objection that the Christian revelation has not remained identically the same through the centuries. This objection is based on the fact that we seem to find, as we look at the history of Christian doctrine, that it has been altered in the course of its growth. This was how the problem appeared to Newman, as he shows in the introduction to the *Essay*. For its solution, we must first of all describe the actual process of growth, study its causes and the laws which govern it; then we must reconcile the facts thus established with the immutability which identity demands. The problem, therefore, takes on a double aspect, that of development and change on the one hand, and that of identity and immutability on the other. Each of these we shall treat in turn.

Furthermore, in examining the manner in which development occurs, we must go on to distinguish two further aspects. On the one hand, development is brought about by the action of the human mind, and so is governed by the same laws of psychology as apply to human thought in general. But in addition this development we are studying works itself out within a society and is effected by it; and so it is subject, not only to the intrinsic laws of the mind, but also to the whole complex of conditions imposed by its social character. This requires a new subdivision of our synthesis: one part will treat of the psychology of development from the standpoint of the individual, another of the life of the idea within society. To assist our exposition, we shall, in dealing

6

with the individual aspect, devote one chapter to the general problems of development, and another to those of a specific nature. A preliminary study of Newman's psychology will serve to throw light on the whole.

Chapter I

NEWMAN AND PSYCHOLOGY

IDEAS grow, multiply and develop in various ways. This is a fact, due to the nature of the human mind. How this growth takes place, and under what influences, is for psychology to determine, in so far as their development is governed by the general laws of mental activity. The way we interpret the life of ideas will, therefore, depend on our views on intellectual life in general. We have just shown, in the introduction, that Newman's theory of development can be understood only in the light of his original views on the obscure and complex processes of the thinking mind. Consequently, before entering upon the psychology of development, we propose to make clear the basic principles of his method, and to show the general nature of the psychology which results; and, in addition, we shall set his conception in relation to all the numerous trends in psychology. Anyone who has ventured at all in the labyrinths of psychology will understand the difficulty of the task. We shall content ourselves with a very summary treatment.

Section A

Method, characteristics and significance of Newman's psychology

The *Grammar of Assent* contains a number of precise and acute observations which are of help in defining the nature of Newman's particular method in psychology; but, in all his writings, there is not a single chapter devoted to it *ex professo*. We will have to rely, therefore, on a view of it drawn, by laborious degrees, from a number of disconnected passages. A reconstruction of this sort, especially when dealing with such an original, penetrating and subtle mind as Newman's, is bound to be, at the same time, an interpretation. Ours, we hope, is justified by what the analysis of his works reveals. For it is only in the manner of execution of his works that Newman's method can be detected and made the subject of reflection.

Newman did not treat explicitly of his psychological methods of research and exposition, because he was not professionally concerned with psychology. He was led to probe into the workings of the mind in order to throw light on certain problems of urgent importance both for himself and others. For the same reason, he never set himself to study psychology in its entirety, but devoted his attention solely to the higher sphere of the intellect, since that alone was involved in the questions before him. The chief reason, however, why he was never fully aware of his own method was its absolute originality. In general, a methodology becomes fully clear only after the body of thought has reached the stage of maturity; it is then that the method used, hitherto apprehended only as a vague sense of a direction followed, becomes, as it were, incarnate in the structure evolved and so can become, itself, a subject of reflection. This very well known circumstance explains why, in defining Newman's method, we are obliged to start with its concrete application in his own works.

Another thing must be noted. A comparison with modern psychology would throw a vivid light on the method and the nature of Newman's. It seems, in fact, that Newman's spirit is in close sympathy with that of modern thought. The Modernists, for instance, appealed to his psychology. His analyses have been compared with those of phenomenalism and existentialism. The most contrasting modern trends find in him their forerunner. To-day, much more than in his lifetime, he attracts general attention. His thought has a contemporary stamp. It is strange, at first sight, yet quite understandable that a writer like Aldous Huxley, an agnostic at the opposite pole to Newman, points to him and to Jung as the greatest psychologists and the chief source of his own ideas.[1] If modern psychology is to be found in Newman's work, we may expect it to assist in understanding him.

We must, however, guard against superficial comparisons and tendentious exegesis. The caricature of Newman drawn by his modernistic admirers should be a warning against hasty and ill-considered comparisons. If we do come to detect certain parallels, it is because our views on Newman's psychology had already taken coherent form before we took into account modern theories; Newman was our way to them, and not vice-versa. They merely help us in the clear expression of some of our ideas about Newman, and in assigning him his proper place in the complicated network of modern psychology. We proceed, then, to emphasise the elements in his theories which are original and peculiar to himself.

His first concern, in treating of psychology, is to establish a fixed point of departure, one quite unprejudiced. He tries to let the facts of the mind speak for themselves, and not to assert anything *a priori*.[2] Just as the grammarian confines his efforts to extracting from actual use the laws of language, so Newman aims at tracing out the structures of thought from his observations of mental life in its entirety, without any attempt at evaluation. His intention is expressed clearly in the title of his chief work, *The Grammar of Assent*. His search for a fixed, unalterable point of departure arose from his own philosophical convictions and aims : if we want to discover the ways by which we arrive at truth, we must start by submission to our intellect as we find it, in all its complexity, and then, by reflection, attempt to find the rules of thought and the signs of truth whose warrant is the nature of our own minds. This is as far as it is possible to go; we cannot look outside our nature for its justification. All we can do is, by close and critical reflection, to draw out of it its rightful laws and, using them as a basis, set out methodically a survey of mental activity strictly in accord with the laws of the intellect. The ultimate guarantee of this first philosophical principle is, at least in a sense, of the religious order; we shall show this later, but we must take notice of it here. All New-

---

[1] Cf. Aldous Huxley, *Proper Studies* (3rd ed.; London, 1939), p.xix: "Among the psychologists who have been of assistance to me, I must give a high place to Cardinal Newman whose analysis of the psychology of thought remains one of the most acute, as it is certainly the most elegant, which has ever been made."

[2] *Grammar*, pp.159-160.

man's fundamental principles, in fact, are finally reducible to the consciousness of duty. The only way open to us is to take nature as it is. We are obliged to conform to this sole possibility; this is what a sound philosophy demands. But, without God, we would be liable to doubt and discouragement. Conscience, however, sees God as the author of our nature. Why He made it thus and not otherwise is His secret. He knows its meaning and purpose in his providential design; and, therefore, in every eventuality, it is adequate to provide us with all the truth we need in life here; provided, that is, we make the best possible use of what we have been given.[1]

Newman was well aware that his point of view was in opposition to that of thinkers like Locke, whose theory of knowledge he dismissed as "theoretical and unreal". Locke does not start with the study of what is actually given in nature; rather, he looks at the mind from the standpoint of an *a priori* ideal, and adopts a scientific method to which he considers the mind, in its every activity, must conform, under pain of being stigmatised as guilty of an irrational and immoral "enthusiasm".[2]

In adopting a psychological standpoint based entirely on an analysis of what goes on in the mind, Newman took pains not to pass beyond it. Not only did he approach the facts without theoretical bias, "pre-judgment," he even refrained from speculating, at a later stage, on their genesis. He is not interested in the power which moves the train, whether steam or any other. All that he is concerned to establish is the fact that the train starts from Birmingham and gets to London.[3] Not that he has anything against speculative psychology; he frankly considers he has neither vocation nor talent for it.[4]

We may, perhaps, wonder if Newman did not overestimate the importance of mere analysis in a critical examination of the process of knowledge. After all, his chief aim was to justify certainty

---

[1] On all these points, cf. *Grammar*, pp.346-352.

[2] *Ibid.*, pp.160-164.

[3] *Ibid.*, pp. 343-344. Cf. especially p.64: "I am only contemplating the mind as it moves in fact, by whatever hidden mechanism; as a locomotive engine could not move without steam, but still, under whatever number of forces, it certainly does start from Birmingham and does arrive in London."

[4] *Ibid.*, p.343. Newman, however, is sceptical about the subject; so many geniuses have ventured into it, yet their opinions are hopelessly confused and at variance.

and the mental processes leading to it. Such a plan, it would seem, involves setting up norms of absolute validity. It is not enough to say that this is, in fact, how the mind works and, in so doing, discovers the truth. The validity of an intellectual method cannot, in the last resort, depend simply on the fact that it is seen to be a natural law of the understanding, as shown by experience. Such a mode of reasoning seems the crudest kind of "psychologism". We shall examine this problem, later on, in a section specially devoted to it.

Newman, then, adopts a purely psychological point of view. He aims at finding out how the intellect normally functions, by allowing our ordinary everyday experience to explain itself to the reflecting mind, and omitting no part of its spontaneous fullness and actual complexity. No prior theory is able to "warp" these observations, no subsequent theory, in explaining, can distort them. But where is to be found the life of the understanding in its full range? His answer to this is precise and explicit : the primary source of psychological knowledge is consciousness itself, the secondary source the testimony of others, and this testimony should confirm the truth of what one discovers for oneself. On the other hand, the knowledge of self has to provide the rules for verifying and explaining the testimony of others.[1]

Thus, for Newman, the chief source for psychology is self-observation, in the most general sense; not only introspection, the simple examination of what actually takes place in consciousness, but also, and especially, the retrospective grasp of past actions and situations, the comprehension of the whole range of the psychic life as a dynamic unity.

The emphasis he puts on self-knowledge may seem rather excessive, a manifestation, even, of a certain egotism not unconnected with his tendency to introversion and his proneness to interpret the world in the light of his own mind. Newman really feels

[1] *Grammar.*, p.385 : "He brings together his reasons and relies on them, and this is his primary evidence; and he has a second ground of evidence, in the testimony of those who agree with him. But his best evidence is the former, which is derived from his own thoughts"; p.389 : "The most authoritative of these three means of knowledge, as being especially our own, is the mind, whose informations give us the rule by which we test, interpret and correct what is presented to us for belief, whether by the universal testimony of mankind, or by the history of society and of the world." It is true that he is dealing here with knowledge of religion, but he points out that all this applies equally throughout the realm of psychology (cf. p.384).

at home only in the deepest part of himself: "in these provinces of inquiry egotism is true modesty."[1] This profound conviction of his, which stamps all his thought, engenders a deep humility. He claims for his views no scientific value. All he aims at is to add his own testimony to the collective experience of mankind. He is convinced that his own experiences are confirmed by those of others, and that they are thereby vindicated. He is also aware that others view the same facts in a different light, but that this difference is capable of explanation. Still, he does not venture to make a downright claim for the absolute value of his own views. His main design is to bring out, with great care, the content of his personal testimony.[2] This "egotism"—a very English quality—provides the key to certain gaps that disclose themselves as soon as we attempt to find in his descriptions a complete account of the general structure of human experience. For example, he sees in the moral experiences of conscience the sole source of the knowledge of God. But are there not other ways by which men come to know God? Modern religious psychology is far from sharing his exclusiveness. Newman would certainly raise no objection, but would probably say that, for his own part, he could speak usefully on the matter from his own experience alone. If, as we shall see, his psychology reveals a profound understanding both of the religious and the rationalistic attitudes of mind, it is because he had undergone the experience of these two tendencies at war within himself, like two personalities coexisting in him and, in his Oriel period, striving for supremacy.

So far we have been concerned with only the most general characteristics of Newman's psychology, its methodological principles. These, in fact, give rise to a whole series of different, even contrasting, conceptions. To understand what is specific in Newman, we shall have to go beyond his first principles and bring to light those concrete factors which govern his thought as a whole.

We have seen how Newman aimed at bringing his scrutiny to bear, by reflection, on the actual working of the mind in its entirety, as it showed itself to him, particularly in his own personal experience of it. The first thing he wished to understand was the life of thought. Now, this cannot be totally compassed by one's own reflection. True, there are mathematical systems that seem

[1] *Grammar.*, p.384.
[2] *Ibid.*, pp.384-386.

to be built up, by the application of strict laws from self-evident principles; such a structure of thought may well be comprehended in itself, for, in these cases, the mind is dealing only with concepts whose meaning it has itself assigned.[1] Consider, however, that ordinary and everyday mode of thinking by which we try to understand our "human condition", to interpret the world we live in, the mystery of destiny and duty. This, surely, is the primary function of thought, the only one that really matters. As a part of our experience, it is inseparably blended with all the other realities for and by which we live. The thinking by which we work out our idea of the world and of life is an expression of what we ourselves are. The course of our thinking shows us the stages, the gradual growth, of what we personally have made of the being we first received. It is, admittedly, possible to discern there certain laws of psychology that may be systematized; but, just as the general biological laws of growth and reproduction in living cells are insufficient to explain the difference between the lily and the rose, so these general laws of thought ignore the innumerable and divergent ideas begotten by the mind of man. We are not referring to true or false reasonings. The crucial element in thought consists of the primary seed from which it goes on to develop. Different seeds, sown in the same ground, assimilate the same nourishment according to the same laws of biology, yet give rise to the immense variety of flowers and plants. It is the same for thought. Its "germs" differ; the first principles, which direct it, are not the same in everyone. Why is this? Because they are not determined, exclusively, by universally valid evidence, but by all the factors at work in our life : temperament, education, family, social environment, the great events of our life, personal experiences, our passions, our actions, our fidelity or infidelity to conscience, our moral attitude to life. All these exercise a secret influence on our thought. They determine our preferences, direct our attention, cause us to accept this or that principle as self-evident. When we say : "That is obvious", it often means simply : "We gladly accept it as certain". Our psychic life, then, is a whole, of which thought is but an aspect, a "moment", a function. Numerous living sources give rise to our personality, as an organic and harmonious whole, and our thought develops simultaneously

[1] *Grammar.*, p.266.

within it. We cannot expect to understand the life of thought if, by an artificial process of abstraction, we try to envisage it in isolation from the rest of life. The life of the soul is an indivisible reality, which abstraction only dismembers. We grasp the real process and meaning of thought only in its relation with the whole personality.[1]

Viewed in this light, thought is seen to be governed by a number of principles, proceeding, as it were, from our personality as a whole, from its many-sided reality. They insinuate themselves in us and we are hardly aware of it. In spite, however, of so many different influences threatening its coherence and unity, our personal thought moves, or at least tends, in a single direction. The one actually chosen from all the possible directions is decided by the combined influence of many principles. The predominant tendency governs the play of influences; repressing some, encouraging others, it allows them to attain full development or transforms them so as to be able to adapt and assimilate them. In this way, it takes hold of a number of intellectual values and draws them into the central current of which it is the absolute ruler. Thus, out of the numerous values originally conferred or subsequently acquired, there emerges, and is gradually built up within us, a vision of the world and of life, characteristic of each of us; it is a kind of translation, in terms of thought, of that personality[2] of which we are the responsible authors. The most diverse principles bring to it their contribution, their relative value and efficacy being determined by the predominant tendency. The latter decides the particular character of the whole, its special value, its depth, its spirit, its atmosphere. All these are what Newman means by "ethos", the characteristic tendency of the living thought of an individual or a society. Newman's psychology is a psychology of

---

[1] See below, pp.114-123.

[2] In what does personality consist? It is the entire complex of our individual psyche, including the essential characteristics of our human nature and our accidental qualities, both innate and acquired. Sometimes, Newman opposes the personal to the natural characteristics, as the singular, the accidental, to the universally human. Cf. *Grammar*, pp.85-86: "To be rational, to have speech, to pass through successive changes of mind and body from infancy to death, belongs to man's nature; to have a particular history, to be married or single, to have children or to be childless, to live a given number of years, to have a certain constitution, moral temperament, intellectual outfit, mental formation, these and the like, taken all together, are the accidents that make up our notion of a man's person, and are the ground-work or conditions of his particular experiences".

"ethos": "it is his special gift to recognise the *ethos* in an individual, a community, a movement, an institution, and, not least, in himself."[1]

Our thought, then, forms an irreducible totality, an "ethos". But "ethos" signifies more than a simple totality, it implies moral responsibility. We are the authors both of ourselves and of our view of the world, and we bear that responsibility. In one respect, it is true, we are something *given*. We did not create our own nature nor determine the greater part of the circumstances and events guiding the course of our personal history. We all live in a situation we did not choose, and it moulds our thought and affects us subtly and without our awareness. Yet our thought is no mere passive result of combined forces. There is a free current of action that takes up the *datum* that we are and that we undergo, giving it meaning and direction. It comes from us, flowing from a source within us, from the deepest part of our nature, from that liberty in virtue of which we affirm our own individuality. This free current impels the *datum* in a definite direction. We are not, however, to regard the *datum* as a kind of lifeless jetsam at the mercy of the current. It has a value and a life of its own, and provides the current with its living content, determines its volume, impact and power; as to the current itself and its direction, it issues from the free self, and is its manifestation. Hence, our *datum*, in one aspect, sheds a portion of its determining agency. The latter persists in regard to a number of accidental characteristics. Many features of the individual life, its poetic quality and beauty, its placid or torrential flow, may well be determined by circumstances, temperament or education. But, as part of the very substance of human life, the *datum* shares in its liberty. Thus, on the one hand, thought is governed by a complex of determinisms and, so far, is passive; on the other, it is sovereignly free, as the very incarnation and expression of human liberty.

There is no doubt that this is how Newman thought of the life of the soul. These are not his metaphors and terminology, but they are true to his conceptions. We are responsible, he says, for the first principles which orientate our thought. Their number is legion and they spring up from every level and from all the recesses of our personality, directing our thought along a certain channel. But it depends on our very first moral dispositions whether this or

[1] P. Sobry, *op. cit.*, p. 46.

that principle prevails over the rest and monopolises the direction of the whole. It is our moral attitude that makes the selection. The direction of our investigations, the angle from which we view life, what we have to assume, the governing principles we accept, all this results from our choice at the outset. The ultimate control rests with the free, living spirit. In the whole course of development we find this active, personal element. Our fidelity to conscience and growth in spirituality purify our fundamental moral tendency, widen the range of its influence, strengthen its power of assimilation, make the mind more sensitive and prompt to discern what accords with it. The "illative sense"—that function of the spirit which perceives truths beyond those furnished by formal reasoning—can only submit itself to the principles which direct it. In it we see the personal instrument by which the intelligence, in the actual circumstances of life, makes continual progress in the direction of its rooted tendency. In the same way, assent and certitude, by which we adopt the results of reasoning, are not the passive effects of a process of argument, but free, personal acts by which we recognise and uphold the truth of an assertion, because reason demands it. If there is one quality Newman assigns to the life of the spirit in every sphere, it is expressed in his view that thought and assent are not passive mechanisms but living and personal acts for which we are ourselves responsible.[1]

"First principles" and "illative sense" are the two fundamental ideas of the *Grammar*, providing Newman with the following clear formulation of his intuition : we think in our totality as persons, active and responsible; our thought is framed by our "ethos"; it is a reflection of the moral character of the thinker. Consequently, it exhibits, with the utmost clarity, the difference between one moral personality and another. We come truly to understand living, concrete thought only after a careful delineation of the principal types of moral personality and their genesis. Newman's psychology was to culminate in an analysis of the inherent dynamism of religious and rationalist thought.

[1] "Certitude is not a passive impression made on the mind from without, by argumentative compulsion, but in all concrete questions, (nay, even in abstract, for though the reasoning is abstract, the mind which judges it is concrete) it is an active recognition of propositions as true, such as it is the duty of each individual himself to exercise at the bidding of reason" (*Grammar*, pp.344-345). "Assent is the free act for which the doer is responsible" (*Ibid.*, p.232).

SECTION B

NEWMAN'S "PSYCHOLOGISM"

The problem stated:

In the preceding section, we have formulated a problem without giving a solution. It must now be examined in more detail. Newman's critique of knowledge starts from the necessity of accepting the realities of thought as they present themselves directly to the reflecting mind, uninfluenced by preconceived theories. Yet he is not satisfied with mere information and description. He wishes to account for, and to vindicate, certain ways in which the mind arrives at certitude and truth.

This brings us to the following question : what principle does Newman use in passing from a descriptive to a normative standpoint? None other, it would seem, than the duty of accepting our mental structure as valid. If we are *obviously* dealing with a normal functioning of our common nature, it is futile to ask if it has validity *a priori*. Every time he wishes to justify one of our intellectual functions or properties, he utters triumphantly the same cry : it is a law of human nature. We find this repeated more than thirty times in the *Grammar of Assent*; it is the hinge on which its philosophy turns. Surely, we have here a kind of "psychologism"?[1] To answer this question let us be clear, first of all, about the term.

Husserl was the chief exponent of a phenomenology set up "under the sign" of a reaction against what he called, pejoratively, "psychologism." Since his time, this word has come to be used only too easily as a weapon in philosophical controversy. The phenomenologists accuse one another of psychologism; and the meaning of the word has become only too confused, elastic and ambiguous in consequence.

Sometimes, the word is used to mean simply a decided penchant for the psychological aspect of a problem. This vague meaning we shall dismiss. The term was, in fact, coined to stigmatize an abuse of psychology; a person is guilty of psychologism if he imagines he has said the last word or discovered the final solution of any

---

[1] Cf. R. Eissler, *Wörterbuch der philosophischen Begriffe* (Berlin, 1929), II, pp.550-555, and, particularly, W. Moog, *Logik, Psychologie und Psychologismus* (Halle, 1920), pp.3-7.

sort of problem when he has explained it in terms of psychology. In the same way, historicism is the claim to deal exhaustively with all intellectual problems by the study of their history.[1]

The unwarranted intrusion of psychology in spheres alien to it is of varying extent.

In its most radical form, psychologism is the logical consequence of nominalism and conceptualism. According to these, thought is completely reducible to the following elements: (1) the direct experience of concrete facts; (2) the formation of the resulting concepts consists merely in the generalisation of certain accidental aspects by which things bear some resemblance to one another; (3) judgment and reasoning, which can arrive at general laws only, similar to those of the natural sciences. The main feature, then, of this epistomology is its conception of abstraction. It regards this as merely a systematic presentation of resemblances perceived in concrete things, not as the apprehension of their essence; and, therefore, it can issue only in statements of general laws based on repeated experiences, and never reach necessary judgments on what reality is in itself.

Applied to the study of the mind or of conscience, this conception confines all investigation into human thought to general laws about the facts. Now, it is a fact that we evaluate judgments as true or false, actions as good or bad, things as beautiful or ugly. The attribution of intellectual, moral, or aesthetic values is a natural law of our minds; we cannot say anything further about them, or affirm their absolute validity. The extreme form of psychologism reasons as follows: values have no validity in themselves, neither are they absolute or necessary; we may do no more than establish the psychological compulsion to affirm them; they simply reflect the laws of the mind.

There is, however, a less extreme form of psychologism. It admits that the values we perceive are absolute and objective and that one and the same act reveals both their knowledge and their validity; in other words, there is genuine knowledge of objective being possessed of value in its own right. But how is this admission to be justified? What seems first discerned by the act of reflection is only the mental phenomenon of an immediate discrimination between opposite values, for example good and evil, which are

---

[1] On historicism, cf. O. Veit, "Geschichtesbild des 19 Jahrhunderts", *Die Tatwelt*, XVII (1942), 126-127.

then judged to be manifestations of the "thing in itself" and, hence, irreducible, objective, absolute. This phenomenon must be examined and justified. Two different methods could be adopted. One would be the metaphysical approach by way of the object, to show that the alleged objective manifestation is, indeed, a partial revelation of the Being who maintains us as conscious and thinking beings. The other would be the psychological approach by way of the subject, to show that the act of affirming objective values is an irreducible function of human nature. To confine oneself exclusively to the latter would be a kind of psychologism.

As regards Newman, we hold the following : (1) Newman is not an example of extreme psychologism because, in the knowledge of values, he does not adhere to a nominalist theory; (2) He does, however, hold to a moderate psychologism; not as a theory, but solely in practice : that is, he does not rule out a metaphysical justification, but considers he is unable to provide it.

Newman and conceptualism:

At first sight, it could appear that Newman was doomed to hold an extreme psychologism, on the ground that his theory of abstraction implies conceptualism. The controversy on his theory has given rise to a number of books, among which is the excellent one by Zeno, *Newman's leer over het menselijk denken*,[1] whose conclusions we adopt, but with one important modification.

Newman's ideas on abstraction may be briefly summarised. He holds that thought takes its rise with concrete experiences, which are then transposed into general concepts. But he views abstraction, which produces the concept, as a generalisation, not as the apprehension of the immutable essence; in his own words, the concept is general, but not universal. It comes into being when the intellect compares, from a given standpoint, several concrete experiences, and then systematically generalises a character they all share; but what corresponds to this character, in the concrete, is only a resemblance between particular elements, which, individually, are never precisely the same. The idea so formed represents a whole class of objects; but, as regards the individual objects taken singly, it does not represent them as such, but furnishes a description sufficiently general to be applicable to each.

This theory of the objective concept is frankly a nominalist

[1] Pp.56-83.

one. At the very most, it allows the induction of general laws, but their applicability, by deduction, to particular cases is of no more than probable validity. Newman affirms this explicitly.

His position, then, would seem highly insecure. When he treats of abstraction formally, he appears to uphold a conceptualist theory. None the less, it would be wrong to classify him as a nominalist. Philosophical error, like heresy, consists nearly always in negation, rather than in affirmation. Newman, in his conflict with "scientism", admits what seems to him true in the description given by the scientist of the general ideas underlying his researches. Now it is a fact that those used in the sciences of observation and measurement are merely generalisations from the observed facts. All that these sciences need is a systematisation of what the senses perceive; they are not concerned with essences. Here lies the explanation of why, in the history of ideas, nominalism turned men's minds from philosophy and directed them to the positive sciences. Conceptualism admits only one aspect of the conceptualisation of experience, namely, systematic generalisation; and this, in fact, corresponds to thought in its spontaneous activity. The conceptualist refuses to allow that, in philosophical abstraction, conceptualisation goes so far as to apprehend concretely an absolute and universal essence. Doubtless, both these aspects of conceptualisation are present and intermingled in the concept formed in direct apprehension; but this does not prevent us, by reflexive analysis, from distinguishing two aspects which correspond to two operations of the mind—generalising abstraction, which is the basis of empirical science, and "eiditic" abstraction, which is the basis of philosophy.

To return to Newman. His description of the nature of general ideas is to be found in the context of an argument against "scientism". Now, we know he always restricted the expression of his mind to the needs of the exact purpose he had in view. He aimed at meeting those needs as fully as possible, but not to go beyond them, or to treat the subject in full. The scientism he opposed affirmed that knowledge obtained by the methods of the positive sciences was the sole valid and certain knowledge. He replied that it was true that these sciences, in their processes of induction and generalisation, were the product of a natural activity of the mind. This he described and, in so doing, was led to analyse the structure of general ideas. As might be expected, his analysis corresponds strictly with the needs of his description, whose object is the generalising abstraction of positive science. Newman could be classed as a nominalist if he had set himself the celebrated problem of universals and had concluded that all our concepts are but systematic generalisations proceeding from the comparison of concrete experiences. But this is not what he did. We can say, in fact, that this was not his view at all, but that he held the exact opposite, as we shall try to show.

Newman's thesis in the *Grammar of Assent* may be stated as follows: I admit, he says, that the mind, starting from sensible experience, proceeds naturally to generalisations expressed by the use of general terms. Science is the exact and controlled use of these. It employs them in its definitions; it distinguishes, compares, orders them, combines them in general statements which it reduces to a system and applies, by reasoning, to the concrete situation. But there is more than this. The same experience gives rise to "real apprehension", and this reveals certain absolute values that we express in the first natural principles. The primary experience, the raw material of our knowledge, comprises not only sensible impressions, but also "mental sensations", in which the higher values, the beautiful, the good, God himself, are, in a manner, made known to our understanding.[1] So it is that consciousness of duty is a specific source, of the highest order, of our knowledge, one absolutely irreducible to sensible experience.[2] The difference is a crucial one. For Newman, the knowledge which proceeds from conscience is not only *sui generis* in virtue of its origin, but it is also the most important and fundamental kind of knowledge. Our internal experience, by which we become aware of the higher values, gives rise to concepts and judgments universally valid, even to those first principles on which all our personal thought is based. It is true that Newman, when he describes generalising abstraction in a nominalist fashion, gives as examples only concepts drawn from sensible experience. On the other hand, in describing the origin within the mind of the higher principles of knowledge, he depicts a kind of conceptualisation that cannot be reduced to the conceptualist theory of abstraction.

Let us examine the texts; they occur in that part of the *Grammar of Assent* where Newman sets out his very original

[1] See below, pp.107-9
[2] See below, Part III, Chapters 1 and 2.

7

views on the first principles. We read that there are certain realities that force themselves on the mind, which apprehends them directly, with absolute and irreducible characteristics, of ultimate validity for all men. A single experience may suffice to recognise this absolute validity; comparison or generalisation is not needed. That is why he speaks of our apprehending this validity by instinct, by which he means *immediately,* without conscious intermediaries of knowledge. This applies to moral values, good and evil. Newman affirms "our instinctive recognition of the immutable difference in the moral quality of acts, *as elicited in us by one instance of them.* Even one act of cruelty, ingratitude, generosity, or justice reveals to us at once *intensivè* the immutable distinction between these qualities and their contraries".[1] The same is true of the opposites: true and false, just and unjust, beautiful and ugly.[2] However, the act by which the mind apprehends these absolute values in concrete experience is not considered by Newman as one of abstraction. It does not belong to the conceptual order, for it is elicited in a real grasp of the singular. It thus forms a part of "real apprehension".[3] We recognise, in this description, what phenomenologists call a *Wesenschau*, and scholastics, abstraction of the *universale metaphysicum*.[4] A single experience is sufficient—so the scholastics agree—and in this one experience the object is seen as possessing a quality of absolute validity, and, therefore, by its very nature attributable, intrinsically and identically, to all possible objects of the same kind, even though the mind has not yet expressly affirmed this universal attribution. The quality perceived is, in the first instance, comprised in the apprehension of the individual object; but, its absolute validity once admitted, it is, in virtue of its own nature, transcendent in relation

[1] *Grammar*, p.65.

[2] *Ibid.*, p.64.

[3] This is of the greatest importance. Newman considers abstract or "notional" whatever does not exist in the concrete, being "drawn away" (in the etymological sense) from the latter. If, then, his study of the concrete reveals in it an element that appears to him absolutely necessary, he refuses to call it abstract. True, he admits the possibility of embracing, in a single act of knowledge, the abstract and the concrete, as in the discovery of a general law, universally valid, in a single instance (*Ibid*, pp.63-64); but this one act is a synthesis of two other, irreducible ones: real and notional conception.

[4] *Wesenschau* has rather a wider and vaguer meaning than the scholastic term.

to the individual in which it happens to be embodied. In this, precisely, consists the abstraction of the *universale metaphysicum*. This mode of abstraction is completed in the *universale logicum*, in which the mind expressly adverts to the possibility of attributing this absolute quality to a whole class of objects. The recognition of its *extensio* is but the addition to the *universale metaphysicum* of a logical relation created by the mind alone, and which is, therefore, called the "logical universal". This explicitation of the universality requires, as a general rule, at least according to Aristotle, a certain "empiricism", or a repetition of experiences. Newman was fully aware of the origin of this "logical universal". He goes on to say in the same place that, in virtue of several moral experiences, we attribute to the quality—whose content and absolute validity we have already perceived in a single act—an unlimited extension, far beyond our particular experience; and here we have a true abstraction, which presupposes some comparison of different experiences. In this way, we arrive at a universal abstract principle. There is moral good and evil; that is to say, there is a world of good and evil, a moral order; good and evil constitute an objective order inherent in all human activity.[1]

This, then, is a special case where Newman clearly admits a quality, necessary and of absolute validity, which the mind apprehends as such without intermediary. It is one of great significance for us. It shows how, for Newman, the moral value revealed by a mental act has its foundation, as a value, not on the psychological necessity of its affirmation, but on its own nature, which reveals itself objectively in each moral act. Apart from contingent experience, the value could not make itself known; but its validity, as such, is independent of our experience of it; it asserts itself in experience by virtue of its objective character.[2]

In the same way, religious values, too, are endowed with ab-

---

[1] For Newman it is only the second phase of the process that is truly abstractive. The first consists simply in an activity of the imagination (see what he says below, on p.110., of the experience to which we owe the conception of an object, of the "thing"). But he did not see that this abstraction, precisely because it universalises an essential characteristic, is a genuine "universal", and admits of no exception. It is quite different from a law of generalisation.

[2] We use the term "objective" not in the Kantian sense, but as defined by, for example, Maurice Blondel: what proclaims itself as a manifestation of being, of the real.

solute validity. How, in fact, do we come to recognise a unique and personal God? By the fact that moral values proclaim themselves not only as absolute qualities recognised by the mind, but also as absolute norms of conduct. Their absolute moral exigence, says Newman, by their essential intentionality, brings us into contact with a personal God who, by their means, speaks to our conscience. Again, a single experience is sufficient.[1] But there is another consideration. Just as repeated experience of material realities forces us to admit the objective existence of a physical world, and as constant experience of moral values obliges us to recognise the existence of a moral order, so repeated contact with God in our conscience compels us to raise our minds to the existence of a universal order, governed by his will and providence. This implies the government of the world by the wisdom of God for the realisation of the purposes of his loving will.[2]

We will now sum up and state our conclusion. There exists a material world independent of our consciousness, and perceived as such by the senses. In describing its elaboration in concepts, Newman seems to confine himself to the generalising abstraction of the exact sciences. This is a grave defect in his theory of knowledge. There exists, however, a world of values which reveals itself in our mental impressions. By this world Newman means, especially but not exclusively, that moral and religious universe of which consciousness receives the first impressions. In this sphere of knowledge are worked out those concepts and principles whose origin the nominalist theory of abstraction is inadequate to explain. They arise, in fact, from the immediate recognition of absolute values, even though they are experienced only once. Newman seems to have been unaware that he is dealing here with a new kind of abstraction. In his view, the apprehension of these values, since it forms part of the experience of the concrete, pertains to "real" knowledge. Hence, in affirming that Newman treated of two kinds of abstraction, that of sensible qualities and that of spiritual values, we state what he really thought, though not his manner of expressing it.

What conclusions may be drawn about the relations between Newman and phenomenology? We must agree with Haecker and

---

[1] *Grammar*, p.62.
[2] *Ibid.*, pp.63-64.

Gladen[1] that some of his descriptions foreshadow, in outline, the phenomenological theory of values later developed by Scheler and Hartmann in Germany, and represented in England by Sorley, Taylor and de Burgh.

Practical Psychologism

We can now see that Newman was innocent of psychologism in its extreme sense. Admitting that objective and absolute values are apprehended and recognised as such in a single act amounts to saying that the judgment of value is made by the mind in the light of objective evidence, under whose influence the act is elicited, rather than by psychological necessity. That is, unquestionably, what Newman meant.

The philosopher, however, cannot rest satisfied with what is basically no more than a distinction, however important, between ultimate elements of consciousness. He would admit that, in fact, everything happens as if man, in his value-judgments, gave expression to objective evidence manifesting itself totally in the acts in question. The subjective act in which a hungry man discerns the value of the food corresponding to his needs differs entirely from the act in which he adverts to the moral imperative obliging him, it may be, to act contrary to his subjective interests. But is this latter case truly one of objective evidence? The phenomenologist perception that the essence of the moral act consists precisely in its being obliged to claim for itself an absolute and objective sphere of application does not settle the question. Husserl saw this clearly. It is one thing to establish that an act manifests itself directly to consciousness as objectively valid, it is another thing to accept the justice of this claim.

A further vindication is necessary, and Newman does not flinch from it. After describing the course followed by thought, and the different ways the mind has of apprehending its object, he proceeds to its justification.

Newman, as we have seen, in seeking to justify the veracity and certainty of our knowledge, turns his attention, not to the object and its evidence, but to the subject, to the nature of man. He does not undertake the metaphysical task of disclosing the ultimate

---

[1] Cf. the translation of the *Grammar* by T. Haecker, *Philosophie des Glaubers* (Munich, 1922), p.439; see also K. Gladen, *Die Erkenntnisphilosophie J. H. K. Newmans* (Paderborn, 1934), p.2.

foundation on which the evidence rests, that is to say the clarity of being, which is not merely one among many clarities that manifest themselves to consciousness, but is the very basis and structure of consciousness, which reveals itself in each portion of evidence as it comes to lodge therein. Newman is less ambitious; he describes his aim, modestly, as a "practical", non-metaphysical, one.[1] A practical standpoint is one that rests on a presumption of common sense which the philosopher cannot escape any more than the ordinary man. This is the presumption that we cannot call in question our human nature. Our first duty is to accept our nature, that is to say those structures of experience common to all. We cannot go outside them in the attempt to judge them; we have no choice in the matter. If we refuse to accept the nature of our minds, we must renounce all thought, for thought implies this nature and makes it known. A man, says Newman, who refuses my principle shuts himself off from the argument, for he cannot allege the validity of any statement of his without, thereby, acknowledging his adversary to be right. We accept, therefore, the general structure of experience and thought, not of our own choice, or by an act of faith, but because we see them as the very expression of our human nature and the only possible access to the knowledge of truth. What we can do is make good or bad use of them. "We use, not trust, our faculties. . . . We are as little able to accept or reject our mental constitution as our being. We have not the option; we can but misuse or mar its functions."[2]

It is enough for Newman to establish that a certain mode of knowledge forms a part of human nature, of the general structure of our experience, for it to be justified as a means to arrive at truth. It is simply a question of acknowledging the requirements of its rightful exercise, in order to make the best use of it.

We have already observed that the supreme principle of Newman's thought is that of Divine Providence. Verbal revelation is not the only means God uses to make known to us his will. As sovereign creator, he is nowise dependent on created nature or its history. Its entire being comes from him. What belongs of necessity to nature and its acts, all that is inevitable in the human situation, is the pure word of the Creator and his Providence.

[1] See what was said above on the *Grammar*; see also *Grammar*, p.344: "My aim, like Butler's in his *Analogy*, is a practical one".

[2] *Ibid.*, p.59.

The religious man, once he sees that any element in the structure of his experience bears the impress of the Divine Wisdom, is thereby convinced that it is adequate for its purpose, even though he may be committed thereby to an involved and arduous task.

Hence it is that Newman never appeals for support to nature, considered philosophically, without at the same time referring to divine Providence. The "principle of nature" and the "principle of Providence" he considers as one and the same, but expressed from different standpoints. To study and describe in close detail the general structure of human experience is, for him, to lend an obedient ear to the creative word of God. Submission to nature is the same as submission to God. Whenever he gives us a description of a common function of thought, and justifies it by an appeal to nature, he directs his gaze towards God of whom nature is the living word and of whose will for us it is the expression.

Of course, I do not stop here. As the structure of the universe speaks to us of Him who made it, so the laws of the mind are the expression, not of mere constituted order, but of His will. I should be bound by them even were they not his laws; but since one of their functions is to tell me of Him, they throw a reflex light upon themselves, and, for resignation to my destiny, I substitute a cheerful concurrence in an overruling Providence. We may gladly welcome such difficulties as are to be found in our mental constitution, and in the interaction of our faculties, if we are able to find that He gave them to us, and He can overrule them for us. We may securely take them as they are, and use them as we find them.[1]

From the philosophical point of view nature is the ultimate ground of Newman's critique of knowledge, once it is granted that the consciousness of duty, by which we come to know God and his Providence, is justified at the tribunal of reason only as "a simple element of our nature", "a constituent factor of knowledge". The principle of nature is the final basis of his philosophical defence of certitude and of the ways that lead to it. But, for the religious-minded thinker, for his own personal certitude, the light of Providence is supreme. His thought, saturated by an experience impossible to communicate in the immediate and compelling evidence

[1] *Grammar.*, p.344.

of the two unique beings, "myself and my Creator," clings to the idea of God rather than to the philosophical principle of nature. After citing nature as the supreme criterion of thought, Newman makes a special approach to all who, like himself, perceive God in their conscience, and he points out another principle of certitude, of greater force and assurance. Since the ways of nature are the ways of God, he says, we may be certain that our faculties of knowing, however strange to us their working, are adequate to lead us to that truth to which he invites us.

From all this it can be seen in what sense Newman may be said to be guilty of psychologism. He undertakes to justify the processes of thought and the attitudes of mind on which our religious and moral certainty is based, not by unfolding and examining the objective evidence that causes them, but by showing, after a radical scrutiny, that they follow from the very constitution of human nature. His treatment is a partial one, since it places the final justification of our thinking in the nature of the subject rather than in the evidence of the object, which is a kind of psychologism. Moreover, he thus pointed the way followed by practically all modern philosophy. For both Scheler and Merleau-Ponty, the common structure of human experience or of "existence" is the ultimate criterion of truth. They, however, consider it the sole philosophical principle. Newman adopted it only for his practical purpose and did not deny the possibility of an alternative approach. (See Appendix C, *The Practical Psychologism of Newman.*)

Chapter 2

THE GENERAL PSYCHOLOGY OF DEVELOPMENT

ONE of the chief principles guiding Newman's thought on
the development of doctrine is that revelation, in its human
setting, follows a course similar to that of other great
"ideas". Its life differs from that of others only in its supernatural
origin and in its inspiration and guidance by the Holy Spirit.[1]
Newman, therefore, in setting out on the study of development,
begins by establishing that this kind of growth is perfectly natural,
since it derives from the nature of the human mind, and it happens to every idea of importance.[2] The psychology of doctrinal
development belongs, then, to the general psychology of ideas,
though possessing certain "personal characteristics" of its own.

This chapter will consist of two parts: one on the general psychology of intellectual development, the other applying its conclusions to the content of faith.

SECTION A

GROWTH AND KNOWLEDGE

Development and reasoning

The special characteristic of man, says Newman, is develop-

---

[1] Cf. *Essay*, p.57: "Christianity differs from other religions and philosophies . . . not in kind, but in origin, not in nature, but in its personal
characteristics, being informed and quickened by what is more than the
intellect, by a Divine Spirit."

[2] He sums up his position in the introduction to the *Essay*: "The expansion and increase of the Christian Creed and Ritual are the necessary
attendants on any philosophy or policy which takes possession of the intellect
and heart and has had any wide dominion; that from the nature of the
human mind, time is necessary for the full comprehension and perfection of
great ideas" (p.29).

ment, the gradual completion of himself :

> What is the peculiarity of our nature, in contrast with the inferior animals around us? It is that, though man cannot change what he is born with, he is a being of progress with relation to his perfection and characteristic good. Other beings are complete from their first existence, in that line of excellence which is allotted to them; but man begins with nothing realised (to use the word), and he has to make capital for himself by the exercise of those faculties which are his natural inheritance. Thus he gradually advances to the fulness of his original destiny. Nor is this progress mechanical, nor is it of necessity; it is committed to the personal efforts of each individual of the species; each of us has the prerogative of completing his inchoate and rudimental nature, and of developing his own perfection out of the living elements with which his mind began to be. It is his gift to be the creator of his own sufficiency; and to be emphatically self-made. This is the law of his being, which he cannot escape; and whatever is involved in that law he is bound, or rather he is carried on, to fulfil.[1]

We have, then, a sacred duty to realise in effect the possibilities of our nature, both as individuals and as members of the human race.[2]

Now, "this law of progress is carried out by means of the acquisition of knowledge, of which inference and assent are the immediate instrument."[3] It is, essentially, the development of knowledge that enables man to reach his specific end; and the root of his intellectual progress is, simply, the nature of the human mind.

The operations natural to the mind which set man on the way of gradual achievement are abstraction and inference.[4] Of its very nature, human knowledge is abstract. Our minds do not take in their objects in a single clear glance. As soon as it perceives them, it starts to form judgments, that is, to compare, abstract, generalize, and so on. In this way, it takes hold of many successive aspects which complete, illumine, and confirm one another and, as they multiply, they approximate to a perfect representation of the

[1] *Grammar*, pp.348-349.
[2] *Ibid.*
[3] *Ibid.*
[4] *Ibid.*, p.34.

reality.[1] The aggregate of the possible aspects of a reality make up the "idea" of it.[2] Development, then, is a characteristic of abstract knowledge.

This development Newman calls sometimes reason, sometimes reasoning. "The Use of Reason in the Investigation of the Doctrines of Faith" is the title of his great Oxford sermon on the Development of Doctrine. The word "reasoning", however, must be taken in its widest sense. "Reason" means, for Newman, any act by which the mind passes from the knowledge of one thing to that of another.[3] The essence of reasoning, then, is its mediate character, the drawing of conclusions from premises.[4] But this

---

[1] Cf. *Essay*, p.33: "It is a characteristic of our minds to be ever engaged in passing judgments on the things before them . . . We compare, contrast, abstract, generalise, adjust, classify"; see also *Ibid.*, p.55; *Idea*, pp.45, 57, 151.

[2] Cf. *Essay*, p.34: "The idea which represents an object, whether real or supposed, is equal to the aggregate of its possible aspects". As we shall have to deal with the different meanings Newman gives to "idea", it might be well to deal with them here. Basically, it signifies the *verbum mentis*, the interior word, the immanent product or effect of thought. "Object" means, generally, the reality indicated by the idea. "Idea", therefore, abstracts from all corresponding reality. Hence, Newman draws the following antithesis, among others, between rationalism and faith: for the rationalist, the words of Scripture refer only to ideas; for the believer, they indicate realities (*Ess. Crit. Hist.*, I, p.35). Moreover, an idea is always more than a mere representation of sense. Newman cites the example of sailors who have seen the entire world, but have never passed beyond the sense to the formation of an idea (*O.U.S.* p.289). The fundamental property of the idea, however, is that it furnishes knowledge, not of a single aspect, but of a many-sided whole. On this basis, the following meanings may be distinguished: (a) an idea can signify, "the sum total of the aspects of an object", and then consists in the totality of rational concepts. That is, for example, its meaning in the title *The Idea of a University*. The various aspects making up the idea are called, as the case demands, concepts, relations, or even judgments. (b) Sometimes the word "idea" takes on an ideal, almost platonic, tinge. Not that subsistence is attributed to it, but it indicates knowledge which is ideal, perfect, beyond that of any individual intellect. The individual approximates to it, but his knowledge is only an imperfect reflection of it, and a partial one. It is refracted in the minds of individuals like light in a prism. It comes to be thought of as if independent of individuals, using them for its own self-realization (*Essay*, pp.34-40). (c) The word may, finally, signify a special mode of knowledge of a total and concrete reality, when this is apprehended, not by the medium of concepts, but by direct contemplation. The idea is, then, that intuition which is the mind's starting point for its abstract functions and which ultimately secures for an aggregate of concepts their inner coherence. It has this meaning especially in the *Oxford University Sermons*.

[3] *O.U.S.*, pp.223, 256: *Stray Essays*, p.71.

[4] *Grammar*, pp.293-337.

sequence of propositions must itself be taken in the widest possible sense. For, in Newman's view, pure and simple abstraction, the passage from concrete to abstract, constitutes reasoning even though, in the case at issue, the *medium* does not belong to the sphere of the abstract.[1] The word "reason", then, denotes every kind of discursive knowledge.

It is, however, used in other, stricter, senses in various contexts. At times, it means skill in logical argument (here it is not a question of natural, spontaneous reasoning). Elsewhere, it is the ability to set out "evidences", that is arguments from history, and then it is contrasted with "antecedent probability". Finally, it is used in a pejorative sense to designate the use of reason to decide questions of religious truth or error apart from serious personal experience in the matter.[2]

The gradual expansion of knowledge is, then, identical with reasoning, with the exercise of reason, in the broadest sense of the word. The study of such development demands, in consequence, study of the process of reasoning.

Implicit and explicit reasoning

The core of Newman's psychology of reasoning is his rigid distinction between its psychological and its logical structure. They do not coincide, and so the full reality of living reason is wider than its logical operations. We must, therefore, distinguish implicit and spontaneous reasoning from what is explicit and technical. Now knowledge in general, just as doctrinal tradition, begins its development by the unconscious, spontaneous activity of living thought. The Oxford sermon, it is true, might give the impression that the reasoning to which tradition owes its expansion is explicit and conscious. Development is there presented as the deliberate unfolding, by analysis and reflection, of the more or less unconscious intuition of faith. In this connection, all the static elements would seem to pertain to intuition, the dynamic ones to conscious reasoning. If the sermon appears to underestimate the part played by implicit reasoning, that is because it deals with the same limited question as the *Arians*, namely, the genesis of

[1] So Newman entitles first principles drawn from experience (*Grammar*, p.65); likewise, in the fifteenth of the *O.U.S.*, the carrying of intuition to the abstract plane is called "reasoning".

[2] These meanings are set forth by Newman in the Introduction to the 1871 edition of the *O.U.S.*, pp.xi-xvi.

the explicit dogmatic formulas, especially the trinitarian and christological ones, and from a definite psychological standpoint (the relations between faith and reason). Newman's attention is there focused on the *relation* between the intuition of faith and doctrinal formulas rather than on the process, the *course*, of the development which issues in these formulas. As befits a preacher, he assembles and sets in clear relief all his explanations in the framework of a single and fundamental antithesis, and leaves the other aspects of his subject in the background. The case is different in the *Essay* and in the *Newman-Perrone Paper*, for there the emphasis is placed on implicit reasoning. In these two works, the problem is treated in its entirety, and so its historical aspect occupies the foreground. The object studied in them is the actual course followed by thought as it proceeds from the intuition of faith to the explicit formulas. The growth of dogma is seen as an *implicit reasoning* : a slow growth, a steady ripening, mostly unconscious, directed by the personal dispositions, moral rather than intellectual, of the reasoning subject; a growth that proceeds from a real apprehension—the soul receiving into itself the realities of the faith, affectively steeping itself in them—and not from a purely intellectual comparison of concepts.[1] Generally, it is the needs of teaching and apologetics that convert this spontaneous process into a logical sequence of propositions and, ultimately, a system in the fullest sense.[2]

This is a distinction of capital importance, and on it depends

---

[1] The analysis that follows is supported by the following passages. The *Essay* (pp.58-59), speaks of the Protestant argument: "They themselves act upon doctrines as implicit and on reasons as little analysed in time past, as Catholic schoolmen ... These doctrines and usages are surely gained, not by a mere exercise of argument upon words and sentences placed before the eyes, but by the unconscious growth of ideas habitual to the mind". Development "is not an effect of wishing and resolving, or of forced enthusiasm, or of any mechanism of reasoning, or of any mere subtlety of intellect; but comes of its own innate power of expansion within the mind in its season, though with the use of reflection and argument and original thought, more or less as it may happen, with a dependence on the ethical growth of the mind itself" (*Essay*, pp.73-74). "It may be questioned whether development could ever be anything other than a logical operation ... An idea grows by inhabiting the intellect; it becomes familiar and precise, its relations come to be perceived: it moves on to other aspects, and from these to others, subtle, abstruse, original, according to the intellectual and moral character of the thinker; thus there forms gradually a whole 'body' of thought, without the mind noticing what happens within it" (*Ibid.*, pp.189-190).

[2] *Newman-Perrone*, p.411; *Essay*, p.190.

the course we will follow in our study. But, before going on to consider Newman's further analyses, we will make our own attempt to realise the nature of the intuition he sets out to define. We saw in the last chapter that, for Newman, thought is no artificial construction, an impersonal network of syllogisms, but a "moment", an inseparable part of our whole personal activity, unconscious as well as conscious. Our thought implies, in some way, our entire life. The confluence of all that shapes and affects our life issues in the slow crystallization, not necessarily conscious, of a more or less coherent body of ideas and convictions which is ours, our particular view of the world, the reflection of our personality, the expression of our total experience. By "experience" we understand our psychic life in its entirety, not only its passive aspect or conscious part, but its active and unconscious side as well. Its individual elements cannot be entirely separated from the whole; we may even say that, as a personal "whole", it cannot be totally separated from the social "whole" of which it forms a part. Our way of looking at things, even many of our most intimate experiences, are due, in part, to the influence of our surroundings. They are determined, also, by our character and abilities, all kinds of feelings and tendencies, moral values, previous experiences, latent memories. Our unconscious propensities, as much as our personal reflections, contribute to the spontaneous growth of our view of the world.[1] This "experiential" thought that arises and develops, of its own accord, in the mind naturally given to reflection, is the expression and instrument of our personality in the process of formation.

Living, personal thought of this kind is contrasted with deliberate, conscious thought, or formal reasoning. This may take place along with spontaneous thought, which still remains, for the most part, unconscious. The ideal would be the use of reason to acquire for consciousness, and to purify by criticism, what has been slowly matured by personal experience. Unfortunately, our reasoning too often lacks organic unity with our personal thought. For example, our conscious opinions may be in accord with certain

---

[1] Newman used no term corresponding to the German *Weltanschauung*, but this word expresses what he meant. W. Dilthey defines it as a conception of entire reality, prior to analysis and reflection, in the spontaneous knowledge of every man. When worked out in logical order and rationally justified, it becomes a philosophy. This is now the accepted meaning, though the relations between it and philosophy are still disputed.

ideas current in our environment, and, at the same time, opposed to our experiences at the deepest level of our being. In that case, we do not possess them by personal experience, we derive from them no real value for living, we take no heed of the silent protest arising, it may be, from the depths of our nature. We may be able to discourse with subtlety and acumen on all kinds of ideas and opinions, while remaining personally indifferent to them, treating them as matters quite extraneous. Our conscious thought is, then, lacking in genuineness, impersonal, unreal. The convictions reflected unawares in our life and conduct may contradict the opinions we consciously entertain. This internal opposition, to which we do not formally advert, betrays its presence at the surface of consciousness according to our character, either in the form of violent oscillations of temper, or of a frivolous scepticism, or of weariness of life. Sometimes, too, it causes in men a sudden upheaval in their whole outlook on life.

In some cases, we see a terrible dearth of real experience and personal conviction accompanied with a reasoning faculty remarkable for its power and penetration. On the other hand, the living thought may have richness and intensity, while the deliberate thought remains clumsy and incoherent. The deepest thinkers, like the greatest artists, are often the least gifted in the power of explicit and "technical" reasoning. True genius is distinguished, not by lucidity of thought, but by an exceptional capacity for experience.

We may now consider how Newman compares these two kinds of reasoning. The one which he looks on as natural, implicit, spontaneous, non-technical, and the other, which is logical and technical. He proceeds to make clear their respective characteristics.

In the first place, implicit reasoning is not necessarily conscious. The act itself, its point of departure, even its results may, as such, escape reflex awareness.[1] On the other hand, explicit and technical reasoning presupposes such reflex knowledge; it is carried out deliberately. The idea of the unconscious plays an important

---

[1] "The process is altogether unconscious and implicit . . . Not only is the inference with its process ignored, but the antecedent also" (*Grammar*, pp.330-331). "Generally, it [implicit reasoning] is hardly conscious of its own exercise, or even of its results" (*Newman-Perrone*, p.411). See also *Grammar*, pp.259-260, 292, and *Essay*, pp.58-59, 190.

part in Newman's thought; and we must bring out exactly what he means by it. "Unconscious" is never used by him in the sense in which it is used in modern depth-psychology. In the latter, the unconscious, strictly so-called, is never itself present to thought, even though it cast its influence on it like a shadow and can, therefore, be tracked down indirectly by a method such as that of psychoanalysis. Hence, it cannot be brought to light by the simple return of thought on itself, or reflective analysis. But what Newman calls unconscious is of itself present to thought and forms part of actual experience, though it escapes scrutiny and eludes attention.

There are two elements in the term "unconscious" as used by Newman that he does not always clearly distinguish; he applies it to the character of the act, and also as a quality of the object. The act of thinking is unconscious when thought takes place in us unaccompanied by that *con-scientia* (conscience in its original meaning), that clear awareness, by which the act becomes the object of explicit perception. An objective element of thought is called "unconscious"—it would be better to say "implicit"— when it is not distinctly perceived by the thinking subject. When Newman speaks of an unconscious idea, he means, rather, a confused idea in the Cartesian sense. There is a pre-history of thought when the whole, whose richness will be later revealed by analysis, is present to the mind only as a global and confused impression.[1] This want of objective clearness is especially characteristic of the knowledge that is, so to speak, steeped in the current of an intense affective life.

Newman bases his assertion that spontaneous thought is unconscious sometimes on the non-conscious character of the act, sometimes on the confused, implicit state of the idea. Generally, he means both at the same time. The statement that spontaneous thought is largely unconscious means, on the one hand, that the reasoning from which it proceeds has no part in the lucidity of explicit self-consciousness; on the other hand, it means that, by this reasoning, an idea, a confused intuition, becomes steadily enriched at the level of experience without, however, attaining the level of intellectual contemplation as a view distinct in all its parts and clearly articulated.

[1] This is the usual psychological meaning of "intuition".

Moreover, the development of implicit thought proceeds slowly and spontaneously, like the ripening of fruit. It cannot be forced. Logical reasoning, on the contrary, is the result of deliberate effort.[1] An idea can, therefore, grow despite the will. We may turn our attention from it and yet it will continue its course in the recesses of our being uninterruptedly, like an underground stream.

At a time of recollection, of interior calm, it may rise to the surface, richer, clearer, more urgent; it draws near to the soul like a piece of music, disturbing yet alluring, till the time comes when it conquers completely. The occasion may be an event of significance or a discussion, and then a secret conviction, slowly matured in the depths of the unconscious, may suddenly take the stage and reveal itself to us as a certitude illuminating the mind and firmly entrenched in it.[2]

Later on, the mind comes to see in this gradual and spontaneous character a guarantee of the rightness of its convictions.[3]

Finally, implicit reasoning is personal; that is, it is carried along and directed by the whole moral and intellectual state of the subject.[4] Consequently, it does not lead to changing opinions, but to personal convictions, firmly rooted in the spiritual substance of the personality. It cannot be communicated. Formal reasoning, on the contrary, is, as such, impersonal. It is precisely the indispensable means by which thought is communicated from one man to another. Our personality, however, can still be a stranger, in its innermost depths, to ideas about which we display much skill in argument.[5]

So Newman outlines, and contrasts, our two modes of thought of which he undoubtedly prefers the first. In his view, implicit reasoning is the more noble, because it involves the whole person, leads to genuine convictions that inform one's life, and shows forth the highest intellectual powers of man. True genius is distinguished by extraordinary capacity for experience, by the power and

[1] *Essay* pp.73-74, 336.

[2] The slow growth of a conviction is described in *Loss and Gain*, pp.56-57, 166-170.

[3] "... the gradual process by which great conclusions are forced upon the mind, and the confidence of their correctness which the mind feels from the fact of that gradualness" (letter of 1879 to W. Froude, quoted in Ward, *op. cit.*, II, p.589).

[4] See below, p.121, on Newman's idea of first principles.

[5] *Essay*, pp.73-74, 189-190, 191.

richness of spontaneous thought, and not by clearness and subtlety of reason.[1]

It only remains for us to bring out in greater detail the mutual relations and interaction of these two modes of thought. We shall do so with the help of the *Grammar of Assent*.

To begin with, implicit reasoning is not illogical. It cannot infringe the laws of logic; it may, in fact, be seen, on reflection and analysis, to embody a logical sequence and an intelligible coherence.[2] Technical reasoning is, then, of the same species as natural reasoning and is its prolongation.

From this it follows that logical deduction, by way of reflection, is of great service to thought. It gives it order, stability, clarity, it makes us fully conscious of our convictions and capable of pursuing them further, and aids us in the correction of mistaken conclusions or faulty methods. By its means we learn to solve certain problems with facility, to judge theories, to refute objections, to eliminate difficulties which, otherwise, would continually haunt and harass the imagination.[3] But, above all, it is explicit reasoning that makes possible the exchange of ideas, and so enables men to enrich, correct, and criticize one another. It is absolutely indispensable when the need arises to make clear and defend our convictions against those of others. Consequently, the expression of living thought in formal propositions is a natural, spontaneous impulse of the human mind.[4]

Although spontaneous reasoning lends itself to expression in

---

[1] "It may be granted that the spontaneous growth which goes on within the mind itself is higher and choicer than that which is logical" (*Essay*, p.191). See also Ward, *op. cit.*, II, p.589, citing a letter to W. Froude.

[2] *Essay*, pp.189-190. In the Essay, Newman emphasizes that the logical order realized *post factum* in development is wider than mere argumentative sequence: "Accordingly, it will include any progress of the mind from one judgment to another as, for instance, by way of moral fitness, which may not admit of analysis into premiss and conclusion" (p.385). But, in the *Grammar*, formal inference is an express syllogism or its equivalent (p.263).

[3] *Grammar*, pp.285-287.

[4] "Our inquiries fall spontaneously into scientific sequence, and we think in logic, as we talk in prose, without aiming at doing so" (*Ibid.*, p.286). The thesis, mentioned above, of the *Essay* and the *Newman-Perrone Paper*, according to which external circumstances require implicit thought to express itself in logical form, has to be modified in some degree. Such logical expression is given "first for our own satisfaction, then for our justification with others" (*Ibid.*, p.286).

technical language, the latter never communicates the full content of living thought. The actual course of its growth and the richness of its significance cannot be compressed into logical form. Two aspects of it must, therefore, be distinguished : one, capable of verbal expression and subject to the control of logic, the other, transcending both.[1] Technical reasoning has for its province only the necessary relations between propositions. But the mind, in its judgments, is moved by a synthetic view itself incapable of division, one which comprises at one and the same time concrete intuitions, various and subtle considerations, personal presuppositions. The whole is so varied and heterogeneous and, in part, so hidden and subtle, that it defies all attempt at analysis and logical recasting. The final judgment is made by the individual person, according to his ability to take a comprehensive view of all the relevant factors.[2]

Logical reasoning cannot, therefore, be separated from the spontaneous act. It must always be, in some way, subservient to the living mind, whose higher logical sense ought to govern the procedures of formal logic. These have to contain themselves, as it were, within a unifying view which is prior in time, and which continues in being including and surpassing them by its clear sense of its own richness and harmony. When the mind reasons perfectly, it leaves thought to express itself in technical language and to control itself by logic in the fullest degree possible; but it does not cease, at the same time, to keep watch over its implicit action, surveying and judging it in its whole range, by means of a single comprehensive view in which experience and "realising" intuition, the personality and the genius of the individual, work to-

---

[1] "Logical inference has for its purpose to provide reasoning with both a means of testing and a common standard. In my view, it succeeds in part, and fails in part. It succeeds in the degree in which it is possible, in fact, to forge words to represent the innumerable varieties and subtleties of human thought. It fails because the initial presumption is false, that everything it is possible to think can be adequately expressed in words" (*Grammar.*, pp.284, 268, 283, 286, 301). By "logic" Newman always means the formal laws of thought.

[2] *Ibid.*, p.303: "The processes of reasoning which legitimately lead to assent, to action, to certitude, are in fact too multiform, subtle, omnigenous, too implicit, to allow of being measured by rule, that they are, after all, personal". See also pp.284, 288, 301.

gether in a hidden manner.[1] This mode of reasoning Newman calls "informal reference".[2] The capacity of judging the whole he calls the "illative sense", the personal ability to evaluate the proofs.[3] Before any intervention of technical reflection, the illative sense has already examined and verified the results of natural and spontaneous reasoning; after its intervention, it accompanies and supervises the work of analysis and technical reasoning and pronounces, finally, on the correctness of its results, completing, by its view of the whole, the work of the impersonal laws of logic.

The disproportion between living thought and logical technique leaves a certain freedom for the personal factor in assessing the worth of an argument; its importance varies according to the object, but is greatest whenever the thought is not purely abstract. This disproportion is absent only in the domain of the abstract sciences, such as mathematics and formal logic, because the concepts they use stand, not for realities, but for creations of the mind.[4]

Newman gives three reasons for this disproportion: (1) the number and the subtle nature of the different factors; (2) the dependence of thought on the intuitive apprehension of the concrete reality; (3) the decisive influence of hidden personal principles on our way of viewing things. The study of these three causes will make clear the whole structure of living reason.

[1] "Verbal argumentation being useful only in subordination to a higher logic" (*Grammar.*, p.303). "Methodical processes of inference, useful as they are, as far as they go, are only instruments of the mind and need, in order to their due exercise, that real ratiocination and present imagination which gives them a sense beyond their letter and which, while acting through them, reaches to conclusions beyond and above them" (*Ibid.*, p.316). "The mind is unequal to a complete analysis of the motives which carry it on to a particular conclusion, and is swayed and determined by a body of proof which it recognizes as a body, and not in its constituent parts" (*Ibid.*, p.292). See also pp. 271, 278, 291, 301, 302, 317.

[2] The chapter of the *Grammar* devoted to inference consists of three paragraphs, relating to formal inference, logical reasoning, informal reference (the whole act of reasoning, which contains two elements, logical and illogical), and natural inference (elementary and spontaneous reasoning).

[3] "It is the mind that reasons and controls its own reasonings, not any technical apparatus of words and propositions. This power of judging and concluding, when in its perfection, I call the illative sense" (*Ibid.*, p.353). See also pp.241, 245, 360. On Newman's "illative sense", cf. especially Zeno, *op. cit.*, which is practically definitive on this point.

[4] *Ibid*, pp.264-268.

Convergence of Probabilities

One of Newman's best-known tenets is that a number of independent probabilities may furnish a certain proof, if they all point to a single conclusion. Here we will consider only the psychological grounds of this theory; later, we will examine its logical structure and its correctness.[1]

This theory arose, in fact, from Newman's study of living thought as it commonly is in the minds of men. Most of our convictions are grounded on reasons and indications of all kinds, gradually acquired in the course of our experiences, which changed, by slow degrees, certain opinions of ours into certainties. In this living and spontaneous reasoning, the mind takes in the whole argument with a single glance, and makes a comprehensive judgment of its value and range of application.[2] This act is indivisible and irreducible. It is possessed inalienably by the individual mind, which is able to produce it owing to its incommunicable power of evaluation (the illative sense). Yet this act of synthesis is, in some measure, open to analysis, not indeed exhaustively, for, in most cases, many of its motives are so subtle and hidden away that they escape reflex attention, or else our awareness of them is so indistinct that we are at a loss to express or employ them openly.[3] The convictions which prevail in a society are often grounded on reasons which remain implicit for years, and are impervious to the scrutiny of the individual thinker who shares in them. If he does succeed in grasping and giving expression to these motives, and incarnates them in precise form, he shows himself a genius in his penetration into reasons that are living and felt all around him. That being so, it is a far more difficult thing to discern exactly, by reflection on the individual consciousness,

[1] See. Part III, chapter 1.

[2] ". . . by a mental comprehension of the whole case, and a discernment of its upshot" (*Grammar*, p.291). "The mind is swayed and determined by a body of proof, which it recognizes only as a body, and not in its constituent parts" (p.292). "We grasp the full tale of premisses and the conclusion, *per modum unius*, by a sort of instictive perception of the legitimate conclusion in and through the premisses" (p.300).

[3] "Too fine to avail separately , too subtle and circuitous to be convertible into syllogism, too numerous and various for such conversion, even were they convertible" (*Ibid.*, p.288). "Such a process of reasoning is more or less implicit . . . The mind is unequal to a complete analysis of the motives which carry it on to a particular conclusion" (p.292). "It forms one of those arguments which, from the nature of the case, are felt rather than are convertible into syllogisms" (p.297).

all the hidden sources of our personal convictions. The motives at work in our minds are often so closely bound up with our very being that we find it extremely difficult to draw them out into the daylight of conscious thought.[1]

If, none the less, we persist in analysing the reasons for our convictions, we discover, as a rule, a number of indications which are independent of one another but point to a single conclusion. Now, if the mind takes each of these factors separately, and puts it in logical form, it will be confronted with no more than a series of probabilities.[2] But no process of logic can transform probabilities into a proof. These probabilities, however, are convergent; they form a single whole in the living mind. It is the mind that integrates them in the synthetic view of consciousness, notes the convergence of their course, observes how they confirm, modify, reinforce one another, and, in the end, is fitted to assess their value as a whole. So it comes about that probabilities pass beyond themselves to become a demonstrative proof.[3]

Our Knowledge of the Concrete

The development of ideas takes place by means of abstraction and reasoning. Abstraction, however, does not operate in a vacuum; it has its origin in concrete experiences. These are not confined to the passive reception of impressions on our sense-organs; they constitute a special department of intellectual activity, and are the centre and source of the entire life of the mind. The development of thought unfolds and extends, so to speak, the riches implicit in certain of our concrete "intuitions".

Human knowledge comprises two quite distinct kinds of apprehension, of singular objects, and of general ideas.[4] In the former,

---

[1] *Grammar.*, p.336.

[2] *Ibid.*, pp.288-293, *passim*.

[3] "The mind itself is more versatile and vigorous than any of its works, of which language is one, and it is only under its penetrating and subtle action that the margin disappears, which I have described as intervening between verbal argumentation and conclusions in the concrete. It determines what science cannot determine, the limit of converging probabilities and the reasons sufficient for a proof" (*Ibid.*, p.360).

[4] "The terms of a proposition do or do not stand for things. If they do, then they are singular terms, for all things that are units. But if they do not stand for things, they must stand for notions, and are common terms. Singular nouns come from experience, common from abstraction. The apprehension of the former I call real and of the latter, notional" (*Grammar*, pp.22-23).

the content of knowledge is seen to inhere, in its entirety, in the perception of a particular reality;[1] in the latter, the content is isolated from the facts from which it is drawn.[2] The formal reason for this difference is to be found in the intentional object of apprehension. By its action, the intellect takes possession, either of *existing things*, or only of general ideas which *have no existence* in the real world. In the first case, the intentional object of my apprehension is, for example, a particular man in his individual reality. In the second, it is something all men have in common, by which they belong to the human species. This "human nature" does not exist as such. Obviously, I can include the two in a single apprehension, and use one word for both, as Aeneas did when he said, thinking of Dido: *varium et mutabile semper femina*. But each of these objects may well be present to the mind without the other. The name of a village brings to the mind of an inhabitant who has never left it a particular, living reality; to me who have never seen it, merely a general notion.

These two modes of apprehension are ultimately irreducible. They share, however, a single origin, a single point of departure, namely, the impressions made by concrete experience; but they use these impressions differently, so that their respective results have nothing in common. The synthesising action of the mind which conceives real objects perpetuates our impressions in the form of images; that which gives rise to concepts transforms these impressions into notions.[3] We have already described the nature of abstract concepts; now we are in a position to treat of the experience by which we apprehend reality in the concrete.

Our experience of the real, according to Newman, begins in the information derived from the sense organs and sensation. We become directly acquainted with concrete realities either through our bodily senses (e.g. when we say, "the sun is shining"), or through our mental sensations (e.g. when we say, "this view is

---

[1] "Something individual and from without" (*Grammar.*, pp.24-25).

[2] "Stripped of the association of the facts from which they are derived" (*Ibid.*, p.22).

[3] "Here we have two modes of thought, both using the same words, both having the same origin, yet with nothing in common in their results. The informations of sense and sensation are the initial basis of both of them . . . We perpetuate them as images in the one case, we transform them into notions in the other" (*Ibid.*, p.34).

magnificent").[1] What sensation delivers, by the agency of our physical organs, are incoherent impressions, partial, passively accepted, "shifting shapes and colours."[2] But what does he mean by such subtle juxtaposition of terms, "mental sensations," or "mental phenomena"?[3] According to their context, the former denotes certain impressions that give rise to aesthetic judgments; the latter, those impressions that are the source of moral judgments. So the data of direct experience are not confined to sensible impressions, but include mental impressions from which we are able to derive a knowledge of values. These values also are irreducible data, directly given by conscience, and not the result of deduction. They are appropriated, therefore, by a "sense of the beautiful" or a "moral sense", in the same way as the act by which the living mind decides on the rightness of reasoning is ascribed to an "illative sense", because such an act is, also, ultimately irreducible and immediate in its execution.

We must, therefore, distinguish different kinds of information about reality within consciousness. These however, do not cover all the elements of our experience of the concrete. Its chief element is an act of synthesis, namely, the active apprehension, through the impressions received, of existing reality. No doubt the unity and the objective existence of the concrete being are not given in our sense-acts, but we apprehend them by means of these, we perceive them by an ultimate action of the mind; and so we come to form, through these impressions, a concrete image of the reality perceived. Our actual perception is, thus, a combination of two things, a passive impression and an active apprehension.[4] So it is that I grasp, I conceive material objects through the varied impressions of sensible knowledge.[5] It is the same with my knowledge of anyone's personality and intellectual and moral character. I

---

[1] *Grammar.*, p.23.

[2] *Ibid.*, p.110.

[3] *Ibid.*, p.104.

[4] This is the case, too, with animals: "The presence of unseen individual beings is discerned under the shifting shapes and colours of the visible world. Is it by sense, or by reason, that brutes understand the real unities? . . . Not by reason, for they have not reason; not by sense, because they are transcending sense; therefore, it is an instinct" (*Ibid.*, pp.110-111).

[5] "By the law of our nature we associate those sensible phenomena with certain units, individuals, substances, whatever they are to be called, which are outside and out of the reach of sense, and we picture them to ourselves in those phenomena" (*Ibid.*, pp.102-103).

have studied the life, I have read the works, of Cicero or of St. John Chrysostom and, from these, I have gained a whole series of impressions. Gradually, their personality reveals itself, individual, original, unique, irreducible.[1] Through the phenomena of moral apprehension, I enter into communion, by an ever closer contact, sustained by obedience and sacrifice, with the transcendant personality of the God of holiness.[2] By the impressions I receive from Scripture, the liturgy, the living voice of the Church, an ever clearer and more certain perception of an invisible world takes shape within me. All this is the province of "real apprehension".

What are we to call this act of synthesis, and from what faculty does it proceed? Newman attributes it to an "instinct" or "intuition".[3] But these are only analogical terms that he applies to all the operations by which we go beyond the pure *datum* to apprehend something without any intermediary—at any rate, any conscious one—of other data or principles that could account for the transition.[4] Intuition and instinct are, then, contrasted with reasoning. The latter, of its nature, requires a middle term, whereas instinct and intuition are characterized by the absence, at least in appearance, of any intermediary. If this absence is only apparent, there can be no question of a true intuition; in that case, we have a process of reasoning whose discursive form

[1] "And so of those intellectual and moral objects which are brought home to us through our senses . . . [Such a man] is not a mere impression on our senses, we know by instinct; that he is such and such, we know by the manner and quality of that impression" (*Grammar.*, p.103).

[2] *Ibid.*, pp.62-63, 103-104.

[3] *Ibid.*, p.62. Newman, however, distinguishes between the two: "By instinct, I mean a realization of a *particular*; by intuition, of a *general*, fact—in both cases without *assignable* or *recognizable* media of realization" (Ward, *op. cit.*, II, p.58). We do not think that he ordinarily keeps to this distinction.

[4] In its primary sense, the word "instinct" is used of all animals; it is "a natural sense, one and the same in all, and incapable of cultivation" (*Grammar*, p.334; cf. also p.260). By a kind of analogy, other cognitive acts, sensory and intellectual, are also denominated instinctive. This analogy is based on the fact that each is a "spontaneous impulse" (p.260). Instinct, then, is "a force which spontaneously impels us, not only to bodily movements, but to mental acts" (p.62). But the chief factor in their similarity is that "each is a perception of facts without the assignable media of perceiving" (p.334). The two psychological characteristics of instinct are, therefore, spontaneity and the absence of intermediate terms. Newman unites them in one formula: "a spontaneous impulse, physical or intelligent, in the individual, leading to a result without assignable or recognizable intellectual media" (Ward, *op. cit.*, II, p.258).

remains implicit.[1] Hence, Newman can speak of "instinctive reasoning", or even of a "ratiocinative instinct".[2]

The act by which we know reality in the concrete Newman calls "perception", whether the reality be spiritual or physical.[3] Intuition is a general category, of which perception is a species.[4] The total act by which we take hold of a real object he generally calls "imagination", and he constantly places "imaginative" and "real" on the same footing.[5]

It follows that, for Newman as for the German romantics, the imagination is not a mode of purely sensible knowledge, but is our entire faculty of knowing the concrete. As we have already shown, intuition of the concrete involves not only accidental elements, but also absolute essential characteristics, which, of their very nature, transcend the individual case.[6]

Newman indicates the same reality by general terms such as "instinct" and "intuition", or by more specific ones such as "perception", "imagination" and "real apprehension", but this does not exclude certain differences in their respective connotations. Applying a distinction of St. Thomas, we can use a technical term in two senses : its original sense, which is the reason why the term is chosen to signify a certain thing (*id a quo est impositum nomen*), and a technical sense attributed to the term to make it signify that thing (*id ad quod significandum est impositum*). Thus, I can signify a man, in the concrete, by terms of a general nature, such as "individual" or "particular", or by more specific terms, such as "substance", "subsistant," or the specific term, "person"; but, although I mean the same reality by these terms, their original

---

[1] There exists, in consequence, an apparent instinct. Implicit reasoning is instinctive, but only on account of its pure immediacy and spontaneity. It is, essentially, reasoning, and so, discursive. On the other hand, our conception of the concrete reality is, essentially, instinctive, "without argumentative media, *through* my senses, but not logically *by* my senses" (Ward, *op. cit.*, II, p.259). Here, again we see how Newman's use of language is analogical.

[2] *Grammar*, p.287, note.

[3] Hence, the act by which we know God in our consciousness is called perception. Cf., *ibid.*, p.62.

[4] "I call *instinct* the general faculty, *perception* a kind of instinct" (draft of a letter to Meynell, quoted in Zeno, *op. cit.*, p.277).

[5] See, e.g., *Grammar*, pp. 34, 63, 87, 119 (imaginary or real assent), 120, 124; "particular experiences of the religious instinct, which are, in the imagination, not intellectually, notices of its presence" (p.63).

[6] See above, p.86.

differences of meaning, for which I chose them, are connotated in my use of them, and will decide my choice of one or the other of them, according to the context. They indicate the same reality, but each emphasises a particular aspect. So, in the case before us, the terms "instinct", "intuition," "perception," "imagination," "real apprehension," are used by Newman to signify the same thing, the function of apprehending concrete reality. But each of these terms emphasises a different aspect, or a certain feature, of this function. "Instinct" and "intuition" bring out its character of immediacy; "perception", the synthetic apprehension of the individual through impressions; "imagination", the activity whereby, starting from the impressions, we represent to ourselves, within the unity of apprehension, the numerous qualities and relations that make up, for us, the concrete being; "real apprehension", the communion of the mind with the existing reality.

It is evident that this single expression, "real apprehension", covers a diversity of acts of the mind that have in common only the highly analogical property of being knowledge of the concrete by synthetic intuition. How far does this analogy extend? All analogy is partial similarity. In practice, Newman attends only to the resemblances and ignores the differences. True, he is aware that there is a problem and, occasionally, expresses himself in a way that points to such differences. He says, for example, that the part played *directly* by sensible phenomena in our knowledge of the outside world is only *indirectly* played, in our knowledge of God, by the interior phenomena of conscience.[1] Through our sensory impressions, we perceive immediately, with the clearest evidence, the existence of material things outside us. But conscience conveys to us, in the first instance, only rules bearing on our conduct of life, whose content does not include direct impressions of the divine attributes. All that can be said is that these rules are revealed to us, in our experience, as absolute obligations, and that this feeling of obligation, with its emotional accompaniments of reverence, fear, etc., implies contact with a Person to whom we are bound by certain duties. At the beginning, however, our sense of the presence of this Person is extremely vague. As a rule, it is only through education and personal fidelity that we attain to a clear and strong perception of the personal

[1] *Grammar*, p.104.

God.[1] There is, in consequence, a great difference between these two ways of perceiving a real being. What they have in common is this; in both, the mind transcends immediate impressions by an act *sui generis*, and attains to a communion with substantial and concrete realities which are not explicable in terms of these impressions. The "grasp" of singular things in the concrete is, with Newman, a highly analogical concept, and he failed to bring out clearly the profound differences in our modes of perception of concrete reality.

Nowhere, for example, did he give a phenomenological description of the great difference between real apprehension of a "thing" or an "object", and that of a "person" or "subject". These are two irreducible kinds of experience; the one, of a world which is at my disposal, like an extension of my body; the other, of a presence standing over against me. All the same, he was fully aware of the difference; in fact, he felt it strongly and refers to it frequently, but I know of no description of it in his writings.

Once more, we must mention the unconscious, this time as one of the properties of real knowledge. This quality he emphasizes particularly in the fifteenth of the Oxford sermons and in the *Newman-Perrone Paper*. An intuition may take root in us without our knowledge. The entire work of a poet may be inspired by an idea of which he was never conscious. Our own spiritual life may be sustained by a vision we have never been aware of. Centuries may elapse without formal expression being given to truths communicated in a contact with the living God and, in spite of this, they have continued, through the whole of that time, to nourish secretly the religious life of innumerable believers.[2] An intuition of that sort makes itself known in ways of living—affectivity, conduct—rather than by exact formulation.[3]

The distinction between the perception of concrete realities and the elaboration of abstract notions is of obvious application in the theory of development. The two modes of knowledge can, moreover, go together,[4] completing and balancing one another:

---

[1] See below, pp.149-154.

[2] All these examples are to be found in the *O.U.S.*, pp.321-323.

[3] *Newman-Perrone*, pp.413-414, 437-438.

[4] "In the same mind and at the same time, the same proposition may express both what is notional and what is real" (*Grammar*, pp.11, 63-64).

Each use of propositions has its own excellence and serviceableness, and each its own imperfection. To apprehend notionally is to have breadth of mind, but .o be shallow; to apprehend really is to be deep, but to be narrow-minded. The latter is the conservative principle of knowledge, and the former the principle of its advancement. Without the apprehension of notions, we should ever pace round one small circle of knowledge; without a firm hold on things, we shall waste ourselves in vague speculations.[1]

This makes it clear how development proceeds on the notional plane, and yet, thanks to real apprehension, this abstract procedure is in continuous communion with reality. The various and abstract aspects which the mind distinguishes in the original experience are expressed in verbal symbols. But there is a danger here; it is only too easy for the mind to let its thought run away with these symbols, without frequently relating them, and turning itself, to the original experience. When that happens, the concepts symbolized come to lead an independent life, without any profound union with the reality from which they arose. So it is that thought is dissipated in empty speculations.

Newman returns incessantly to the dangers of abstraction. Our concepts are imperfect and partial approximations of reality; they are true, but only up to a certain point. If we attend to them alone, they tend to cut us off from reality, and so we reach conclusions, logical enough in relation to the notions in question, but no longer corresponding to the real.[2] The scientist who confines himself to a single subject is bound to fall prey to this danger. For a given science is a systematization of a special aspect of the real, and of that alone. Its version of reality has to be broadened and completed by that of the other sciences, if it is not to be misleading. Now, the greatest desire of the intellect, its deepest impulse, drives it towards a perfect knowledge of reality; and so our partial knowledge, if unaccompanied by a wider sweep and a philosophi-

---

[1] *Grammar.*, p.34.

[2] "Our notion of a thing may be only partially faithful to the original; it may be in excess of the thing, or it may represent it incompletely and, in consequence, it may serve for it, it may stand for it, only to a certain point, in certain cases, but not further. After that point is reached, the notion and the thing part company; and then the notion, if still used as the representative of the thing, will work out conclusions, not inconsistent with itself, but with the thing to which it no longer corresponds" (*Ibid.*, pp.46, 47).

cal spirit, sets itself up as a complete account of the whole, and so turns into a philosophy, unilateral and false.[1] It is against these dangers of abstract knowledge that we are protected by the close, inner knowledge of reality in the concrete. This gives depth to our thought, and keeps it sane and balanced. It is, in one sense, the touchstone and guarantee of notional thinking. Whenever we reason, our minds must never lose sight of the concrete as a whole, which is the subject of analysis.[2]

Yet this is not the whole extent of the influence of the intuitive element of the development of knowledge. In addition, it helps to enrich abstract thought; the firmer the mind's hold on the real, the wider and clearer becomes its perception of the different aspects. Hence, the intelligence gains both in range and in depth, and the further it penetrates the recesses of the real, the richer becomes the material at the disposition of abstract thought. What is more, things in the concrete make their appeal to the heart, something which abstraction cannot do; they draw us into a deep, interior recollection, more or less unconscious, in which the different aspects of reality slowly disengage themselves, take firm outline, and imprint themselves on the understanding. Then it is that the mind seems no longer to reason from abstraction to abstraction, but travels, as it were, all round the thing and takes note of the various aspects brought to its view.[3] "Realising is the very life of true developments."[4]

First principles

Impersonal, analytical logic cannot take the place of the syn-

[1] This is the fundamental idea of the fourth lecture on the *Idea*; cf. especially, pp.73-76.

[2] "Real apprehension has the precedence, as being the scope and end and the test of the notional" (*Grammar*, p.34).

[3] "The fuller is the mind's hold upon things or what it considers such, the more fertile is it in its aspects of them, and the more practical in its definitions" (*Ibid.*, p.34); see also, *Ibid.*, pp.314-315, for a fine description of this mental process. Here are some extracts from it: "Ordinarily speaking, such deductions do not flow forth, except according as the image is cherished within us with the sentiments which it necessarily claims of us . . . Such a one is able to pronounce about the great sight which encompasses him, as about some visible object . . . he is not inferring abstraction from abstraction, but noting down the aspects and phases of that one thing on which he is ever gazing". A very full description will also be found in *Newman-Perrone*, pp.409-411.

[4] *O.U.S.*, p.337. See also *Apologia*, p.194: "Developments arising out of a keen and vivid realizing of the divine *depositum* of faith".

thetic judgment of the personal intellect. From the outset, personal judgment perceives the upshot of a complex of reasons too
rich, subtle, or hidden to be transposed into abstract reasoning.
The very indications disclosed by analysis possess, especially in
the sphere of the concrete, in addition to the probability assigned
to them separately by formal logic, a stronger demonstrative force
as elements of a whole within which they converge along with
other factors to one and the same conclusion. The evaluation of
this synthetic proof depends, ultimately, on individual competence, experience, common sense, or a special form of wisdom.
Further, the exactness and the power of our reasoning derive
from a close contact with the real, whose influence escapes the
scrutiny of logic. Do we, in fact, bear in mind all the aspects we
should in our examination of a given problem? Logic cannot
possibly decide. The answer rests with a mind that has familiarized
itself, by profound experience and receptiveness with the numerous aspects of reality.

There is a third reason why logic must be held more or less
impotent in the majority of reasonings. It is that every process of
reason ultimately rests on first principles and, on these, all men, by
the very nature of their personal condition, differ to such a degree
that no set of impersonal rules can possibly furnish a general
criterion of truth.[1]

We must, therefore, consider more closely the theory of first
principles. Here we are concerned only with their psychological
aspect, ignoring for the time being the epistemological problems
concerning them.

What are these first principles? The question is, at one and the
same time, simple and complex. It is obvious what Newman generally means by them throughout his writings. Reasoning presupposes premises. These are either ultimate or depend on
others. But it is impossible to regress indefinitely. We finally arrive,
then, at first judgments, incapable of demonstration. These are
the "first principles".[2] Newman, however, views them always
from a psychological, never from a logical, standpoint. Conse-

---

[1] Cf. *Essay*, p.90; *Present Position*, pp.260-261; *Grammar*, p.269; "First
principles, the recondite sources of all knowledge, as to which logic pervades
no common measure of minds, which are accepted by some, rejected by
others". "In which men are, in fact, in essential and irremediable variance
one with another" (p.362).

[2] *Grammar*, pp.269-270; *Present Position*, p.256.

quently, he holds to be first principles not only positions logically irreducible—immediately evident to all minds—but also all those judgments which, in fact and for whatever motive, we presuppose absolutely, and which we neither can prove, nor even care to try, since we accept them—no one knows how or why—as obvious and unquestionable. The notion of "first principles" then, is itself a very wide, analogical concept, covering a multitude of analogues, whose common character is that they are, *in fact*, the *first* grounds of our thinking and judging.

This is the sense in which Newman uses the term "first principles" in practically all his works. Take, for example, his famous seventh lecture, in the *Present Position of Catholics*, where he expresses himself on the subject in the most explicit, concrete and vivid terms. He makes his meaning perfectly clear. He draws a distinction between prejudice (pre-judgment or presumption) and "first principle". The first two derive from motives; but, whereas the prejudiced man clings obstinately to his opinions, the man who "assumes" a thing is ready to modify his views on the evidence of the facts. A first principle, on the other hand, has no reasons to support it[1]; it belongs to a different species altogether.

Newman devotes his attention especially to those first principles which are characteristic of a group of terms and are accepted uncritically because they are shared by all. These are what determine the spirit of one community as opposed to that of another. They inspire its collective attitudes and common judgments, and explain what its members, immersed in the group, regard as the expression of common sense.

Now, when we come to that part of the *Grammar* in which Newman expounds the different kinds of notional assent, we get the impression that those "first principles" against which he warns us in the *Present Position* are there described under the heading of "credence"[2], instead of "first principle".[3] Moreover, the term "speculation" embraces a whole assembly of axioms, aphorisms, and even the principles of theology.[4] It would seem, then, that in the *Grammar* he uses "first principle" in a restricted sense.

This, however, is improbable; for, in the same work, he asserts

---

[1] *Present Position*, pp.255-256.
[2] *Grammar*, pp.53-58
[3] *Ibid.*, pp.60-71.
[4] *Ibid.*, p.73.

that first principles are primary judgments from which we set out to reason on any subject at all. Being very numerous, they differ from one person to another, according to the particular mentality of each. A few only of these first principles are admitted universally.[1]

Newman's study of them is very suggestive, and he discusses some in detail. Those he selects are not those first principles of metaphysics or logic, as generally understood; but those judgments of existence, in which we affirm the reality or the objective validity of various "worlds", spiritual and material, in which human life is involved: e.g. that there exists a corporeal world external to us; that the distinction between good and evil, beauty and ugliness, truth and falsity is an expression of absolute values, incumbent on us but independent of us, in other words, objective; that there is a supreme, transcendent Lord, whose presence fills all, whose providence rules all; that there exists in the world a universal order of finality and causality. It is a question, then, of certain general conclusions of our experience, interpreted from the standpoint of an objectivist ontology. They are judgments which enter rarely, if ever, as conscious premises in a particular course of reasoning. They are, rather, the expressions of our awareness of certain elements encompassing our experience of the real, or one of the chief spheres of that experience. We are conscious of them in each fresh experience, and the judgments expressing them are presupposed in each of our thoughts and acts. They indicate the ultimate meaning of experience, stimulate thought, impel to action, and determine the mental climate of the conscious life of each man.

Are the distinctive characteristics of first principles to be traced to their mode of origin? Newman, in the *Grammar* gives an emphatic affirmative. First principles, he says, are drawn from concrete events, they are generalisations of our experience of the real.[2] Given certain cognitive acts by which I conceive transsubjective realities through the medium of sense-impressions, I arrive, by a process of generalisation, at the knowledge of an external world.[3] Similarly, it is from certain moral experiences that

[1] Thus, almost literally, in *Ibid.*, p.60.
[2] "These so-called first principles are really conclusions or abstractions from particular experience" (*Ibid.*, p.65)
[3] *Grammar.*, pp.61-62.

I come to be aware of a whole universe of good and evil.[1] In each case, he emphasizes the identity of structure. We have here a striking feature of his thought. Are we, then, in a position to distinguish clearly the first principles from other acts by which ideas are formed? Actually, "profession" and "credence" do not take their origin in any concrete knowledge of the real. They are affirmations or opinions, borrowed, so to speak, from the social environment, not personal convictions springing from living contact with reality.[2] As to "opinion", the question does not arise, as it is merely a moral judgment, and its subject is not reality, but the validity of an argument.[3] What about "speculation"? This is distinguished by reflex self-consciousness, it presupposes a critical examination of our mental activity; it consists in a firm, conscious acceptance of the truth of a proposition.[4] First principles, on the other hand, are spontaneous convictions, usually unconscious, whose existence is derived from our personal experiences at the deepest level of our being.[5]

What are we to conclude from all this? For Newman, first principles are those abstract judgments which, viewed psychologically, form the lowest stratum of our mental constructions, regardless of their origin or our awareness of them. This is the general meaning he gives in the majority of instances, even in the *Grammar*. When in the course of that work, he makes clear the impotence of logic to determine first principles, he has in mind not only the presuppositions which arise from our personal nature, but also a whole crowd of subtle convictions due to the spirit of

---

[1] *Grammar.*, pp.64-65.

[2] "Profession" is a weak form of assent. It consists in words devoid of genuine content, such as slogans, empty formulas, and the like. It is an assertion "with the pretence and without the reality of assent" (*Ibid.*, p.43). "Credence" is more serious. It consists in all those acts of superficial acquiescence, in various spheres of knowledge, which make up the culture of a given group at a particular period: "It is never more than the furniture of the mind, it is never thoroughly assimilated with it" (*Ibid.*, p.55).

[3] "An assent to a proposition, not as true, but as probably true, that is, to the probability of that which the proposition enunciates" (*Ibid.*, p.58).

[4] "The contemplation of mental operations and their results as opposed to experience, experiment, or sense. . . . Those notional assents which are the most direct, explicit, and perfect of their kind, viz., those which are the firm, conscious acceptance of propositions as true" (*Ibid.*, p.73).

[5] "The recondite sources of all knowledge" (*Ibid.*, p.269); "Recondite and untractable principles" (p.272); "They are hidden deep in our nature, or, it may be, in our personal peculiarities" (p.277).

the time, environment, religion, social habits, the experiences and history of the individual.[1] Finally, when he comes to treat of the rôle of the illative sense in the genesis of first principles, he once again makes choice, as examples, of certain conceptions we share with our social surroundings.[2]

We return now to the problem stated above. Did Newman, in the classical passage of the *Grammar* where he expounds the different kinds of notional assent, use the expression "first principle" in a more restricted sense? We do not think so. Only—and the importance of this will be seen later—there are two main kinds of first principles. The one comprises those which arise from a genuine experience of the real, one which is, at the same time, the most personal and the most universal among men; the others are the expression of a kind of public or social "ego", which shares unconsciously the prejudices, the estimates, the attitudes of a particular society, in a given place and time, into which it is born and whose influence it undergoes. These latter principles, in fact, share the nature of "credence". But every credence is not a first principle. A credence assumes the value of a first principle only from the time when it comes to play in the life of the mind the part of first mover, which is the characteristic of a first principle.

There is a similar relation between first principles and speculation. The latter is a notional assent given to a proposition which is the outcome of methodical, critical thought. However, in the first instance, first principles appertain to spontaneous thought; but they may be subjected to critical reflection, and so be raised to the dignity of speculative truth. "First principle," then, is a psychological expression, "speculation," an epistemological one. The first principles of science, philosophy and theology, once established by methodical reflection, become speculative truths.

Whence do we get these first principles? Newman is rather elusive about this. In the first edition of the *Grammar* he wrote: "It must be recollected too that the first springs of thought are so obscure that at times experiences and reasonings may be indistinguishable from each other; and sometimes it is impossible to say whether an apparent first principle is an elementary truth or rather the exhibition of some sensation or sentiment in the

---

[1] *Grammar.*, p.270.
[2] *Ibid.*, pp.375-381.

shape in which the illative sense represents it to us."[1] Whence arise these innumerable "recondite sources of all knowledge"? "The very sense of pleasure and pain inevitably translates itself into intellectual assumptions."[2] In the *Grammar*, Newman expresses himself quite clearly: "First principles are abstractions from particular experiences . . . they are abstractions from facts, not elementary truths prior to reasoning."[3] But he seems to contradict this in the *Present Position*: "First principles are not drawn from facts . . . they proceed immediately from the mind . . . the holder considers them to be a part of himself."[4] That is exactly what distinguishes them from a prejudice or a presumption. According to the *Grammar*, they are the product of a discursive act of reason, abstraction or induction; according to the *Present Position*, they are characterised by not having such an origin. How are these contradictory views to be reconciled? Did the lecturer in the *Present Position* simplify the problem, in practice equating the lack of *conscious* motives with the absence of *any* reason, whereas for the philosopher of the *Grammar*, with his acuter vision, the first principles flow, secretly and spontaneously, from experiences so profound as to be often unconscious? Or did the guard against Protestant prejudices build up his theory in function of its purpose, with an eye to those collective convictions which are based on no personal experience, but derive their power of persuasion from the tendencies common to a group; whereas the analyser of notional assents attends to another class of acts altogether, as we have just seen? This latter explanation seems the best.

For the expression "first principles" covers a number of analogous things in the psychological order, whose real nature and origin are profoundly different. Hence their theoretical explanation varies as the writer envisages, according to the context, now one kind of reality and now another. In the *Grammar*, Newman's design was to draw out those first principles with which we express that experience in depth, that awareness we have of a containing and enclosing element that accompanies each of our particular experiences, and issues in the affirmation of the various objective worlds on which our existence depends. In the *Present Position*,

---

[1] *Grammar*. (3rd ed., 1870), p.355. This passage is omitted in later editions.
[2] *Ibid.*, p.377.
[3] *Ibid.*, p.65.
[4] *Present Position*, p.255.

on the other hand, he uses the introduction, which treats of the first principles in general, to prepare the ground for our understanding of the psychological interplay of those first principles characteristic of the Protestant mentality, whose origin is to be sought, not in the experience of individuals, but in the collective mind.

The same kind of treatment is to be seen in Newman's theory of the experience of the real. When, in his *University Sermons*, he uses it to explain the development of reasoning in theology, the object of concrete intuition appears as an unconscious idea. In the *Grammar*, however, where he is chiefly concerned to show how, through abstract formulas of belief, we come into vital contact with realities of religion, it is the apprehension of the concrete by the imagination that takes up the foreground. To understand so subtle a mind as Newman's, who invariably expounds his views and directs his investigations in relation to a particular design, we must continually bear in mind his standpoint in writing the work in question.

Our study of the origin of first principles leads to the same conclusion as the preceding analysis, namely, that the very term is highly analogical. All first principles are primary movers giving to thought its impulse and direction. But there are certain very general, we might say transcendental ideas which, by our very constitution, imprint themselves on our minds by a kind of spontaneous generalization from experiences that are typically human. Others, however, are implanted by the nature of a particular department of experience, and are valid only within it.[1] Yet others are inspired by the spirit of the age, of a school of thought, or the mental climate of a certain milieu. Some are "awfully personal", and derive either from individual value-experiences, or from practical concerns, from professional bias, a one-sided culture, temperament, character, personal talent, routine. A speculative statement that, for one thinker, is but one tenet among several others becomes, for another, a basic principle from whose standpoint he attacks all his various problems and which, by its dominance and penetration of his entire thought, determines the original structure of his personal philosophy.[2] It is not possible to include all these contents of the mind in a single description. They differ in

[1] *Grammar*, pp.275-276.
[2] *Essay*, p.179.

every way, in their origin, their range of meaning, their sphere
of application.

This minutely detailed examination has brought to light, little
by little, the essential characteristics of the first principles of
thought. All together, they are the expression of our personality.
Our common nature, social position, individual gifts, personal
acquirements, these are what our mind expresses in the form of
first principles. Character, temperament, personal cast of mind,
practical attitudes, the level of culture, the history of the individual,
his moral condition, all these factors, and others too, combine in
the setting up of our first principles.[1] Now, if these are personal
so is thought as a whole. For, in fact, the majority of men, even
the least cultured, habitually reason correctly, if it is to their interest to do so.[2] If, in spite of this, they reach such different conclusions, the sole cause lies in the principles governing their mental
operations. Truth and error actually exist, but our attainment of
truth depends less on our power of reasoning than on the prior
determination of the first principles directing our individual
judgments.[3] This shows clearly the insufficiency of logic as a controlling agency of thought.[4] All of which is magnificently expressed by Newman in these words :

> The fact remains that, in any inquiry about things in the
> concrete, men differ from each other, not so much in the
> soundness of their reasoning as in the principles which govern
> its exercise, that those principles are of a personal character,
> that where there is no common measure of minds, there is
> no common measure of arguments, and that the validity of

[1] "[They]constitute the difference between man and man; they characterize
the individual. His religion, his Creed, his worship, his political party, his
character, correspond to his first principles. In short, they are the man."
(*Present Position*, pp.260-261). See also *Grammar*, pp.270, 277, 364, 367-369,
413.

[2] "If their mind is really interested, men, as a rule, do not reason ill"
(*O.U.S.*, p.211). See also, *Grammar*, p.413.

[3] "The problem how to arrive at truth is one whose solution depends
entirely upon first principles, and not on syllogistic exposition" (*Grammar*,
p.296); "Syllogism, then, though of course it has its use, still does only the
easiest and minutest part of the work, in the investigation of truth, for when
there is any difficulty, that difficulty commonly lies in determining first
principles, not in the arrangement of proofs" (p.270). See also p.277.

[4] "How impotent logic is to deal with these indispensable first principles"
(*Ibid.*, p.272). See also pp.269-270, 367.

proof is determined, not by any scientific test, but by the illa-tive sense.[1]

There is one property of first principles that is closely related to their personal character. It is that we are unconscious of them. We do not see ourselves. Consequently, it is highly probable that precisely the most deeply rooted elements of our personalities, those that most effectively govern our thought, escape most easily our reflection. "They are hidden for the very reason they are so sovereign and so engrossing. They have sunk into you, they spread through you; you do not so much appeal to them as act upon them. And this, in great measure, is meant by saying that self-knowledge is so difficult; that is, in other words, men commonly do not know their First Principles."[2] These are the despots which, crouching in the most hidden recesses of our personality, govern the bustling world of our thoughts and actions, without ever show-ing themselves in the open. They are idea-sources rather than idea-objects.

Newman's doctrine of first principles is the cornerstone of that section of his psychology that treats of the genesis of human know-ledge. Our thought receives impulse and direction from our prin-ciples as its first movers. So it comes about that one and the same doctrine develops divergently in different individuals or groups, according to the nature of their first principles.[3]

SECTION B

FAITH AND DEVELOPMENT

Let us return to our dominant theme : the development of faith and of dogma takes place according to the same laws as the devel-opment of ideas in the natural order. However, the origin of this development from revealed data, its supernatural character, and its fulfilment under the influence of the Holy Spirit, give rise to certain problems of its own. In the first section, we have described the general psychology of development. Here it will be enough to

[1] *Grammar.*, p.413.
[2] *Present Position*, p.261.
[3] "Doctrines expand and spread differently, according to the mind, individual or collective, which receives them. The peculiarities of those who profess them are their regulative force, their norm of organization or, it might be called, their evolutionary form" (*Essay*, p.178). See also p.180, and *Present Position*, p.263.

show briefly that Newman explains the development of doctrine in the light of this psychology, and then we shall go on to consider its special problems.

Faith and theology

Faith is, first of all, an experience, a real knowledge of supernatural realities, and this intuition of faith is transposed by theology into notions. This is the main thesis of the famous sermon on the development of religious doctrine and of the first part of the *Grammar*.[1] Here Newman does not consider faith in the supernatural aspect proper to it, that is, in its formal object. Considered in this aspect, faith "is assenting to a doctrine as true, which we do not see, which we cannot prove, because God says it is true, who cannot lie".[2] But this supernatural act of faith can also be considered from a purely psychological standpoint, in its material object.[3] Then the question arises, "Of what nature is the apprehension which inspires the act of faith?"[4] The answer is that faith being a religious act, attains its object in a real apprehension. It is, therefore, a "real assent", affective.[5] In Newman's terminology, it might equally be called an act of "devotion" or of "religion".[6]

---

[1] "A dogma is a proposition . . . To give a real assent to it is an act of religion; to give a notional, is a theological act" (*Grammar*, p.98). He might equally have said an act of faith or of piety. See pp. 124, 135, 140, 146-147.

[2] *Disc. M. Cong.*, p.194. See also *Grammar*, pp.99-100: "Faith, in its theological sense, includes a belief, not only in the thing believed, but also in the ground of believing; that is, not only belief in certain doctrines, but belief in them expressly because God has revealed them".

[3] "Here I am engaged only with what is called the material object of faith . . . not the formal" (*Ibid.*, p.100).

[4] *Ibid.*, p.99.

[5] In addition to these two chief meanings, the word "faith" has many others: (1) the object or content of belief, the Creed (*Diff. Angl.*, II, p.26); (2) the virtue: "faith is a state of mind, a habit or character of mind" (*Disc. M. Cong.*, pp.193-194); (3) the implicit reasoning which brings a religious man to belief: "faith is the reasoning of the religious mind, acting according to presumptions rather than in virtue of proofs" (*O.U.S.*, p.203); (4) the whole Christian attitude to life and the world. The two latter meanings of the word are closely analyzed by J. A. Elbert, *The Evolution of Newman's Conception of Faith Prior to* 1845, (Philadelphia, 1932).

[6] In *Diff. Angl.*, II, pp.26-28, faith is opposed to piety as objective truth, not yet "realized", to subjective, or "realized", truth. Faith and piety are, therefore, regarded as two phases, as it were, of one and the same act as it tends to its perfection. Faith is the simple acceptance of the Creed; piety is its flowering within the whole personality, and this expansion comes about by slow degrees, under the influence of the acceptance of the Creed.

As an apprehension of concrete reality, faith is contrasted with theology. The latter term is used generally, by Newman, not in the restricted sense of discursive reasoning from dogma,[1] but to embrace all that pertains to the notional expression of religious truth, including dogma itself. Often enough, it is expanded to include natural theology. In that case, it comprises natural and revealed elements, dogmatic pronouncements and free speculations, implicit reasoning and the explicit science of the faith.[2]

It is true that the object of faith is the truth of God, and thus simple and immutable; but it becomes multiple and progressive once it is assimilated by the intellect.[3] In the *Arians* and the *University Sermons*, Newman outlines a psychological scheme of doctrinal development. First of all, he says, the object of faith is an intuition or "idea", of which we are not necessarily aware. This "idea" is a contact with the concrete living objects of faith, an "impression" of objective revealed truth. This "idea-impression" is then spontaneously analysed and reflected upon. We rethink it accordingly, in the form of successive judgments, each the complement of the others.[4] But this transposition into abstract terms never exhausts the richness of the intuitive "idea".[5] So it is that theology never ceases to develop; its inner vital principle and its guarantee is the concrete vision of faith.[6]

The development of doctrinal tradition starts with a very gradual process of implicit reasoning in the minds of believers: "Development is the fruit, neither of a wishing and resolving, nor

---

[1] Later, he accepted this meaning, too (*Via Media*, I, p.94, note of 1877).

[2] At times, this meaning is confined to scientific analysis. For example, in the *Idea*, pp.222-223, 441-442, where theology as a technique is compared to physics.

[3] *Newman-Perrone*, p. 405.

[4] "Revelation sets before it certain supernatural facts and actions, beings and principles; these make a certain impression or image upon it; and this impression, spontaneously or even necessarily, becomes the subject of reflection on the part of the mind itself, which proceeds to investigate it, and to draw it forth in successive and distinct sentences" (*O.U.S.*, p.320).

[5] *Ibid.*, pp.331-332.

[6] *O.U.S.*, p.334: "Though the Christian mind reasons out a series of dogmatic statements, one from another, this it has ever done, and must always do, not from those statements taken in themselves, as logical propositions, but as illustrated and "as I may say, inhabited by that sacred impression which is prior to them, which acts as a regulating principle, ever present, upon the reasoning, and without which no one has any warrant to reason at all". See also, *Grammar*, p.98: "No theology can start or thrive without the initiative and abiding presence of religion".

of a forced enthusiasm, nor of any rational mechanism, nor of any subtlety of intellect; it proceeds from an innate power of expansion within the mind in its season, though making use, more or less according to circumstances, of reflection, argument and original thought, with a dependence on the ethical growth of the mind."[1] Development of the faith is, then, in the first instance, an implicit and vital reasoning.

It is only subsequently that formal reasoning and systematic statement come to impose their order on thought.[2] The inequality existing between the two forms of reasoning is greater here than in other cases, because the ideas in question here are, much more than elsewhere, mere shadows of the realities which they are obliged to stand for[3], realities which, in any case, are mysterious. Our reasoning moves in the twilight of mystery, then, at least partially.[4] The mind, therefore, makes, in the process of development, transitions which subsequent logic is unable to justify.[5] Theological proofs form part of an intellectual process of a high order; sometimes, they suggest and point a direction rather than demonstrate.[6] Logical competence, however subtle and forceful, is insufficient for the understanding of theology. To be capable of estimating it, we need to steep ourselves profoundly, and over a long period, in its universe of ideas and to let them penetrate our being. Hence it is that the greatest theologians, as, for that matter, the greatest men of learning, owe their eminence to a special kind of

[1] *Essay*, pp.73-74.

[2] *Ibid.*, p.190.

[3] This sets a special problem, to be dealt with later.

[4] "All mystery implies a partial manifestation. Because it is then in a measure understood, it can so far be developed, though each result in the process must partake of the dimness and confusion of the original impression." (*Essay*, pp.59-60). See also *Diff. Angl.*, II, 81.

[5] "In my terminology, 'logical coherence' is opposed to the scientific principle which classifies, in hierarchical order, the developments already effected. It includes, therefore, every progression of the mind from one judgment to another, that made, for example, in virtue of moral suitability, which does not lend itself to dissection into premises and conclusion" (*Essay*, p.383). See also *Newman-Perrone*, pp.424-425.

[6] *Essay*, p.338 (dealing with the influence of the principle of faith on theological method): "We come to consider the arguments as suggestions and indications for our guidance, rather than as logical proofs, and the developments as a moral growth, slow and spontaneous, of existing opinions and not as results scientifically compelling". Cf. *Ibid.*, pp.73-74.

instinctive judgment, in this case, theological judgment.[1] Within this instinct there is collaboration between the mind of the Church and a subtle and divine gift of reasoning.[2] That is why the writings of theologians seem so strange to the profane.[3] Here we have a clear echo of Newman's theory of the illative sense.

Argument by convergence of probabilities also has a part to play in the development of doctrine. Though its application is not expressly formulated in the *Grammar*, it is still to be found there. Newman adduces, for example, historical developments, but these are wholly reducible to the evaluation of concrete facts, the determination of the canon of Scripture being a case in point.[4] The slow growth of opinion, the effect of controversies and the comparing of testimonies, by which Newman explains the determination of the canon, is best regarded as a gradual accumulation and convergence, in the Christian consciousness, of all kinds of indications, simple and complex, telling in favour of this or that sacred book. As regards the "analogy of faith"—for Newman the capital rule of doctrinal development[5]—what else is it than an accumulation of probabilities, more or less strong, in favour of one or other article of doctrine, and based on the requirements of harmony with doctrines already professed? Newman himself has recourse to this method of convergence, in the *Essay*, to demonstrate the infallibility of the Church.[6]

The theory of first principles has a special application to the problem of the development of doctrine. Just as the intuition of consciousness gives rise to principles that direct and foster thought more or less unobserved, so the intuition of religious faith raises

[1] See the letter of 1879 to W. Froude in Ward, *op. cit.*, II, 590-591. Newman there claims for theology the same rights as physics, and draws a parallel: "Our teaching, as well as yours, requires the preparation and exercise of long thought, and of a thorough imbuing in religious ideas. Athanasius, Gregory, Leo, Augustine . . . have, from our estimate of their theological instinct, that honour with us".

[2] The Church "has recourse also to other sources of information, Scripture, Tradition, the sense or *phronema* of the Church, and a subtle power of reasoning, in its origin a gift of God" (*Diff. Angl.*, II, pp.312-314).

[3] "It will account for the charge of weak reasoning commonly brought against those Fathers; for never do we seem so illogical to other as when we are arguing under the continual influence of impressions to which they are insensible" (*O.U.S.*, p.334).

[4] *Essay*, p.47.

[5] *Newman-Perrone*, p.412.

[6] *Essay*, pp.75-92.

up a series of principles which determine, in a manner, the spirit, the atmosphere and the direction of true and accepted theology. These principles are abstract presuppositions, of the moral and practical order, not concrete elements of the data of revelation. They are the causes of the growth of doctrine, but they themselves do not grow.[1] What appears to be a development is, in reality, a wider application of them.[2] From its beginning, they were at work in the Church, but were mostly below the surface; it is only later that they come into full view, in the history of theology, on the occasion of some dispute or other.[3] Newman assembles those relating to the doctrine of the Incarnation,[4] and enumerates ten :[5]

(1) *The dogmatic principle*: There is one revealed truth, definitive and irreformable. It possesses a determinate content, able to be grasped by the mind, despite the inadequacy of the language in which it is conveyed. Its acceptance or rejection is of decisive importance for the life of man.[6]

(2) *The principle of faith:* We are obliged to believe unreservedly the revelation made by God, whatever the difficulties placed in the way by ordinary experience and natural reason. It is true that these are logically prior to faith but, psychologically, they follow it. Some have seen in this principle a sign of fideism, but this interpretation of it is mistaken. For the term "faith" is not used by Newman generally, in the *University Sermons* and *Essay*, to denote the supernatural act, but the psychological act in its totality, which comprises both the motives and the assent in their living, spontaneous unity. The faith that precedes reason is, therefore, an act which includes its own rational justification, but rather

---

[1] *Essay.*, p.178: "Principles are abstract and general, doctrines are concerned with facts; doctrines develop, while principles, at first sight, do not; doctrines grow and expand, principles are permanent; doctrines are of the intellectual order, principles of an order more directly moral and practical".

[2] *Ibid.*, p.180: "It is often said that principles develop, when they are but exemplified."

[3] *Ibid.*, p.179: "We might expect that, in Catholicism, principles develop later than doctrines, since they are more deeply engrained in the mind, and they are to be viewed as presumptions rather than objective professions"; "Before the Church had fully matured her doctrines, she had already taken root in her principles" (p.361). Cf. also p.360.

[4] "For reasons of order, I will consider the Incarnation as the central truth of the Gospel, and the source from which flow the Gospel principles" (*Ibid.*, p.324).

[5] For the enumeration, cf. *Ibid.*, pp.325-326.

[6] *Ibid.*, pp.346-352, 357-368.

as lived and implied; the reason which follows faith is the conceptual and scientific analysis of that justification.

Faith, then, is an act of the entire personality, an expression of our moral disposition and of our love, and implicitly contains our rational motives. It is only subsequently that these latter come to be adequately expressed by analysis and reflection, and this is the peculiar task of reason. Fideism, therefore, is excluded, except in the view of those who hold the opposite opinion that faith becomes reasonable only after its acceptance has been logically and explicitly demonstrated. The principle of faith is a clear application to supernatural religion of the basic ideas of Newman's psychology. Its value becomes evident, once spontaneous knowledge is vindicated.[1]

(3) *The theological principle:* Faith is an act of the intellect. It is open, therefore, to analysis and systematization in scientific language. But this analysis can never exhaust the reality. Here lies the work of theology.[2]

(4) *The sacramental principle*: By the Incarnation God, who is invisible, appears and communicates himself, together with his invisible gifts, in a visible, bodily form. We may, therefore, expect that the manifestation and communication of the divine through the intermediary of the visible world is a universal law of the divine plan in the Church and the world.[3]

(5) *The principle of the mystical sense of Scripture:* Just as the visible humanity of Christ is related to new supernatural realities beyond it, so the revealed word has a sacramental function; it contains a hidden meaning that the Holy Spirit discloses to the faith of his Church. The mystical sense of Scripture has always been the corner-stone of orthodoxy, while its literal sense has been the weapon of heretics.[4]

(6) *The principle of grace:* God makes himself like to us, in order to make us like to him, that is to sanctify us inwardly.

(7) *The principle of asceticism:* Sanctification involves mortifying our lower nature.

(8) This confirms the principle of the natural conscience, namely, *the intrinsic and absolute evilness of sin.*

---

[1] *Essay.*, pp.326-336. Newman refers the reader to *O.U.S.*; and, in a note added later, to the *Grammar*, for a detailed exposition of the principle.

[2] *Essay*, pp.336-338.

[3] *Ibid.*, pp.368-382.

[4] *Ibid.*, pp.338-346.

(9) *The principle of the possibility of the sanctification of matter:*
The physical nature of Christ proves that matter is an essential
principle of our being and that, equally with spirit, it is capable
of sanctification.[1]

(10) *The principle of development:* In the edition of 1870, Newman added in a footnote this principle: Revelation was given,
according to the divine plan, as a seed destined to grow in the
course of centuries.

These, then, are some of the principles which, from the beginning, gave impetus to Christian thought, without its being aware
of their action; only later, and by degrees, did it come to realise
what it owed to them. From certain among them Catholic doctrine derived vigour and vitality, together with a strong power
of assimilation. The dogmatic and theological principles, for
example, allowed the recognition and the integration into the body
of doctrine of those truths and prefigurations, in the natural
order, that divine Providence, before the Incarnation, had dis-
pensed throughout the world.[2] The sacramental principal permits
the recognition, in a number of cults and rites alien to Christianity,
of an original religious inspiration and of their being turned to the
profit of Christianity, after being purified.[3]

Thus we see true dogmatic theology growing steadily according
as it surrenders itself to loving contemplation of supernatural realities. It draws its life from the principles it carries deep within it,
perhaps without awareness of them. It advances along a way
which logic is unable to analyse completely or control entirely.
Here again, the last word is spoken by the illative sense of the
believer, the personal judgment of the Church, in whose possession
is the gift of faith, and which lives by its principles.

Concrete intuition or fact of revelation?

There seems, however, to be a contradiction between intuitive
knowledge by faith and Newman's principle of dogma, according
to which the Christian religion derives from a definite revelation
of certain truths, given at a particular moment in time. Where
lies, in fact, the real guarantee of the doctrines we actually possess?

[1] This is developed further in *Essay.*, pp.401-407.
[2] *Ibid.*, pp.357-368.
[3] *Ibid.*, pp.338-342.

Is it in the vision of the living faith of to-day, or in some *deposit* bequeathed from the time they arose? Or is it possible for the two criteria to act jointly and, if so, how?

George Tyrrell was of the opinion that here Newman's ideas underwent development, or rather became equivocal. According to the Oxford Sermon, the Church of today teaches revealed truth, not because it has kept the memory of it, but because it has an actual apperception of it. In the *Essay*, on the other hand, the other point of view makes itself felt and ends by supplanting the first; it asserts the identity of the faith of today with the *depositum* of the past. Newman, he held, overlooked the insoluble opposition of the two.[1] We are not concerned to defend Newman against this criticism, because it would take us far afield. Our aim is merely to see if and how he succeeded in reconciling these two conceptions. Nothing is more certain than Newman's constant fidelity to the dogmatic principle; it was the basis of his intellectual activity for sixty years. It is almost equally certain that he invariably held faith to be a quasi-vision of supernatural realities.[2] But this vision is

---

[1] G. Tyrell, *Through Scylla and Charybdis* (London, 1907), pp.139-154. According to him, the ideas of the Oxford sermons coincide in principle with those of the new liberal theology: "For in this view, the subject matter of development is not a formulation of the object revealed, but the object itself ever-present to experience—or at least present in the same way that material objects are present . . . So that the Church of today speaks from *vision*, not from *memory*, of revealed truth" (pp.41-42, 144). In the *Essay*, on the other hand, "The conception throughout is clearly that of an unchanging dogmatic nucleus round which 'additional' propositions ever group themselves into a doctrinal system, ever the 'same', because its central beliefs are *actually*, its subsidiary beliefs *virtually*, apostolical, i.e., identical with the 'deposit of faith'" (p.150). Tyrell's criticism amounts to this: as an historian, Newman realized that the identity of the faith could not be justified by the scholastic method; and so he wished to overcome his liberal opponents by their own weapons. "What he did not see, perhaps, was the intimate connection between methods and their results; that the new could not defend the old, nor the old the new; that to give his adversaries the choice of weapons was to give them the victory" (G. Tyrell, *Christianity at the Cross-Roads* (London, 1909), p.31).

[2] Here are a few examples: "To see him in some sort intuitively constitutes the very promise and gift of Him who is the object of intuition. Such is, undeniably, the characteristic of divine faith considered in itself" (*Disc. Arg.*, p.367). For Catholic faith, supernatural realities are "as present as if they were objects of sight" (*Grammar*, p.76). As a Catholic, Newman preached a magnificent sermon, affirming that unregenerate man is, in matters of faith, spiritually blind; he can only reason and form opinions, whereas grace endows us with a spiritual view which brings certainty. ("Illuminating Grace", in *Disc. M. Cong.*, lect. 9).

itself conditioned and guided by dogmatic teaching. In the order
of supernatural knowledge, therefore, intuition does not enjoy, as
it does in the natural order, priority either of time or importance;
it is not normative. We have seen how Newman, in the Oxford
sermon, takes up again the problem of the *Arians*. Now, in the
latter book, the relation between dogma and the intuition of faith
is parallel to that between dogma and Scripture.[1] One of the
principle theses Newman takes over from the Fathers is that the
faith, in its entirety, is in the Bible, though it does not appear on
the surface. Scripture is a book of devotion; it is anything but
systematic. The truths of faith lie there dispersed, without connection or cohesion, expressed in concrete terms, with a practical aim.
Reading and meditating on the Bible bring our life, by degrees,
into touch with the higher realities.[2] So arises, as a function of
devotion and *praxis,* a concrete vision of supernatural realities;
but this view, limited in its range, is entirely due to what is
communicated by Scripture. The development of doctrine simply
consists in the transposition of the "object of scripturally-informed
piety" into an abstract language and system.[3] That is Newman's
thesis in the *Arians.*

He maintains this position in the Oxford sermon, though he
gives greater emphasis to intuition, on account of the psychological
standpoint he there adopts. Besides, it is natural that, in a public
discourse, some aspects receive particular notice, while others are
dealt with summarily. Here, Newman compares the development
of doctrine from the intuition of faith to that of rational, purely
natural, knowledge from sensory perception. But he brings out,
also, the differences; in the absence of an organ for the immediate
perception of spiritual objects, the intuition of faith has to reach

---

[1] After describing the relations of intuition and dogma, he concludes:
"If this account of the relations between theological systems and the implications of Scripture is correct" (*Arians*, p.145).

[2] See above, Chapter 2, p.45. In 1838, Newman published a whole
treatise on this subject, "Holy Scripture in relation to the Catholic Creed",
in *Disc. Arg.*, pp.109-253.

[3] *Arians*, pp.145-147: "The test of Scripture being addressed principally
to the affections and of a religious, not a philosophical character . . .
Scripture being unsystematic, and the faith which it propounds being
scattered through its documents, and understood only when they are viewed
as a whole . . . The systematic doctrines of the Trinity may be considered
as the shadow projected for the contemplation of the intellect of the Object
of scripturally-informed piety".

us through the study of Scripture and of dogmatic theology.[1] We have no direct, independent intuition of faith. In contrast with the process of natural knowledge, we normally require, to obtain contact with the realities of faith, a certain verbal expression, as an indispensable condition.[2] The intuitive "idea" must be communicated by the Bible and its subsequent analysis will expand into theology. Scripture, then, marks the first step towards a dogmatic theology, of whose construction the words of the Bible are at once the source and the warrant.[3]

If, in the *Essay*, less stress is laid on intuition as the starting-point of development, and more on Scripture,[4] that is, obviously, due to its historical standpoint. The whole of the *Essay* turns on one central idea, the apostolicity of dogma in its existing state. Moreover, it is highly significant that Newman, in the document written for Perrone, in which he proves no thesis but simply explains his theory of doctrinal development, sets intuition again in the foreground, ascribing it, in this case, to the "ears of faith".[5]

The last word on the problem, however, is to be found in the *Grammar*, according to which the two kinds of knowledge, the real and the notional, may interpret, independently of each other, one and the same proposition.[6] Take, for example, the formulas of the Creed attributed to St. Athanasius. We may compare them one with another and examine their logical coherence. That is what theology does, and it concludes with the conception of dogma as a mystery, as an aggregate of notional judgments whose internal coherence cannot be comprehended. Dogma, so understood,

[1] *O.U.S.*, p.333: "The senses are direct, immediate and ordinary informants, but no such faculties have been given us, as far as we know, for realizing the objects of faith. The secondary and intelligible means by which we receive the impression of Divine Verities are such as the habitual and devout perusal of Scripture, the study of Dogmatic Theology". See also *Ibid.*, p.338.

[2] *Ibid.*, p.333: "The obvious distinction follows between sensible and religious ideas, that we put the latter into language in order to fix, teach, and transmit them, but not the former".

[3] "One thing alone has to be proved from Scripture, the Catholic idea, and in it all dogmas are included . . . Revelation itself has provided in Scripture the main outlines and also large details of the dogmatic system . . . The Scripture statements are sanctions as well as informants in the inquiry; they begin and they do not exhaust" (*Ibid.*, pp.335-336).

[4] *Essay*, pp.56-57. The nature of Scripture proves the necessity of a development.

[5] *Newman-Perrone*, pp.413, 416, 437.

[6] *Grammar*, p.10.

"says" nothing to the religious imagination. But we may, also, examine each formula of the Creed separately; they are, then, enabled to bring us into contact with living realities which, by imparting to us life and vigour, give impetus to our spiritual faculties.[1] Now, in Scripture and the liturgy, these are living truths, bearing a high spiritual potential, closely related to the life of man, and conveyed in an imagery wonderfully apt to communicate living experience. We find these truths implied everywhere. The very tone of St. Paul's words, in speaking of Christ's crucifixion and death, presupposes the true divinity of the Son.[2] This is how Scripture, the Creeds and the liturgy may, independently of any theological activity, be transposed into a concrete vision of supernatural realities. But these same formulas, vitalized in this way by the real perception of faith, may themselves be treated from the notional standpoint; and this gives rise to dogmatic theology. The latter furnishes for the reason of man, being prompted by its special needs, what Scripture and the liturgy provide, in their own way, for his religious needs. It analyses, clarifies, compares, arranges and connects together all these elements of Scripture and the liturgy in a structure of rational ideas, the whole depending on certain principles and hypotheses.[3] In this process, it is natural for the religious imagination to perform the same function as was exercised, in the building up of notional thought, by the perception of concrete reality.[4] On the other hand, notional theology is itself always indispensable for the protection and guidance of living religion. For the objects of our religious knowledge are not evident in the way material things are.

[1] *Grammar.*, pp.125-127; 140: "Religion has to do with the real, and the real is the particular; theology has to do with what is notional, and the notional is the general and systematic. Hence theology has to do with the dogma of the Holy Trinity as a whole made up of many propositions; but Religion has to do with each of those separate propositions which compose it, and lives and thrives in the contemplation of them. In them it finds the motives for devotion" See also *Ibid.*, pp.146-147.

[2] *Ibid.*, pp.137-139 (for Scripture), 139-140 (for the liturgy). Cf. *Ibid.*, p.76, for remarks on meditation on the Bible.

[3] See especially *Ibid.*, pp.146-148: "Far different, certainly, is the nature and duty of the intellect. It is ever active, inquisitive, penetrating; it examines doctrine and doctrine; it compares, contrasts and forms them into a science; that science is theology". A description of these different functions follows.

[4] Newman says, for example: "We apprehend more strongly theological truths according as we possess habits of personal religion" (*Ibid.*, p.115).

Reason, therefore, has to direct the religious imagination and preserve it from degenerating into fantasy.[1] Consequently, living faith and abstract theology exercise a reciprocal control.

From all this we may draw the following conclusion. Nowhere, not even in the Oxford sermon, does Newman represent the intuition of faith as a contact with supernatural realities, independent of verbal revelation. It is arrived at by degrees through Revelation as manifested in Scripture, the Creeds and the liturgy. Such a manifestation is itself, in a manner, notional and is bound to be if it is to reach us. This is a consequence of Newman's whole doctrine, according to which only what is notional can be communicated in words, and the experience of perceiving concrete reality is always inexpressible.[2] None the less, the notional element is not applied in Scripture according to the dictates of reason, which demands clarity, logical connection, and strict ordering. It is used there to stir the imagination by the description of facts and deeds in the concrete, by the expression of sentiments, dispositions and practical attitudes that only the real is able to arouse in us. The intuition of faith arises, then, from these various elements by a comprehensive act of the religious imagination, which Newman sees as a combination of sensible imagination and spiritual contemplation.[3] It does not create its own object, but only the manner of knowing it; it assembles the elements provided in a concrete synthesis, living and arresting. In its working, the notional elements are not eliminated, but do not function *as such*; they are not made use of *as notional*. We are not to consider this act of the religious imagination as purely natural; on the contrary, it is elicited under the influence of that illuminating grace which is the cause of faith.[4] This grace effects a mysterious contact

---

[1] *Grammar.*, p.121: "Devotion must have its objects; these objects, as being supernatural, when not represented to our senses by material symbols, must be set before the mind in propositions ... Sentiment, whether imaginative or emotional, falls back upon the intellect for its stay, when sense cannot be called into exercise; and it is in this way that devotion falls back upon dogma". As regards the blind and fantastic impulses of disordered devotion, they are described by Newman in his *Letter to Pusey* (cf. *Diff. Angl.*, II, pp.26-31, 77-88).

[2] This contrast is described in the *Grammar*, pp.83-87: "Real assents are of a personal character; notional apprehension is, in itself, an ordinary act of our common nature" (p.83).

[3] See above, p.110.

[4] See the sermon "Illuminating Grace", *loc. cit.*

between the depths of the soul and the supernatural realities, between the spirit of man and the living God who reveals himself to it. To believe is not to accept dispassionately, but to live in the moving presence of Christ. To believe is to confront Christ in a living relationship of person to Person. For Newman, Christianity is Christ. The living image of Christ, as imprinted on the soul of faith, is the vital secret of Christianity and the sole explanation of the extraordinary and miraculous success of the Church in the world, which furnishes a convincing proof of its being authentically divine.[1]

Under the influence of the grace which gives faith, the religious imagination forms a preliminary synthesis of tradition, one that takes hold of concrete reality, bringing about a real knowledge of God as Saviour. Subsequently, another act of synthesis, that of abstraction by reason, expresses this tradition in notional terms corresponding to the processes of reason. In this way, tradition is unfolded and amplified, and dogmatic theology is born. Hence the development of religious tradition is, precisely, the transposition by the mind of the unordered sources of faith into a rational system, making progressive use of the full wealth of the idea by bringing out all that it implies. Now, thought does not live in books, but in minds; the content of faith has, therefore, to become first a personal, subjective life, in the form of an *idea* which perceives the concrete reality. It is this intuition that alone can give theological thought the impulse to grow and guarantees, when its expansion has come about, that its conclusions accord with the idea intuitively perceived as a whole. Faith, though an intuition, is always *fides ex auditu,* it rests on the authority of God. Notional development expresses only what was implicit, from the first, in the real apprehension, which, in turn, received it from the living sources of Revelation. In consequence, what doctrine gains in lucidity is not at the expense of the unchanging truth.[2] These views of Newman are, ultimately, the application, in terms of

---

[1] Cf. *Grammar*, pp.456-458. In these magnificent pages, Newman shows, against Gibbon, that the spread of Christianity is due to one cause only, the living and divine image of Christ. See also pp.364-365: "It is the image of Him who fulfills the one great need of human nature, the Healer of its wounds, the physician of the soul, this Image it is which both creates faith and rewards it . . . This central Image as the vivifying idea both of the Christian body and of individual in it".

[2] See below, Part III, chapter 2.

psychology, of the characteristically Thomist thesis that no one can be a genuine theologian unless he possesses a living faith.

We are now in a position to estimate Newman's attitude to the problem of whether it is spiritual insight or theology that is the guiding principle of the life of doctrine in the Church. It is neither one nor the other, but both together. One balances the other, and each has precedence, but in a different relationship. The intuition of faith acts as a counterpoise to theological reasoning, to prevent its losing contact with reality. Notional theology points the direction to be followed by devotional imagination, and counteracts any tendency to extravagance.

Finally, let us consider the dilemma put by Tyrrell. Present intuition governs dogma, but is itself nourished at the historical source of the faith, and even by the study of dogmatic theology. Within this intuition there are many elements, relations and conclusions, not yet drawn out by the abstraction of reason. Hence, there lives within the Church, in addition to her explicit dogmatic tradition, a tradition of truths not yet formulated by reason, and thus virtual as regards their notional expression, existing germinally in the intuition of faith, a faith which, through the grace of God, springs incessantly from the great living sources of the Church, Scripture, the Fathers, the liturgy, devotional practice, the ordinary *magisterium,* the life of the Church, and all the rest.[1]

Relation between faith and the realities of faith

A difficulty arises from the fact that the vision of faith is communicated in the form of words and concepts, and Newman treats it in detail in the latter part of the Oxford sermon.[2] It is this : in order to set forth our knowledge of supernatural realities, we make use, not of supernatural ideas, but of purely natural words and concepts. Now, nothing can communicate what it does not contain; we can transmit only what we have. Consequently, human language can convey only those natural concepts of experience to which it owes its origin; its terms cannot be used as

[1] It is especially in *Newman-Peronne* that the concepts of "evolution " and of "tradition" are compared (pp.409, 418, 431, 436-437).

[2] *O.U.S.*, pp.338-351.

symbols,[1] that is, indications to draw attention to independent realities of a higher order.[2]

In answering this objection, Newman begins with two preliminary observations: (1) we do not know how far divine grace may refine and elevate our natural ideas; (2) in combining certain natural ideas, we may raise up new ideas, though still of an earthly nature.[3] Then he gives the answer. There can be a resemblance between natural ideas and their heavenly *archetype,* such that natural ideas are true representations of supernatural reality. This representation, however, is always an "economical" translation, inadequate, one conforming with the possibilities of our earthly condition. In arguing this, Newman exhibits the highest degree of intellectual subtlety. He combines analogies in order to draw from them an intricate argument *a priori* and *a posteriori.* Intercourse between men itself requires the use of representations that are practical, "economical," so that mutual understanding

[1] In the Oxford sermon, Newman says of the intellectual expressions of faith: "They are but symbols of a Divine fact . . . august tokens of most simple, ineffable, adorable facts . . . they are but specimens and indications of it" (*O.U.S.*, pp.332, 334, 336). It would, obviously, be most fallacious to interpret these passing expressions in the light of a later philosophy, and to tax Newman with "symbolism". By the term "symbol", he expresses the relation words have with what they signify: "Science uses words only as symbols . . . verbal symbols of things" (*Idea,* pp.275-276); "Words are but symbols of ideas" (letter to Froude, cited in Ward, *op. cit.,* II, p.591). What does he mean by such statements? The direct, spontaneous knowledge we have of concrete reality is too rich, multiform and subtle to act as a basis for exact thought. Our intellect has to replace it by signs which extract from the many-sidedness of the concrete and indicate the object in a general and abstract way: it can then work with precision: "Without external symbols to mark out and to steady its course, the intellect runs wild; but, with the aid of symbols, as in algebra, it advances with precision and effect. Let, then, our symbols be words: let all thought be arrested and embodied in words" (*Grammar,* p.263). The word "symbol" means, then, that a conventional verbal sign is substituted, in the mind, for real things and, indicating them, serves as a basis for intellectual activity—exact, but inadequate about the real. The same may be said about the words which express the concrete intuition of faith.

[2] Here is the statement of the objection: "The idea of a supernatural object must itself be supernatural, and since no such ideas are claimed by ordinary Christians, no knowledge of Divine Verities is possible to them . . . How can human words, how can earthly images, convey to the mind an idea of the Invisible? They cannot rise above themselves . . . The metaphors by which they are signified are not mere symbols of ideas which exist independently of them, but their meaning is coincident and identical with the ideas" (*O.U.S.*, p.338).

[3] *O.U.S.*, p.339.

may be possible. All our means of expressing reality in human ways—even mathematics and music which show forth eternal relations—are fraught with inadequacy. How do we know if our sense-knowledge itself is more than an "economical" expression of invisible, eternal realities, one adapted to our condition of beings whose knowledge comes through the intermediary of the senses? It follows that the communication of divine ideas by Revelation must, *a fortiori*, be highly "economical" and inadequate. This inadequacy, arising from the nature of things, is perfectly admissible.[1] Any vestige of concern we may feel disappears if we but remember the Providence of God. What does it matter if we go to God by means of shadows and images, if this is the way He has appointed?[2] Analogy, the very nature of things, divine Providence —it is all a splendid example of Newman's apologetic. Here he appears at his best.

The relation between the intuition of faith and dogmatic formulas

The relation between the intuition of faith and dogma involves one more difficulty, which is also treated in the Oxford sermon. The chief purpose of this sermon, we have seen, was to defend theology against the liberal view denying any real correspondence between interior faith and the formulas of dogma, the latter being a kind of disguise, indispensable indeed, but variable according to places and seasons, whereas the view of faith is ever unchangeable.[3] The delay and difficulty we find in reaching a more or less satisfactory expression of an idea, our natural repugnance to

[1] We give the substance of a very detailed exposition: "There may be a certain correspondence between the idea, though earthly, and its heavenly archetype, such that the idea belongs to the archetype, in a sense in which no other earthly idea belongs to it, as being the nearest approach to it which our present state allows . . . The nearest approach to truth, compatible with our human condition" (*O.U.S.*, pp. 340, 360).

[2] "Should anyone fear lest thoughts such as these should lead to a dreary and hopeless scepticism, let him take into account the Being and Providence of God, the Merciful and True; and he will at once be relieved of his anxiety . . . What is it to us whether the knowledge He gives us be greater or less, if it be He who gives it? What is it to us whether it be exact or vague, if He bids us trust it? What have we to care whether we are or are not given to divide substance from shadow, if He is training us heavenwards by means of either" (*Ibid.*, p. 348).

[3] Newman propounds the liberal objection thus: "There is no natural connexion between certain dogmas and certain impressions; and theological science is a matter of time and place and accident, though inward belief is ever and everywhere one and the same" (*Ibid.*, p. 327; cf. also p. 319).

acknowledge a theory to be a true expression of our most intimate conviction, the obstacles we meet with in trying to grasp in its profound unity an idea that is presented to us piecemeal and dismembered—all these factors, described by Newman with a wealth of detail, could easily give the impression that his opponents were right.[1]

His reply is, once again, very detailed. The very instinct impelling us to formulate our belief implies the conviction that such a process is both possible and legitimate.[2] Moreover, all philosophy and science have to contend with the same kind of difficulty, but their possibility is not open to doubt. Difficulties, therefore, form no obstacle to the natural and universal correspondence between faith and dogma.[3] This correspondence may be justified on the following lines. God is ever identical with himself, and it is as such that he reveals himself to us. Hence, faith, the effect of grace, shares in this identity; and, since it is our nature to progress according to fixed and stable laws, the notional expression of the vision of faith must, in all its parts, be consistently uniform with it.[4] Dogma is unchanging, and, as Newman says in the *Essay*, is as fixed and invariable as the objective fact of which it is the expression.[5]

Conclusion

Summing up the conclusions reached in this Section, we see that there is a considerable obstacle in applying the way our knowledge develops, as outlined previously, to the development of the Christian tradition; for the latter process does not originate in the immediate experience of supernatural objects, but in their communication to us by Revelation in human terms, concepts and

---

[1] *O.U.S.*, pp.323-327.

[2] *Ibid.*, p.327: "Surely the instinct of every Christian revolts from such a position; for the very first impulse of his faith is to try to express itself about the great sight which is vouchsafed it".

[3] *Ibid.*, p.327-328, for a detailed account.

[4] *Ibid.*, p.328: "If Almighty God is ever one and the same, the true inward impression of Him must be one and the same; and, since human nature proceeds upon fixed laws, the statement of that impression must be one and the same, so that we may as well say that there are two Gods as two Creeds".

[5] "If Christianity is a fact, if it penetrates our minds with its proper idea, this idea will multiply in the course of ages, will expand into a multitude of ideas and aspects of them, correlative and concordant, fixed and invariable in themselves as is the objective fact represented by them" (*Essay*, p.55).

"signs". Newman overcomes this obstacle by the following three considerations :

(1) There is an intuition of faith, sustained by the living language of the sources of Revelation and by doctrine, and expressed in words, acts, and sentiments. It is the effect of illuminating grace, though it uses the psychological process of real knowledge.

(2) Although a vast distance separates supernatural realities from the images and notions of the natural order in which they are expressed, these are, however, sufficiently analogous and are warranted by revelation itself. Consequently, the faith which makes use of these forms of expression does, in fact, attain, by their means, to the truths it envisages.

(3) God being immutable, any contradiction between impressions truly received from him by the human mind is ruled out. There is, then, only one religious truth given to mankind, and the analysis of it by theology, following the universal requirements of human reason, is able to attain to, and express, this unchanging truth.

Chapter 3

THE SPECIFIC PSYCHOLOGY OF DEVELOPMENT

THE most striking feature of Newman's general psychology of reasoning and of development of thought, is its organic character. His conception of the whole governs every detail. Thought is a function of the person, the expression of his experience in its entirety, and this experience involves the whole complex of tendencies and dispositions, innate and acquired, which make up the personality. Now the structure of experience follows a certain guiding principle, of the moral or ethical order. Newman uses the word "ethos" to indicate the characteristic shape taken by the developing experience of an individual or a group of persons. It signifies that the development of human experience and thought follows a course fixed, as it were, from the outset, by a deep-seated moral agency.

Since thought is such a personal matter, we cannot hope to understand the psychological process of its exercise and growth by abstracting from the differences between individuals. As we have already shown, any psychology that views each kind of human action as an element in the whole personality is bound to concern itself with the study of human types. It is quite certain that one of Newman's chief preoccupations, as a psychologist, was to arrive at an understanding of certain types of thought. Throughout his life, he strove to penetrate to the very depths the "ethos" both of the religious man and the rationalist. We have now to examine in detail his investigations.

At this stage, we shall confine ourselves to a psychological description, and will refrain as far as possible, from passing judgments. Newman's account of the different types is governed by his assessment of each. For him, the religious man is, primarily, one who is receptive and faithful to moral experience. Conscience is, according to him, an essential element of human nature, and, when unimpeded in its exercise, guides us into that order of truth of whose knowledge it is the instrument. We will, however, postpone our vindication of this judgment to our treatment of his apologetic.

Section A

Nature and culture

Men differ in their ideas and convictions, not because of faulty reasoning on the part of some, but because they do not all start from the same first principles. The orientation of thought varies with the personality that controls it. For, ultimately, our first principles are an expression, on the abstract plane, of our personality. There are different types of thought and the reason for their divergencies is to be found in the personal sphere, that of first principles.

On many occasions, Newman speaks of some first principles as deriving from our human nature, and of others as due solely to the personal qualities of the individual.[1] He distinguishes, in fact, between nature and person. "To be rational, to have speech ... belong to man's nature; to have a particular history ... a certain constitution, moral temperament, intellectual outfit, mental formation, these and the like, taken all together, are the accidents which make up our notion of a man's person, and are the ground-work or condition of his particular experiences."[2] Principles of the second type are numerous and proceed from the most various individual qualities. Thus, for example, a profession which uses "exact" methods fosters a spontaneous tendency

[1] "Pre-existing beliefs, hidden deep in our nature or in our personal peculiarities" (*Grammar*, p.277). The most explicit passage is on p.270. See too, *Present Position*, pp.263-264. In many places, he affirms the natural character of the principles of conscience.

[2] *Grammar*, pp.85-86.

to use the same methods in all problems.[1] In the same way, the intuitive mind of Niebuhr would furnish him with ideas of historical method other than those of a positive and analytic mind like that of Sir George Lewis. The latter is satisfied with what is clearly expressed in the sources, and refuses to go beyond the letter; whereas the former seizes on the slightest indication to divine what is not clearly contained in the texts.[2] Our philosophical outlook can be a decisive influence on our historical researches, and direct them accordingly.[3] To one brought up in Protestant surroundings, the principle of the sole authority of Scripture in matters of faith is naturally accepted as a truism.[4] Newman is particularly insistent on the existence of all kinds of "subtle assumptions not directly arising out of these primary conditions of our nature, but accompanying the course of reasoning step by step, and traceable to the sentiments of the age, country, religion, social habits and ideas, of the particular inquirers and disputants, and passing current without detection, because admitted equally on all hands".[5]

The difference between the two kinds of first principles is not difficult to grasp, now that we have studied Newman's theory. The one kind originates in a few simple experiences, common to all; in favourable circumstances, such principles take root in the mind of their own accord, in virtue of their own intrinsic power of growth. Though notional themselves, they are yet, in some way, incorporated into a concrete experience of the real. The other kind, however, is most often exclusively notional. These principles consist of attitudes of mind, points of view, norms of judgment and of value, whose origin lies in a group-mentality, the spirit of the time, the "cultural" environment; they insinuate themselves, as it were, by stealth, and are thus unresisted and unquestioned. It is not by personal experience that we first acquire them or, later, for the most part, "realise" them. We take them for granted, because we breathe them in as part of the surrounding

---

[1] *Grammar.*, p.81.

[2] *Ibid.*, pp.364-371.

[3] *Ibid.*, p.373.

[4] *Ibid.*, pp.379-380.

[5] *Ibid.*, p.270.

atmosphere. In the aggregate, they constitute what may be called, in a special sense, our "culture".[1]

It follows that our personality, in the concrete, as shown in our first principles, comprises a central, essential core, which pertains to our nature and is the deepest, most intimate part of our being, and, at the surface, a kind of covering, accidental to our nature and pertaining to our "culture". The individual subject, viewed in its entirety, in other words the personality, implies, in some sort, a double ego—one that is profound, individual, drawing sustenance from its contact with those realities and values whose existence and claims make up the life of man in this world; another that is superficial and social, sustained by the opinions of its environment. The question arises, what is the bond of union between these two strata of our personality?

Here we meet with an important problem in the philosophy of culture. Unlike many modern philosophers, Newman does not set nature and culture in irreconcilable opposition. As author of *The Idea of a University*, he is a clear protagonist of general culture. He is aware both of its dangers and its merits; he is too well-balanced and realistic to outlaw it. Living, as we do, in a highly developed culture, it is impossible to escape its influence. It fashions us unawares, and by it "our bare and barren nature is overrun and diversified from without with a rich and living clothing".[2]

It stimulates our activity of mind and the expansion of our thought, helps us in forming a varied and reasonable judgment

[1] Here the word "culture" has a very restricted sense. A culture is the whole complex of attainments that raise a man's life to a higher level than its natural state, and enable him to extend indefinitely his possibilities of self-realization. They are the result of the exercise of our natural powers. True culture, therefore, consists in the perfecting of man on the natural plane; but it involves the danger that a one-sided intellectual development may stunt, and even suppress completely, our deepest natural instincts and experiences. That is a salient theme of modern culture-philosophy. Our education, in a given cultural milieu, loads us with all sorts of information. We are subjected to a standardized training, so that our thought and conduct are moulded independently of our own personal efforts. What we are to think and feel is imposed on us ready-made by outside agencies, and our creative powers decay. Hence arises the opposition between "culture" and "nature", and the former comes to mean an acquirement that fails to express our true personality as embedded in authentic experience. In this sense, "culture" is practically synonymous with "credence".

[2] *Grammar*, p.54.

on a number of theories and events, gives refinement to life, ease and elegance to society. All this is of value, and there is no call to despise it. Admittedly, even the most talented are, necessarily, superficial in the greater part of their knowledge, but breadth of culture may be of great service to the specialist in his department.[1]

Newman considers that the young student should start by accepting, in a spirit of loyalty and docility, whatever he is taught.[2] To begin with universal doubt is to condemn oneself to arrive nowhere.

> I would rather have to maintain that we ought to begin with believing everything that is offered to our acceptance than that it is our duty to doubt of everything. The former, indeed, seems the true way of learning. In that case, we soon learn to discover and discard what is contradictory to itself; and error always having some portion of truth in it, and the truth having a reality which error has not, we may expect that, when there is an honest purpose and fair talents, we shall somehow make our way forward, the error falling off from the mind, and the truth developing and occupying it. Thus it is that the Catholic religion is reached, as we see, by inquirers from all points of the compass, as if it mattered not where a man began, so that he had an eye and a heart for the truth.[3]

This passage shows us the obverse of the relation between the authentic core and the cultural "envelope" of our thought. Intellectual culture serves the search for truth, provided that we really devote our minds and hearts to truth; in other words, if our thought is consistently directed by certain natural principles, grounded on genuine experiences of reality, by those "personal first principles and judgments which may be fairly pronounced to be common conditions of human thought".[4] If these "intellectual moorings" are wanting,[5] we are doomed to be tossed about by the fickle currents of opinion, without ever reaching firm

---

[1] *Grammar.*, pp.53-58; *Idea*, Disc. VII.

[2] *Ibid*, p.54.

[3] *Ibid.*, pp.377-378.

[4] *Ibid.*, p.402.

[5] *Ibid.*, p.88: "Till we have them [real assents], in spite of a full apprehension and assent in the field of notions, we have no intellectual moorings, and are at the mercy of impulses, fancies, and wandering lights, whether as regards personal conduct, social and political action, or religion".

ground and, in that case, our vessel's elegance and its wealth of equipment are of little account.

The two classes of first principles may be viewed as two sources of power impelling our life and thought in different directions, according as one or the other prevails. Some men are so absorbed by their surroundings that their true personality is, as it were, dissolved in them. They disappear in the impersonal crowd. Others strike root, independently, in their own experiences and principles; little by little, by their own original and personal qualities, they come to assimilate, critically, the common culture or, at any rate, that part of it that concerns the essential problems of human life. Our intellectual history may be either a progressive "realisation", a gradual testing, a vital essaying of a number of notional ideas, originating from the environment, and soliciting our assent; or else it may display the slow parasitic growth of external opinions and habits at the expense of what is native and original. The up-shot of it all is the opposition between the personal and profound thinker and the superficial and impersonal type. For the former, his view of the world becomes something organic and stable, animated by an immanent principle; for the latter, it is imposed from without and, like a fashionable garment, always liable to be discarded.

Thought that is strongly engrained, deeply rooted in real experience, is ultimately religious, even though this character may long remain only implicit. That which is not so rooted is nothing more than the play of abstract reason. The former develops in a genuine and continuous process of growth, slow but sure, and leading on to certitude; the second is spasmodic and fitful, dazzling at times in its speed, but never stable, ever in pursuit of the latest idea, the most recent argument.[1] It is evident how the first is directed, above all, by living and implicit reasoning, while the second is the work of explicit and formal argument with no solid connection with personal experience. Though both comprise at once unconscious procedures and those which are technical, personal

---

[1] "True religion is slow in growth, and, when once planted, is difficult of dislodgement; but its intellectual counterfeit has no root in itself; it springs up suddenly, it suddenly withers" (*Idea*, p.202); "They who have no religious earnestness are at the mercy, day by day, of some new argument or fact, which may overtake them, in favour of one conclusion or the other" (*Grammar*, p.425).

experience, because it is more living and profound, possesses a more vigorous and spontaneous power of expansion, though it is more resistant to expression in conceptual form. Thought which is impersonal and purely notional, being received more passively by the mind, does not arouse the same unconscious and spontaneous stirrings, though it furnishes reason in its deliberations with more tractable material, for, unlike intuition, it is unaccompanied by a painful awareness of the inadequacy of its concepts to represent reality.

Section B

The Religious Man and the Rationalist

The religious man alone is genuinely human and personal; the rationalist is superficial, impersonal. The difference between the two, however, must not be accounted for in a too empirical manner, itself superficial. A man with a deeply rooted, personal life may yet lack a clear perception of the religious truths implied by his first principles, or he may have been misled by circumstances, education, even various experiences, so that he makes no profession of religion. Even so, he has a real, if confused, notion of the divine, which shows itself in his humble and conscientious regard to duty; this fidelity of his reveals the living, if unacknowledged, presence of religion in his soul. On the other hand, a man whose outlook is merely superficial may perform his religious duties as a matter of routine or social conformity, and so imagine he has "some religion", though he never really gives serious consideration to religious values.

At this point, it is fitting to view more concretely the types we have just considered in an abstract fashion. Their features are incarnated in the "ethos" of the religious man and the rationalist, described so often by Newman in various ways with all his acuteness and subtlety.

The development of the religious man is a dialectic of fidelity to conscience. The philosophy of the rationalist is wrought by reason to the exclusion of conscience. Conscience, therefore, first claims our attention.

A moral conscience is a part of human nature.[1] Newman insists repeatedly that conscience is no accidental possession of an individual or society, but an essential function of man. Later we shall see his reasons for this assertion[2]; at the moment, we are concerned only with the psychological side of the question. Conscience is the organ of a specific experience of a higher order, comprising two elements, the moral sense and the sense of obligation.[3] Like the aesthetic sense, the moral sense is a recognition, immediate and irreducible, of properties and values of a higher order, inherent in objects and acts. It judges of what is fitting and what is not. Certain acts excite our approbation, others we condemn; we qualify them respectively as "good" or "bad".[4] In the application of this distinction, the moral judgment is susceptible of wide variations. Faced with a particular situation, one person will consider good what another holds to be bad. The "material" content of the moral sense is not the same for all;[5] but the moral judgment itself is not relative. A single act is enough to enable us to perceive the moral difference, absolute and invariable, between this act and its opposite.[6] Formally, therefore, the moral judgment is absolute, so long, at least, as it retains its native force; but education, habit, and other factors, by deforming it, increase its liability to all sorts of "material" errors in its exercise. The moral sense itself is "instinctive" and immediate; its judgments cannot be reduced to more simple elements out of which it is compounded.[7] All the same, reason may subsequently analyse these judgments up to a point and bring arguments to support them. In other words, a science of morals is possible.[8]

[1] "We have by nature a conscience" (*Grammar*, p.105). Also in the *Idea*, p.191, and *P.P.S.*, I, p.216.

[2] See below, pp.203-212.

[3] *Grammar*, p.105: "The feeling of conscience is twofold; it is a moral sense and a sense of duty". Cf. *O.U.S.*, p.20.

[4] *Grammar*, pp.64, 105: "There are things which excite in us approbation or blame, and which we in consequence call right or wrong . . . a certain keen sensibility, pleasant or painful, attendant on certain of our actions, which in consequence we call right or wrong" (p.105).

[5] *Ibid.*, pp.106-107; *Occ. Ser.*, pp.64-65; *O.U.S.*, p.20.

[6] *Grammar*, p.65.

[7] *Ibid.*, p.105; *O.U.S.*, p.185: *Diff. Angl.*, II, p.248.

[8] *O.U.S.*, p.183: "Conscience is a simple element in our nature; yet its operations admit of being surveyed and scrutinized by reason"; "Reason generalizes the judgments of conscience" (*Grammar*, pp.64-65). So Newman calls the moral sense the "judgment of reason" (*Ibid.*, p.105). Cf. also *O.U.S.*, p.66.

Conscience consists also, and above all, in a feeling of obligation which is not reducible to the moral sense. The latter may be crude, or subject to all kinds of error, even scarcely perceptible; even so, the sense of obligation regarding what is left of the moral sense may be no less intense. On the other hand, a highly acute moral sense may be present without any feeling of obligation.[1] In each of these cases, we see conscience in a mutilated state. For the moral sense and the feeling of obligation are, in fact, essentially two elements of one and the same moral act.[2] In so far as it is moral sense, conscience has its root within the individual. It is autonomous. Considered solely in this aspect, in abstraction from the sense of obligation, conscience is, so to speak, an aesthetic sense of what is fitting and what is not; its standard is our human nature and nothing beyond it.[3] The feeling of obligation, on the other hand, is, in a way, imposed on us from outside; it makes itself felt as proceeding from a higher source, from a transcendent sphere. Its commands are absolute, its law inflexible, and there is no escape from it. We may react against its orders, interpret them wrongly; but it is rare that anyone entirely eludes its dominion. It is within us from the beginning, prior to reasoning, and testifies to our state of radical dependence. So the sense of obligation, unlike the moral sense, does not leave us shut up within ourselves. It guides us of itself, though vaguely at first, above and beyond ourselves towards a sanction deriving, not from ourselves, but from a Lawgiver, a Master who uses the voice of conscience to speak to us and to assert his absolute rights over us. Conscience, as a sense of obligation, refers us by its very essence to one who is higher than itself, that is, to God.[4]

---

[1] "Though I lost my sense of obligation . . . I should not in consequence lose my sense that such actions were an outrage offered to my moral nature. Again; though I lost my moral deformity, I should not therefore lose my sense that they were forbidden to me" (*Grammar*, p.106).

[2] "Of course, its act is indivisible; still it has these two aspects, distinct from each other" (*Ibid.*, p.105).

[3] *Ibid.*, pp. 108-109, where conscience is compared to the sentiment of beauty: "Conscience, too, considered as a moral sense, an intellectual sentiment, is a sense of admiration and disgust, or approbation and blame" (p.109). To the moral sense, sin is "an offence to my moral nature" (p.106); ". . . his conduct has not been beautiful" (p.108).

[4] *Occ. Ser.*, pp.64-65: "A peremptory command, not a simple sentiment, any more than a mere opinion or impression or view of thing, but a law, an authoritative voice; this is more even than the intimate being of a man.

This relatedness of conscience is shown more clearly in the comprehensive experiences we indicate when we speak of having a "good" or a "bad" conscience.[1] The experiences of conscience are, in fact, always and by their very nature emotional. Emotion is more than a mere sentiment. As distinct from the sense of obligation, the moral sense, like the aesthetic, is accompanied by such sentiments as admiration, revulsion, approbation, disapproval. If we act against our moral sense, we have feelings of shame.[2] And we reproach ourselves even though we no longer hold the moral law as absolutely binding. But these sentiments, of themselves, do not imply any heteronomy, any dependence on a transcendent reality. They are merely sentiments. The "emotions", however, are sentiments whose very essence involves a relation to a transsubjective term.[3] Now conscience, as connoting an experience of obligation, is distinguished in kind from other value-

Man himself has no power over this command, or exercises it only with extreme difficulty; he did not create it, he cannot destroy it. He may silence it in some cases or in part: he may deform its expressions; but, save with rare exceptions, he cannot throw it off. He may disobey it, refuse to heed it; but it remains. This is conscience; and, by its nature, its very existence leads our thought towards a Being external and superior to us". See also *P.P.S.*, II, p.18; *O.U.S.*, pp.18-19; *Grammar*, pp.106-110.

[1] For an analysis of the good and the bad conscience, cf. *Ibid*, pp.106-115.

[2] Cf. *Ibid.*, pp.108, 110, where Newman includes shame among the specific emotions of conscience. On the other hand, he says, in the *Idea*, p.191 : "Fear carries us out of ourselves, whereas shame may act upon us only within the round of our own thoughts". Such apparent contradictions are inevitable in a psychologico-literary account. The emotional life is so rich, and certain sentiments are so closely related that they are described in the same generic terms, and specified only by the addition of certain qualifications. The scientist indicates their meaning with minute precision, while the man of letters leaves it, at times, to the "illative sense" of the reader or his sense of the context. This is the case here. There are several kinds of shame. We may, for example, be thoroughly ashamed of ourselves, when we make the unpleasant discovery of our mediocrity, are surprised to find ourselves meaner than we thought, and are, at the same time, secretly ambitious for a nobler life. Real shame, however, the violent emotion which makes the cheeks burn, supposes, besides, that we feel or imagine another's gaze fixed on us, or, at least, that our knowledge of what diminishes us is shared by another. There are, obviously, other kinds of shame as well, such as bashfulness, but their definition is of no consequence here.

[3] Newman does not state expressly, but evidently presupposes, this distinction between emotions or sentiments that are "intentional", related to another, and mere sentiments, pure and simple.

judgments as pertaining to that special class of moral emotions by which man, whether consciously or not, feels himself in the presence of a Person who penetrates and governs his inmost being.

Inanimate things cannot stir our affections; these are correlative with persons. ... If, on doing wrong, we feel the same tearful, broken-hearted sorrow which overwhelms us on hurting a mother; if, on doing right, we enjoy the same sunny serenity of mind, the same soothing and satisfactory delight which follows on receiving praise from a father, we certainly have within us the image of some person, to whom our love and veneration look, in whose smile we find our happiness ... in whose anger we are troubled and waste away. These feelings in us are such as require for their exciting cause an intelligent being; we are not ashamed towards a stone, nor do we feel shame before a horse or a dog; we have no remorse or compunction on breaking mere human law : yet, so it is, conscience excites all these painful emotions, confusion, foreboding, self-condemnation; and on the other hand, it sheds upon us a deep peace, a sense of security, a resignation and a hope, which there is no sensible, no earthly object to elicit. ... If the cause of these emotions does not belong to this visible world, the object to which his perception is directed must be supernatural and divine.[1]

The clearest intimations are given by the bad, the sinful, conscience. The experience of sin is not a mere sentiment of moral ugliness, but of an outrage, an injury, to love. The fact that an act is unseemly does not suffice to explain this sense of sin which is as strong as if an act of impurity, untruthfulness, or cruelty were in question. These three faults disturb us profoundly, though all men are not equally sensitive to them.[2]

If he has been betrayed into any kind of immorality, he has a lively sense of responsibility and guilt, though the act be no offence against society, of distress and apprehension, even though it may be of present service to him, of compunction and regret, though in itself it be most pleasurable, of confusion of face, though it may have no witnesses. ... 'The wicked flees, where no one pursueth'; then why does he

[1] *Grammar*, pp.109-110.
[2] *Ibid.*, p.417.

flee? Who is it that he sees in solitude, in darkness, in the hidden chambers of his heart?[1]

All this is incomprehensible, if we do not acknowledge that, in our conscience, the eye of God rests upon us.

It follows that conscience, as the sense of obligation, is the natural bond between man and God. It is the creative principle of religion, just as, considered as the moral sense, it is the creative principle of morality.[2]

God, then, is shown in the conscience as a personal Being, present in the depths of the heart, spiritual and intelligent, since the most secret places of the soul are as an open book before him.[3] In addition, he is our absolute Master, for the first aspect in which he confronts us is that of a severe judge, rewarding good and punishing evil.[4] He is also the perfectly moral Being, for he commands what is morally good. This good does not appear to us as such uniquely because God wills it. The determination of what is good does not stem, in the first instance, from an exterior law; it depends on our moral sense, an interior and autonomous authority. God, then, demands of me actions that I feel and know to be good, through my autonomous moral sense. But this means that we naturally conceive God as totally good and the source of goodness. He not only excites in us hope and fear, as a despot might, but inflames our hearts with love and veneration. Now, love is essentially directed to the good. And, since all the qualities he demands of us—truth, purity, justice, kindness, etc.—are so many aspects of the good, God appears, ultimately, as perfect Goodness, uniting in himself, in an eminent manner, perfectly and indivisibly, all the aspects of the good.[5]

The idea of God gained by the simple analysis of conscience is,

---

[1] *Grammar.*, pp.108-110.

[2] *Ibid.*, p.117: "Conscience is the connecting principle between the creature and his Creator": "It is the creative principle of religion, as the moral sense is the principle of ethics" (p.110).

[3] *Ibid.*, p.113: "It involves the impression on his mind of an unseen Being with whom he is in immediate relation . . . who can hear him, wherever he happens to be, and who can read his thoughts".

[4] *Ibid.*, p.420: "Retributive justice is the very attribute under which God is primarily brought before us in the teachings of our natural conscience". See also pp.380-391; *Occ. Ser.*, p.67.

[5] *Grammar*, pp.113-114.

in the first instance, living and concrete, an object of experience and of real apprehension.[1] Obviously, the numerous aspects of it remain, for the most part, implicit in our spontaneous knowledge. The object of religious intuition is not endowed, at the outset, with a clearly defined form for the mind to perceive. In the beginning, it is more of a vague sentiment of a higher reality to which we are subject.[2] At first, it is felt but weakly and unobtrusively.

> The sentiment of good and evil, which is at the origin of religion, is something so delicate, so easily disturbed, so quickly confused, obscured, degraded, so subtle in its persuasions, so amenable to education, so liable to yield to the influence of pride and passion, so insecure in its course, that, in the battles of life, among the innumerable feats and triumphs of human reason, this sentiment reveals itself as at once the most sublime and the least distinct of all masters.[3]

The question naturally arises whether our knowledge of God could grow into an explicit and clear representation without the intervention of outside factors. Of his very nature, man is a social being; and so it is difficult to know if the conscience, left to itself, could ever lead us to God.[4] But in any case, the light of conscience increases and, if lovingly submitted to, becomes, by degrees, a powerful beam illuminating all the recesses of the soul. Moral and religious realities then become the chief concern of our lives. They are lovingly received into the soul, and there they gather up all its faculties into a single living force, directed, tranquilly and unremittingly, to its religious good. Under this profound, affective impulse, living, implicit thought develops and, by degrees, brings into being a religious conception of the world and of life. The contributions of education, books, and social life serve strongly to bring out what is intuitively perceived, but always subject to the critical view of conscience itself. The profound concrete experiences of conscience give rise to fundamental insights and principles of value, of general application, and in their light we come to

---

[1] *Grammar.*, pp.62-63.

[2] "Conscience does not repose on itself, but reaches vaguely forwards to something beyond self, and dimly discerns a sanction higher than self for its decisions" (*Ibid.*, p.107).

[3] *Diff. Angl.*, II, pp.253-254. See also the fine description, a classical one, in the *Idea*, pp.513-514.

[4] *Grammar*, p.115.

consider and judge all categories of beings and their problems.[1] The following are among these principles : the primacy of conscience in the search for truth and the judgment of values;[2] sin as a formidable reality of life;[3] goodness and badness as ultimate qualities of every human action;[4] the meaning and value of life found in moral action, in holiness, rather than in a high state of culture;[5] our whole life as surrounded by mysteries, and our having to be content with the degree of evidence afforded by our earthly condition.[6] All these come to be profound convictions colouring and directing all our thoughts, all our judgments; but the main element in our view of the world is the idea of God. God, manifesting himself in my conscience as a just and good Master, I come to regard, in virtue of a growing experience, as the Lord and Ruler, just and omnipresent, of the entire universe.[7] I see in all things the expression of his Will and his wise Providence, both in their being and essence, in the laws of nature and the casual occurrences of life.

It is true that, in the beginning, the world and conscience are in opposition, this strange "outside" world, that seems, at first sight, so desperately confused, so devoid of meaning, so remote from God. Soon, however, it too is illumined in an extraordinary way by conscience. In the depths of our being, the consciousness of our culpability witnesses to the abyss between God and the world of men. Though wrought by man, it cannot be crossed by man. The mystery of the world is a mystery of alienation from God. God abandons it, more or less, to its own devices, the sport of the enormous and insane force of its pride and passions. God hides his face, and is silent. So it is that the religious attitude is, at first, one of compunction, of abasement before the supreme Judge whose avenging hand is raised against us. Yet, on the other hand, our conscience affirms the essential goodness of God, and his merciful designs for us. That is why the world-view of natural

---

[1] *Grammar.*, pp.115-116; *Occ. Ser.*, p.65; *O.U.S.*, pp.18-19.

[2] "Obedience to our conscience in all things, great and small, is the way to know the truth" (*P.P.S.*, I, 227). This celebrated principle of the primacy of conscience is the very first constitutive principle of the religious man.

[3] See, for instance, *Present Position*, p.263.

[4] An example of a first principle given in the *Grammar*, p.65.

[5] Well-known utterances of Newman "Holiness first", and "Life is action" (explained in the *Grammar*, p.95).

[6] Cf. Janssens, *op. cit.*, pp. xiii-xx; we shall return to this point later.

[7] *Grammar*, p.63.

religion has, also, its luminous side. Already, before any Revelation, we "hope against hope". We pray, we offer our gifts, even though none of our acts in themselves can bring about our reconciliation; but we go to him no less, because in the depths of our hearts we know him as the Lord of love and we are confident that, at the final reckoning, not only distributive justice, but goodness, too, will have its say. We even expect him to take the initiative in giving a revelation that will reconcile us with him and bring him near.

Finally, the idea of Providence is the key to the enigma of the world and the uneasy state of religion in it. It shows us the world and its darkness as part of a divine economy using it as a test and tempering of our fidelity, which will be ultimately rewarded. The religious man recognises that everything has its part in the plan of Providence, though the darkness is never entirely dissipated. All serves as material for a religious conception of the whole, and the outward appearance of the world, at first so alarming and dismaying, comes, in the end, to bear striking witness, if involuntarily, to the early intuitions of conscience.[1] It is this very growth of a religious view of the world that brings up the problem of Christianity, for all genuine religious feeling reaches out to, and demands, Christianity and the Church. This is a subject we will develop later, in discussing Newman's apologetic.[2]

The "ethos" of the religious man is, then, a resultant of his fidelity to conscience; a real experience of God, received in the soul with entire submission, gives rise to a complex of ethical and religious principles, which, of themselves, by the steady workings of implicit reasoning, develop within the mind a religious conception of the world impervious to invasion of any kind. In contrast, the "ethos" of the rationalist is the outcome of the clouding over of conscience. Conscience begins as a feeble glimmer, and its normal development requires a favourable social environment. A non-religious education, or one hostile to religion, may be enough to prevent the principles of conscience exercising their normal influence on the development of a person's convictions. Is the individual to blame in such a case? Newman does not give a simple answer. We are, admittedly, responsible for what we are and for our principles; but this is a general statement, and only

[1] *Grammar.*, pp.116-117, 394-400, 402-403.
[2] See below, pp.229-234.

part of the truth. A case of irreligiousness or total scepticism, without personal fault, is doubtless not impossible, though it is exceptional. Were not W. Froude and Mark Pattison, along with many others of the kind, among Newman's personal friends? They were men of upright character, good will, and absolute integrity, utterly devoted to the highest truth; and yet, under the influence of "scientism", they fell irretrievably into religious scepticism. Therefore, when Newman, in the *Grammar*, sets about the problem of defectiveness in regard to one's first principles, he expresses himself generally with extreme caution, and reserves the possibility of inculpable error.[1]

Apart from this restriction, Newman asserts roundly that, as a general rule, personal infidelity to conscience is the reason why religious experience fails to expand in the heart and remains barren in the mind. A person who infringes, consciously and habitually, the moral law, comes by degrees to lose sensitivity of conscience. He adapts himself, more and more, to his feeling of uneasiness which eventually becomes less acute. He succeeds better in ignoring it.[2] Sin, by itself, would not be enough to degrade our conscience; but we have an unfortunate tendency to align our thought with our conduct, and a subtle power to achieve this effect. The intrinsic evil of the world is that it reasons against God and provides sin with the support of an intellectual system.[3] Man rebels against feeling himself in the wrong, in an inferior position; he prefers to act as he pleases, in independent fashion, his mind at rest. Like the Pharisee in the Gospel, he desires to be contented with himself.[4] Very well, then; his intellect will be the go-between to arrange the matter and to build, with the help of a number of ingenious theories and subtle arguments, a vast substructure from which, admittedly, it does not exclude his higher, ineradicable convictions, but where they are prudently adjusted and

---

[1] *Grammar*, pp.375, 386, 402 ("till these principles are deliberately or accidentally lost"), p.413 ("whether he is responsible to his Maker for being mentally crooked, is another matter").

[2] *Ibid.*, pp.115-116, 123. Finely described in *Callista*, p.97; most explicitly described in "The Self-Wise Inquirer", *P.P.S.*, I, p.222-225.

[3] *Ser. Subj.*, p.93: "The world has many sins, but its peculiar offence is that of daring to reason contrary to God's word and will . . . It goes wrong on principle, and prefers its own way of viewing things to God's way".

[4] Newman describes the religion of the self-satisfied in "The Religion of the Pharisee, the Religion of Mankind", *Occ. Ser.*, pp.15-30. "It has as foundation self-sufficiency, and for result self-satisfaction" (p.25).

"explained", allowing falsehood a placid co-existence with a religious veneer to a life in accordance with the maxims of the world. Conscience cannot be totally silenced, for it is an essential part of human nature; but we are able to misdirect it, to interpret it in various ways, to overlay it with plausible ideas and arguments. In this way, it comes to lose its early precision, its direct and simple penetration. Weakened by sin, deceived by an arrogant reason, it ceases to speak for itself and from the standpoint proper to it. We succumb to a "judicial hardness and blindness". Reason, then, enjoys free play in defining, on principles borrowed from the world, what is true and good without undue interference from this conscience so insistent on having a say in everything. Reason creates its own view of the world, which will be less burdensome, rigid and dogmatic.[1]

The first thing reason has to get rid of is the sense of obligation, absolute and formidable, whenever we hear the voice of God. For this purpose, conscience is reduced to one of its elements, the moral sense; and morality is divorced from religion. The transcendental aspect disappears, and only the human aspect of morality remains. Its centre, then, is no longer God the lawgiver, but the man of sense. The content of conscience is taken from its original sphere, which was theocentric, and transferred to one purely anthropocentric; for a voice which commands and threatens is substituted a delicate feeling for human perfection. Henceforth, sin is no more than an injection of rules created by a purely human ideal; repentance and a religious sense of shame, penetrated with fear, degenerate into self-criticism and self-discontent, we feel diminished in our dignity as men; humility becomes a kind of modesty, likeable indeed, but so often hypocritical; and so with the rest of the virtues. In short, the moral imperative with its firm foundation in God gives place to a humanist ethic.[2] But the moral sense itself forfeits its finality and

---

[1] In infidelity to conscience, Newman always distinguished two elements —sin, and pride of intellect. See *P.P.S.*, I, pp.220-225. It is a complex process which substitutes, by degrees, "for our instinctive sense of good and evil, our weak and infatuated reason" (p.219). He describes it magnificently in "Intellect, the Instrument of our Religious Training", *Occ. Ser.*, pp.9-11. He shows there the decay arising from an unhealthy curiosity, the first form taken by intellectual pride in youth. In the *Idea*, p.191, he says: "A false philosophy has misinterpreted emotions which ought to lead to God".

[2] This is shown especially in the eighth lecture of the *Idea*, pp.191, ff.

its original authoritativeness. The instinct of conscience, at first so certain, is subjected to reasoning; its principles are replaced by motives foreign to it. Everything becomes uncertain and relative. It is soon discovered that morality consists only of fluctuating opinions. What remains, in the end, is a certain number of social sentiments, varying according to time and circumstance, a creation of human culture, and equally relative. A more or less radical scepticism prevails.[1]

What is the general aspect of this worldly morality? It can take many forms, since, as far as possible, it is disengaged from conscience and depends on a reason divorced from its roots. Now, this reason comes to base its arguments on rules currently accepted in the world—theories and slogans in force in various places—and it can prove anything by emphasising one aspect to the exclusion of others. In addition, the world's philosophy is, by its very nature, shifting and changeable, for it is made up of theories and opinions, such as those of literature and science. Besides that, the cultivated mind is always on the look-out for the purely intellectual pleasure that it obtains from novel and interesting ideas. This superficial enjoyment, however, is short-lived, and soon leads to boredom. As in literature, the worldly man continually seeks for new and arresting ideas in the moral and religious sphere: "New objects in religion, new systems and plans, new doctrines, new preachers, are necessary to satisfy that craving which the so-called spread of knowledge has created. The mind becomes morbidly sensitive and fastidious, dissatisfied with things as they are, desirous of a change as such, as if alteration must be of itself a relief".[2]

Yet, in spite of its instability, this worldly philosophy clings to a few fixed principles and doctrinal tendencies. Newman sees it as claiming to be realistic, as declining to be led by the feelings, such as those of conscience, which it considers too remote from reality. It aims at recasting conscience on the line of principles drawn from tangible reality. It takes the human situation as it finds it. Man is endowed with a given nature, and he has to exercise his function ("métier d'homme") in a determinate sphere, which is the visible world. This is a certain and universal fact, which must be looked at objectively, not "from within", by

[1] *Idea*, pp.202-204.
[2] *P.P.S.*, I, p.313.

conscience, but "from without", by the organs of sense and by common sense; man ought to act in accordance with his nature and to discharge his function in the world. The first principles of ethics, then, are to be sought not from an inner, irrational voice, but from the objective data of general experience and from the conditions of success in the life of this world.[1]

Let us look at man objectively, as we would a stone or a plant. He has a definite nature to which correspond equally definite tendencies. Since these are not bad, it cannot be sinful to follow them.[2] Individually, no doubt, they may inflict harm on the whole, but it is precisely for that reason that we have to use them rationally, that is to say in the degree and with the foresight required by the good of each person and the common good. We triumph over physical nature by yielding to her laws, and using her rationally. That is how we should act in regard to human nature; we are not to seek our ideals in the clouds, or abandon ourselves to visionary illusions, or to imagine man as other than he is; let us confine ourselves to following nature, reasonably and in due measure.[3] Where is this reason, this measure, to be found, but in the utilitarian demands of life and of earthly happiness? Leave out all that transcends this life. Let us not be drawn by the passions as their slave, but set them within the bounds required for a balanced life and happiness. The only sin recognised by the world is exaggeration, disorder, lack of self-control.[4] Bring into life balance and harmony, and it will become a thing of beauty. Then, the higher the level of civilisation, the more refined and

---

[1] The principles of the world have as their norm the organs of sense, usefulness, even, in a highly cultured society, refinement of manners. See P.P.S., I, p.224: "As to the code of morals, they acknowledge it in a measure, that is, as far as its dicta can be *proved* by reasoning, by an appeal to sight and to expedience, and without reference to a natural sense of right and wrong"; "Conscience is replaced, partly by love of the beautiful, partly by motives of fitness" (p.312). See also *Ser. Subj.*, pp.96-97; *Occ. Ser.*, p.21.

[2] "They reason themselves into the notion that to sin is their nature and therefore no fault of theirs, that is, that it is not sin" (*Disc. M. Cong.*, p.97; see also pp.148-149). *Ser. Subj.*, p.97.

[3] *Ser. Subj.*, p.97.

[4] *Disc. M. Cong.*, p.148: "It sees that nature has a number of tendencies, inclinations and passions; and because they are in nature, it thinks that each of them may be indulged for its own sake, so far as it does no harm to others, or to a person's bodily, mental or temporal well-being. It considers that want of moderation, or excess, is the very definition of sin". Cf. also P.P.S., I, p.312.

delicate becomes our feeling for all that pertains to style and beauty of living. The man of culture is shocked by any gross instance of sensuality, cruelty, and so forth. With moderate enjoyment of the objects of sense he combines the higher, more delicate, pleasures of the imagination and reason, the innocent pursuit of art, letters and philosophy.[1]

The highest moral obligation recognised is that each should play his part in the world, in the sphere appropriate to him. The good of all is the first condition of the good of the individual. Hence, the world's idea of virtue is different from the Christian idea. Patience, humility, a sense of guilt, purity of heart, gentleness, chastity are unproductive in the eyes of the "realist". They are commodities the world can well do without. It needs more muscular virtues, manliness, vitality, ambition, courage, initiative, perseverance, retributive justice, etc. These are the qualities which make for worldly advancement, and lead to the highest positions.[2] In addition, it recognises those virtues whose practice makes life more secure and pleasant, such as exactness, honesty, moderation, agreeableness, good manners, cheerfulness, loyalty, readiness to co-operate.[3]

Whoever possesses these qualities which the world applauds is virtuous.[4] He may act as he likes as regards his thoughts, even in his outward conduct, provided others are not affected.

Provided he does his duty in the world, according to his calling, he cannot fail to gain heaven, even if he confines his efforts to what has just been said, yes, even though he be guilty, in other spheres, of acts obviously bad. For example, a soldier must be loyal, obedient, and brave; all the rest is of no account. A businessman must be honest; a worker, industrious and content; a gentleman, truthful, courteous, self-respecting; a statesman, nobly ambitious; a wife, a good house-keeper; an ecclesiastic, worthy, benevolent and moderately active.[5]

This worldly ethic does not exclude God. Is he not the author of our nature? Has he not placed us in this world as our sphere of

---

[1] *Idea*, pp.184-190.
[2] *Grammar*, pp.248-249.
[3] *Ser. Subj.*, p.101.
[4] *Occ. Ser.*, pp.22-23.
[5] *Ibid.*, pp.24-25; *Ser. Subj.*, p.103.

action? If so, it is his will that we give free rein to our nature, as far as our human condition allows, and within the bounds imposed on it by the requirements of a "good" life in the world.[1]

The world, then, has its idea of God, its religion even, but one from which all anxiety, oppressiveness and severity has been eliminated. It is all unction, joy and consolation. God is sought, not in the fearful experiences of conscience, but in the external world, in the sun, moon, stars, in the splendour and immensity of nature. In it everything speaks of benevolence and harmony, of natural bounty and creative life. God made the world; from him every creature, man included, has received its nature. Under his fatherly gaze, and with his benign approval, we allow our nature to develop within us, as it follows its spontaneous inclinations. As far as lies within us, we try to shape our universe, so as to make it as "good", as pleasant, as possible. If there is a future life, those, certainly, will enjoy it who, in the present life, have continued the work of God, the creator of natural beauty, by adapting it with delicacy and taste. He is a God of nature, not of sinners. Because he is a God of the world, our duties towards him are comprised in our duties to the world, the gaining of money, the upbringing of a family, fighting for one's country, and so on, according to our place in society.[2] The "God" conceived in this way tends easily to become merely the primary source, unsubstantial and impersonal, of nature. We can understand why, all through his life, Newman waged war on Natural Theology, that pseudo-religion, an alibi, an excuse, a veneer stuck on by the world in revolt against the living God of conscience.[3]

Finally, we may notice that this contrast between the rationalist and the religious man is found in a number of great religious thinkers, in Pascal, Dostoievski, Schlegel and Kierkegaard. In this respect, Kierkegaard is the closest to Newman. He contrasts the "crowd", whose ideas reflect public opinion, with the man of personal religion who, in fear and trembling, stands before the living God.

[1] *Disc. M. Cong.*, p.149; *Ser Subj.*, pp.102-103.
[2] This religion is well described in "The Religion of the Day", *P.P.S.*, I, pp.309-324.
[3] A violent attack on purely natural theology, or deism, is to be found in "The Tamworth Reading-room", *Disc. Arg.*, pp.254-305, especially pp.298-305. It is treated with greater calm and depth in the second lecture of the *Idea*.

Analogous ideas, too, though in great part secularised, are to be found in some modern philosophers, most of whom are indebted for their leading principles to Kierkegaard. The fundamental tenets of contemporary philosophy are drawn from such concepts as *das Man* of Heidegger, the *moi public* and the *moi privé* of Le Senne, the "man enselved" and the "alienated man" of Ortega y Gasset, the *être* and *avoir* of Marcel, the *individual* and the *person* of some present-day personalists; all these antitheses turn round a like intuition, obviously interpreted in many different ways, on account of the different standpoints adopted and the varying ideas of the authors. (See Appendix D, *The philosophy of conscience.*)

SECTION C

ORTHODOXY AND HERESY

This account of Newman's theory of types may seem to have led us far from the subject and to be little connected with the development of doctrine; but its relevance will soon be clear. The religious man becomes, in the context of Christianity, the bearer of orthodoxy, the rationalist becomes heretical. Now, orthodoxy and heresy are, as it were, the two poles of the dynamic of tradition. *Oportet haereses esse.* There are two main causes of the development of the faith into a dogmatic theology ever more clear and exact. First is the theological instinct, the spontaneous tendency of the believer to analyse and draw into himself, by reflection, the riches of intuitive faith. Then comes heresy which, by setting forth ideas and statements contrary to the faith, obliges the Church to oppose it with more precise expressions of doctrine.

The orthodox thinker lives by his intuitive faith, by the concrete idea he carries within him of Christ and the economy of salvation. It is an idea he owes to the sources of revelation, and the gift of faith has deeply imprinted it in his heart and mind. The part played by conscience in the development of the religious spirit is paralleled by the intuition of faith and the dogmatic spirit in the orthodox development of doctrine.[1] The apprehension of

[1] *Essay,* p.361.

the real, of the singular, is the vital principle of all
true development.[1] This intuition becomes the centre of the ordinary, daily concerns of the believer. Hence his faith takes on a
definite significance in his life; it is, from now on, a valued possession, not only of his mind, but of his heart.[2] It naturally results
in a continual meditation bringing home the realities of faith, a
spontaneous and affective dwelling upon them, a constant sense
of the presence of God, of Christ, his Mother and the saints; it all
takes place so freely and tranquilly as almost to escape reflex
awareness. By this means, the first principles of Christianity,
already described, settle in the mind "of themselves". They are
all, in fact, rooted in the dogma of the Incarnation, in the central
teaching of faith that the Son of God took to himself a real human
nature to redeem us and make us like to him.[3] These principles
are subsequently fertilised by the spontaneous, implicit process of
vital reasoning by which the various aspects of Christian truth
are imparted to the mind in all their mysterious fulness and
coherence. Ultimately, as occasion demands, and particularly
in reaction against heresy, these insights come to be expressed
in exact form and, as far as possible, to be logically interconnected.[4]

This does not by any means involve a complete absence of
error, however. We have the greatest difficulty in bearing continuously in mind all the aspects of reality. Admittedly, the mind
in contact with the real, senses the full richness of its object, but
cannot immediately transpose it fully into the terms of explicit
thought. That is a work that needs years, centuries, in fact the
whole of Christian history. The Fathers themselves who express
one or other aspect of the Mystery with an almost miraculous
exactitude, put forth, at times, alarming statements on other points
not then under discussion. We find, for example, especially in the
ante-Nicene theologians, expressions which, if taken literally,
imply a kind of subordinationism, an inferiority of the Son to the

---

[1] *O.U.S.*, p.337: "The very life of true development is *realizing*". Cf. also
Apologia, p.194.

[2] *Essay*, p.358.

[3] See above, pp.127-128.

[4] This process is described in *Newman-Perrone*, pp.436-439.

Father.[1] Even St Athanasius and the Alexandrine Fathers, who corrected this error with real supernatural genius, used formulas which are far from making sufficiently clear the human nature of the Son.[2] In the long run, however, one Father makes good the inadequacies of another; and in this way apparent errors are eliminated. They are, in any case, simply examples of clumsy expression in notional thought and do not impair the truth of that "realising" apprehension which takes in the mystery of faith in its entirety.

The process is analogous to that of the upright conscience. Its orientation is correct from the beginning, but, at first, there is considerable hesitation in the explicit recognition of various duties. It does not escape, from time to time, material errors, but these are gradually rectified as the man of good faith follows his interior light and brings it to maturity.[3] Newman saw the Fathers of the Church as men whose minds were steeped in the depths of an ineffable knowledge, and urged on by a burning love for the object of their contemplation. Their thought ripens slowly, falls easily into obscurity and confusion, advances haltingly and timidly, is difficult and hesitant in expression, for it is aware of the chasm which separates human concepts from the mysterious life they are brought in to express. In Newman's eyes, then, the Fathers seemed as if they felt out of their depth in the sphere of abstract thought and as if, in their constant dissatisfaction with their theology, they returned over and over again to the same problems, ever rectifying, adding to, and explaining their statements. Their thought is penetrated with reverential fear; prayer is the accompaniment of their reflections, and their minds seek to probe the mystery which claims their devotion and holds their affection. Each of them advances tradition in a very modest degree only, but their contribution is the product of deep and mature thought, and their constant care is to show that the little they do bring is

---

[1] *Essay*, pp.135-137. The ante-Nicene theology gave Newman many a headache. His changing views on the ancient theologians are set out in detail by Guitton, *op. cit.*, pp.149-166. His solution is, finally, given by the principles of his epistemology: "Error would be, from this point of view, like the first state of a confused vision which failed to observe the difference of planes" (p.162); "their opinions were in opposition to their implicit faith" (p.159).

[2] *Essay*, p.367.

[3] *Ibid.*, p.361.

nothing new or original, but simply a more exact expression of the ancient faith. Each Father hands on the torch to his successor. After one man's lifetime's work, the formulation of dogma has taken a step forward; and so development goes on, slowly, but, considered in its entirety, with infallible certainty.[1] This certainty comes from the profound vision that the gift of faith excites within us. That same vision which had sustained the constancy and intrepidity of the martyrs in a former generation is now, in the patristic period, the strength and stay of Christian thought.[2]

Heretics, however, are rationalists. Newman came to see this at the time when, just after his experience at Oriel, still haunted by the memory of the detached intellectualism of the Noetics, he set out on the study of Arianism to write his first great work on the ancient Church. Arians and Noetics were hewn from the same block. Those subtle Aristotelians of Antioch, who admitted no other than the literal sense of Scripture, were, for Newman, born heretics. Undoubtedly, he did them less than justice.

What heresy lacks is a real apprehension of the content of revelation, and the religious assent that holds it continually present to the heart. It has no feeling of subjection to a transcendent mystery, for it holds that the truths of religion are perfectly capable of being fitted into the categories of reason. In fact, for heresy there are no mysteries at all. This view is not always consciously present to the mind; its action is more that of a first implicit principle, and it shows itself repeatedly in the way heresy treats the truths of faith.[3] What differentiates the heretic from the orthodox

---

[1] *Essay.*, pp.266-367: "The theology of the Church is no random combination of various opinions, but a diligent, patient working out of one doctrine out of many materials. The conduct of the Popes, Councils, Fathers, betokens the slow, painful, anxious taking up of new elements into an existing body of belief. St Athansius, St Augustine, St Leo are conspicuous for the repetition *in terminis* of their own theological statements . . . Here we see the difference between originality of mind and the gifts and calling of a Doctor in the Church; the holy Fathers just mentioned were intently fixing their minds on what they taught, grasping it more and more closely, viewing it on various sides, trying its consistency, weighing their own separate expressions. And thus, if in some cases they were left in ignorance, the next generation of teachers completed their work, for the same unwearied process of thought went on".

[2] *Ibid.*, p.359.

[3] *Ibid.*, p.87. In 1835, Newman already saw in the acceptance or denial of mystery the capital difference between the rationalist and the believer. Cf. "On the Introduction of Rationalistic Principles into Revealed Religion", *Ess. Crit. Hist.*, I, pp.30-99.

thinker are his first principles.[1] The heretic invariably admits a
number of orthodox doctrines; at times, he even contributes to the
formulation of doctrine. The Fathers themselves took over many
useful conceptions from heretics.[2] Every error contains a part of
truth. Error breeds in the spirit of heretics, their cast of mind, the
atmosphere of their thought; all these find expression in their
first principles. In so far as they are heretics, their thought is controlled by principles diametrically opposed to those, enumerated
above, of orthodoxy.

Arian and Nestorian schools denied the allegorical rule of
Scripture interpretation; the Gnostics and Eunomians for
faith professed to substitute knowledge, and the Manichees
also, as St Augustine so touchingly declares in the beginning
of his work, *De utilitate credendi*. The dogmatic rule, at least
so far as regards its traditional character, was thrown aside
by all those sects which, as Tertullian tells us, claimed to
judge for themselves from Scripture; and the sacramental
principle was violated, *ipso facto*, by all who separated from
the Church, was denied too by Faustus and Manichee when
he argued against the Catholic ceremonial, by Vigilantius in
his opposition to relics, and by the iconoclasts. In like
manner, the contempt of mystery, of reverence, of devoted-
ness, of sanctity, are other notes of the heretical spirit.[3]

The principles of heresy, like those of erroneous philosophies,
are not the outcome of a profound intuition of the real, but are
the product of reason, acting on a purely superficial view of things.
Ultimately, the first principles of heretics are the same as those of
false philosophies.

That truth and falsehood in religion are but matter of
opinion; that one doctrine is as good as another; that the
Governor of the world does not intend that we should gain
the truth; that there is no truth; that we are not more acceptable to God by believing this than by believing that; that no
one is answerable for his opinions; that they are a matter of
necessity or accident; that it is enough if we sincerely hold
what we profess; that our merit lies in seeking, not in possess-

---

[1] "Pagans may have the same principles as Catholics; heretics not.
Principles are a better touchstone of heresy than doctrines". *Essay*, p.181.

[2] *Essay.*, p.362.

[3] *Ibid.*, p.354.

ing; that it is a duty to follow what seems to us true, without a fear lest it should not be true; that it may be a gain to succeed, and can be no harm to fail; that we may take up and lay down opinions at pleasure; that belief belongs to the mere intellect, not to the heart; that we may safely trust our-selves in matters of faith, and need no other guide,—this is the principle of philosophies and heresies, which is very weakness.[1]

It follows that the principles of heresy are permanent, while what it teaches is a set of fluctuating opinions.[2] These are lifeless, without power of growth; they lack continuity and organic rich-ness. They abound only in the multiplicity of their ceaseless varia-tions.[3] Heresy does not ripen by degrees, does not develop in orderly fashion; it is the product of deliberate mental activity. The heretic is a producer of novelties, of resounding and bewilder-ing theories, of sensational ideas in theology.[4] His thought soars into space, light and free; at times brilliant and subtle, it unfolds with breadth and lucidity like an exercise in pure logic. He is unencumbered by any profound intuitions, undisturbed by any instinct for reality. Taking hold of the real in haphazard fashion, he substitutes for it one of its many aspects, and uses that to sketch out, in broad, sweeping strokes, a brand-new system. But it is like a soap-bubble, beautiful in itself, but expanding only to burst.[5] A few years later, it is forgotten. Basically, what heresy most lacks is a serious spirit; its animating principle, whether concealed or evident, is scepticism.

[1] *Ibid.*, pp.357-358.

[2] *Ibid.*, p.181: "The doctrines of heresy are accidents, and disappear rapidly; its principles are everlasting".

[3] *O.U.S.*, p.318: "Its formulae end in themselves, without development, because they are words; they are barren, because they are dead. If they had life, they would increase and multiply . . . It develops into dissolution; but it creates nothing, it tends to no system".

[4] *Essay*, p.351: "The very characteristic of heresy is this novelty and originality of manifestation".

[5] *O.U.S.*, p.337: "Here we see the ordinary mistake of doctrinal inno-vators, viz., to go away with this or that proposition of the Creed, instead of embracing the one idea which all of them together are meant to convey; it being almost a definition of heresy, that it fastens on some one statement as if the whole truth, to the denial of all others, and as the basis of a new faith". Cf. also *Essay*, p.181; *Newman-Perrone*, p.412; *Diff. Angl.*, II, p.81-82. In the *Essay*, p.336, Newman emphasizes the heretic Tertullian's fecundity, comprehensibility, originality, in comparison with the orthodox Fathers.

Newman, in his study of heresy, evidently had no plan to treat every false doctrine, but confined his strictures to those who stubbornly clung to their own opinions. No one is a formal heretic unless he rebels against the Church.[1] Newman would not deny that there are, in many heretical communities, persons in good faith, sincere believers, but misled. The heresies of the earlier centuries are generally admitted, by historians of theology, to be rationalistic, certainly those of the Arians and Manicheans, the Nestorians' doubtfully, the fifth century Monophysites' even more doubtfully. These, however, were less familiar to Newman, whose special object of study was Arianism.

Chapter 4

THE SOCIAL PSYCHOLOGY OF DEVELOPMENT

NOW that we have described the psychology of development in its individual aspect, it remains to consider it from the social standpoint. This distinction is, however, somewhat artificial, for social development is "incarnated" in individuals, and individual development is dependent on the life of society. Consequently, we have already, in the preceding chapter, touched on various social elements of the psychology in question.

Once again, we will devote the first section to a study of its general aspect, and a second to its applications in the Catholic Church.

Section A

The Idea in Society

We have seen in the preceding chapters how thought is a function of the whole personality. The different elements of our personality exercise of themselves, though in no blind, deterministic fashion, an influence over our thought, acting spontaneously to form certain first principles of varying efficacy, which dominate us unconsciously. We are social beings, and the place we occupy in our environment is one of the elements which make up our personality. The effect on us of our environment varies in extent. It may equally well promote or thwart our experience of the concrete and the fruitfulness of our authentically personal principles. There is no necessary opposition between our true personality and the child of the age which co-exist in each of us. Their concord is impaired only when the traditional culture is not taken up and regained by personal reflection; and, when that is the case, culture is only a superficial layer and a meaningless ornament of the empty mind. It happens, especially, when our own infidelity or neglect severs our contact, in the depths of our being, with the mystery of reality. This contact alone is able to assure balance, solidity and consistency to our thought. Without it, we are incapable of directing our own course, and we are soon at the mercy of the variable currents of the age.

It is possible, therefore, for the action of our minds to be incorporated with collective thought and, at the same time, to keep its own distinctive stamp.

By this incorporation, we can be associated with a "cultural" milieu, an ideological trend, a philosophical school, a social movement, a political party, a class of society, a nation, a Church. Newman was keenly aware that social life, even in the sphere of the mind, is a kind of higher organism, in which the intellectual life of the individual is comprised as a particular function. In the first part of this work, we have set out the circumstances of his life to which he owed this conviction.[1]

General sociology of the idea

An idea develops and matures within a society in the same way as a thought in the mind of a philosopher.[2] All kinds of individuals are active in a society, which is therefore indebted to them for what their personalities contribute to it. The community, none the less, has its own objective existence, and its basic idea follows a determinate curve, in spite of—but, also, exactly because of—the diverse activities of its members.[3] For this reason, every society is seen to be, even as regards its ideas, a living unity of a higher order and from its collective life the idea itself draws its own sustenance. Just as all the faculties of a person contribute to the development of his thought, so an idea develops in its social setting through the influence of all the various agencies which determine the course of history.

The dominant factor, on every occasion, is the idea itself. It

[1] See above, p.38.
[2] *Newman-Perrone*, pp.414-415.
[3] See below, pp.173-174.

is (in the aristotelian sense) the *form,* the principle of unity; it uses individuals as its instruments for expansion.[1] Consequently, in Newman's eyes, it attains to a kind of independence such as Plato would have given it. Once embodied in a society, it creates in it an intellectual atmosphere and, in that way, stamps its principles on the individual mind, though the person is more or less unaware of the process. This is how a living tradition comes to perpetuate the development of an idea in accordance with its original spirit.[2] A community, a movement is thus seen to have a life of its own, whose spirit and guiding principles are reflected in its conduct.[3] The unity of a society derives from the fundamental idea bound up with it.[4]

The course of its life is regulated by "first principles", whose action is as secret and authoritative as in the thought of individuals.[5] In a community, too, thought develops unperceived, coming to maturity by slow degrees and as if by instinct. The life of a society, then, is seen to be the expression and realisation of an idea.[6]

We have now to describe the successive phases of this development, using, for the purpose, Newmans's own analysis in a passage

---

[1] Newman wrote about the Oxford Movement in *Diff. Angl.,* I, p.101, thus: "It has been formed on one idea, which has developed into a body of teaching . . . When I thus represent the idea of the movement . . . I am speaking of what may be called its *form*"; "We could say rather that the idea makes use of Christian intellects" (*O.U.S.,* p.317); "An idea develops through and by means of human communities, their rulers and leaders; it uses their minds as instruments and, in so doing, is dependent upon them" (*Essay,* p.38).

[2] See above, pp.144-148.

[3] Cf. *Diff. Angl.,* I, pp.54-56: "It, as every religion, has a life, a spirit, a genius of its own, in which doctrines lie implicit, out of which they are developed and by which they are attracted into it from without and assimilated to it (p.54) . . . the religious life of a people is of a certain quality and in a certain direction, and this quality and this direction are tested by the mode in which it encounters the various opinions, customs, and institutions which are submitted to it" (p.55).

[4] Cf. *Essay,* p.186: "A living idea becomes multiple, while remaining one. Principles stimulate thought, an idea focuses it".

[5] Newman wrote thus in connection with the Oxford Movement: "Life consists or manifests itself in the activity of principle. There are various kinds of life, and each kind is the influence or operation in a body of those principles upon which the body is constituted. Each kind of life is to be referred, and is congenial to its own principle" (*Diff. Angl.,* I, p.43-44).

[6] That is why Newman gives for the first criterion of the identity of the idea throughout its development the maintenance of the type, that is, of the external structure and action typical of it.

of the *Essay*.[1] For the sake of clarity, we will single out certain elements from his copious treatment.

There are ideas, both true and false, whose nature is such that they take deep root in the human mind, and so come to rule the life of men. They may be called living ideas.[2]

If it is the case that the mind can only be degrees unfold the content of any real idea whatever, this same slow growth is even more characteristic of living, social ideas.[3] What ultimately causes them to develop is that they seize upon the spontaneous thought of a community of persons. At first, each member of it, according to his nature, character, culture, interest, and so on, is struck by this or that aspect of the idea; and, in his absorption by it, is blind to the others. Thus, the idea begins to be assimilated by various thinkers under different aspects, and the order in which these are assimilated is different in each case.[4] This, naturally, gives rise to a certain amount of disturbance and confusion, particularly as the expression and unfolding of the idea are, at first, extremely defective and inexact.[5] Criticism then ensues, both friendly and hostile, together with the collision of all kinds of opinions and incompatible theories;[6] and so we have a period of conflict and chaos. In the surge of opinions, no one can tell the direction of the ship.[7] These clashes, however, inaugurate, in time, a new phase, in which their significance is brought to light, their differences composed, and order established. After much discussion and explanation, apparent contradictions are resolved into complementary aspects of one and the same idea which give mutual support. New points of view are found and adopted; and the idea takes

---

[1] *Essay*, pp.33-40.

[2] *Ibid.*, p.36: "When an idea, whether real or not, is of a nature to interest and possess the mind, it is said to live in the mind that is the recipient of it".

[3] *Ibid.*, p. 16: "The more an idea may be said to be living, the more varied are its aspects; the more social and political its nature, the more complex and subtle are its consequences and the more extended its career". Cf. also *Ibid.*, pp.36-37.

[4] *Newman-Perrone*, p.409. Cf. *Essay*, pp.37-39.

[5] *Ibid.*, p.37: "At the beginning we do not fully apprehend what moves us; we express and explain ourselves inadequately".

[6] *Ibid.*, p.37.

Ibid.: "There will be a general agitation of thought, and an action of mind both upon itself and upon other minds. There will be a time of confusion, when conceptions and misconceptions are in conflict; and it is uncertain whether anything will come of the idea at all".

on firm outline. All sorts of opinions and ideas are sifted and tested, some accepted, others rejected; and thus an articulated system rises, by degrees, out of this chaos, and the idea that was, at first, dissected in its various aspects within the society is reconstituted as a whole, and becomes the property of each member.[1]

The social development of an idea, therefore, is brought about, primarily, by the conflict and reconciliation of the various aspects in which different people at first envisaged it. Yet the origin of this tension is not to be found solely in the conflicts between individuals; collective disagreements, too, play their part. At times, the needs of the masses leads ideas in a direction different from that prescribed by the intellectuals. In cases where a society comprises several nations or races, it receives from their various endowments a greater variety of forms. In a very large community, certain necessary functions are present from the outset, exercised by different individuals or groups whose interests do not naturally coincide. The theorist tries to develop the idea on speculative lines, according to the demands of logical consistency. The statesman looks at things from a practical standpoint. The moralist is engaged in a search for values to enrich our emotional and moral life. Theory, politics and ethics are not always in agreement, and, consequently, do not invariably draw the idea along the same course of development.[2] These various opposing factors, individual, social, national, functional, excite a continual struggle and an internal tension in the intellectual life of the society. Yet such factors are mutually compensatory; tension between them protects the idea from the danger of exaggerating one aspect and from the resulting impoverishment; they are, therefore, indispensable to its harmonious development. The crises caused by their opposition may be alarming, but, in view of human nature, they

---

[1] *Ibid.:* "New lights will be brought to bear upon the original idea, aspects will multiply, and judgments accumulate . . . After a while, some definite form of doctrine emerges; and, as time proceeds, one view of it will be modified or expanded by another, and then combined with a third, till the idea in which they centre will be in each mind separately what at first it was only to all together . . . The multitude of opinions concerning it, in these respects and many others, will be collected, compared, sorted, sifted, selected or rejected, and gradually attached to it, or separated from it, in the minds of individuals and of the community".

[2] In the second section of this chapter, we shall examine in detail these collective differences.

are still the sole guarantee of balance and harmony.[1]

The second factor of development is the *milieu*. A movement, like a community, is born and lives in an environment already occupied by other ideas and institutions with which it has to reckon. It has to compare itself with them, the better to understand its real nature; it has to decide its attitude to them, measure the possibility of absorbing, combining with, or tolerating them.[2] Some it will have to reject and oppose, or else adopt them after giving them a fresh significance and direction.[3] It cannot, in fact, exempt itself from outside influences. It takes on the vesture of the ideas it finds prevailing. Principles alien to its nature may insinuate themselves. In the conflict it may be overcome, or it may become enfeebled and deteriorate as the result either of violence or some hidden cause.[4]

Finally, the idea has to be translated into the terms of practical life, and here we have the third cause of its development. Its practical consequences must be pursued to the end. It must be "incarnated" in visible form, create an organisation, lay down a line of moral conduct. It cannot continue to live, unless it has a form of government and a political attitude. It must provide itself with weapons of defence, with instruments to strengthen and propagate it. For this purpose it has, once more, to adopt, adapt, or reject many possible means of action, bearing in mind the situation as a whole and a thousand particular circumstances.[5]

This explains why development takes, simultaneously, many different courses. They meet from time to time, and diverge, and

[1] These ideas are set forth especially in the great Preface to the (new) edition of the *Via Media* in 1877. Cf., also, *Apologia*, pp.238-239.

[2] *Essay*, p.37: "It will be surveyed, too, in its relation to other doctrines or facts . . . How it stands affected towards other systems, how it affects them, how far it coalesces with them, how far it tolerates, when it interferes with them, will be gradually wrought out".

[3] *Ibid.*, p. 37: "Since its province is the busy scene of human life, it cannot develop at all, except either by destroying, or modifying and incorporating with itself, existing modes of acting and thinking . . . It develops . . . in giving them a meaning, in throwing off from itself what is utterly heterogeneous in them".

[4] *Ibid.*, p.39: "It may be interrupted, retarded, mutilated, distorted, by external violence . . . coloured by the received tone of thought into which it comes, or depraved by the intrusion of foreign principles".

[5] Newman agrees with Guizot that Christianity came to the world "as an idea rather than an institution, and had to furnish itself with weapons of its own manufacture, forge itself methods and means for its own well-being and warfare" (*Ibid.*, p.77). See also pp.37-39, *passim*.

co-operate in setting up the living structure of the idea in its doctrinal, institutional and practical aspects. At its origin, the idea
may be sound and vigorous, or feeble and sickly; it is tempered
and proved in the heat of conflict. The greater its power, the more
freely it unfolds itself. The more formidable the obstacles, the
more clearly it reveals its persisting identity by carving its own
way, coherent and consistent, through the thoughts which beset
it. As it grows, it becomes increasingly itself. Doubtless, it runs the
risk of alteration and deterioration, but this is inherent in life on
the earth.[1] There is no development exempt from danger.

Typical forms of development

We have just seen how Newman describes the general process
of the development of ideas in their social context. It is extremely
complicated, being a dialectical movement of synthesis and antithesis, originating in the free play of thought in the individual
and the community, influenced by the relations between the new
idea and those already current in the environment, and by the
practical necessity of its embodiment in a particular place and
time by the creation of a moral code and a juridical organisation.
The whole community takes part in this process; but this does not
exclude the preponderance of any one individual. In view of such
a variety of causes and influences, it is understandable that a
reality so many-sided and subject to chance events may take on
all kinds of forms. In fact, there are certain typical forms of
development which appear according as the dominant factor is
the community or the individual, the cultured few or the mass,
the unconscious maturing of thought or deliberate reflection, political circumstance, moral necessity, or logical coherence. Newman does not enter on a detailed and systematic analysis of all
the possibilities, but limits himself to five types, which we shall
now describe.

He begins by ruling out any kind of mathematical development,
on the ground that it follows by strict demonstration, and so lacks
any element of chance. He considers it not to be development

[1] *Essay.*, pp.40, 188-189. In the tenth lecture on Anglican difficulties
("The Differences between Catholics no Objection to the Unity of the
Church"), the same general ideas appear again, viz., all these conflicts and
disorders only go to show the profound unity of the Church, since, through
these precisely, it attains to balance and cohesion—"Her trials are her
proof" (*Diff. Angl.*, I, p 313).

in the proper sense, but "simple evolution".[1] This strictness in his use of terms shows that he viewed development as a psychological event, and not a logical operation. For him, the word "development" always indicated the fortuitous and complex reality of concrete thought, influenced, as it is, by all kinds of unforeseeable factors.

The first type of development in the strict sense is called by Newman "political", because influenced, chiefly, by external and social happenings. It is seen, especially, in connection with ideas and theories about society itself, its form of government, its different classes and interests. So it was that, in the twelve-year struggle between Charles I and Parliament, it gradually became clear that the general good required some limitation of the royal power. Being influenced by the chance of events, political developments are often highly capricious. "They are influenced by the character of sovereigns, the rise and fall of statesmen, the fate of battles, and the numberless casualties of the world. Perhaps the Greeks would be still involved in the heresy of the Monophysites, says Gibbon, if the Emperor's horse had not fortunately stumbled".[2]

It may be that the idea itself brings the events in its train. In other cases, the doctrine is formulated subsequently, after the logic of events has been analysed. The fact that a development pertains to the political order by no means implies that it has no logical connection with any leading ideas prior to it, but indicates that external events are mainly responsible for the unfolding and acceptance of certain of its consequences.[3]

Development is said to be "logical" when pure reason, conscious and logical thought, is the main influence at work. A given doctrine may be worked out to its final consequences in a closed environment, a school of philosophy for example, normally liable to be affected by certain controversies or other factors, and then accepted, without much difficulty, by the whole community.[4]

"Historical" development is the kind that results in decisions bearing on facts, persons or events, for example the canonization of saints or the formation of the canon of Scripture. As a rule,

[1] *Essay*, p.41.
[2] *Ibid.*, p.43-44.
[3] The preceding paragraph on political development is a summary of *Essay*, pp.42-45.
[4] *Ibid.*, pp.45-46.

such decisions are the outcome of a long process of growth, during which a particular view emerges from a mass of signs, indications and testimonies, to spread and take root in the mind of the community. In these cases, the chief factor is the collective judgment.[1]

"Moral" development is governed principally by a basic attitude to life that is directed by moral considerations. It originates in certain needs and principles within ourselves which we come to realise as a result of our moral disposition and formation. In this way, a set of observances, based on the knowledge of the Object of religion, may come to spread within a society and, on the other hand, the knowledge of God, as we have already seen, may itself result from a moral and emotional experience. Some of our ideas about the nature of God are due to inner experiences, but, at the same time, what we think of God determines, ultimately, the nature of our religious practice.[2]

Finally, there is that mode of development that Newman calls "metaphysical", described in the fifteenth Oxford sermon. It consists in a growing awareness, brought about by analysis and reflection, of all the riches inherent in a concrete idea.[3] It is characterised, therefore, by the fact of an intuition of reality; and so is different from a purely logical analysis, being distinguished from it as the result of a process of implicit reasoning, of the kind we have already described. Yet this same knowledge of the concrete, this implicit reasoning are, obviously, present in other forms of development, moral development for instance. This shows how difficult it is to draw exact distinctions in psychology. Moral development is partly metaphysical, but metaphysical development is not necessarily moral; and so a distinction is necessary.

These different kinds of development combine to form a single social development. They are not absolutely distinct in kind; they differ, rather, according to the influence which predominates in each. They all form one powerful movement which unfolds the aspects and the practical and theoretical consequences of a living idea. This process, therefore, taken as a whole, cannot be reduced to the simple analysis of an idea. Doubtless, it all hinges on the central intuition : in the case of Christianity, on that of the

---

[1] *Essay.*, pp.46-47.
[2] *Ibid.*, pp.47-52.
[3] *Ibid.*, pp.52-53.

Incarnation; but the relation is only a general one and, at times, remote, the matter having so many different aspects. Take the case of Christianity; we find in it not only a fundamental doctrine concerning divine reality but also the whole practical organisation of the Church. Sometimes, we are engaged in establishing facts or estimating their value, at other times in determining a moral or religious line of conduct. Influences of all kinds come to bear on it, events and personalities, evidence, conscious thought and unconscious growth, moral dispositions and principles of every order—in short, all the factors at work in history.

Section B

Doctrine in the Church

The general theory applied to the doctrine of the Church

The descriptions given in the preceding chapter have been taken from the *Essay*, where they are used to explain the development of doctrine. It would, therefore, be superfluous to show their application to it in detail. Christianity is the expansion of what has been revealed. At the beginning, it was an idea rather than an institution.[1] Though the Church, from the outset, exercised its functions, their structure only gradually achieved finality. Thus the dogmatic principle produced certain effects in the Church before the Councils and the Pope, the guardians and instruments of that principle, had found their place and their true function within the movement and organisation of the Christian community.[2] In a broad sense, it may be said that Christianity at first spread among the lower classes, and as a form of worship. Next, it conquered the higher levels of the Empire, and raised up a theology there. It finished by taking its place among the rulers, and so was led to set up an ecclesiastical polity with its centre in

---

[1] See above, note 4, p.175.

[2] *Essay*, p.360: "Councils and popes are the guardians and instruments of the dogmatic principle; they are not that principle themselves . . . the principle might act even before they had their legitimate place, and exercised a recognized power".

Rome.[1] The actual, living Church is, therefore, the expression of an animating idea which created its own structure. This idea is what determines its outward behaviour; and the consistency of its visible conduct, its essential continuity down the centuries, constitutes, precisely, the first and chief criterion of the identity of its doctrine persisting throughout its development. Its conduct was, equally from the outset, inspired and directed by the unconscious and profound principles in which its supernatural personality found expression;[2] the second criterion, therefore, is the abiding influence of these same principles.[3] Newman's account of the life of doctrine in the Church is a striking illustration of his psychological standpoint, which envisages the whole reality.

Particular aspects of the doctrinal tradition in the Church.

Though the tradition of the Catholic faith develops on the same lines as ideas of the natural order, it still has certain characteristics of its own. These derive from the circumstance that the faith is a product, not of any natural experience, but of a revelation; and, in addition, the gradual growth of its understanding in the minds of believers is governed by the action of the Holy Spirit.[4] Consequently, the course of its development is affected by a new set of factors, which penetrate, direct, lead and elevate the natural forces of development in such a way as to modify, in some degree, its whole tenor. These new factors are the following :

(1) *Dogmatic authority:* This is the most important of them all. Christianity is a revealed religion, and as such, addresses all mankind. Its governing principle, then, is not the conscience everyone possesses by nature, but an external authority.[5] This authority resides, primarily, in Scripture, the principal source of Revelation. Since, however, Christianity rests upon the principle of authority,

---

[1] Preface to *Via Media*, 3rd ed., p.xli: "Although Christianity exercised substantially these three functions from the beginning, their full development, one after the other, was the work of centuries. Christianity was seen first as a cult introduced into the world and spread among the lowest classes of society. Next, it took possession of the intellectual and cultivated, raising up a theology and schools of learning. Finally, it took its place among the princes as an ecclesiastical polity, and chose Rome as its centre".

[2] See above pp.128-130.

[3] These two criteria will be treated in greater detail below.

[4] See above, p.128.

[5] *Essay*, p.86.

it goes without saying that this principle must govern, and be the warrant for, its entire development. Besides this, as we shall see later, Christianity—considered not as a supernatural religion, but simply one of authority—is seen to be precisely what is needed in the world, for the perfecting of natural religion. For, in the world as it is, no genuine form of religious life can have any stability if its only basis is the purely internal one of the individual conscience. Conscience itself, by its very condition, requires a divine authority over it. Now, the central authority of the Church affirms its own infallibility and its special guidance by the Holy Spirit.[1] Its function is to guard the process of development from the dangers of deformation and deterioration to which it is, of its very nature, exposed. Doubtless, infallibility pertains to the Church as a whole, because we can conclude that, if the feeling of the faithful is unanimous, or a doctrine is universally taught, an infallible judgment has been formed within the Church. But the "teaching Church" alone has the power to pronounce a final and unchangeable judgment, settle the bearing of tradition, and give it permanent form by a definition of dogma.[2] The existence in the living Church of an infallible authority as its governing principle and guarantee of truth is bound to give a special character to the development of its doctrine.

So it is that doctrinal thought, as it develops, passes, by the agency of infallible authority, from a subjective condition to an objective rule, which is universal and immutable.[3] The intervention of the *magisterium* concludes a period of ripening, in the course of which the apostolic tradition is shown forth, in various ways, in the consciousness of the Church, sometimes by the utterance of bishops, sometimes by that of doctors or by the voice of the people, but also by the liturgy, ritual, customs, even, too, by movements and happenings of all kinds—in short, by all that

[1] See below, p.233.

[2] *Uber das Zeugnis der Laien*, pp. 210, 206: "The agreement of the faithful is for us a 'pointer', nay an 'instrument', of this Church which is infallible . . . But I grant, at the same time, that the gift of judgment, discrimination, definition, proclamation, injunction, regarding any element whatever of tradition pertains exclusively to the teaching Church alone". In *Diff. Angl.*, I, p.218, Newman views doctrine as developed by the "infallible working of the entire body". See also *Ibid.*, II, p.314.

[3] *Newman-Peronne*, p.415.

13

goes to form history.[1] We have already seen how Newman, through his experience within the Church and his struggle with ultramontanism, came to examine more closely the doctrinal consequences of social institutions and of political attitudes in the Church. The method is characteristic of his genius, for he was concerned to define, as clearly as possible, the actual structure and processes by which the Church expresses herself as a "whole". The frankly controversial attitude he adopted, with admirable courage, gave him the opportunity to sketch, not only the actual life of the Church, but also some features of her ideal state. These reflections of his are a fitting completion of his psychological description of the development process.

(2) *Heresy:* Heresy is an important factor in the working-out of Christian doctrine. We have already noticed its psychological roots and its "ethos";[2] so we confine ourselves here to examining its role in the Church. Heresy, which is an adulteration of the Gospel, is inevitable, considering the nature of man.[3] The danger of heresy arises from the abstract character of human knowledge. The risks attendant on abstraction have been pointed out previously,[4] and they become greater still when it is a question of expressing in abstract terms the profound and mysterious realities which are the life and soul of Christianity. It is, no doubt, the case that the experience of faith—intuition of reality—together with certain intellectual qualities such as the "philosophic sense", described by Newman in the *Idea,* help to counteract the dangers of abstract reason. But there will always be men, deficient in personal religion, who yet reason about religion, while men of common sense and a philosophic sense are not often found.[5]

---

[1] *Uber das Zeugnis der Laien*, p.206: "I am justified, I think, in saying that the apostolic tradition is expressed at different times in various ways: sometimes by the mouth of Bishops, sometimes by Doctors, the faithful, the liturgy, rites, ceremonies and customs, but also by events, conflicts, movements, and all the other phenomena to which we give the collective name of history".

[2] See above, pp.166-169.

[3] *Diff. Angl.,* I, p.348: "It lies, for what we know, and to all appearance, in the very constitution of the human mind; corruptions of the Gospel being as necessary and ordinary a phenomenon, taking men as they are, as its rejection".

[4] See above, pp.113-114.

[5] See the letter to Pusey in *Diff. Angl.,* I, pp.81-82: "Theology is concerned with supernatural realities, and it invariably issues in mysteries that reason

Together with the theological instinct, heresy makes the greatest contribution to the development of tradition.[1] Without it, many of the dogmas that have been defined in the course of centuries would have remained implicit.

If we want to give an example of the actual method by which the subjective Word, living in the Church, becomes objectively and unchangeably valid, we need only to observe the ordinary conduct of the Church, from the outset of a heresy till the pontifical anathema. No sooner does a heterodox teacher put forward some heretical thesis than the Bishops feel ill at ease. The answer needed is not clearly evident to them. Their internal experience of the subjective Word leads them to detest and reject the opinion, but they are wanting in arguments to refute it. They refer to dogmas already defined, go through Scripture, consult the Fathers, and hastily seize any defensive weapon they chance to discover. In the meantime, those who are virtually apostate, hidden from one another, become aware of their unity; they seek out one another, assemble in groups, form a party. A few of the faithful join the heretical camp; others are hesitant; some, through ignorance are seduced for a time. The struggle is hard. But soon appeal is made to Peter; his decision is urgently requested; a Council assembles. The matter is discussed calmly, a number of opinions is expressed, the problems are considered in all their aspects. Bit by bit, by means of conciliation or elimination, all differences on doctrine between the Fathers of the Council disappear. Dogmas already defined are examined with care, slowly, attentively. All this complex activity of minds is like a fertile soil, in which, gradually, the apostolic definition germinates and grows, till, under the secret impulse of the divine Spirit, at the end of a

can neither explain nor reduce to its own measure . . . But logic stumbles forward as well as it can, though thick darkness. The Arians advanced, taking logic as their guide, and so they forfeited truth. With St Augustine, however, common sense and a wide view of the truth corrected logic. So we reach the final conclusion of the whole matter, for common sense and a panoramic view of the truth are very rare gifts, while all men are obliged to holiness, and most of them try their hand at argument and reasoning".

[1] In the *Essay*, Newman indicates as causes of development, "the investigations of faith and the attacks of heresy" (p.68).

road that bristles with difficulties, the new dogma makes its entry into the world.[1]

The role of heresy in the Church does not consist solely in causing itself to be rejected. Sometimes, it is the premature form of a development justified later on. The thought of the Church unfolds slowly; in it is involved the whole life of the community. Heresy, however, prefers to take a short cut, it walks alone, in isolation from the Church. What it takes as decisive is not the authority of the Church, but the personal prestige of the heresiarch. So it is that its statements often contain much that is true, but expressed in an exaggerated manner and prematurely, and so impairing the fullness of the faith. Heresies, therefore, often point out the direction to be followed by theology. The thought of the Church, as it makes its way slowly, reaches only at a later date the point which, here and now, heresy annexes to itself, without awaiting the time of ripeness.[2]

(3) *The faithful:* Of their own accord, the faithful revolt against heresy; they might be said to be guided by an instinct given them by the Holy Ghost.[3] Between the Councils of Nicaea (325) and of Constantinople (381), when the episcopate was hopelessly divided, and in great part conquered by heresy, the faith of the people remained generally unshakeable, and caused the triumph of orthodoxy.[4] The unanimous testimony of the faithful, in matters of faith, may, therefore, be considered a sign that an infallible

---

[1] *Newman-Perrone*, pp.416-417.

[2] *Ibid.*, p.420. See also *Apologia*, pp.231-232, and *Essay*, pp.362-365: "Heresies in every age may be taken as the measure of the existing state of thought in the Church, and of the movement of her theology; they determine in what way the current is setting, and the rate at which it flows".

[3] In "On Consulting the Faithful, etc.", Newman distinguishes five ways in which theologians express the relation of the testimony of the faithful to the fixing of tradition. The second, which he ascribes to Moehler, is as follows: "A kind of instinct or *phronema* (a state of mind, a mentality) in the inmost being of the mystical body of Christ". The last is a "feeling of hostility to error, seen from the outset as a scandal" (p.215). On the latter, he refers the reader to *Diff. Angl.*, I, Lecture 2.

[4] This historical thesis is amply proved in the article cited above, which is printed, in the edition of Newman's works published by Longmans, Green and Co., as an appendix to the *Arians*. The same thesis recurs in *Tracts Theological and Ecclesiastical* as an essay of 1872, called "Causes of the Rise and Successes of Arianism".

judgment is in the course of formation within the Church.[1] This
applies particularly in the case of those articles of faith which foster
the life of religion and "speak" to the senses. The Church, then,
in its doctrinal decisions, will normally take into consideration the
laity, as a *locus theologicus*.[2]

Yet ecclesiastical authority must be constantly on the watch to
restrain the excesses and deviations of popular devotion. The
nature of man is such that the grossness of the masses, the blindness and violence of their passions, their infatuations, inevitably
incline them to illuminism and superstition.[3] Theology, certainly,
is a counterpoise, but it is not sufficient. Popular devotion will
always transgress the limits allowed by dogma;[4] that is the very
law of its life. The Church has to be vigilant in its regard, just as
she has to guard against the deviations of reason. She may even
appear too severe in her attempts to strangle every dangerous tendency at birth. Newman prefers the Church to be tolerant in the
beginning, to give full liberty to the spontaneous flow of ideas,
before prosecuting abuses.[5]

(4) *Theology* : Doctrinal developments seemed to Newman to be
caused mainly by the theological instinct, that loving curiosity

[1] See above, p.180-181.

[2] *Uber das Zeugnis der Laien*, p.237: "In most cases where a definition is
considered, the testimony of the laity is important; but, if there was ever a
case where it was a duty to consult them, it was when it was a question of
doctrines directly related to the sentiment and devotion of the faithful".

[3] *Via Media*, I,p.40, note of 1877: "Truths as potent as those of Catholicism
are certainly liable to the danger of exciting, in the ignorant, the weak, or
the carnal-minded, a fanaticism or superstition whose correction requires
and effectively provokes the constant vigilance of the Church". A detailed
exposition of this may be found in *Diff. Angl.*, II, pp.77-88.

[4] *Diff. Angl.*, II, p.81: "The religion of the multitude is ever vulgar and
abnormal; it ever will be tinctured with fanaticism and superstition, while
men are what they are. Nor is it any safeguard against these excesses in a
religious system that the religion is based upon reason, and develops into a
theology. Theology both uses logic and baffles it". Cf. *Grammar*, pp.120-121,
where Newman describes the protective function of theology with regard to
religious sensibility.

[5] *Diff. Angl.*, II, p.79: "Life in this world is motion, and involves a
continual process of change. No rule of art will suffice to stop the operation
of this natural law, whether in the material world or in the human mind.
Life has the same right to decay as it has to wax strong. This is especially
the case with great ideas. You may stifle them; or you may refuse them
elbow-room; or again you may torment them with your continual meddling.
For myself, I prefer much wherever it is possible to be first generous and then
just; to grant full liberty of thought, and to call to account when abused".

which prompts men to analyse and study the faith in a spirit of due reverence.[1] A science of theology that expresses and systematises in rational terms the content of faith is possible; that is a fundamental and characteristic principle of Christianity.[2]

Newman, as a Catholic, held theology to be a broad and free application of one's own personal thought to the faith. A number of schools came into being, differing in their point of view and methods.[3] There is, in theology, besides a kernel of revealed and certain truth, a wide expanse of free thought which has nothing in it of finality.[4] Theology, like science, advances precisely by taking note of its basic uncertainties. The Catholic theologian may excercise his mind freely on all that authority has not yet defined as forming part of the *depositum*.[5] The supreme *magisterium* does not keep watch on all that he writes; on the contrary, it leaves the field open to controversies. A particular thesis may be discussed for a long time, in specialist circles such as universities, before Rome decides to speak. The matter is later brought before lesser authorities than the pope and, generally, the point in dispute is practically resolved by the theologians before Rome intervenes to close the debate. The Church, then, acts in a way favourable to liberty and even encourages the enterprise of the individual theologian or apologist.[6]

[1] Cf. *O.U.S.*, pp. 313, 317-318, 329; *Essay*, p.337.

[2] *Essay*, pp.325, 336-337: "This constant tradition and habit in the Church of scientific analysis is an ecclesiastical principle rather than a note of any kind, and it is hardly known outside Christianity".

[3] *Newman-Peronne*, p.411.

[4] *Grammar*, pp.236-240: "Such on the whole is the analogy between our knowledge of matters of this world and matters of the world unseen: indefectible certitude in primary truths, manifold variations of opinion in their application and disposition" (p.240). See also *Via Media*, I, p.91, note of 1877.

[5] "What then you say of mechanical science I say emphatically of theology, viz., that it makes progress by being always alive to its own fundamental uncertainties. We may allowably argue, and do argue, against everything but what has been ruled to be Apostolic" (letter to W. Froude of 1879, cited in Ward, *op. cit.*, II, p.591).

[6] *Apologia*, pp.237-238, gives a vivid description which concludes as follows: "It is manifest how a mode of proceeding, such as this, tends not only to the liberty, but to the courage, of the individual theologian or controversialist. Many a man has ideas, which he hopes are true, and useful for his day, but he wishes to have them discussed . . . He would not dare to do this, if he knew that an authority which was supreme and final was watching at every word he said, and made signs of assent or dissent to each sentence as he uttered it".

Theological speculation, bold and untramelled yet ever liable to correction by infallible authority, is not merely permitted, it is indispensable to the life of religion as manifested in the actual circumstances of history. The Catholic Church is like an arena where the interplay of authority and reason never ceases. The keenness of the latter is not blunted, but accentuated, and the Church, for her part, finds her doctrine and life brought to full flowering by the action of reason. So the expression of the faith owes its growth to the constant interaction of study and authority.[1] Reason supplies the initial impulse, and executes the task; the infallible *magisterium* intervenes only to restrain and guide its impetuosity. The great geniuses of Christian thought are not to be found in high places of the Roman hierarchy. In the councils, it was often clerics of the lower ranks whose role was predominant (Athanasius at Nicaea, Salmeron at Trent). The divine gift of infallibility is not under the dominance of reason; but in the course of the investigation which precedes its exercise, the primacy, on the whole, falls to the reason and genius of the individual thinker.[2]

All this must not blind us to the defects of reason. We have already seen, in speaking of heresy, how history shows that the unbridled use of reason invariably leads away from doctrinal truth. Were it subject exclusively to the free exercise of reason, Christian thought would be doomed to irreparable division, issuing, finally, in the break-up of all dogma and principle. Newman sees in this

---

[1] *Apologia.*, pp.225-226, 236: "The energy of the human intellect 'does from opposition grow'; and is never so much itself as when it has been lately overthrown . . . It is the vast Catholic body itself, and it only, which forms an arena for both combatants in that awful, never-dying duel. It is necessary for the very life of religion, viewed in its large operations and its history, that the warfare should be incessantly carried on".

[2] *Ibid.*, p.236: "It is individuals, not the Holy See, who have taken the initiative and given the lead to Catholic minds, in theological inquiry. Indeed, it is one of the reproaches urged against the Church of Rome that it has originated nothing, and has only served as a sort of *remora* or brake in the development of doctrine. And it is an objection which I embrace as a truth; for such I conceive to be the main purpose of its extraordinary gift. Ecumenical councils . . . have been guided in their decisions by the commanding genius of individuals, sometimes young and of inferior rank. Not that uninspired intellect overruled the superhuman gift which was committed to the council; . . . but that, in that process of inquiry and deliberation which ended in an infallible enunciation, individual reason was paramount".

fact the strongest proof of the need for an infallible authority.[1]
(5) *Ecclesiastical government:* This plays a most important part
in the development of doctrine. Already in the *Essay*, Newman's
keen interest in "political" development appears. In his preface to
the new edition of the *Via Media*, he showed it at work in the
actual structure of the Church. The Church, in fact, has three
principal functions, theological, religious and administrative; and
their guiding principles, respectively, are truth, piety and practical
usefulness. Reason is the instrument of theology, worship makes
use of that which appeals to the senses, command and coercion
are the means employed by administration. Each of these functions has its peculiar danger; that of the first is rationalism, of the
second superstition, of the third despotism.[2] They may impinge
on one another, and one may even flagrantly violate the territory
of another. For example, the administrative may, in arbitrary
fashion, interfere in the rational progress of theology, in virtue of
the principle that no action that is obviously essential to the
Church's unity, holiness and peace can ever be theologically
erroneous.[3]

The application of this principle demands a high degree of
prudence and insight. It has sometimes been mistakenly applied,
as by Popes Liberius and Honorius;[4] but, in other cases, it has
produced excellent results. It obliged Leo IX to tone down his
judgment on simoniacal ordinations.[5] It settled the controversy on
the validity of heretical ordinations in the fourth century, and
those of the schismatic Donatists in the fifth. In the latter case,

[1] This idea is constantly recurring in Newman. We have already alluded
to it in connection with heresy. "I know that even the unaided reason,
when correctly exercised, leads to a belief in God, in the immortality of the
soul, and in future retribution; but I am considering it actually and historically; and in this point of view I do not think I am wrong in saying that its
tendency is towards a simple unbelief in matters of religion". *Apologia*, p.219.

[2] *Via Media*, I, p.xli: "Truth is the guiding principle of theology and its
investigations; piety and edification, that of worship; utility and suitability
does the same for government. The instrument of theology is reasoning; that
of worship, our sensibility; that of government, command and coercion.
Furthermore, for man as he is, reasoning tends to rationalism, piety to
superstition and fanaticism, power to ambition and tyranny".

[3] Newman expresses it thus: "No act can be, from the theological standpoint, an error, if it is absolutely and undeniably necessary to the unity, the
holiness and the peace of the Church" (*Via Media*, I, p.lxxxiii).

[4] *Ibid.*, p.lxxxiii.

[5] *Ibid.*, p.lxxxv.

Rome and St Augustine were obliged, under the pressure of the facts, to abandon their own views in favour of those of the majority of the African bishops.[1] It was decisive, too, in the long dispute, lasting from the third century to the fifth, on the validity of heretical Baptism.[2] In the same way, new needs, born of a slackening in the spiritual life, brought about successive mitigations of the penitential discipline, contributed to clarify the distinction between the precepts and counsels of the Gospel, between mortal and venial sins, and between the internal and external forum. Later still, the weakening of primitive fervour had, as an indirect result, the development of the doctrine of Purgatory and the institution of monasticism.[3]

From all this Newman draws the conclusion that the needs of the Church are, on occasion, more effective than theology to prepare the way to the exact formulation of doctrine; and that greater certainty is obtained by this means. This results from the very nature of the ecclesiastical institution. The Church's progress would be frequently retarded, if practical needs were never allowed to decide a speculative problem. Divine Providence is a sufficient guarantee that the logic of facts—even against the apparent evidence of the other factors at work—issues in the truth, even in regard to matters properly belonging to ethics and theology.[4] Obviously, this does not imply that practical necessity gives rise to propositions which could be inserted, in defiance of logic, like floating bodies, into the systematic structure of Catholic doctrine. The fact is that such needs bring to light principles hitherto unperceived which temper the application of other acknowledged principles and so prevent the working of the system from being too rigid and uniform.

(6) *The diversity of nations:* In the *Apologia*, Newman mentions

[1] *Via Media.*, p.lxxxvii.

[2] *Ibid.*, pp.lxxxvii-lxxxix.

[3] *Ibid.*, pp.xci-xciii.

[4] *Ibid.*, p.lxxxvi: "In this case, God willed that a problem of theology should be resolved—in a manner appropriate to the catholicity of the Church and the edification of the faithful—by the logic of facts; it happens, in fact, that this prevails over all laws and positive prerogatives, and that its efficacity extends to the very frontiers of immutable truth, in the religious, moral and theological sphere"; "This shows us once more the theological schools yielding to ecclesiastical suitability; in this case, too, the needs of peace and unity lead more surely to conclusions of doctrine than more directly theological methods" (*Ibid.*, p.lxxxvii). Cf., also, p.lxxxix.

one more factor at work in the development of doctrine, namely, the difference between nations in their mentality, their mode of reasoning, their gifts and virtues, all of which are taken up into the Church and used in the work of sanctification. In his view, the loss of the Anglo-Saxon and Germanic elements gravely impaired the resources of the Church. The multiplicity of nations and of their particular traditions protects the rulers of the Church from narrowness of mind and arrogance in connection with dogmatic "directives"; they are to be looked upon as a providential counterpoise to the eventual and natural influence of Italy on the See of Peter. So we are led to envisage the ideal of a future theology: it would not be all the reflection of a single mentality but, bearing the imprint of the spirit of various nationalities, it would come to form a part, in some degree, of the living thought of each national culture. That would be, Newman considered, of the utmost benefit to the Church.[1]

These opinions of his are obviously in accord with his persevering attempt to adapt, as far as he could, the Roman Church to the English mind. His efforts were directed chiefly to making the outward forms of devotion more congenial to English tastes. The faith is the same for all, but the piety of each varies according to his personal and national characteristics. Some devotions do not appeal equally to all persons and nations. Newman's aim led to disagreements with Father Faber, a highly gifted and attractive character, whose ardour impelled him to let loose on the Catholics of England a flood of pious manuals and edifying stories more suitable to the simpler dwellers by the Mediterranean sea.[2]

---

[1] See *Apologia*, pp.238-239: "The multitude of the nations who are in the fold of the Church will be found to have acted for its protection against any narrowness, if so, in the various authorities at Rome, with whom lies the practical decision of controverted questions . . . Then again, such national influences have a providential effect in moderating the bias which the local influences of Italy may exert upon the See of St Peter . . . Assuredly I think that the loss of the English, not to say the German, element, in its composition, has been a most serious evil. And certainly, if there is one consideration more than another which should make us English grateful to Pius IX, it is that, by giving us a Church of our own, he has prepared the way for our own habits of mind, our own manner of reasoning, our own tastes, and our own virtues, finding a place, and thereby a sanctification, in the Catholic Church".

[2] Ward, *op. cit.*, I, pp.211-212.

CONCLUSION

We have given a succinct, but accurate, account of Newman's views on the various forces affecting the development of the Church's tradition. These ideas of his are not to be found set forth systematically in a single work, but occur in different passages of his writings, each of which is complementary to the others. We have now to attempt to penetrate to the interior of that single idea of his that informs such a variety of works, each dealing with its own problem, each having its own particular mentality and standpoint. Where must we look for this centre of gravity, and how reconcile affirmations that seem incompatible? At one moment, theology appears to be governed by a slow and infallible process of reflection which, after a lapse of time, submits to the *magisterium* its solution of problems. At the next, Newman looks on this process with misgiving, as if beset with the peril of rationalism, from which it can be saved only by the intervention of an infallible teaching authority. Sometimes, he exalts the faith of the masses as guided by an almost infallible instinct of supernatural discernment. In other places, the multitude is a source of perilous superstition, requiring the perpetual vigilance of the Church. But, if that is the case, how does God guide his Church and preserve it from error? This is the question that has to be examined from every angle. Doubtless, the faithful as a body possess an infallible instinct of orthodoxy; but its action, as described by Newman, is mainly negative, that of causing their spontaneous reaction against doctrinal innovation. This instinct is far from being "progressive"; it is, in fact, ultra-conservative, and quite unsuited to the creation of formularies hitherto unknown. The ordinary Christian perceives concrete reality by means of images of his own creation, but he lacks the ability to criticize them. But, as we know, the experience of reality tends to be enclosed in a narrow range of familiar and accepted ideas, and if the imagination, emotionally affected, is not restrained by reason, it easily degenerates into superstition.

As to theology, it is the supreme instrument of development; for, in clarifying the faith, it makes use of reason, which is the source of advance in knowledge. True theology, which is animated by a profound intuition of faith, reaches slowly, but with certainty, the precise solution of doctrinal problems by means of the devious processes of the intellect. Even it, however, is not infallible. Its method is human and very imperfect, leading at times to the use of expressions which, if not erroneous, are ambiguous or only partially true. The Monophysites, it may be recalled, pressed into their service formulas that originated in the greatest and holiest of the Alexandrine Fathers.

Besides, the true theologian is somewhat rare. There are many who apply themselves to theology, without having that supernatural reasonableness, that intense contemplative gift, that wide sweep of the mind characteristic of, among others, St Augustine. When we look at theology from a historical point of view, and see it as it actually exists in the Church, we are bound to admit that it embraces a number of contradictory trends, and is ever producing more or less rationalistic tenets that lead in the direction of heresy.

It may be said that theological disputes of themselves bring about the eventual triumph of orthodoxy. *A priori,* that is not so likely as might be thought. No doubt, an orthodox party is gradually formed, and works out the true solution of the questions in dispute : but how can its strange and subtle reasoning, which with the greatest difficulty clears a way towards a mystery which is accessible to the "interior" vision alone, how can it prevail over the reason of the "natural man", judging on the basis of ordinary evidence accessible to all? We may well wonder how this solution could come to be accepted by the Church as a whole. For if theology is allowed to pursue its course unbridled, the result will be irreparable divisions and schisms without end.

Besides, what kind of certitude may we expect from theology? Its principal sources are the Scriptures, the Fathers and reason.

> But history and the patristical writings do not absolutely decide the truth or falsehood of all important theological propositions, any more than Scripture decides it. As to such propositions, all that one can safely say is that history and the Fathers look in one determinate direction. They make a doctrine more or less probable, but rarely contain a statement, or suggest a conclusion, which cannot be plausibly

evaded. The definition of the Church is commonly needed to supply the defects of logic.[1]

This applies equally to the other conclusions drawn by reason from the Scriptures and the Fathers.[2] Does this mean that theology offers no guarantee of certitude? To answer this question, we must recall the distinction between implicit and explicit reasoning. Theology advances in virtue of implicit reasoning, which is sustained by a living communion with supernatural reality, and cannot be adequately expressed in formal propositions and proofs. Consequently, it can never compel assent in a purely objective manner.

Every theologian arrives at his personal convictions and certainties as a result of his reflection on his own living thought; but if we view the logical process from the outside only—abstracting, that is, from the personal element the intuition of faith and the synthetic judgment of the illative sense—we seldom meet with a strictly conclusive proof. However convincing the evidence may be for the true theologian with his wide intuitive view, it cannot be presented as such in a purely rational demonstration. This is the interpretation implied by Newman's whole theory of knowledge.

The role, therefore, of ecclesiastical authority is to compensate, as regards the general public, the defects of logic. The infallible authority is a guarantee that is simple, evident to all, designed to buttress reason, as it were, in the external sphere, where reason is incapable of giving any kind of absolute assurance. It acts infallibly in this sphere, since the Holy Ghost has endowed it for the purpose with a special *charism*. It raises a theological conclusion to the rank of a certain truth whose acceptance is of universal obligation. In this way, it is restricted to ratifying the conclusions of genuine theology and, to that extent, is dependent on it. It is not an instrument of investigation and discovery but, in virtue of its own divine authority, it sets a seal on tradition. Yet this seal is not a simple declaration of authenticity which certifies the value of a proposition which, in its completed state, falls into the hands of the teaching authority. The latter, in fact, puts the finishing touch on the process of development by eliminating the final and, as it

---

[1] *Via Media*, I, p.38 (note of 1877). Cf., also, *Diff. Angl.*, II, pp.311-315 for a fuller development of this idea.

[2] *Ibid.*, II, pp.303-304, 314.

were, extrinsic uncertainty which remains with every theological product so long as it has reason alone to defend and warrant it. This uncertainty needs to be removed so that the outcome of the reflection of the faithful may form the firm and unquestioned basis of a great society founded on the faith. Since authority thus completes the development, the new doctrinal propositions become true objects of faith : "In all cases there is a margin left for the exercise of faith in the word of the Church. . . . It is the Church's dogmatic use of history in which the Catholic believes. . . . The immediate motive in the mind of a Catholic for his reception of doctrines is not that they are proved to him by reason or by history, but because Revelation has declared them by means of the high ecclesiastical *Magisterium* which is their legitimate exponent".[1]

On this question, it is evident that Newman's thought is extremely complex and subtle. To avoid misunderstanding it we must, more than ever, take his whole philosophy into account. All the ordinary factors of history contribute to the development of the Christian tradition, but the supreme direction and the final judgment belong to authority alone. The instinct of the faithful is infallible in matters of faith, but its action is negative and defensive; and, besides, the Church has to intervene repeatedly to prevent the rank growth of superstition to which human nature is always prone, regenerated, it may be, in principle, but not in its whole range of action. The Spirit of God guides theology, giving it its own certitude and cohesion. But theology cannot provide its conclusions with the evidence and solidity indispensable for their open and universal acceptance in the Church; and, in addition, as far as theology in general is concerned, authority has to intervene repeatedly to restrain rationalistic trends which are a constant danger to the faith, the tares which are always mixed with the wheat in the fields of God. Authority is thus the fundamental principle controlling the growth of the life of faith. It makes use of theology and popular devotion, but is not involved in them; otherwise, it would be open to the same dangers. It preserves its liberty in regard to the instruments it uses even to the point of superseding them.

Here, then, we have the supreme organ by which the Holy

[1] *Via Media.*, II, pp.312-313.

Ghost carries into effect the promise made by Christ to the Church. The Spirit which guides the Church is active, in varying degrees, both in the community of the faithful and in all orthodox theology, but not in such a way that the collaboration of these two can be a sufficient guarantee of lasting unity of faith in the entire Church alongside the fertile and varied expansion of tradition. Here, as in other spheres, the grace of God acts in a secret and unobtrusive manner. It may foster in a few souls a supernatural force and purity, together with an almost infallible clearsightedness into the faith, but the rest of men remain far below that level. In spite of the persistent working of grace, human nature is ever hostile to supernatural light. Just as healing grace cannot at once remedy the evil tendencies of the heart, so the illuminating grace of faith does not suddenly remove the intellectual prejudices and bias of the ordinary man or the theologian. Consequently, the natural course of historical development, however purified and led by grace, is not the means God chose for keeping tradition unchanged as it developed. Instead, the Holy Ghost has provided the Church with a new organ, an infallible teaching authority. It draws support from theology and the instinct of faith, though independent of theological reasoning and of popular devotion, and is endowed with a special gift of infallibility in its formal pronouncements as to what is the truth. When, therefore, it is said that infallibility is found "in all the members of the Church, but especially in her hierarchy",[1] we may be allowed to interpret the sentence as meaning that infallibility belongs simultaneously both to the community and to the hierarchy, as to a single body, but is exercised fully only by the supreme teaching authority.

Furthermore, since the pronouncements of authority are the result not of a private revelation, of a miracle, still less of an arbitrary decision, but follow on a series of interchanges between the *magisterium,* theologians, and the ordinary faithful—that is to say, the study of what has slowly taken shape within the Church—we must conclude that the events leading up to the definition also participate in infallibility, in as much as they are guided by the Holy Ghost as a preparation for the infallible

[1] *Via Media.*, II, p.314. (The author seems to have misunderstood the passage in question. Newman there speaks of "the legacy of truth, of which the Church, in all her members, but especially in her hierarchy, is the divinely appointed trustee". *Translator's Note.*)

pronouncement, and they provide for it the necessary material. The infallibility of the entire process of both the preparation and the formulation, appears, and its acceptance by the whole Church becomes obligatory, only when authority, making use of its prerogative, issues its solemn declaration. This account of the whole matter is, we believe, the one which best corresponds to Newman's ideas.

PART III

The immutability of faith and doctrine.
The problem of tradition and its continuity.

INTRODUCTION

I N the preceding part of this work, we have studied the way in which doctrines come to be clarified. We have examined the factors, individual and social, by virtue of which tradition springs up in the mind of man, grows and comes to fruition in new dogmas. In so doing, we confined our efforts to describe, to elucidate, and to understand. We now confront a fresh problem : how does the faith remain unchanged in the course of the development of doctrine, and what is the guarantee of its continuing identity?

That it does, in fact, remain the same is a truth of faith. The necessity of this is beyond question, but it brings up the basic problem of Christianity, namely, its historicity. A revealed religion, which claims to be authoritative, presupposes the communication by God of certain truths at a given moment of history and, in addition, the handing down of these truths complete and unchanged in the course of the subsequent centuries. There has been no new revelation in the Church since the time of the Apostles, and she confines herself to the maintenance and teaching of the faith delivered to her. Hence, the problem we are about to treat concerns the very essence of Christianity.

In this third part, therefore, we adopt a new standpoint, one of criticism, for the problem to be resolved is one of apologetics. Though different from the preceding, it yet makes use of the analyses already given.

The problem before us figures very largely in Newman's works. In setting out, shortly before his conversion, to write a book on the development of doctrine, his main object was not to determine the manner in which the Church's tradition grows, but to prove that its growth does not impair the immutability of divine Revelation. As he proceeded, this development, as it actually took place within the Church under the direction of an infallible authority, appeared to him a positive sign of its divine origin. The apologetic significance of development is, therefore, twofold : it is a positive demonstration of the divinity of the Church, and it refutes the accusation of a change in doctrine.

We pointed out, in the introduction, that Newman's theory of the development of doctrine forms part of an apologetic system of a highly personal character and that the arguments he employs represent an apologetic method which constantly recurs throughout his works. It seems, therefore, both useful and necessary to give a preliminary analysis of this method, to set forth its principles and its special character, and to determine its place in apologetics generally, particularly as this has never yet been done in sufficient detail. To the lack of such a study is due the frequent confusion of Newman's ideas with others more or less contemporary, whereas it is their originality that requires to be emphasised.

Chapter 1

GENERAL VIEW OF NEWMAN'S APOLOGETIC

Section A

The Dilemma

NEWMAN'S method is aptly described by Jean Guitton. He speaks of it as a combination of two logical processes, of which one confronts the mind with an unavoidable dilemma, and the other leads it to the discovery that it already contains within itself, though unaware of it, the solution.[1] Newman's starting point is the assertion that there is no middle term between Catholicism and atheism. As an Anglican, he had outlined a *via media* between Catholicism and Protestantism, and he considered the latter logically bound to issue in liberalism and, finally, disbelief. Now this *via media,* by an inherent necessity, leads to Catholicism; and, in consequence, Newman was led to deny the existence of a middle term between Catholicism and irreligion. This view of his already appears in the *Essay on Development;*[2] it is found at the conclusion of his first Catholic publication, a study of Keble's *Lyra Innocentium,* where he states that the principles underlying that poem draw the Anglo-Catholics, in spite of themselves, towards the Church of Rome. If they do not pursue the logical course of their attitude, they run the risk of retrogression; they may even come to deny the religious principles which point to Rome, to fall at length into rationalism and scepticism.[3] This assertion reappears, in one form or another, in

[1] J. Guitton. *op. cit.,* pp.xxvii-xxx.
[2] *Essay,* p.182.
[3] *Ess. Crit. Hist.,* II, pp.448-452.

many of his works.[1] In 1880, Newman defended its true sense and upheld its validity;[2] before finally ceasing to write, he repeated it for the last time in 1887.[3] Ward regards it as his principal thesis, from 1845 till his death.[4]

It is closely bound up with the theory of religious types already examined. There are men whose complete development naturally brings with it a corresponding fullness of inner religious experience. Hence, their intellectual life flows, whether consciously or not, under the direction of religious principles. Others, however, are strangers to such experience, and so their whole intellectual life leads them, gradually and perhaps unknowingly, to a vision of the world from which religion is absent. These two types of thinker develop in their several ways as a result of their principles. Newman was convinced that the first, being animated by principles of religion, is on the way, at least by his essential inclination, his internal dialectic, towards ultimate religious truth, in other words Catholicism. It matters little what religion such a man professes; he may, in fact, remain all his life outside the Church, without ever thinking of being converted to it. He is possibly quite ignorant of Catholicism and incapable, through the prejudices of his surroundings, of making any serious inquiry into it. None the less, his very attitude of mind and the inherent logic of his "ethos" make him already a part of the family of Catholicism, in spirit. Now take a person of the second type : his cast of mind turns him in the opposite direction, since he is wanting in those living principles which are the only possible basis of a true sense of religion. His own "ethos" sets him on the way towards absolute disbelief, even though, through a conscious or unconscious habit of conformity, he remains outwardly faithful to the religion in which he was

---

[1] Here are a few passages: "In the long run, it will be found either that the Catholic Church is, really and effectively, the advent of the invisible world in this, or that there is nothing positive, nothing dogmatic, nothing real, in any of our notions concerning our origins and destiny" (*Disc. M. Cong.*, p.282); "I came to the conclusion that there was no medium, in true philosophy, between atheism and Catholocity, and that a perfectly consistent mind, under those circumstances in which it finds itself here below, must embrace either the one or the other" (*Apologia*, p.186, 190). See also *Diff. Angl.*, I, p.393; Ward, *op. cit.*, p.238; Harper, *op. cit.*, p.80. The most vigorous exposition is to be found in *Disc. M. Cong.*, pp.260-283.

[2] Note added to the last edition of *Grammar*, pp.495-501.

[3] J. Guitton, *op. cit.*, p.xxxvii.

[4] Ward, *op. cit.*, II, p.158.

brought up.[1] Newman held that religion must always be personal to be genuine and must be sustained by personal contact with God, however vague and implicit. This is true, too, of Catholics. Unless their religious education either accompanies or fosters some kind of personal experience of religion, they are already unbelievers, in virtue of their personal "ethos", even if they keep up a merely routine, and therefore lifeless, connection with the Church. On the other hand, the man who, by his fidelity, fosters in his conscience that first living contact with God, becomes, by the actual logic of his personal position, a Catholic *in via,* no matter what religious body he belongs to. This, then, is Newman's dilemma : there exist "two characters of mind and two standards and systems of thought each logical when analysed, yet contradictory of each other, and only not antagonistic because they have no common ground on which they can conflict".[2]

In his day, it did not appear very difficult to acknowledge this dilemma. It was accepted by the great positivists, Thomas Huxley and Auguste Comte, who decided in favour of the atheistic alternative.[3] The important thing, then, was to vindicate the other; and this presupposed two things—a critical justification of the objectivity of religious experience and the drawing out of the logical consequences of the natural sense of religion.

SECTION B

THE JUSTIFICATION OF CONSCIENCE

A. The account given by Newman

Newman's apologetic starts from the knowledge of God given by

---

[1] *Grammar*, p.499: "There is a certain ethical character, one and the same, a system of first principles, sentiments and tastes, a mode of viewing the question and arguing, which is formally and normally, naturally and divinely, the *organum investigandi* given us for gaining religious truth, and which would lead the mind by infallible succession from the rejection of atheism to theism, and from theism to Christianity, and from Christianity to Evangelical Religion, and from these to Catholicity. And again, when a Catholic is seriously wanting in this system of thought, we cannot be surprised if he leaves the Catholic Church, and then in due time gives up religion altogether". In the *Grammar*, Newman shows in detail how one may go through a whole series of conversions with no substantial change of certitudes, whose logical implications are simply brought out. See pp.240-255; 313-314, 377-378.

[2] *Ibid*, pp.311-312.

[3] J. Guitton, *op. cit.*, p.xxviii.

conscience. He considered it a primary and most evident truth that man's conscience sets up a living contact between him and a personal God, Creator, Lord of the universe, strict Judge and guiding Providence of his rational creatures. For the religious man the moral ideas and norms present to his mind admit of no doubt; and he is aware that these norms are of absolute validity and obligation, as commandments from on high. The experience and its absolute objectivity are manifested simultaneously; and the religious man can no more doubt its value as a means to the knowledge of reality than he can doubt his own existence. The existence of God, like his own, is "luminously self-evident".[1] He believes in God, because his own existence, which is undoubted, would seem to be denied if He who lives in his conscience does not Himself exist.[2] It is conscience that is our ground for our existence as human beings.

Did Newman consider this an adequate basis on which to erect an apologetic? Undoubtedly, his own experience, with its accompanying religious evidence, was sufficient for his personal conviction and life; and for others, who possess the same interior evidence, their own experience is enough. He could, then, have confined the cogency of his reasoning to those kindred spirits whose own experience attested the validity of its initial assumption. As Pascal says, "We often make assertions that can be proved only in so far as they impel men to reflect on themselves and so to discover their truth".[3] Newman would certainly agree with this, at least in the sense that, in default of a sound personal conscience, no abstract proof could bring conviction.

Surely, however, it is desirable, even necessary, that this inner and vital certainty should be carried beyond the limits of personal and incommunicable experience to the region of notional and communicable knowledge, and so not only made explicit in its content, but also justified as valid, at the bar of reason. This is what the mind of man instinctively requires; for it is natural for man to aim at being fully conscious of his own certitudes and at justifying them, however imperfectly, by reasons that can be

---

[1] *Apologia*, p.31.

[2] *Ibid.*, pp.186, 217.

[3] B. Pascal, *Discours sur les passions de l'amour* (Paris: Hachette, 1941), p.129.

expressed.[1] Moreover, it is not everyone who discovers in himself a knowledge of God by conscience. The real apprehension of which Newman speaks is denied by many, or held to be illusory; in a number of people it remains in its initial state, hesitant and confused, or merely rudimentary; often it is attacked and its existence threatened by prejudices or partisan reasoning. On account of these, religious knowledge needs to be justified by rational argument which will serve to buttress the religious sense against any weakness and to dissipate, as far as possible, the prejudices of unbelievers. Newman was clearly aware of these necessities. At the same time as, in the *Apologia,* he testifies to the luminous evidence of conscience, he goes on to say, "I have not expressed myself with philosophical correctness, because I have not given myself to the study of what others have said on the subject; but I think I have a strong true meaning in what I say which will stand examination".[2] He admits, therefore, the possibility of a rational examination based on an objective study of religious phenomena; but he holds its execution to be, in fact, very difficult. Of this we have one striking piece of evidence in his inability to work out a proof of the existence of God which would satisfy his mind;[3] just where the interior evidence is most forceful, reason harasses him with its most numerous and powerful objections.[4] Yet, if a given piece of knowledge is to be vindicated, it must be capable of harmonious adjustment with all the rest.

Does this mean that Newman refused to admit the validity of any rational proof of the existence of God? The external world, surely, abounds in convincing signs of God; was he ignorant of the classical "ways" of theology? He knew them and did not deny their intrinsic value. There are many ways by which we come to know the existence of God; not only by conscience, but also by the witness of mankind and history, by deduction from the facts

[1] For the relations between real and notional knowledge, see above, pp.103 and 113.

[2] *Apologia*, p.186.

[3] *Ibid.*, p.217.

[4] *Ibid.*, p.216. In *Disc. M. Cong.*, pp.264-276, Newman puts these difficulties in the strongest way.

of nature, and by metaphysics.[1] There is, then, a "cumulative proof of the existence of God".[2] But none of these ways of arguing makes a real impression on Newman's mind. So long as reason alone surveys, in its aloof fashion, the varied spectacle of history and of the human race, he considered the evidence against God's existence outweighed the signs in favour of it. A careful examination of the external world, in the hope of finding traces of a universal purpose which gives a meaning to things, discloses only obscure and isolated indications. Conscience alone gives us the key to the mystery of the universe. Newman held that the classical proofs were insufficient to assure him the settled conviction that there is a God who is living and personal, and not just the "soul of the world" or a deification of invisible forces.[3] As to the metaphysical proofs, he never felt at his ease in such matters; he seems never to have understood the real nature and the absolute character of metaphysics. It is true that he gives an outline of a proof of the existence of God, based on the principles of causality and of order.[4] Causality, he says, is one of our first experiences; we discover it in the results of our own acts of will and in the resistance set up by the wills of others. In this way, we reach the general principle that every event is the effect of some will; and from that we go on to posit a supreme will at the source of the whole creation. Order, too, is something we experience, leading us to the principle that there is a universal order, which is one of the foundations upon which natural science rests. Now, order presupposes intelligence. The order of the universe, therefore, requires a supreme Spirit, who assures the cohesion and harmony of the whole. These two proofs, however, are far from metaphysical. The principles they are based on are neither self-evident nor of absolute validity; they are just hypotheses of a general nature, assuming an analogy

---

[1] *Idea*, p.25: "Is not the being of God reported to us by testimony, handed down by history, inferred by an inductive process, brought home to us by metaphysical necessity, urged on us by the suggestions of our conscience?"

[2] *Ibid.*, (edition of 1852), p.186. See, also, *Disc. M. Cong.*, p.261.

[3] For all this see *Apologia*, pp.217-218. The world may speak to us of God, but, apart from conscience, the consideration of nature leads only to a vague religiosity; it does not set man's life under the regard of God to whom he is responsible. Newman saw a general tendency to substitute that kind of natural theology for Christianity; and it is with that in view that we have to take account of his constant and penetrating attacks on natural theology. Cf., Przywara, *J. H. Newman*, in *Christentum*, IV, pp.44-51.

[4] *Grammar*, pp.66-72.

between the cosmic process and human action. Arguments of that sort are simply more or less probable.

Judged in its historical context, Newman's attitude on this matter is very understandable and shows his perspicacity. The proof of the existence of God from the world of nature was known in his day only in the form it took in the philosophers of the Enlightenment. Newman took it mainly from Paley's *Natural Theology*, a classic republished in his time with commentaries by Lord Brougham and Sir Charles Bell. It is a treatise on nature rather than God, a synthesis of the natural sciences to prove finality in nature. Such a proof of God, in the complete absence of meta-physical argument, loses its cogency; and so Newman's distrust of it is very largely justified.

All things considered, we may say that Newman's view was that, since conscience provides convincing, but purely personal, evidence of God, the classical "ways", along with other arguments, more or less justify, at the bar of impersonal reason, the objective value of religious experience as a means of attaining reality, but they are not absolutely conclusive. Moreover, it is the case that, in his works, he rarely resorts to these kinds of proof.

Cannot the existence of God be proved from conscience itself? After all, it is a mode of knowledge. It has, of course, an emotional side, but that is but an aspect of what is essentially an act of apprehension. Cannot this cognitive act be rationally grounded on itself, and so the objective nature of its object assured? The passage from the *Apologia* cited above seems to imply that it is possible to work out a proof of the existence of God from conscience which would be strictly philosophical, by taking into account the evidence of other persons. In the *Grammar of Assent*, Newman's aim, pre-cisely, was to provide a justification of religion from the evidence of his own conscience, reinforced by that of others. Surely we have here an attempt to explain the first religious experience we undergo. In the passage on faith in God, Newman states that, starting from the fact of conscience, three things can be demon-strated—the existence of God, the nature of God, the possibility of reaching God, not only as an idea, but as a living reality. His investigation, however, stops at this point. If, he says, he had to prove the existence of God, he would do so from conscience; but, in fact, he does not intend to do so. He cannot, he continues, forego entirely an examination of the first two points, and he goes on to say that the proof of the existence and the nature of God would be based on the fact that we possess a conscience by our very nature; in other words, that conscience, with its double function, moral and religious, is an essential constituent of human nature.[1]

We will now put together all that Newman says on this question. The cognitive act of conscience is a specific function of the mind; it is not reducible to other, more elementary, acts of which it would be a combination. It is *sui generis*.[2] It is a question here of conscience in the full sense Newman gives to the word. Judgments of moral value are of imperative force as absolute norms of conduct. They belong essentially to the emotional sphere, that is, they are accompanied by affective qualities that imply relationship with a person. They involve, therefore, the acknowledgment of a personal Legislator; and, in this way, the act of conscience is specifically distinct from other cognitive acts.[3] Now, Newman says that conscience, including knowledge of religion, is a universal property of the human race;[4] consequently, it must be considered an essential operation of the mind, of human nature as such, on the same grounds as sense-knowledge, reason, and the aesthetic sense.[5]

But how does he come by this conviction? He is well aware that his notion of conscience is in flagrant contradiction with the views of his contemporaries, men of science and letters as well as with public opinion.[6] Current philosophy does not recognise conscience as the voice of God; it sees it as only a moral sense, produced by

[1] *Grammar.*, p.104-105.

[2] *Diff. Angl.*, II, p.248: "They would not allow, any more than we do, that it could be resolved into any combination of principles of our nature, more elementary than itself"; "Conscience is a simple statement of our nature" (*O.U.S.*, p.183).

[3] The specific character of conscience as an act of the mind is set out at length in the *Grammar*, pp.107-110, and contrasted in particular with the apprehension of aesthetic value.

[4] *Ibid.*, p.385: "As it is given to us, it is given to others, too."; "It is the same in the mind of each, whatever the particular errors in individual intelligences, as to the acts it enjoins to do or avoid" (p.103).

[5] *Diff. Angl.*, II, p.248: "A constituent element of the mind, as our perception of other ideas may be, as our powers of reasoning, as our sense of order and the beautiful and other intellectual endowments". Cf., also, *Grammar*, p.105.

[6] *Diff. Angl.*, II, p.247.

the mind of man. To it, sin, divine command and the voice of God are pure illusions. As for freedom and responsibility, these are fallacies to anyone who realizes man is ineluctably involved in a network of causal determinism.[1] Nor are the ideas of men in general any closer to those of Newman; if they make any claim to conscience at all, it is, generally, to assert the right to act and think as they see fit.[2]

These views of Newman on his contemporaries are rather too pessimistic. They occur in a context where he vindicates for the Church the quite legitimate right to supplement, by its objective judgment, the individual's subjective norm of good and evil, and to rectify its errors. His rhetoric leads him into slight exaggerations which, however, are largely true. But how does he prove that the cognitive function of conscience, as he understands it, is an original element in the human mind?

When he gave utterance to the views we have just stated, Newman had in view only the irreligious masses of his day. He excepts from their application the majority of those belonging to religious bodies. All who are genuinely religious share his idea of conscience.[3] The greater part of those who speak of it mean not only a rule but also a sanction.[4]

Moreover, it is a fact that, in all popular religions, most of all the primitive, it is the dark, depressing, oppressive aspect that predominates. Natural religion is, in fact, founded on fear and the feeling of guilt. Man, in his natural state, finds himself a sinner before the just God; this alone explains the greater part of religious institutions and practices in the world at large. The ways in which natural religion manifests itself correspond perfectly to the data of conscience, as Newman sees them; they imply, in consequence, in spite of their errors, the spontaneous activity of conscience.[5]

Another line of argument is still more compelling. If a child has spent his early years in an atmosphere not definitely irreligious, and has had the usual religious teaching, he acquires, from his first glimmerings of reason, a personal grasp of the truths of

---

[1] *Diff. Angl.*, p.249.
[2] *Ibid.*, pp.249-250.
[3] *Ibid.*, p.247-248.
[4] *Grammar*, p.106: "It is the ordinary sense of the word. Half the world would be puzzled to know what was meant by moral sense; but everyone knows what is meant by a good or bad conscience".
[5] *Ibid.*, pp.390-396.

religion, with a spontaneous and sensible attachment to them. His inner attitude towards God is a proof that he has an idea of God which is shown by analysis and reflection to comprise the chief elements of the same idea as fully developed in the mature conscience. This, surely, indicates that the human mind, even in infancy, has a latent endowment which, at the first opportunity, springs into action and makes its first religious teaching something of profound personal significance. Here we see a proof of the basic affinity of the religious knowledge issuing from conscience with the true nature of the mind of man.[1]

The most natural and spontaneous exhibitions of the human mind testify thus to the religious character of moral experience. No doubt it is equally a fact that in highly civilized societies such evidence is easily obscured and even disappears altogether. Yet the validity of the primordial evidence in favour of what belongs to human nature everywhere is not in the least weakened by rebuttals based on a later stage of development. Progress "must subserve the elements from which it proceeds, in order to be a true development and not a perversion";[2] this, as we shall see later, is one of the laws of true development. Hence, if the cultivated mind rejects what is universally held about human nature, its denials must be ruled out as deviations from the truth.

Moreover, these deviations are easily explained. What we call "civilisation" is not, in fact, the harmonious development of human nature in its entirety, but one side of it only, its power of abstract reasoning, which is what makes man capable of progress. Now this, by itself, takes hold of experience only notionally, of that aspect of it alone which lends itself to abstraction and generalization. It fails to take into account all the personal and incommunicable side of experience, all that can be grasped only in real apprehension. This means, in regard to conscience, that the educated reason has no difficulty in recognising it as the activity of the moral sense. But, as the source of obligation and of an experience of the invisible world, developing in the depths of the mind in proportion

---

[1] *Grammar.*, pp.112-115: "If a child of five or six years old, when 'reason is at length fully awake, has already mastered and appropriated thoughts and beliefs, in consequence of their teaching, in such sort as to be able to handle and apply them familiarly, according to the occasion, as principles of intellectual action, those beliefs at the very least must be singularly congenial to his mind, if not connatural with its initial action".

[2] *Ibid.*, p.395.

to our fidelity, and there giving rise to various hopes and fears, conscience is unknown to the logical mind that views only the surface of things.

Reason, in fact, is a willing servant of pride, with its secret desire to elude whatever lays down obligations or demands respect and fear. Pride sets up a tendency for the mind to see in conscience only what accords with its wishes; a partial and one-sided idea of conscience comes into being, and its characteristics gained in earliest experience are lost.[1] These explanations, since they account for the exceptions, confirm the rule.

From all this it follows that the cognitive act of conscience is specific and irreducible and proceeds from the very constitution of human nature. If, then, in the case of other acts of knowing, such as sense-perception, we have no choice but to accept their objectivity as given in their very exercise, it would be illogical to deny such objectivity to the acts of conscience.[2] If acts of a certain kind are seen to be essentially related to an object outside them, we are bound, by the first principles of any sane philosophy, to accept the existence of that object. We may admit to a number of errors in particular acts; but to admit the absurdity of a natural and basic function of the mind would be equivalent to asserting the intrinsic absurdity of human nature itself, which is contrary to the whole of our experience. There is, in nature, no being below man that has a natural function devoid of meaning. It is, therefore, impossible that, in the highest of creatures, one of the noblest natural functions should also be meaningless.[3]

There remains one more consideration which helps to justify rationally the value we attribute to conscience as manifesting God to us. The knowledge of God given by conscience is one of many similar cognitive acts by which we apprehend concrete reality.[4] Now, if these reveal to us something objective, why should we refuse to admit the same of conscience? Take, for example, our

---

[1] *Grammar.*, p.395-396. Newman has some interesting reflections on civilization and barbarism in the seventh of his "Lectures on the History of the Turks", *Historical Sketches*, I, pp.159-182.

[2] *Grammar*, p.105: "Conscience has a legitimate place among our mental acts; as really so, as the action of memory, of reasoning, of imagination, or as the sense of the beautiful; that as there are objects which, when presented to the mind, cause it to feel grief, regret, joy or desire, so there are things which excite in us approbation or blame".

[3] See what Newman has to say about the illative sense, *Ibid.*, p.348.

[4] See above, pp.107-112.

knowledge of material things or of some person. No more than conscience is, is this knowledge an immediate intuition of existing realities. We grasp them instinctively, that is without other intermediary, "in and through" the impressions they make on our sense-organs or our mind, just as we apprehend God immediately "in and through" the moral law he imprints on our mind. The cognitive act of conscience exhibits practically the same characteristics as other acts by which we know the concrete. Why, then, should not conscience, too, place us in contact with reality.[1]

In conclusion, we may observe that, although Newman never claimed to have analysed and discussed exhaustively his view of conscience as giving knowledge of objective reality, his later writings contain numerous and clear indications of his mind on the question. From these it is possible to construct, in broad outline, his vindication of conscience as a faculty of religious knowledge.

B. Criticism of Newman's theory

For a complete estimate of Newman's theory of conscience and its place in the history of the philosophy of religion, a detailed study would be needed. A shorter treatment, however, is all that our purpose requires. Some aspects demand special attention, since we here come to the very core of Newman's apologetic and philosophy of religion.

No one can deny that, as a fact, it is conscience, in the main, that paves the way to religion, that many conversions originate in a serious regard for moral values. For the ordinary faithful, this is obvious, for conscience is the voice of God speaking to the soul. Tertullian, at the end of the third century, appeals to the spontaneous testimony of the average man, whether Christian or pagan, not to the mind formed in the schools, libraries and academies, but to the simple mind, uncultured and illiterate.[2] Whatever philosophers may say, the conscience, in its natural state, testifies clearly that there is a God, a single God, a good God, but a Judge too, who sees us and judges us.[3]

Tertullian holds this monotheism to be "a doctrine inspired by nature, and tacitly entrusted to the conscience innate in

---

[1] *Grammar*, pp.102-104.

[2] Tertullian, *De testimonio animae*, P.L. vol. I, col. 610.

[3] *Ibid.*, cols. 611-612, 618.

us".[1] No philosophy may prevail against this intuition, for man is first man, and only subsequently a philosopher or poet.[2] Conscience, being the same in all, is a surer guide than learning, for nature cannot lie.[3]

Literature gives us some striking examples in this connection, for instance the dialogue between the two assassins of Clarence in Shakespeare's *Richard III*, or the last chapters of *Anna Karenina*, where Tolstoy describes the conversion of Levin. The history of philosophy, too, brings strong confirmation. That the living conscience confronts us with the living God is the final conviction of Kierkegaard, Schlegel, and even Kant.[4]

Conscience, then, leads man to God. To know Him, it is above all necessary to admit the absolute nature of good and evil. The religious character of conscience can be denied only by a superficial rationalism. But a number of problems arise at this point. In the spontaneous experience of a religious man, the link between conscience and God is seen as immediately evident, as a kind of intuitive fact. That is what is meant by the metaphors we use when we say that conscience is the voice of God speaking within us, or his eye in the depths of the soul. These descriptions, however, tell us nothing about the actual structure of the religious and moral elements in man. The word "intuition" is used in this context in the sense given to it by descriptive psychology; it means a vague general impression,[5] a kind of psychological immediacy characteristic of spontaneous thought and applicable even to complicated mental processes by the student of their logical structure. The voice, or the eye, of God, are simply imaginative expressions, of great practical value, but quite unphilosophical.

What is the precise relation between moral experience and the knowledge of God? In trying to answer this question, we run the risk of being involved in a labyrinth of tangled opinions on a subject of current religious philosophy. Kant's well-known argument in the *Critique of Practical Reason* has reawakened interest in the

---

[1] *Ibid.*, col. 616.

[2] *Ibid.*

[3] *Ibid.*, col. 617.

[4] Kant's final conviction is found in his *Opus Postumum*. Cf. E. Adickes, "Kants Opus Postumum", *Ergänzungshefte der Kantstudien*, No. 50, 796-846.

[5] Spearman says that the word "intuition" usually signifies a "general impression": "It does not really denote how a person comes to know anything, only that he does not know how he knows" (*op. cit.*, I, p.83).

deontological proof of the existence of God. Since his time, none of the classical proofs has been so often set out, defended or attacked, under such a variety of forms.[1]

A critical examination of all these arguments would involve an enormous amount of work, and has never yet been attempted. Some reject the moral argument, others consider it the most convincing of all, if not logically, at least in practice.[2] Some grant it only a high degree of probability;[3] others see in it the most profound and solid metaphysical proof of the existence of God.[4] Here we will give only a summary view of the different ways of setting out the relation between the experience of duty and the knowledge of God.[5] Four classes may be broadly distinguished, though each of them is by no means homogeneous.[6]

(1) The first group consists of those who hold that conscience does not acknowledge any absolute obligation, so long as the existence of God is not known and admitted beforehand. Hence, any argument based on the absolute nature of duty is reducible to a *petitio principii*. From the psychological point of view, most people, perhaps, arrive at an explicit acknowledgment of God by way of awareness of absolute obligation; but such awareness itself rests upon an implicit acknowledgment of God, based on reasons outside the moral order. Logically speaking, it is impossible to infer the existence of God from the fact of absolute obligation.[7]

(2) The second group comprises, among others, the phenomenologists influenced by Max Scheler, who follow Newman

[1] W. G. de Burgh, *From Morality to Religion* (London, 1938), p.155: "The moral argument, like that from religious experience, is distinctive of modern thought. It could hardly have been formulated until the time of Kant . . . The moral argument has been more fully discussed, especially in Britain, during the last hundred years, than any of the other arguments to theism".

[2] A. Sertillanges, O.P., *Dieu ou Rien?* (Paris, 1933), I, p.193.

[3] de Burgh, *op. cit.*, p.151. All the same, according to de Burgh and many other English thinkers, no demonstrative proof of the existence of God is possible. Our certainty of it rests on cumulative probability. Cf. *Ibid.*, pp.153, 182.

[4] P. Descoqs, S. J., *Praelectiones Theologiae Naturalis* (Paris, 1932), I, pp.463-464, 468.

[5] We purposely omit the proof founded, not on obligation, but on the necessity for sanction.

[6] In his *Ethica* (III, pp.275-281), E. De Bruyne distinguishes three groups, corresponding, more or less, to our first, third and fourth classes.

[7] To the first group belongs a number of neo-scholastics of the extreme right: Franzelin, Billot, Gredt, Van der Meersch, *et al.*

closely.[1] It holds that, in our moral experience, the fact of absolute obligation is evidently given and must, therefore, be accepted without question. Further, the existence of a personal God is immediately perceived in the emotional experience conscience has of moral values. This perception, however, results from a religious experience which accompanies the moral one. Acts which, of their nature, are related to different orders of values are themselves specifically distinct and irreducible. Moral experience doubtless gives some inkling of the existence of a religious order, since moral values, like all the objective values on which human civilization is based (the true, the good, the beautiful), have a profound significance, an ontological dimension, which can be understood only in the light of the central value, which is that of religion; but moral experience, by itself, tells us nothing of God. Only experience of a specifically religious nature can effect a positive contact with God. A spontaneous knowledge of God is given in conscience only when the latter is already orientated to religion by a genuine experience of God.[2]

(3) A third group considers that it is possible to prove absolute moral obligation independently of any religious sanction. It accepts, too, the possibility of a proof of the existence of God from the fact of duty. These views are shared, among others, by a few great English theists[3] and a number of neo-scholastics. There is a danger here, which many fall into, that, while they start from the fact of obligation—a characteristic, especially, of conscience—they lose sight of it in their reasoning and produce an argument in which obligation, as such, has no part. Thus, they come to pursue one or other of the traditional "ways" based either on the natural

[1] Especially in his account of conscience in *Vom Ewigen in Menschen* (Leipzig, 1921), I, pp.5-6.

[2] Cf. Stoker, *Das Gewissen*, pp.158-160; J. Hessen, *Die Werte des Heiligen* (Regensburg, 1938), pp.60-61. Stoker expresses himself with greater precision than Hessen. The moral is distinguished above the other "cultural" values as being a "proto-phenomenon" of religion.

[3] The relations of morality and religion have often been dealt with in the Gifford Lectures: in 1914-1915 by W. R. Sorley, *Moral Values and the Idea of God* (Cambridge, 1921); in 1926-1928 by A. E. Taylor, *The Faith of a Moralist* (2 vols; London, 1931); in 1938 by W. G. de Burgh, *op. cit.* The argument varies in detail but is broadly the same, namely that, with absolute obligation, we enter an order of personal values, irreducible to that of physical necessity; that reason shows this order to be as real as the other, and so postulates the existence of a supreme personal spirit.

order or on the idea of the good.[1] The arguments of Père Descoqs, S. J.[2] and Professor de Bruyne are designed to base an absolute metaphysical proof of the existence of God on the fact of moral obligation.[3] They are founded on contingent being, but are quite different from the usual proof. Obligation presupposes two essential conditions : (a) the person obliged is, of necessity, summoned to follow the moral good; (b) he may, however, refuse this good, and pursue his selfish inclinations. This opposition within the mind and will of a person shows the imperfection inherent in his spirit. It presupposes, however, as a basic requirement, the action, at the deepest level of the moral subject, of a perfect spiritual Being, who is unable to tend to the moral good only because He is Himself pure freedom and moral goodness. This perfect Being must be intimately present to the imperfect person, while transcending him. There can be nothing in common, either materially or formally, between Him and the imperfect. This immanence-transcendence must, therefore, be understood as a total dependence of the imperfect moral being on the perfect moral Person who created him.

[1] Thus the excellent argument of Sertillanges, *op. cit.*, I, pp.220-224, and *Les sources de la croyance en Dieu* (Paris, 1904), pp.278-293, seems simply a variation of the Fifth Way of St Thomas; R. Garrigou-Lagrange, *Dieu* (5th printing; Paris, 1928), pp.308-312, reduces the proof from ethics to the Fourth Way.

[2] P. Descoqs, S.J., *op. cit.*, pp.444-523.

[3] Cf. E. De Bruyne, *op. cit.*, III, pp.229-391, on which our short account is based. He does not regard himself as one of the "reasoning" group to which Descoqs belongs. All he tries to do is, by a strictly critical approach, to analyze what is implied in the fact of obligation. His proof, however, is clearly a metaphysical one. He does not make use of any metaphysical principles previously established; they are only implicitly contained in his principle; that conditions whose existence it is necessary to confirm so that a given assertion is not self-contradictory are themselves as certain as the latter (p.348). Every true metaphysical proof rests on this principle. In the traditional *Viae* themselves, if they are properly understood, the metaphysical principles are not established beforehand, independently of the actual thesis. They appear only in the course of the metaphysical analysis of the given proposition. The mania of the textbook writers for condensing every argument into logical form often prevents this character of metaphysical thought from being sufficiently evident. A "metaphysical proof of God" is not a reasoning in the strict sense De Bruyne gives the word. G. Rabeau, in *Species Verbum: L'Activité intellectuel élémentaire selon saint Thomas d'Aquin* (Paris, 1938), pp.173-179, has rightly shown that the theistic arguments of St Thomas are not real deductions, but "reductions", that is, operations of the mind that penetrate to the infrastructure, the essential conditions of a given concept.

(4) A fourth group, embracing thinkers of various kinds, holds that the experience of absolute obligation itself involves an experience of God.[1] It is very difficult to condense their views in such a way as to do justice, even approximately, to them all. We might best express their common ideas in the following way. In the living experience of conscience, moral good is presented as of absolute obligation and as placing upon us a certain responsibility. The ideas of obligation and responsibility are simple and ultimate. They imply our subjection to someone who lays on us the obligation and to whom we are responsible. The highest reality of all is the person, and a person can be subject only to another person. Moral experience, therefore, contains an element of genuine religious experience, which may, however, remain implicit. If this moral experience is allowed to develop in the right fashion and its nature to become clearer, the religious element in it will arise of its own accord to explicit awareness. No reasoning takes place; all that happens is that which was previously latent now becomes manifest. Mere reflection is enough to convince a conscientious and unprejudiced person that the spontaneous workings of his conscience put him in touch with the unseen God. Here, then, we are not engaged with a purely moral experience that has to be justified by reason before it can serve as foundation of an argument for the existence of God. The experience of conscience is indivisibly ethico-religious, even though the strictly religious element lies at the deepest level, and thus is most hard to discern, so that self-will and prejudice may easily blind us to its presence. Our judgment has to take account of the ethico-religious fact as a single whole.

This view lends itself to many differences of emphasis. Ollé-Laprune puts in the forefront the idea of obligation; Newman and Rosenmoeller the emotional accompaniments of conscience, such as reverence, fear, shame, remorse. God may be thought of anthropomorphically, as supreme Lord, absolutely transcendent, or, more profoundly, as Creator at once immanent and

---

[1] In addition to Newman and the later Kant, this group comprises aristotelians and scholastics such as M. Wittmann, "Ethik", *Philos. Handbibl.* (Munich, 1923), VII, pp.274-311, and Schiffini, *Ethica Generalis*, n. 141; Catholics of augustinian tendencies, such as B. Rosenmoeller, *Religions-philosophie* (2nd printing; Munster, 1939), pp.50-87, 137, and L. Ollé-Laprune, *Le prix de la vie* (46th printing; Paris, 1925); and moderns such as R. Le Senne, *Traité de Morale générale* (*Collection Logos*; Paris, 1924), pp.363-374.

transcendent, as Judge and, at the same time, the essential source of our freedom and responsibility. Under this aspect, however, it is not easy to draw a hard and fast distinction between this group and the preceding one. Le Roy tells us that "the data . . . do not so much involve, as constitute, an affirmation of God";[1] and this immediate "posting" of God could mean anything we like, apart from a logical deduction. After all possible misunderstandings are allowed for, it would appear that the intellectual process of which Le Roy speaks is simply metaphysical argumentation.

A detailed criticism of these opinions would be outside our purpose. The fact that ordinary, unsophisticated persons of upright life have a spontaneous awareness that conscience is a link between themselves and God, that God speaks to their heart, seems of great moment for whoever sets out to study the phenomena of religion. We feel that this experience points to certain latent realities of the metaphysical order, which it is the task of reason to disclose. They lie at the root of the spontaneous experience of conscience, and are not perceptible to a cursory view; yet, even in their implicit state, they form an essential basis for that experience. Expressed in clear, logical form, they would furnish a metaphysical proof of the existence of God; but Newman stopped short of this. With all his varied attainments, he was never drawn to metaphysical problems. We need not be surprised that he always showed himself more or less distrustful of metaphysics, for he had a horror of empty phrases, and this, the most noble and comprehensive of the sciences, is the most prone to degenerate into vague verbosity and formulas so abstruse as to be unintelligible. Newman was acquainted with metaphysics only in its decadence; his instinctive repugnance for "unreal words" prevented any serious concern with a science that had lost inspiration and its contact with reality.

Newman lacked the opportunity to become acquainted with the great metaphysical tradition. His solution to the problem of the relation between religion and ethics was in line with the members of the fourth group we have mentioned. His importance in the history of this problem must not be minimized, for his influence was at work in the most eminent of these thinkers. His description of the emotional side of conscience, together with his

---

[1] E. Le Roy, *Le problème de Dieu* (2nd ed.; Paris, 1930), p. 54.

analysis of the religious conscience, its spontaneous generation, its development in the individual, forms his special contribution to the psychology and the phenomenology of ethics and religion. He drew a clear and precise distinction between the two essential elements of conscience—the moral sense, which apprehends the specific qualities of good and evil in human acts; the sense of obligation, which commands the good as an absolute duty. With a power of suggestion unsurpassed by any other writer, he describes how knowledge of a supreme Lord and Judge arises out of the fulness of personal experience of conscience; for the experience of his own responsibility is the starting-point whence the man of good faith advances steadily—at first vaguely groping, then, in proportion to his fidelity, with growing clearness and certainty —to the recognition of a Creator and Judge, apart from whom consciousness of duty and obligation is inexplicable. It is this experience, in solitude, of conscience, that gives rise to those deep and powerful emotions, fear and reverence, shame and remorse, which show that such a man feels himself under the regard of a supreme Majesty, even when his attention is mainly directed elsewhere.

Newman's attempt to give a rational account of conscience is modern. Many of our contemporaries adopt an attitude indistinguishable from his : J. Hessen, for example, who, in turn, cites Goehre and Scheler.[1] The latest results of the science and the phenomenology of religions, allied with Newman's theories, might be used to furnish an argument which, though not absolutely conclusive, would possess great cogency and permanent value. (See Appendix E. *The proof of God from conscience*).

SECTION C

THE DIALECTIC OF CONSCIENCE

In the last chapter of the *Grammar*, Newman reaffirms that his proof of Christianity is addressed to those only who agree with his principles. These are the truths of natural religion, and our knowledge of these truths has its source in conscience.[2] By means of conscience we come into possession of principles which, logically,

[1] J. Hessen, *Die Werte des Heiligen*, pp.255-261.
[2] *Grammar*, pp.415-416.

lead to Christianity and thence to Catholicism. Newman could say, in the *Apologia* : "I am a Catholic because I believe in God".[1]

Conscience, then, points the way to the Catholic Church. The man who follows his conscience and whose whole life is impregnated with religion comes, by degrees, to look upon the world in the light of God. For this, a deliberate and methodical process of thought is not required. The first principles of conscience take root of themselves in the mind, where they steadily expand, often without the knowledge of the person himself. They draw their strength from active life and, as occasion arises, produce their mature effects in the form of fully conscious convictions.[2] It is in the course of the attempt to work out a coherent philosophy of life that the conscience—unless prevented by prejudice or ignorance—comes to accept Christ and Catholicism.

Reflection, however, may lead to a recasting of these data of conscience in order to give them cohesion and rational justification. In this consists entirely Newman's apologetic. It is comparable, not so much to a straight, man-made canal of abstract reasoning but to a winding stream with numerous tributaries, made up of all those elements in concrete thought whose entry is permitted by reason. He is not primarily concerned to examine, in a controversial spirit, the external side of Christianity; his method is that of an inquiry conducted by conscience to throw light on its mysterious and baffling situation in the world of man, and to set it on the road to truth.[3] The religious man, as he tries to work out a view of life consistent with his first principles, is forced to recognize that there is no correspondence, either in his own condition or in that of the world, present or past, with what one would naturally expect if the world was governed by Providence. The contradiction of which he is deeply conscious is resolved only by his acceptance of the Church and its claim to be entrusted with a divine mission. The Church alone offers a solution to the problems encountered by conscience in its contact with the world.

In setting out Newman's apologetic system, we shall start by noting the first principles furnished by conscience in working out a general view of the world. Next, we shall concern ourselves with his method and, after that, give a broad outline of the resulting

[1] *Apologia*, p.186.
[2] See above, pp. 154 *ff.*
[3] *Grammar*, pp.424-425.

synthesis. Finally, we shall estimate his exact significance in regard to Catholic theology.

A. Apologetic principles:

The first principle of conscience is that all things are governed by the Providence of their Creator. No one who reads Newman with attention can doubt that this conviction is the most fertile element in his thought. In virtue of it, he belongs to the spiritual lineage of St. Augustine. Whatever the severity of the Judge before whom our guilty conscience trembles, we are assured, by the hope that we experience even in our fallen state and which is confirmed by all kinds of blessings we receive, that God is no pitiless despot. No doubt, it is his justice that conscience emphasizes the most; yet, to the mind of the religious person, the chief attribute of God is goodness.[1] History shows that sacrifice and prayer have, in all ages, formed the principal acts of religion. It is evident from this that the human race has always retained the idea of God as a Father, in spite of the corruptions introduced by pagan imaginings and superstitious practices.[2]

A religious view of the world always has as its foundation the idea of a Providence guiding all things and seeing to the punishment of evil and the reward of the good.

> It is possible to give an interpretation to the course of things, by which every event or occurrence in its order becomes providential; and though that interpretation does not hold good unless the world is contemplated from a particular point of view, in one given aspect, and with certain inward experiences, and personal first principles and judgments, yet these may be fairly pronounced to be common conditions of human thought, that is, till they are wilfully or accidentally lost.[3]

A salient feature of Newman's greatest works is that they are all centred on the idea of Providence. In the *Essay on development*, the last of the *University Sermons*, and the *Grammar of Assent*, he appeals to divine Providence as the ultimate basis of all his certainties.[4] Most especially does he make use of the

---

[1] *Grammar.*, p.400.
[2] *Ibid.*, p.401 ff.
[3] *Ibid.*, p.402.
[4] *Essay*, pp.111-112; *O.U.S.*, pp.348-349; *Grammar*, pp.351-352.

principle of a Providence in his proof of the truth of religion.[1]

This primary and supreme principle of his makes use of two others—that of the nature of things, and that of analogy. We have already alluded to their connection and now it must be made quite clear. God directs the world inasmuch as he is its Creator. Both its contents and their relationships proceed from him. Consequently, all nature and all created beings are the expression of his designs and intentions. His ways and his will reveal themselves in everything that nature as it actually is and the inevitable conditions of life involve for man. This principle is the axis of Newman's thought. The way he applies it gives him a distinguished place among the greatest exponents of the traditional Christian philosophy. His use of it, however, is highly individual. Take, for example, the proof he gives in the *Grammar of Assent*. "Scientism" alleges that it is wrong to accept as true a proposition that cannot be clearly proved by the rules of mathematical physics. Newman's rejoinder can be summarised as follows. It is true that, in mathematics and the related sciences, the *very nature* of the subject forbids us to accept a conclusion not proved in strict logic; but, in history, ethics and religion, the *very nature* of the subject and the condition of the human mind require another method. In these three departments of knowledge, the *kinds* of subjects treated forbid us to expect strict proof, and oblige us to be content with a certain number of probabilities, more or less explicitly realized, that furnish no apodeictic certainty until we see them converging and centring on an identical conclusion. Further, in matters of ethics and religion this convergence can be estimated only by the personal intelligence, and our intellectual judgment is, in the event, a function of our whole personality.[2] "Perplexing as

---

[1] *Grammar*, pp.411-413.

[2] The following passage sets out clearly the whole situation in its relation to Providence: "Since a good Providence watches over us, He blesses such means of argument as it has pleased Him to give us, in the nature of man and the world, if we use them duly for those ends for which He has given them; and that, as in mathematics we are justified by the dictate of nature in withholding our assent from a conclusion of which we have not yet a strict logical demonstration, so by a like dictate we are not justified, in the case of concrete reasoning and especially of religious inquiry, in waiting till such logical demonstration is ours, but on the contrary we are bound in conscience to seek truth and to look for certainty by modes of proof which, when reduced to the shape of formal propositions, fail to satisfy the severe requisitions of science". (*Ibid.*, pp.411-412).

we may find it, this phenomenon is a normal and inevitable characteristic of the mental constitution of a being like man on a stage
such as the world".[1]

Later, we shall see how the argument in the *Essay on Development* rests on the same basic principle. The objection that development infringes the identity of doctrine and of Christianity is answered by the consideration that it is a natural and necessary consequence of the fact that a living idea is entrusted to the human
mind whose thought proceeds by logical steps. Development,
therefore, is willed by Providence. It follows from the very nature
of human society that any idea of importance keeps its identity
only in so far as it is living, in other words, by developing.

Another principle and essential element of his method and
thought is that of analogy. Newman derived his use of this delicate but dangerous instrument of thought from the celebrated
work of the Anglican Bishop Butler. Butler used it to refute objections to supernatural religion. Anyone who admits the natural
order, he argued, cannot reject the supernatural on account of
the difficulties it involves; for the same difficulties are shared by
the natural order. Newman, however, extends considerably the
range of the argument from analogy. Not only does he admit it
as decisively refuting objections,[2] but he frequently uses it to show
how certain probabilities and presumptions lead to a given conclusion.

The principle of analogy is closely connected with that of Providence. It may be stated in the following way. All the works of
God bear the imprint of one and the same divine Wisdom. The
nature and order of things manifest a design governed by a few
important, but simple, principles of consequence, which give to
the whole a wonderful harmony and majesty. The fundamental
principles of the divine plan are revealed, more or less, in creation.
Whatever happens according to its laws comes, in all probability,
from God himself.[3] The theory of development is the most typical
application of this principle. All the great works of God known to
us, whether interior or exterior, in nature or human history, take
place according to the law of development. God brings nothing
into being in a completed state. He lets everything realise itself

[1] *Grammar.*, p.350.
[2] *Ibid.*, p.382.
[3] *Essay*, pp.74-75, 84-85.

little by little, succeed by degrees, grow towards perfection. For this reason, the development on such a large scale of the doctrinal tradition constitutes *a priori* no objection to the truth of Christianity. On the contrary, it forms a presumption that it is God who directs the history of doctrine; whereas the sterility of its doctrine is a presumption against the truth of Anglicanism.[1]

The chief use of the argument from analogy is, however, as with Butler, to refute objections. Newman's attitude towards difficulties in matters of faith is determined by the three principles mentioned. It is a fact that the capital truth perceived by conscience, the existence of God, is at once absolutely evident and opposed by all kinds of difficulties in logic. This gives rise to the presumption that, right to the end of its journey, religious thought will encounter many similar obstacles. Everything in religion that is clear has its obscure side. It follows that difficulties, as such, do not impair certitude at all. In fact, certitude and difficulties belong to different planes. Ten thousand difficulties do not make one doubt.[2] It is, therefore, quite natural for there to be apparently insoluble difficulties against faith. Furthermore, conscience teaches us the profound significance of this state of things, in showing that difficulties make for growth in the life of religion. Even in the depths of conscience, God leads us to the light only by degrees. Understanding comes as the reward of our humble, fervent and persevering fidelity; the light graciously conceded is always bordered by darkness. Providence evidently wills this as part of our trial here below. Without difficulties, it would be impossible for fidelity to be deserving or trust to be practised. In relation to religious truth, these difficulties require, even alongside adequate evidence, a humble submission to the mystery of God, the renunciation of that pride of intellect which claims to be the judge of all, and an acknowledgment of the divine transcendence, since the being of God and the light he gives surpass our understanding. This humble submission is an essential part of the truly religious attitude. Difficulties, then, are a necessary condition of the life of religion here. They are present in every kind of religious knowledge, as well as in knowledge by faith.[3]

---

[1] See below, pp.249-250.

[2] *Apologia*, p.215.

[3] This is admirably expressed in *Disc. M. Cong.*, XIII: "Mysteries of Nature and Grace", pp.260-283.

It is true that our mind, by a natural instinct, seeks to resolve difficulties as far as possible; but the religious man pursues his way tranquilly in spite of them. His certainty does not depend on their complete solution; and so it is unnecessary to force one, at any price. We continue to uphold the absolute requirements of the intellect; the solution will appear when God wills. It can now be seen why Newman welcomed intellectual culture in all its forms with such breadth of mind and flexibility and strenuously defended the independence and freedom of science. The progressive tendencies of true science gave him no cause for fear; he was a total stranger to obscurantism. As a Catholic, he made himself the upholder of intellectual progress, for he was convinced that anyone deeply religious was immune to the dangers of the intellect and the difficulties it revealed. Certainly, no one ever saw and analysed the dangers of higher culture so acutely as he. No one felt intellectual difficulties more keenly. Nor yet was anyone so utterly convinced of the need and duty of accepting integrally with all its conditions, the life given us by God; and, if this life is beset with dangers, the Creator and Lord of all will not fail to help us to surmount them and to draw from them the most signal triumphs of religion.

These are the great principles of Newman's system. They give it that religious atmosphere which is its essential characteristic and condition of its being. A mental atmosphere, in fact, consists precisely in the living energy of the principles at work.[1]

B. The method of apologetics:

How can religious thought attain to the acknowledgment of the truth of Christianity and the Church? The sole aim of Newman's apologetic is to analyse and justify the spontaneous expansion of a religious conception of the world which, when fully developed, should lead to the Church. This means that his method is not rigorously logical; for, as we have already seen, spontaneous thought cannot be adequately expressed in syllogisms. The mind, in its living activity, makes such use of signs and allusions—at times, highly subtle ones—that the use of an impersonal technique would be quite inappropriate. Nor will his system be based entirely on a philosophy of history, one that makes use exclusively

[1] See Appendix F.

of miracles, prophecy and the visible signs of historical Christianity. Its primary source, in fact, consists in the problems arising in the human conscience. Yet Newman does not disregard the signs and events of history. He is no extreme advocate of the method of immanence which seeks to uphold the truth of Christianity and the Church by the sole testimony of religious experience. Christianity is a contingent fact of history; its course is dependent on the free dispensation of the divine mercy. That God actually conceived and ordained this dispensation can be definitely established only by objective and external evidence. It was Newman's firm conviction that even the most powerful presumptions of reason are insufficient to demonstrate a fact.

His apologetic, therefore, proceeds by an accumulation of probabilities, independent of one another, but converging to a single result and reciprocally confirming and elucidating each other. We are presented with a mode of argument whose validity rests ultimately, not on formal logic, but on a personal power of evaluation, or the "illative sense". Whereas Newman holds that anyone who admits the principles of conscience ought, if he is consistent, to accept Catholicism as well, we know in advance that the logic in question is not that of formal reasoning, but the higher logic of the "illative sense". Does that mean that a "proof of the Church", strictly objective and demonstrative, is impossible? It is not ruled out altogether. Yet arguments of the sort, however valuable, can always be declined by reason. Further, they make no impression on us, unless we already possess some concern with the things of religion. It is more practical, therefore, to allow the "illative sense" of the sincerely religious man to direct the course of the argument. For such a man is prepared by his inner experience to receive the conclusion and so is disposed to see all the factors of the historical demonstration converge harmoniously to one inevitable result. In any case, this is the way Newman chooses.[1] His own cast of mind moves him to put his trust in a variety of probabilities forming, as it were, a flexible cord, rather than in a rigid syllogistic bar which either resists without bending or else breaks.[2]

Newman distinguishes two classes of probability—antecedent

[1] *Grammar*, pp.410-411.

[2] This simile occurs in Ward, *op. cit.*, II, p.43.

probability and evidence.[1] When they supplement and reinforce one another, we have the most conclusive possible proof.[2] What is the relation between the two? Both are necessary; but, in apologetics, antecedent probability is, more or less, the principal factor.[3] Indeed, it may be so strong that a prudent man ought, at least in practice, to admit it without factual proof.[4] The probability of a divine revelation is so strong for the conscience that expects it that, if there existed only one religion claiming to be revealed, very many would thereby be satisfied that the religion was the only true one. Anyhow, as soon as the mind entertains a rational presumption of such force, there is no need to resort to a number of facts to settle the whole question.[5] For, if we examine the facts in the light of a previous probability, rationally justified, we rightly approach the matter in a confident spirit, ready to explain the obscure points by what is already clear, and resolved not to be frightened by difficulties.[6] Antecedent probability ought to provide the key to the facts, whatever our personal disposition in regard to the possible results. That is merely what a sound method demands.[7]

In this way, Newman's apologetic consists of an accumulation of probabilities, some proceeding from established principles, others from facts, but with the emphasis on the former. Obviously, he needs to justify his method and he does this chiefly in the *Essay on Development*. We find in it a striking example, in which the validity of the principles we have just outlined is clearly shown.

[1] The terms "antecedent probability" or "antecedent reasoning" on the one hand, and "evidence", on the other, are of frequent occurrence in the *O.U.S.* and the *Essay*. Newman often substitutes "presumption" or "verisimilitude" for "antecedent probability". When he speaks merely of "probability" he generally means "antecedent probability".

[2] H. Tristram, "Cardinal Newman's Theses *de fide*", *Gregorianum*, XVIII (1937), 247.

[3] The value of antecedent probability is brought out mainly in the *O.U.S.* and the *Essay*. In a letter of the same period, he declares: "The kind of argument which brings moral certainty is not proof, but antecedent probability" (H. Tristram, *loc. cit.*). In the *Grammar*, he does not express himself so emphatically.

[4] *Grammar*, p.383; *Essay*, pp.113-114.

[5] *Grammar*, p.423.

[6] *Essay*, p.101.

[7] *Ibid.*, pp.108-110: "If strong presumptions recommend to us a doctrine, we ought to receive it without suspicion, and use it as the key to the proofs it appeals to, or to the facts it claims to systematize, whatever judgment we may ultimately form about it".

In the religious, as in the secular, sphere, we have to adjust ourselves to the laws of our being.[1] Now, in some disciplines, in physics, for example, the mind can rely entirely on facts, because it has them always at its disposal and can apply itself to adequate research and experiment. Here it would be unreasonable to depend on anything other than the data furnished by the senses. Other disciplines, such as theology and history, do not enjoy this advantage, for the facts are wanting. We must, therefore, judge with such means as we possess, opinions, traditions, analogies, parallel cases, previous considerations, etc., not using them arbitrarily, but sifting them and examining them critically and sensibly.[2] It is, inevitably, a matter of moral proof, and so early foreshadowings, personal character,[3] upbringing, even genius, are relevant factors, though they may be irrelevant in physical science.[4]

The complementary theme is, once again, divine Providence, to which our mind owes its various instruments adapted to the needs of different kinds of knowledge. Through divine help, each of these instruments, applied in its own sphere, will lead to an adequate degree of truth and certitude. This is particularly true in matters of religion, where our relations with God are involved.[5]

[1] "In the religious domain, as in the others, we ought to be content to follow the law of our nature" (*Essay.*, p.115).

[2] *Ibid.*, p.111: "The facts of the physical order are present; they are subject to the senses, and may be sufficiently tested, corrected, verified. To trust anything but the senses, in dealing with objects of sense, is irrational. But it is not the same with history, where the facts are not present . . . In such sciences, we cannot rely on facts alone, for we do not possess them. We must do the best with what is given us, but also seek support in other spheres; in such circumstances, the opinion of others, agelong tradition, commands of authority, previous intimations, analogies, parallel cases, and other factors of the same order, not selected at random but, like sensible proofs, sifted and closely scrutinized, acquire obviously great importance.

[3] In connection with "antecedent reasoning", he says, (*Ibid.*, p.381): "In great measure, these antecedent probabilities are our own product and pertain to our personal character".

[4] *Ibid.*, p.112: "When it is a question of moral proof, as in history, antecedent probability may have a real weight and a power of conviction it would not have in the experimental sciences".

[5] *Ibid.*, pp.111-112: "If we start with the hypothesis that a merciful Providence has furnished us with the means to acquire the truth that concerns us, in various spheres, but with different instruments, the question is simple: what are the instruments designed for a particular case? If they are given us by divine Providence, let us be certain that, such as they are, they will bring us to the truth. The least exact among the methods of reasoning will suffice to do his work as well as the best, if he blesses them".

This is the main line of Newman's justification of his method. It is reinforced, however, by an accumulation of analogous or parallel cases, taken from the most various spheres, where the same method is taken for granted. It follows from this that the method has the support of the common sense of all men.[1] The three first principles he makes use of here are the same as those governing the whole body of his thought: the nature of things, analogy and the idea of Providence.

Later we shall take a typical example of his method; but to understand its significance it is necessary to analyse his entire work. Nearly all his important conclusions are reached by following a number of different paths, and are gained by the same skilful tactics of encirclement.[2]

Newman's apologetic, then, centres on the human conscience, which gives his whole argument its unity, its internal movement, its orientation and its characteristic structure. The contribution of conscience is not simply one probability alongside the others, but rather a current impelling and directing the whole. At the same time, it expresses the existential condition governing his thought. His whole apologetic is most appropriately described as the existential dialectic of conscience, which is the reason why we are chiefly concerned with this aspect of his thought.

C. The course of the apologetic:

We are now in a position to set out, in broad outline, the course of Newman's apologetic. First of all, we have to see how a strong presentiment of conscience prepares the way for the acceptance of divine Revelation; next, how such acceptance leads to belief in the Catholic Church. To understand his demonstration, we ought first to "realise" the actual, existential place of conscience in the world. Newman's apologetic gives the answer to the question how, in the state in which we are inevitably placed, can our conscience grow naturally to become what it ought to be, the sun whose brilliance lights up our whole conception of the world? We know God by our conscience, but this knowledge is, at its origin,

---

[1] *Essay.*, pp.101-106, 113-115.

[2] There are excellent examples of these forms of argument even in Newman's Anglican period; for example, in his first *Essay on Miracles*, in 1825-1826, when he defends against Hume the scriptural miracles. Another, highly successful, example is in Tract 85, "Scripture and the Creed", *Disc. Arg.*, pp.109-253.

a feeble, confused glimmer, ever endangered by our weakness and unfaithfulness. It gains in vigour and clarity as we are faithful, but how agonizing is our solitude when we try to live according to our conscience. For the world all around us precipitates itself towards its idols, and seeks to draw us along with it. It is impossible to avoid the world. It rises up against our conscience like Goliath before David, and we cannot elude the fight. We are unable to take refuge permanently within the four walls of the interior life, for our life is necessarily in the world.

Now, this world is in flagrant contradiction with the admonitions of conscience. We have only to look around to see that the world of man is entirely one monstrous edifice, as it were, which, day by day, is built up by the strength of those instincts, passions and activities which conscience warns us against. It is ruled by egoism, cruelty, pride and sensuality—passions which inspire the maxims daily dinned into our ears. To all appearances, the Lord of this world is not the God whose voice is dimly heard in conscience, but a hostile despot. The religious man, as he considers the world, sees no sign of the divine image he bears *within himself*, but only a monstrous giant *before him,* staring at him with mingled pity and contempt, and ready to annihilate him.[1]

Yet this world is not completely external to us, but lives and works in each one of us. In one aspect, we are of the world, we are the world. The very passions that give rise, at each instant, to the "world" make themselves heard, and their impulses felt, inside ourselves. We bear them as hidden and mighty accomplices of the world. Besides, it is in the world that we are brought up and receive our formation. We live in it as our natural and necessary element. We accept, unaware, and take for granted, a number of opinions held as true, which do not come from our conscience and are at variance with it. What the world owns in us, the part of the world to be found in us, makes up a good part of our personality; it is the surface of our being, the outside layer, the most visible and clamorous. It does not proceed from our inner, authentic nature, but is a kind of sediment which, with the tacit collaboration of our

---

[1] *Apologia*, pp.217-218; *Grammar*, pp.396-400. Naturally, this pessimistic view of the world is expressed in many sermons; for example, *Disc. M. Cong.*, pp.273-274; "The Church and the World", *Ser. Subj.*, p.119: "The whole visible course of things, nations, empires, states, polities, professions, trades, society, pursuits of all kinds, are, I do not say directly and formally sinful (of course not), but they 'come of evil' and have in them the nature of evil".

lower nature, is, so to speak, deposited on us; it clothes us with a
sort of public, impersonal character. It constitutes us as children
of the age, of a given nation, culture, class and family. The world
infests our mind with its own first principles, which seek to govern
it in as hidden and forceful a manner as those of conscience. They
infiltrate quietly, because they live "in the atmosphere of the time";
we breathe them in unawares. Every child is subject to their mortal infection.[1] What kind of resistance can our conscience put up
against the attraction of this great world? How can it make its
voice heard amid the din within and around us? Surely we are
inevitably doomed, if conscience has only itself to count on.
Immersed in the world, conscience finds itself in an impossible
situation. Normally, it lacks the power to accomplish its essential
task. In the long run, it seems impossible for us, no matter how
keen our attention, to distinguish always the voice that speaks in
us, whether it is that of conscience or that of the world and the
passions. We are conquered in advance.[2]

What is still worse is that, with all our efforts, we fail at times
to follow the clearest injunctions. We sin, and the light becomes
even dimmer. We are terrified, as we feel the impending sentence
of the invisible Judge. We have deserved it, and there is no escape;
we are lost.[3] We see ourselves drawn down to the mysterious
depths of evil. Clearly, we belong to a race that is, somehow or
other, far removed from God.[4] It is not he who abandons us, but
we who withdraw from him; and so he hides his face from us.
My bad conscience and the strange spectacle of the world speak

---

[1] All this is set forth most vividly in the sermons. "Faith and the World",
Ser. Subj., pp.89-107, and "The Religion of the Pharisee", *Occ. Ser.*, pp.15-30,
describe the philosophy of the world in forceful terms. The hidden influence
of the world on the man with a religious upbringing is splendidly analysed
in "The Contest between Faith and Sight", *O.U.S.*, pp.120-135.

[2] *Occ. Ser.*, p.66; *O.U.S.*, p.131. Kierkegaard says, for example, "Even
with the best, the voice of conscience is too often mixed with many others,
and it is easy for this solitary voice to be drowned in a crowd of others"
(*Purity of Heart*).

[3] *Occ. Ser.*, p.67; *P.P.S.*, II, p.20; *Grammar*, pp.423, 486, 487.

[4] Like Pascal, Bossuet, and many others, Newman considers that the
spectacle of the world irresistably suggests to the religious mind the doctrine of original sin: "*If* there be a God, *since* there is a God, the human race
is implicated in some terrible aboriginal calamity. It is out of joint with the
purposes of its Creator. This is a fact, a fact as true as the fact of existence;
and thus the doctrine of what is theologically called original sin becomes to
me almost as certain as that the world exists, and as the existence of God"
(*Apologia*, p.128).

plainly on this point. The only possible explanation of the silence of God in the world, and of the desperate anguish in the hearts of all, is the fact of sin.[1]

It follows conclusively that, in the world as it is, conscience cannot exercise its full rights; the light it affords can never become intense enough to give us a pure, integral knowledge of God and his will. The life of religion is bound to be stunted. Such a catastrophe, however, cannot be final, so long as the course of events is governed by Providence. Sin and error notwithstanding, conscience continues to testify to the fact of a benevolent Providence. We must, therefore, wait upon the intervention of God. It is to him that conscience turns in absolute confidence, imploring his light and clearer tokens of his Being and will, a firmer hold on those great truths of which it possesses only vague intimations. In its guilt, the soul hopes for mercy and forgiveness from him. In its intolerable, yet inevitable, situation, conscience, encouraged by the thought of Providence, hopes for aid from above.[2]

What will God's intervention be, if it is to counter the influence of the world? Our very condition evidently requires that he should send against it an antagonist equally tangible and visible, and endowed with proportionate strength; and this would be nothing other than a visible institution, teaching authoritatively what has been divinely revealed, and possessed of the same communal strength which the world enjoys against the isolated individual. Conscience, weak as it is and endangered, would find itself reflected objectively in a revealed religion where, in its moments of hesitation, it would see, as in a mirror, a counterpart of its true self. In Revelation it would see the fullness of that sublime truth of which, left to itself, it has but a vague surmise; and, in addition, it might discover that deeper knowledge of God and his will, which is beyond its natural powers, though it is the object of its infinite aspirations. Thus it is that conscience "realises" its need of a religion of authority, revealed and dogmatic. Under the pressure of this need, the religious man has only to be presented with

[1] *Grammar*, pp.397-399.

[2] *Ibid.*, pp.422-424, supplemented by *P.P.S.*, II, pp.17-21, and *Occ. Ser.*, pp.66-68. These two sermons bring out the disadvantages of conscience as situated in the world, the practical impossibility of a sufficient knowledge of God and his will, and the practical impossibility of avoiding sin. This is what impels it to see the necessity of revelation.

Christianity, with its revealed doctrine—so pure in itself, so harmonious with the promptings of conscience—and to hear its message of salvation and perceive its historical grounds of authenticity, in order to recognize it, spontaneously, almost intuitively, as the message he had hoped for, the Good Tidings of the God whom he hears in his conscience.

Further, anyone who admits the truth of Christianity is logically bound to acknowledge the Catholic Church. For a revealed religion has to speak with authority, to assert itself against a hostile world, keep itself unchanged under the impact of external influences. All this requires an infallible authority in command. With mankind as it is, a revealed, dogmatic religion is inconceivable apart from an infallible authority. Let us suppose that, at a given moment of history, God presents man with a Revelation destined to endure for centuries and entrusts it to the free play of human intellects; it is easy to foresee the inevitable result.

On the one hand, this Revelation would spread and develop in an intellectual élite; but, delivered over to reason, it would not be long in deteriorating and would end in hopeless confusion, so that a chaos of opinions would finally replace what was originally given. That could be foreseen, given the nature of man, and it is confirmed by the history of Protestantism. Reason—not in itself, but as we see it at work in history—avowedly tends to confusion and scepticism in religion.

On the other hand, this Revelation will be incorporated with the practices of popular devotion. Now, it is a fact that the religious practices of the masses, who seek their own satisfaction, clearly tend to degrade religious values to the level of superstition in various forms. Consequently, to rectify these two tendencies, a divine organ of truth must be set up over them. Without it, a dogmatic religion could not possibly survive; and, if this authority were to disappear, the world, to which Revelation should be a counterpoise, would speedily engulf it.

The only religion to claim a living, infallible authority, is that taught by the Catholic Church. It is, too, the only one which furnishes the spectacle of a continuous development leading, under the guidance of ecclesiastical authority, not to a hopeless fragmentation, but to a theology of increasing precision and clarity. Hence, conscience may rightly presume that in this Church alone the authentic form of Christianity is perpetuated.[1]

D. Critical observations:

We will conclude this chapter with some critical observations and with an attempt to place Newman's system in the general scheme of Catholic apologetics.

As regards method, the proof by convergence of probabilities is one of the most valuable elements in Newman's system and marks a real progress in apologetics. Once it is understood that the force of the argument comes, not from each piece of reasoning individually, but from the convergence of all to one point, its value is easily seen. It was Newman's great merit to have methodically analysed and applied this mode of proof in the "moral sciences". Yet it was not entirely unknown before. The great scholastics point out, on occasion, that a fact of history can be proved with certainty by means of a number of considerations of which each, taken separately, points only to a probability.[2] The Jesuit, Michael d'Elizalde, outlined a whole system of apologetics proving the fact of revelation by the convergence of many separate arguments.[3]

Pascal, in his clear and precise way, had already formulated the method, and he based the plan of his *Pensées* on the encounter between conscience, with its sense of guilt, and historical Christianity.[4]

At the beginning of the 18th century, a start was made to apply the calculus of probabilities, or at least its principles, to moral problems.[5] Amort, an authority on the theory of probability, used it in apologetics; Newman quotes him in the *Grammar*.[6]

---

[1] This argument is stated with force and at length in the *Apologia*, pp.219-225. The latter part, which might be called a *demonstratio catholica*, is restated in greater detail in the *Essay*, pp.55-98. We shall return to this point below.

[2] Cf. for instance, St Thomas on the Resurrection, *S.T.*, III, qu.55, a.6, ad.1.

[3] For Elizalde (*Forma verae religionis quaerendae et inveniendae* (Naples, 1622)), the fact of revelation is morally evident. He speaks of the evidence arising from a comprehensive view of numerous arguments, each of which contributes to the conclusion. Cf. F. Schlagenhaufen, S.J., "Die Glaubensgewissheit und ihre Begründung in der Neuscholastik", *Zietschr. fur Kath. Theol.*, LVI (1932), p.317.

[4] Jeanne Russier, *La foi selon Pascal* (Paris, 1949), pp.319-329.

[5] H. Pinard de la Boullaye, *L'Etude comparée des religions* (Paris, 1925), II, p.397, note 1.

[6] *Grammar*, p.411.

But Amort only aims at showing that the truth of Christianity is more probable than its falsity.[1] Moreover, this method was already known in England; and Newman observes that it is used in philosophy as well as in astronomy, physics, law, and literary criticism.[2] Butler has some penetrating observations on its use in apologetics.[3] Newman, however, starting from the outline given by Butler, was the first to venture a strict analysis and defence of this complex procedure. His explanation is still, it would seem, the most balanced that has yet been given. Pinard de la Boullaye seems to reject it as being carried to extremes,[4] but he obviously failed to understand Newman; and his own theory, which makes the proof equivalent to a *reductio ad absurdum* is an undue simplification and beside the point. Newman asserts that seeing the convergence of probabilities and apprehending its force is an irreducible act, "instinctive" or "intuitive", and by it the full significance of the whole is grasped *per modum unius*.[5] It does not, however, follow, as Pinard seems to think, that there takes place, by instinct, a "leap", rationally indefensible, beyond the limits justified by the facts. There is, certainly, a leap beyond what could be deduced by formal logic, but not beyond what is drawn by the higher logic of the illative sense. This logic reaches further than formal logic—a position that is quite defensible. Hence, Newman's argument cannot be impeached except by those who hold that valid conclusions are to be obtained only by syllogisms. For Pinard, the proof by convergence is simply a *reductio ad absurdum,* and that concludes the matter.[6] The convergence of a number of signs, he says, requires a sufficient reason, and the only one that can be given is the truth of the one conclusion to which each of them, individually, points. Of course, this is so, and Newman does not say otherwise;[7] but he is aware that, in asserting this, he has yet explained nothing. Once we are certain that a convergence is so binding on us that the only sufficient reason for it is the truth of the conclusion, the work is already done. It is then easy enough

---

[1] *Ibid.* Actually, Amort's argument is identical with that of Elizalde.

[2] *Grammar*, pp.316-329.

[3] *Ibid.*, pp.319-320: *Essay*, pp.108-109.

[4] H. Pinard de la Boullaye, *op. cit.*, pp.398-400.

[5] *Grammar*, pp.275, 291-292, 301-302.

[6] H. Pinard de la Boullaye, *op. cit.*, pp.400-405.

[7] *Grammar*, pp.295, 300, 319-320.

to subsume this under the major premise : to admit anything without sufficient reason is absurd. Therefore.... But the difficulty lies in the minor—when do the convergent probabilities reach the state that the conclusion they point to cannot be denied without absurdity? Where is the precise frontier and how is it to be drawn? That is the whole question. Newman replies that, faced with this problem, logic is silent, and, when it withdraws, the thinking personality takes over.[1] The practised eye, right judgment, experience, proper disposition, natural sense, all come into play. Ultimately, technique is no substitute for the vigour of personal thought; that is the main proposition of the *Grammar*. Does that mean that, in the event, it is impossible to obtain absolute certainty altogether? Not at all, but in most cases, no doubt, the evidence will not be complete. A good detective novel is enough to teach us that. Everything points to the principal character— his revolver, his handkerchief, his personal relations with the victim, the witnesses who saw him, at the time of the murder, roaming nervously in the neighbourhood of the crime. Everyone sees him as guilty, yet, in the end, he is not the murderer at all. Yet such cases are quite consistent with the convergence of probabilities, at other times, quite rightly leading us to a truth which cannot be gainsaid. There may not be metaphysical certainty, but there is moral certainty, which excludes all positive doubt.

In contemporary thought, the method of proof by convergence of probabilities enjoys great authority. History uses it as a matter of course, but it is accepted as well in other sciences, even in philosophy. Burloud, for example, considers it a scientific instrument of great importance in psychology;[2] Bergson prefers it to abstract reasoning as a means to arrive at solid conclusions in philosophy.[3]

[1] *Grammar.*, p.369: "Men become personal when logic fails them; it is their way of appealing to the primary elements of their own thought, and to their own illative sense, against the principles and judgment of others".

[2] A. Burloud, *Principes d'une psychologie des tendances* (Paris, 1938), pp.83-92. Burloud calls this method "restrospective induction", to distinguish it from the usual "amplifying induction". Neither brings absolute certainty (p.85), but "convergence brings about a probability practically equivalent to certainty" (p.92).

[3] H. Bergson, *Mind Energy, Lectures and Essays* (London, 1920). Bergson sees himself as a philosopher, confronted with the choice between pure deduction and the weighing up of the real, in all its aspects. He declares himself in favour of the second method, and describes it thus: "We are drawn, with the widening of our experience, to an ever higher probability, and so to the ultimate limit of final certainty".

What distinguishes Newman's apologetic, as well as that of Pascal's *Pensées,* is that the probabilities he makes use of are not derived solely from history, but are also presumptions that conscience needs to justify *a priori.* These antecedent probabilities are the chief ones. They give his system its characteristic structure, which entitles it to be defined as an existential dialectic of conscience. A "dialectic", that is, a mental process by which an initial proposition takes on a fuller significance by the reduction of antitheses to a more concrete synthesis; a dialectic "of conscience", since what conscience makes known to us constitutes the starting-point of the dialectical movement; an "existential" dialectic, because it does not originate in an apparent contradiction of ideas, but in an actual experience of opposite tensions—a universal experience arising out of the very nature of man.

Newman's method has sometimes been compared to modern existentialism.[1] J. Willebrands, the first to do so, was careful to point out their differences. Still, their points of agreement are remarkable. In both cases, we find the fundamental distinction between a knowledge which is prior to reflection and implicit, and explicit thought, the product of reflection. Equally with the existentialists, Newman asserts the radical dependence of the second on the first. Reflection is not creative; it merely takes up on the plane of conceptual analysis the activities of an "experiential" thought to which it can never be equal: "No thinking is able to comprise all our thought".[2]

This, however, leads to a very ambiguous position. Granted that the relations between the spontaneous life of the mind and its reflective activity may be expressed identically from the point of view of either, yet the idea we form of this spontaneous life may vary considerably, and so the processes of reflection take on a quite different meaning. Whereas Newman attempts to clarify and estimate a development carried through by the moral personality by translating it into conceptual terms, Merleau-Ponty, for instance, tries to look beyond cultural developments and disguises to a primitive state antecedent to reflection which would be human life in its purity. In this matter, Newman's approach is shared by M. Blondel and G. Marcel, just as Newman himself continued, without being aware of it, the kind of thought

---

[1] J. G. M. Willebrands, *op. cit.,* pp.383-384.

[2] M. Merleau-Ponty, *Phénoménologie de la perception* (Paris, 1945), p.ix.

characteristic of St. Augustine, who held that it was the function of reflection or *cogitatio* to bring to consciousness a *notitia*, a pre-conscious knowledge of God, whose clarity is proportionate to our love and fidelity, and in whose light everything is viewed.

Newman is still closer to existentialism, in the widest sense of the word, in his distinction between the self at the deepest level, the source of true personality, and the worldly, superficial self, alienating man from himself and his rightful mode of being. This distinction occurs throughout modern philosophy, in Heidegger with his well-known *on*, which cloaks and stifles the original person, in the *moi public* and the *moi privé* of R. Le Senne, *le moi de l'être* and *le moi de l'avoir* of G. Marcel. Once more, these resemblances are misleading; they hide differences which are radical. To a Marxist, religion is the sphere of alienation, the *regio dissimilitudinis,* the place of dissemblance, in the words of St Augustine. For Newman, however, as for Kierkegaard, it is through conscience and faith that man is aroused to his true life, and his alienation from it is consummated in atheism. On this point, Newman is clearly very close to Kierkegaard.

We can see from this how Newman's method may be called an "existential" one; for it starts out from a "fundamental situation" —another existentialist concept[1]—brought about by the opposition between the true self of conscience and the godless world that tries to stifle it by cloaking it with a superficial personality formed according to its ideas. Newman's whole apologetic is designed to clarify this fundamental situation of man's life, and to understand it in the light of the primary certitude of conscience, namely, the existence of a God whose Providence governs the whole world and the course of events in it. We can, therefore, call it "existential", provided we attach to the word an exact meaning.

Newman's position in the history of Catholic apologetics can now be determined. His method is clearly distinct from the traditional one, which also begins with the existence and nature of God, and natural religion. Following St Thomas, it shows the necessity of a revelation if all men are to attain a knowledge of God adequate for them to live according to the requirements of natural religion.

[1] Cf. for example, G. Marcel, "Situations fondamentales et situations limités chez Karl Jaspers", *Recherches Philosophiques*, II (1932-1933), pp.317-348; "Aperçus phénoménologiques sur l'être en situation", *Ibid.*, VI (1936-1937) pp.1-21.

This is the core of Newman's argument from conscience; hence, his ideas are not so unheard of in the Church as is sometimes thought. In the traditional method, however, they are presented as a logically connected sequence; but, with Newman, we have a concrete description of the dialectical movement of the anguished conscience seeking, in the light of its early convictions, a path through a hostile world. Newman's apologetic starts from the experience of God in a specific situation, an existential one, fraught with anxiety and distress of mind; and its procedure is one of "realization", by which the conscience strives to understand its plight, and thus to regain and fortify, in despite of the world and its confusion, its certainties, by reconciling the sorry condition of man with the existence of a Providence. This is what gives the whole demonstration its motive power, its impulse, its unity and its inwardness. We have seen that Newman had no intention of discarding the traditional arguments. The presumptions given by conscience are not conclusive, apart from external signs; but the objective factors are all drawn in, as by a powerful current, to the personal movement of the religious mind.

In so far as it is an existential dialectic of conscience, Newman's apologetic cannot be equated with the later systems of Cardinal Dechamps and Maurice Blondel.[1] Bremond wrote that, "Had he been born sixty years later, Newman would not have written either the *University Sermons*, nor the *Grammar*; he would have written *Action*".[2] This opinion is without foundation. We do not deny the affinity of the two geniuses; a valuable study could be devoted to it, as well as to Newman's influence on Blondel. The latter, however, remains a quite independent and original thinker. The main lines of his philosophy have not changed since his first

[1] For a comparison of the two thinkers, the reader would do well to read the short work of Blondel, "Le problème de la philosophie catholique" *Cahiers de la nouvelle journée* (Paris, 1932). On pages 61-112 of the work, Blondel takes up the theme of the magnificent articles on Dechamps by F. Mallet. On Dechamps, cf. the historical study of Alfred Deboutte, C.SS.R., *De apologetische methode van Kardinaal Dechamps* (Bruges-Brussels, 1945), and also, Maurice Becqué, "Le fait intérieur dans l'apologetique du Cardinal Dechamps", *Eph. Theol. Lov.*, XXI (1945), 97-166.

[2] H. Bremond, "Apologie pour les Newmanistes français", *Rev. Prat. d'Apol.*, III (1906-1907), p.665, note. In *Nouv. Rev. Apol.*, XXXVI (1939), M. Hayot has published an article in which he calls Newman a precursor of that "*apologetic of the threshold* which questions the profound desires of the human soul, finding there an aspiration, ineffective perhaps, but *essential*, towards the *true* Good it postulates and which transcends it" (p.219).

publications, written when he was completely ignorant of Newman. No doubt it is very striking that their conceptions of the relations between real and notional thought are so similar; but, though Blondel makes use of the same terms as Newman, he did not borrow the idea from him. His philosophy of thought, worked out entirely on the basis of a powerful and conscious metaphysic, is far more comprehensive than the sober and purely psychological descriptions of the English thinker.

In any case, the central idea of the "apologetic of the threshold" is not to be found in Newman. What Blondel teaches is a dialectic of the "profound will", that ontological tendency whose hidden working permeates all the life of man. His apologetic seeks to equate the *volonté voulue,* or the empirical will, with the essential propensity he calls the *volonté voulante.* It leads to Catholicism precisely inasmuch as the Catholic religion offers us the supernatural possession of God. Newman's method, on the contrary, is a dialectic of conscience. The soul, its gaze fixed on Providence, seeks a state in which the seed of religion, already present in conscience, may grow, and it finally accepts Catholicism as an ecclesiastical institution, revealed, dogmatic, governed by an infallible authority, abstracting from the content, natural or supernatural, of the Revelation it transmits. Newman cannot be accorded the honour of being the forerunner of Blondel.

Chapter 2

INVARIABILITY AND DEVELOPMENT

NEWMAN'S passage from Anglicanism to Catholicism implied a profound change in his conception of apostolic tradition. From a strict application of the rule stated by St. Vincent de Lérins, he went over to the theory of development, substituting a dynamic for a static conception.[1] Yet apostolic tradition was still, for him, the single source and primary norm of the faith; and the dogmatic principle remained the cornerstone of his view of the world. The idea of development, however, brought about a change in his conception of the *depositum*[2] and of tradition. His theory of development starts from the proposition that all dogmatic development forms part of the apostolic tradition, and, though there is growth, there is no addition or discovery of new truths.[3] The fruits of development belong to the original Revelation;[4] they form, with it, one single truth;[5] they are themselves revealed,[6] descended from heaven,[7] divine,[8] willed by the Author of Revelation himself.[9] These are the different expressions used by Newman, in the *Essay*, to express the one basic

[1] This is exactly what is stated and justified in the Introduction of the *Essay*.

[2] The word *depositum* itself acquires a more or less dynamic sense. See *Newman-Perrone*, pp.404, 417.

[3] *Ibid.*, p.418.

[4] *Essay*, p.92.

[5] *Ibid.*, p.169.

[6] *Ibid.*, pp.79-80.

[7] *Ibid.*, p.93.

[8] *Ibid.*, p.120.

[9] *Ibid.*, pp.63, 74, 75.

requirement. Once he has discovered the law of development, he is faced with a new task, which consists, mainly, in reconciling the two elements of tradition, invariability and development, tradition and growth. He has to determine how they can be consistent with each other, to set out how we can hold that the faith, as it is professed today, is identical with the original. This is the precise object of the *Essay*.

As we have already seen, Newman was still on the defensive when he wrote the *Essay*. He was concerned to show that the doctrinal increment gained by the Church over the centuries was no alteration or deformation, but a genuine development[1] in no wise infringing the essential permanence of the Christian Revelation and its continuing identity. It was only at a later date that he perceived clearly that the theory of development could serve as a basis for a positive apologetic, that the continuous development of tradition, as taking place in the Church under the guidance of an authority claiming to be infallible, is, of itself, a positive sign of the divine authenticity of that Church. Some time after his conversion, when he made his summing-up of Anglicanism and the Oxford Movement, he gave additional emphasis to this thesis.[2] In the previous chapter, we have already expounded it, and allotted its place in his apologetic. Here we shall deal chiefly with the first problem, the reconciliation of the invariability of doctrine with its development.

Our account will be divided into three parts. First, we will briefly examine what the reconciliation of the two ideas, identity and development, involves. It is a question of philosophy, and it has to be resolved before studying the historical problem of doctrinal identity in Catholicism throughout the course of its development.

In the two sections which follow, we shall see what reasons Newman put forward in seeking to justify the historical identity of current doctrine with the faith as originally proclaimed. We have already seen that, in re-editing the *Essay* in 1878, he clearly distinguished two parts, each of which corresponds to a different

---

[1] We use the term "development" in the following senses: (1) the way development happens, or its fruit; (2) development in general, apart from fidelity, or otherwise, to the original ideas; or development in particular, true development as opposed to corruption.

[2] *Diff. Angl.*, I, pp.392-396.

argument.[1] The first makes up his characteristic proof. It takes as presuppositions the principle of conscience and the dogmatic principle of Christianity, and draws from them a preliminary presumption. If God has given the world a dogmatic revelation, we may expect *a priori* that it should not disappear. But mankind being as it is, it is bound to grow, like something living, within a religious communion. In other words, it will keep its essential immutability only by a continuous and gradual development. This thesis, established *a priori,* is then confirmed by examples taken from history. His proof, then, is based on *historical* and *religious* considerations.

In the second part, Newman adopts a different standpoint. He renounces here any Christian or religious presupposition, and examines rationally the history of doctrine in the Church. He then attempts to establish the criteria in a sound philosophy for distinguishing authentic developments from corruptions, and applies them to the history of the Christian Revelation. This time, we have a *historico-philosophical* proof.

Each of these has its special function. The first, from "within", makes up a part of that inner movement of his thought we have called the "existential dialectic of conscience". It is decisive for the religiously-minded person. But, supposing difficulties are still present, they have to be dealt with, as far as possible, by pure reason; and this gives rise to the second, the "extrinsic", argument. Its aims are negative and its force is not compelling. All that it furnishes is a probability.

Section A

The Compatibility of Ideas

To a philosopher, the coupling of the two concepts, invariability and development, is an obvious paradox. Stated in the most general terms, it is reducible to the opposition of being and change, one of the oldest problems in western philosophy. How can a being be identical with itself, in other words, not change, and yet grow and develop, and so be, in some degree, modified? That is the fundamental problem of metaphysics. As such, it did not claim Newman's attention, for he was not naturally disposed to treat of

[1] See above, pp.51-52.

such questions. He did not, therefore, study expressly the general problem of identity in development. Rather, he assumed the conclusion as a basis of his theory, or, we may better say, he sensed that the two problems went together. His analysis never envisaged the general question, but he must have entertained, at least implicitly, some idea of the correspondence or coincidence of the two. Certain elements of the solution were bound to emerge here and there; and we shall see how this occurred.

According to the *Essay,* we can speak of "development" only if those aspects which make up the developed idea are truly a part of the original, and included in it.[1] Development is the passage from implicit profession to formal expression.[2] Here we have a first formula to express identity, that is, the *inclusion* or *implicitation* of all the aspects of the idea in the original—it may be, as we have seen, in a kind of real but obscure "apprehension" whose richness finds later expression in abstract concepts. This inclusion may be apparent in various ways. The concrete idea does not dwell only in the imagination, but finds expression in sensibility and in conduct. Sometimes, it is a pure "source-idea", unrelated to an object of thought, and making its presence known only through its influence on action.[3] If the idea does not represent something external, the development it undergoes is, as we have seen, moral.[4] Newman, however, did not always expressly distinguish different kinds of inclusion from one another.

The second formula is more of an organic one. It governs the analysis of the seven norms, as will be explained later. It is of less value for each of the doctrines taken separately than for Catholic doctrine as a whole. The final doctrine is the *perfect fulfilment of a preliminary imperfect state,* as the man is the perfect form of the child. When, therefore, we come to consider the doctrine as a whole in a purely analytical way, we may agree that something has been added, and that the mutual relations of the parts have been modified. To a synthetic view, however, it is evident that the points of departure and arrival are, respectively, the imperfect

---

[1] *Essay,* p.38: "This process will not be a development, unless the complex of aspects constituting the most recent form really belong to the primitive idea, may be held to be included in that idea".

[2] *Ibid.,* p.439: "The continued and firm progress of sacred science, starting from implicit faith to issue in the formal pronouncement".

[3] See above, pp.111-112.

[4] See above, p.178.

and perfect forms of the same being, which, consequently, is more perfectly itself in the second stage than in the first.[1] Later on, we shall be in a position to pass judgment on the real nature and meaning of this idea.

Finally, there is a third formula, this time one of the logical order: *the conclusions are already present in the preceding propositions*. This is the reason why what is deduced as a conclusion from the *depositum* is not, strictly speaking, something new. In one sense, the conclusions are, certainly, additions, but, in another aspect, they really form part of the *depositum*. Newman makes use of this formula only in his later works, occasionally, and in the context of scientific theology.[2] He no longer draws a distinction, as he seemed to do in the Oxford sermons, between two types of reasoning: those whose outcome is something new, and those which result in nothing really new.[3] However, it is all too little worked out and examined by him for us to draw any firm conclusion. Can we apply this third formula to the entire doctrinal development in so far as Newman regards it as a reasoning in the broad sense of the term? Perhaps; and, in that case, we would have, roughly speaking, another aspect of the first formula. It would be necessary, however, to distinguish clearly between the *fact* of identity and its *justification*. Defending and justifying the identity of the result and the starting-point is, then, equivalent to showing that the first is a conclusion correctly drawn from the second. But we have seen that, with living thought, logical tests can apply only in part. The work of logic needs to be completed by the illative sense; what it lacks has to be supplied by the

---

[1] This idea is never found expressed in strict form, but it follows from a number of observations. For example, *Essay*, p.419: "It has been observed already that a strict correspondence between the various members of a development and those of the doctrine from which it is derived is more than we have any right to expect. The bodily structure of a grown man is not merely that of a magnified boy; he differs from what he was in his make and proportions; still manhood is the perfection of boyhood".

[2] *Idea*, p.441: "As the conclusion is always contained in the premises, such deductions, properly speaking, add nothing". Cf. also, *Ibid.*, p.223, and *Grammar*, p.147: "In a sense, these deductions are a portion of the *depositum* of faith or *credenda*, while in another sense they are additions to it".

[3] Newman there affirms: "Ideas and their developments are commonly not identical, the development being but the carrying out of the idea into its consequences. Thus the doctrine of Penance may be called a development of the doctrine of Baptism; whereas the developments in the doctrines of the Holy Trinity and the Incarnation are mere portions of the original impression and modes of representing it". *O.U.S.*, pp.329-330.

personal ability to estimate proofs, and, in the case of doctrinal developments, the final decision rests with the *magisterium* of the Church. This has been adequately explained above.[1]

SECTION B

THE HISTORICO-RELIGIOUS SOLUTION

The method we are about to use has just been described in the previous chapter.[2] We will now study a typical application of Newman's argument from the convergence of antecedent probability and historical evidence. As far as concerns the method, it will be enough to recall how Newman envisages the relationship of the two factors. In his opinion, the reasonable presumption of a religious intelligence is so strong as to make historical evidence almost unnecessary : "From the claims of a sound logic, I think it right to insist that, whatever early testimonies I may bring in support of later doctrinal developments, are in great measure brought *ex abundanti,* a matter of grace, not of compulsion."[3] He even considers he has the right to interpret the facts of history in the light of this presumption. The identity of Christian doctrine is so strongly guaranteed by anterior reasoning that we may retrospectively expound the primitive state of the truths of faith in the light of the whole subsequent course of their development.[4]

There are three phases in the process of establishing the presumption that the primitive faith and developed Catholic doctrine are identical. First, it has to be made clear that, before any investigation into the facts, a development of Christian tradition, conformed to the plan of God, is to be expected. Next, we prove, still *a priori,* the probability of an infallible external authority guiding and guaranteeing the development. Finally, we show, in broad outline, that Catholicism today alone claims a development of the kind, directed by an infallible authority. In reproducing New-

---

[1] See above, pp.191-196.

[2] See above, pp.225-229.

[3] *Essay,* p.120.

[4] *Ibid.,* p.107: "The primitive state, and the proofs, of each doctrine considered ought always to be interpreted in the light of the development finally attained"; cf. also p.114.

man's demonstration, we have to confine ourselves to the essential; it would be impossible to analyse the entire proof with all its convergent parts, and to estimate the force of every element in detail.

A. A true and faithful development of doctrine is to be expected:

The first principle on which Newman bases his demonstration is the dogmatic one, that God has, in the course of time, revealed a definite and changeless supernatural truth, in order to effect the salvation of man by faith in this truth. Thus it is immediately guaranteed that the truth in question can neither disappear nor be substantially altered.[1] His second principle is that this revelation lives within our intelligence and follows the natural laws of the intelligence. This is based on the general theory, borrowed from Butler, according to which the divine governance of the supernatural order follows the same principles as in the natural order.[2] These two principles govern the procedure in the first part of the thesis.

The human mind is unable to grasp immediately the idea of an objective reality, but arrives at it by degrees. If, moreover, the idea is a living one, its aspects will be all the more numerous; if it has a social and political application, its development will be correspondingly complex and dependent on events. Now, Christianity is an idea of this sort; it is objective, living and social. We may, therefore, presume at the outset that human thought can possess the full wealth of such an idea only in the course of a highly complicated development,[3] which, far from altering or corrupting it, will, in accordance with the will of God, result

---

[1] In the Introduction to the *Essay* (p.10), Newman sweeps aside the suggestion that there could have been real changes in Christian teaching and that, in this way, Christianity adapted itself constantly to differences in time and place: "It is difficult to understand how such a view would be compatible with the special idea of a revealed truth; in fact, those who defend it more or less reject the supernatural claims of Christianity; we have not, therefore, to concern ourselves with it here".

[2] See *Essay*, p.57. This first part concludes with a long quotation from Butler on the analogy of nature and religion, in regard to the progressive character of the relations of God with men (pp.74-75).

[3] *Ibid.*, pp.55-56. This is simply an application of the psychology of the idea described above. Newman concludes his description as follows: "Among these great doctrines, we Christians will surely not refuse a capital place to Christianity. Before any study of the later facts of history, we ought to expect this, merely from our observation of its beginnings" (p.56).

in a more perfect possession of the original revelation.[1]

In this consists the essence of the proof. Newman, however, devotes the greater part of his treatment to the special problems arising out of the unique character of the case in question; for Christianity, in fact, came into the world in a unique manner, by a Revelation set out, by divine inspiration, in Holy Scripture. The question thus arises, whether inspiration does not make development quite unnecessary. Newman considers it in every possible light. His first answer is that ideas live in the mind, not in the written word, and, therefore, we have to ask if the word discloses its entire content at once, or only by degrees.[2] The Scriptures, in their unsystematic form, their diversity, their use of metaphor, make up an inexhaustible source of new discoveries, a kind of oracle, whose content is not at once apparent, but which confirms, in a most astonishing way, ideas maturing in a later age. An instance of this is how the Church found in the words of Christ, "Whose sins you shall forgive they are forgiven them", a striking confirmation of Confession.[3]

Besides, no words could express all the subsequent forms the divine would assume in its life in the community where it would be, as it were, incorporated; particularly as Christianity is destined to subsist in all ages and countries, with the result that its tone and mode of application vary accordingly. This helps on the elucidation of the meaning of Scripture and also extends it in different directions, with both good and bad results. Everyone appeals to

----

[1] This section concludes with the following observation: "From the necessity of the case, from the history of all sects and parties in religion, and from the analogy and example of Scripture, we may fairly conclude that Christian doctrine admits of formal, legitimate and true developments, or of developments by its Divine Author" (Essay., p.74).

[2] Ibid., p.56: "It may be objected that inspired documents, such as the Holy Scriptures, at once determine its doctrine without further trouble. But . . . that idea is not in the sacred text, but in the mind of the reader; and the question is, whether that idea is communicated to him in its completeness and minute accuracy, on its first apprehension, or expands in his heart and intellect, and comes to perfection in the course of time.

[3] Cf. Ibid., pp.71-73: "It is in point to notice also the structure and style of Scripture, a structure so unsystematic and various, and a style so figurative and indirect, that no one would presume at first sight to say what is in it and what is not . . . It may be added that in fact all the definitions or received judgments of the Church rest upon definite, though even sometimes obscure sentences of Scripture". There follow eight examples.

the Bible, that is, he reasons from its premises, or wrings from it evidence, in support of this or that opinion derived from his personal reflections on the text itself. The only way to control this spontaneous life of the mind and to avoid confusion is for there to be a means of distinguishing between true and false interpretations.[1] In addition, if Scripture is to provide us with clear-cut ideas, it can be only through development. For example, every term in the sentence, "The Word was made flesh", raises a problem whose solution gives rise to fresh ones.[2]

Finally, the Bible leads us to ask many questions it leaves unanswered, even though, as time goes on, the need for an answer becomes imperative. One of these, for instance, concerns the canon of Scripture, the list of inspired books of which it is composed. Had the apostles known of it, they could have left the answer in so many words; but, in fact, God in his wisdom preferred to let it be fixed in the slow process of time.[3] All these considerations point to the conclusion that Scripture, of its very nature, confirms rather than opposes our presumption about the correspondence of doctrinal developments with the designs of God.[4]

Newman concludes, in characteristic fashion, with a whole

[1] *Essay.*, pp.58-59: "Principles require a very various application according to persons and circumstances, and must be thrown into new shapes according to the form of society which they are to influence. Hence all bodies of Christians develop the doctrines of Scripture . . . the fact of false developments or corruptions, involves the correspondent manifestation of true ones. Moreover, all parties appeal to Scripture . . . but argument implies deduction, that is, development".

[2] *Ibid.*, p.59: "When we turn to the consideration of particular doctrines on which Scripture lays the greatest stress, we shall see that it is absolutely impossible for them to remain in the mere letter of Scripture, if they are to be more than mere words. or to convey a definite idea to the recipient. When it is declared that 'the Word became flesh', three wide questions open upon us on the very announcement. What is meant by 'the Word', what by 'flesh', what by 'became'? The answers . . . will suggest a series of secondary considerations".

[3] *Ibid.*, p.60: "This moreover should be considered, that great questions exist in the subject-matter of which Scripture treats, which Scripture does not solve; questions too so real, so practical, that they must be answered. Such is the question of the Canon of Scripture and its inspiration. These difficulties . . . it is quite conceivable that an apostle might have dissipated them all in a few words, had Divine Wisdom thought fit. But the decision has been left to time, to the slow process of thought, the influence of mind upon mind, the issues of controversy, and the growth of opinion".

[4] *Ibid.*, p.74.(Text quoted above, p.248, note 1.)

sheaf of analogies taken both from the revealed and the natural order, to show that development is a universal characteristic of the dealings of God with men. Revelation itself is given only by degrees. The prophecies of the Old Testament do not form a group of disconnected and independent predictions, but are a slow growth in clarity and concreteness of one and the same view of the future. The principal doctrines of the Old Testament—for instance, the kind of sacrifice pleasing to God—became known only by degrees; and even the Jewish theocracy develops politically through the centuries.[1]

The same is true of the New Testament, and of the sayings of Christ and the apostles; and so we may expect them to be subject to the same process of development.[2] It is impossible to point to a time in the history of the early Church when development came to an end and the rule of faith was fixed once and for all.[3]

This account of the matter is supported by the analogy of the physical and moral order where, as Butler described it, everything advances by degrees towards perfection.[4] We may conclude that it was the will of God that the law of development should govern the sphere of revelation as well as that of creation.

B. An infallible governing authority is to be expected:

Revelation being committed to the working of the human mind, it must, necessarily, branch out in various directions. Who is to decide how far these developments accord with the primitive revelation? Looking at the question in the abstract, we might

---

[1] *Essay.*, pp.65-71.

[2] *Ibid.*, p.66-68: "The *affata* of Our Lord and his apostles are of a typical structure, parallel to the prophetic announcements above mentioned . . . It is probable antecedently that those doctrinal, political, ritual, and ethical sentences, which have the same structure, should admit the same expansion".

[3] *Ibid.*, p.68: "We shall find ourselves unable to fix an historical point at which the growth of doctrine ceased, and the rule of faith was once for all settled". This might give the impression that Newman did not distinguish precisely two developments, that of Revelation itself, and that of doctrine after revelation had ceased, especially as he never speaks of this cessation on the death of the last of the apostles. Still, this distinction was taken for granted by him since, as an Anglican, he considered that Revelation had been especially entrusted to the apostles and was wholly to be found in Scripture, though not on its surface.

[4] *Ibid.*, pp.74-75.

think that a theologian, completely at home in the history of dogma, could distinguish, without difficulty, true developments from corruptions. In fact, this is not so. All men, learned or simple, are caught up in the movement of life, and their judgments are bound to be affected, to some extent, by their temperament, character, inclinations and prejudices.[1]

Moreover, development, in the various forms it takes, as a living thing, is extremely obscure and subtle. The intellectual activity of a community spread over the whole world is continually productive of effects, true and false, important or insignificant. An unchanging rule is essential to find a path in this virgin forest.[2]

Of special complexity and delicacy are certain forms of development. Christianity came into the world primarily as an idea. It had to create for itself, little by little, a complete social framework, and abstract reason, with its strictly logical methods, is little suited to this task. Other kinds of development are moral ones and depend ultimately on the moral sense, which is so delicate and fluctuating. As to political developments, designed to govern the relations of Church and State, they are prone to all sorts of influences of an emotional nature, from chance events or arbitrary will. Where should we be if, in all these spheres, the decision was left to theologians?[3]

In any case, the Church is not a monastic cloister in the desert. It is caught up in the stress of the world, with its passions and its ideas. The opinions current in the world lay siege to it and penetrate its most hidden and sacred recesses. Without the firm guidance of authority, it would soon be caught in the toils of the world, its doctrine adultered and impaired, to end up in a scepticism from which there would be no escape.[4]

A living *magisterium*, under divine direction, is thus seen to be imperative, and this is confirmed by the agelong experience of Christianity. The rejection of infallible authority is followed, inevitably, in the passage of time, with a breakaway from unity, as is the case with Protestantism; or else the dogmatic principle is violated, as in Anglicanism, to the point of tolerating, within

[1] *Essay.*, pp.75-76.
[2] *Ibid.*, pp.76-77.
[3] *Ibid.*, pp.77-78.
[4] *Ibid.*, pp.89-90.

one and the same community, all kinds of contradictory opinions.[1] This shows the ineffectiveness of those norms of authority substituted by other religions for the infallible living authority. Protestants tried to set up the Bible as their authority and the distressing consequence is to be seen in Protestantism itself, which has emptied itself both of doctrine and of life. The Bible is clearly inadequate to direct and guarantee the course of development. In addition, modern criticism deprives it, more and more, of its authority.[2] The Anglicans, for their part, preferred an Establishment, a State Church, with the result that liberalism has become firmly entrenched within it, and religious indifference is widespread.[3] Newman had tried to set up the Oxford Movement on a patristic foundation, but no firm support could be found in the writings of the Fathers, who point the way to follow, but whose conclusions are not incontestable.[4]

Theology, it might seem, could settle questions of development by determining the essential characteristics both of true development and of corruption. That is true, but subtlety of argument is not decisive in matters where human passions are involved; and, in any case, the arguments of theology do not provide a sufficient guarantee. They serve to confirm a proposition, to refute objections, but not to demonstrate conclusively the truth of each development that occurs.[5] The nature of man requires a living infallible authority as the only means of curbing the excesses of the mind, and of providing sure guidance for the faithful against the deceptions of the world. If, then, God gave a dogmatic revelation

---

[1] *Essay.*, pp.90-91: "If Christianity is both social and dogmatic, and intended for all ages, it must, humanly speaking, have an infallible expounder. Else you will secure unity of form at the loss of unity of doctrine, or unity of doctrine at the loss of unity of form. By the Church of England a hollow uniformity is preferred to an infallible chair; and by the sects of England an interminable division. Germany and Geneva began with persecution, and have ended in scepticism".

[2] *Ibid.*, pp. 87-88; *Apologia*, p. 220: "Experience proves surely that the Bible does not answer a purpose for which it was never intended. A book after all cannot make a stand against the wild living intellect of man, and in this day it begins to testify, as regards its own structure and contents, to the power of that universal solvent, which is so successfully acting upon religious establishments".

[3] *Apologia*, p.220.

[4] See above, p.192.

[5] *Essay*, p.78.

for a momentous purpose, we may rightly presume that he provided us, too, with an infallible authority.[1]

This first argument is based on an analysis of what is essentially involved in each individual case taken in its entirety. A second proof Newman gives makes use of the principle of analogy. Christianity is a revealed religion. It exhibits visible signs of its divine origin and so requires everyone to accept its teaching as the infallible word of God. From its very beginning, it rests on the principle of authority. If Revelation includes truths which become manifest only at a later period, we should expect that the task of defining, guaranteeing, and teaching them should devolve, not on the reason of individuals, but on authority.[2] It is a general principle of the working of Providence that God continues his work in the same way as he initiated it. God proceeds always in a perfect manner; that is, his designs of such momentous consequence do not depend on a miscellaneous collection of principles, but form an "order", that is a fully coherent system, built up on a single fundamental principle. This applies to the present case. Revelation rests on the rock of authority, and so the entire order proceeding from it is based on the same principle: "As creation argues continual governance, so are Apostles harbingers of Popes".[3]

It might be objected that the radical difference between the natural and the supernatural order makes it impossible *a priori* to argue by analogy from one to the other. This objection, however, can be easily refuted. Admittedly, we cannot prove either the fact of a divine dispensation or the form it would take did it exist; but once we are assured a revelation has been given, it is perfectly permissible, by the use of analogy with the natural order, to make certain presumptions about it, not, indeed, as to its content—the Incarnation, for example, has no counterpart in nature —but as to its possession, in its structure, of the same marks of

---

[1] *Essay.*, pp.78, 88-89; *Apologia*, pp.220-221.

[2] *Essay.*, pp.79-80: "Christianity is a revelation which comes to us as a revelation, as a whole, objectively, and with a profession of infallibility; and the only question to be determined relates to the matter of the revelation. If then there are certain great truths or proprieties or observances, naturally and legitimately resulting from the doctrines originally professed, it is but reasonable to include these true results in the idea of the revelation; to consider them as parts of it, and if the revelation be not only true, but guaranteed as true, to anticipate that they will be guaranteed inclusively".

[3] *Ibid.*, p.86.

the divine wisdom as are to be found so abundantly in nature.[1]

In this connection, natural religion provides a useful comparison. For just as it is wholly based on conscience, an immanent and subjective principle of authority, demanding complete obedience at all times, so is revealed religion based wholly on its own proper principle, which is that of an external, objective authority, and the difference between the two forms of religion runs throughout their respective structures.[2]

These two arguments establish a strong probability that the dogmatic side of the Church's life is to be governed by a living authority with divine sanction. There are, however, certain objections, or arguments in the contrary sense, against the *a priori* probability of such an authority.

Is the principle of authority really effective, and does it provide the certainty required? We have to accept revelation as a whole on the word of authority; but, first of all, it is necessary to accept the authority itself and this we cannot do on the word of the same authority. We are thus driven back to reason, and this, at the most, can only furnish moral evidence that the authority of the Church does, in fact, speak in the name of God Revealing. But moral evidence leads only to a probable conclusion. If, then, the validity of the authority is not absolutely certain, all that it presents for our acceptance is likewise uncertain. To claim infallibility for what authority teaches, while the authority is itself only probable, is to assert what is contradictory.

Newman's reply is cautious. He begins with a few arguments *ad hominem*, drawn from analogy. The objection, he says, applies not only to ecclesiastical authority, but against the principle of authority itself, and so against Scripture, the apostles, and every authority to whom the objector appeals, or could appeal.[3] It, therefore, proves too much. Moreover, we accept as certain, quite apart from authority, many things which are supported only by probable arguments. He then proceeds to set aside the objection as logically fallacious. It rests on the assumption that probability, certainty and infallibility are predicated in the same way; whereas

[1] *Essay.*, pp.83-86.

[2] *Ibid.*, pp.86-87.

[3] The objector here is, especially, Newman himself, who had raised the same objection in *Via Media*, I, p.122; it was current among non-Catholics in England. In the *Grammar*, p.226, Newman attributes it to Chillingworth.

infallibility is a property of an objective function, evidence and probability belong to propositions, and certainty is a property of subjective assent to a certain proposition. To say that the Church is probably infallible is simply the same as saying that it is probable that the Church has the gift of judging infallibly in matters of faith, and there is no contradiction in that. An authority may be infallible, but I may have only a probable knowledge of this; yet I may submit to the authority in absolute faith and obedience because I know it is highly probable that it is infallible.[1]

This reply of Newman's undoubtedly refutes the objection in its extreme form that the idea of a probable infallibility is self-contradictory; but it does not eliminate every difficulty. He himself gives the following counter-argument: "Granted that the gift of infallibility be adapted, when believed, to unite all intellects in one common confession, it is as difficult of proof as the developments which it is to prove, and nugatory therefore, and in consequence improbable in a divine scheme".[2] Newman requires an infallible authority on the ground that reason can distinguish only with a certain probability true development from corruption; but the existence of this authority, also, it can prove to be only probable. In other words, Newman *recule pour mieux sauter*; he does not solve the problem, but moves it on to another plane and, though the *Essay* gives no definite answer, the want can easily be supplied from the *Grammar*. Arguments that, in isolation, produce only a probable conclusion, in their convergence may provide adequate proof and justify absolute certainty; and since their probative force is essentially derived from the universal and connatural principles of conscience, we may conclude that every man of right disposition as regards religion, may reach certainty, whether his reasons be implicit or explicit.[3]

There is yet another objection, that infallible authority sets the life of reason in order, but at the expense of spontaneity, that it enslaves the mind, and does away with personal responsibility. For I am thereby obliged to accept blindly whatever it pleases this authority to enjoin, without having any say in the matter, and so, in the end, it deprives my faith of the merit that comes

---

[1] *Essay*, pp.80-81; *Grammar* pp.224-227.

[2] *Essay*, p.80.

[3] In the *Essay*, Newman does not seem to be absolutely clear about the relationship between certainty and probability.

from its being a trial. Consequently, the existence and exercise of infallible authority destroys all the values the divine plan was intended to foster.

This was a very common argument in England, and so Newman applied himself to answer it in detail in the *Apologia*.[1] We will summarize what he says in the *Essay* and the *Apologia*. In the first place, my acceptance of infallible authority is not merely passive. On the contrary, my whole moral being, my freedom and responsibility, share in the act, which is perfectly consistent with responsibility, as my acceptance is always a free act. Next, even after submission, there is still a wide field open to free and independent study, and authority, far from preventing it, presupposes it, only curbing its exaggerations and extravagances. The Church is like an arena in which the continual conflict of reason and authority promotes the development of doctrine. A rider does not repress the vigour of his mount, but, by use of the bridle, guides and stimulates it. Likewise the goad of authority does not paralyse reason, but urges it on and directs its course. Besides, the sphere of action of infallible authority is limited by the bounds of tradition. I ought not to accept blindly whatever the Church might choose arbitrarily to impose, for it cannot create anew, it is restricted in its definitions to the living tradition. There is no need to be afraid of novelties or of violent measures inspired by caprice; the Church can define only what I might have long foreseen. Besides, her own history testifies that my mind will not be subjected to pressure of a humiliating kind. The Church has always been very chary of exercising her infallible authority. In any case, there is nothing less desirable than absolute freedom and independence of reason; for it is incapable of deciding by itself, for each individual, what is true or false, in every contingency. Finally, the partial surrender of reason to authority involves the continuous practice of obedience and humility in faith.

It follows that there is no compelling reason for rejecting the probability of a living infallible authority in the Church. In the above argument, infallibility is considered from the standpoint of apologetics, as a reasonable hypothesis demanded by doctrinal development in its actual course. It is, however, an article of faith as well, and can, therefore, be considered in a strictly theological

---

[1] *Apologia*, pp.221, 225-229, 235-239; *Essay*, pp.82-83.

way.[1] From this angle Newman treats of it in his letter to the Duke of Norfolk, in which he interprets and defends the definition of the Vatican Council.

C. Both these expectations are fulfilled in the Catholic Church alone:

Before any study of the facts, we have already established that, if God has given a revelation to the world, it will steadily grow till it reaches its perfect expression, without in the process losing its unchanging character as something "given"; and, further, that, in the existing state of human nature, the only means for it to reach that state is an infallible living authority. Where do we find all this realised in fact? If it is anywhere, it must be in the Catholic Church, for it alone claims to be anything of the kind. A single glance is enough to show that it has no rival in the matter, for it alone, looked at from the outside, exhibits those features essential to establish the truth of what we have supposed. It alone has a history that unfolds to our view the sight of a continuous growth of doctrine, in which the centuries, as they pass, add new threads to the elaborate texture of doctrine, without ever rending it. Ever renewing its youth, it moves with assurance through the turmoils of the world and, in its ceaseless struggle against the philosophies of the world and against one heresy after another, gains fresh insights into the ancient treasure of the faith.[2] The fact of such development is known to everyone. It has gone on now for centuries, and the ideas that have resulted make up a single harmonious system which logic obliges us either to accept or reject in its entirety.[3] Heresy, on the other hand, is sterile; it is wanting in any theology worthy of the name and is well aware of this. It even boasts of it and reproaches Catholicism for possessing a system of doctrine. In so doing, it condemns itself and, after its own fashion, bears witness to the truth.[4]

[1] *Essay*, p.91.

[2] *Ibid.*, p. 93: "When we are convinced that the idea of Christianity, as originally revealed, cannot but develop, and know, on the other hand, that large developments do exist in matter of fact, professing to be true and legitimate, our first impression naturally must be that these developments are what they pretend to be".

[3] *Ibid.*, pp. 93-94 (one of the finest passages in the book).

[4] *Ibid.*, pp.94-95.

The Catholic Church is the only religious body to claim infallible authority[1] and therefore, it is no use looking elsewhere for the two *a priori* indications of a revealed dogmatic religion. Divine revelation is either there or nowhere. Since then, it must exist somewhere, it follows that the Catholic Church is its rightful agent, and that God's action within it, by virtue of infallible authority, develops the tradition of revelation, without in the least impairing its original character.

D. Historical complement of the proof:

We have now established, antecedently to the examination of the facts of history, that the gradual development of traditional doctrine cannot be a departure from what was given originally; and the argument will be completed by factual evidence. The facts, however, are so numerous and involved that, if the proof from history were unsupported, it could never be shown to be conclusive. The task is greatly facilitated by the preceding demonstration, for the reasonable presumption afforded by conscience is, in fact, so strong that an exhaustive study of the facts is unnecessary. A few soundings taken on the way will be enough to transform the *a priori* hypothesis into a definitive proof. Newman starts by pointing to a few examples *en passant* : the canon of the New Testament, original sin, infant baptism, the *Homoousion.*[2] He goes on to treat more in detail, first the development of the doctrine of the Incarnation and, in particular, mariology[3] and the worship of the saints, then the Roman primacy.[4] These are not to be viewed in isolation. But, "since the doctrines all together make up one integral religion, it follows that the several evidences which respectively support these doctrines belong to a whole, and must be thrown into a common stock, and all are available in the defence of any".[5] An examination of these arguments would take us too far afield, and, as their function is only accessory, they may conveniently be omitted from our survey.

[1] *Essay.*, pp.95-96.

[2] *Ibid.*, pp.123-126, 127-129, 129-133, 133-134.

[3] *Ibid.*, pp.135-148.

[4] *Ibid.*, pp.148-165.

[5] *Ibid.*, p.107.

SECTION C

THE HISTORICO-PHILOSOPHICAL SOLUTION

Problem and method

Newman's argument, in the preceding section, was conducted from a particular standpoint, that of conscience and faith, and it would carry entire conviction to any religiously-minded person. There still, however, remain certain difficulties to human reason. It might, for example, be said that, though it is possible that some Catholic doctrines agree with the convictions and practices of primitive Christianity, and that, in consequence, the doctrinal succession may be *natural,* it does not follow that more recent doctrines are likewise true and contained in what went before. After all, nature itself gives rise to factors making for corruption, and degeneracy naturally follows on growth and maturity. Hence, reason cannot accept natural succession as a guarantee of changeless integrity. To meet this difficulty Newman had recourse to a second argument, which, though taking up almost two thirds of the *Essay,* was left unfinished.[1]

It was necessary for him to prove that later doctrines were not deviations, but developments agreeing with the original. To do so he had to determine the characteristics proper to genuine developments, which would then serve to distinguish them from corruptions. He thus came to enumerate seven criteria and to show, in copious detail, how they are satisfied in the development of the Catholic tradition.

The theory of the seven criteria is well known and has often been examined. Yet it is one of the most misunderstood parts of Newman's work, owing to the failure to perceive how he viewed the process of social development as a whole. His critics fail to consider this part of his thought in the context of the intuition

[1] *Essay.,* pp.169-170: "I might be answered that it is not enough that a large system of doctrine, as that which goes by the name of Catholic, can be referred to the beliefs, opinions, and usages current among the first Christians for me to be logically justified in including the later teaching in the earlier. I might also be told that an intellectual development may be in a sense natural, and yet unfaithful to its original. Finally, it may be affirmed that the causes which foster the growth of ideas may also disturb and deform them".

which guided him throughout, and so mistake both his stand-point and purpose. All, however, agree that his account of the seven criteria is, in itself, a masterpiece of historical and philo-sophical analysis. They admire the psychological depth and exacti-tude of individual elements, but miss, for the most part, the signi-ficance of the whole, especially of the use to which Newman puts it in his apologetic. They do not seem to see its relevance. Con-sider, for instance, the very detailed judgments of J. B. Mozley and V. F. Storr.[1] They assume that each criterion is meant to show the derivation of certain particular contemporary doctrines from articles of the primitive faith. Consequently, some of these criteria seem to them applicable, but most are rejected as quite beside the point. As we read their criticisms, we can sense their surprise that Newman should have had recourse to arguments of that kind. Obviously, if they expect of his theory the solution to a problem it did not envisage, it is not surprising that they are disappointed.

Others, like Père Gardeil, consider that Newman misunder-stood the laws governing the intellect; and these do not take into account that the life of the mind is quite other than a biological process.[2] It is true that Newman is guided, in his study of the criteria of development, by a comparison of intellectual develop-ment with growth and corruption in organic nature, but is this analogy really a decisive factor in his account? Is every psychology that tries to understand the significance of the parts by setting them in the living unity of the whole inevitably committed to biologism? This is the crux of any discussion on Newman's theory.

The seven criteria are the outcome of a phenomenological study of the entire living reality of the development of ideas in a com-munity. To understand Newman, we must continually bear in mind his description of the psychology of development analysed in the second part of this book. It is a spontaneous process, set in motion more or less unconsciously, and directed by "first prin-ciples", whose origin is to be found either in human nature or in the characteristic qualities of individuals or groups. As it pro-ceeds, there gradually emerges a group of ideas which seek to harmonize with one another without doing violence to logic. It has its own *ethos,* giving rise to a characteristic mode of behaviour,

---

[1] J. B. Mozley, *op. cit.,* and V. F. Storr, *op. cit.,* pp.305-316.
[2] A. Gardeil, *Le donné révélé et la théologie* (Paris, 1910), pp.156-157.

and always at odds with opposing ideas and forces. This whole complex movement which results in either the corruption or the ever purer development of the original idea is closely examined by Newman under every aspect, and so he comes to detect the notes of genuine development in contrast with those of corruption. It is a question, then, of analysing a complex phenomenon, grasped initally by a comprehensive intuition, and emerging to the view of an experienced thinker from a large number of observations. In some cases, a corruption will be perceived at once by a mind accustomed to take a wide intuitive view. Vast learning, combined with sustained reflection, has gradually brought to light, from an abundant variety of instances, the philosophical idea of genuine development together with its essential difference from the false. Newman had only to analyse what his mind already perceived in a single view, in order to take note of all its aspects, and his examples are carefully chosen to set them in a clear light. In this way, he set himself to the task and discovered the seven criteria.

These, therefore, constitute the different aspects of a single, complex, but unique and indivisible, phenomenon, namely, true development. For this reason, Newman, in applying them to the life of Catholic tradition, begins by devoting his attention to the doctrinal life of the Church as a whole. His intention, at this stage, is not to create a technique of reducing this or that piece of current doctrine to the creed of the apostles, but to lay a firm foundation for judging the Church's living tradition viewed as a whole. With Newman, the synthetic view always holds pride of place; it takes precedence of the analytic view, the distinction of the various elements. It is not surprising, then, if some of the criteria, those, in fact, he held to be the most important, are inapplicable to a particular doctrine in isolation. This, of course, does not mean that he completely neglected this field, for some of the criteria can be used to judge the nature of development in particular cases; but this, the analytical point of view, is only secondary. For this type of mind, the main thing is that doctrinal development should be shown to be homogeneous as a whole. If, after that, there still remain problems of detail and individual difficulties, that does not trouble him at all.

In building up his induction of the seven "notes", Newman chooses to be guided, more or less, by the analogy of the life of ideas with that of organic nature.[1] This comparison needs to be properly understood. In our mental processes, analogy may serve functions of greater or less importance. The analogue may be, as it were, an archetype, a symbol, which I use to gain access to a reality it represents for me, but of which my knowledge is only vague and indirect; in that case, I am taken up wholly by the consideration of the figurative image. But I may also make use of analogy for purposes of instruction only, and then its function is merely accessory. I myself possess a clear knowledge of the real nature of the thing I wish to describe, but it is more or less remote from matter and inaccessible to the generality of men. Here the words ordinarily used to describe it signify properly something analogous, but more tangible and open to the observation of all. Consequently, I make use of this better known reality as a parallel and image of the other, an imperfect one, no doubt, but eminently useful. This is what happens here. It is a procedure particularly adapted to Newman with his genius for "realization". His own attention remains fixed on the living mind as it manifests itself in its own effects, and he uses physical life as a remote, but striking, analogy to facilitate the description of the processes of the mind. "Thus, without considering the analogy as strict, or sufficient to rest an argument upon, we may use it to introduce several rules for drawing the line between a development and a corruption".[2] The image of physical life does not for a moment distract his attention, so alert and watchful, from the one reality he wishes to clarify, but this is so immaterial and difficult to grasp that he readily employs the biological analogy to explain his meaning. For the life of the body is much easier to understand than that of the mind, besides bearing a striking resemblance to it, at least in the eyes of one who, like Newman, considers the latter in its concrete and spontaneous reality. To maintain, after studying Newman, that he argues from biology to the life of the mind and the development of ideas would be both unjust and ridiculous.

[1] Newman introduces his study of the seven criteria by a description of development and corruption in organic nature, and continues: "Taking this analogy as a guide, I venture to enumerate seven notes, varying in their cogency, autonomy and range of application, in order to distinguish between sound developments of an idea and its state of decadence and corruption" (p.171).

[2] *Essay*, 1st ed., p.63.

First criterion: Preservation of type

This first note embodies one of Newman's favourite ideas, for it has to do with a social, collective *ethos*. The application of this norm to Christianity takes more than a hundred pages.[1]

Its explanation and justification are somewhat confused, as we can see by comparing the first and second editions of the *Essay*. In the first, Newman begins by considering, and then rejecting, a note which he calls "unity in type". It was to consist in the elements making up the idea and their interrelations remaining unchanged in the final stages of development. This norm, he admits, seems at first sight the most obvious of all; but he goes on to show, by a number of examples, that this is not supported by experience, for an idea may, in fact, remain the same under very different appearances.[2] From this he concludes that we must look deeper. It is then that, after a general account of the biological analogy, he begins his analysis of the seven criteria, the first of which he calls "Preservation of the essential idea," which means that, despite apparent change, the impression the object actually makes on the mind that considers it objectively remains essentially the same. This criterion, he goes on to say, is difficult to apply, because it involves the ability to grasp, beneath all appearances, the essential idea of an institution, whereas it is often the case, especially with a historical phenomenon so complex as Christianity, that this idea is defined in a purely theoretical and arbitrary fashion.[3]

In the revised edition of the *Essay* Newman suppressed the

[1] *Essay.*, pp.207-322.

[2] *Ibid.*, 1st ed., pp.58, 62: "Here the most ready test is suggested by the analogy of physical growth, which is such that the parts and proportions of the developed form correspond to those which belong to its rudiments ... Unity of type is certainly the most obvious characteristic of a faithful development". There follow examples, with the following conclusion: "Natural then as it is at first sight to suppose that an idea will always be the exact image of itself in all stages of its history experience does not bear out the anticipation. To discover the tests of a true development, as distinguished from a corruption, we must consider the subject more attentively".

[3] *Ibid.*, pp.64-66: "That the essential idea or type which a philosophical or political system represents must continue under all its development, and that its loss is tantamount to the corruption of the system, will scarcely be denied ... This test however is too obvious and too close upon development to be of easy application in particular cases. It implies an insight into the essential idea in which a system of thought is set up which often cannot be possessed and, if attempted, will lead to mere theorizing".

initial discussion on unity in type and, joining this first note, rejected in the first edition with the second we have just mentioned,
"preservation of the essential idea", he presents us with a new
first criterion, called "preservation of type". Here, the word "type"
signifies the interrelation of parts within the whole, as manifested
externally.[1]

He points out that this invariability of type is not to be taken
too strictly, for 1) an idea may remain the same though expressed
in very different forms; 2) even when the outward form is little
changed, there may yet be corruption. This, however, does not
prevent the typical structure, especially when it persists in the
face of considerable developments, from being a reliable indication
of the genuineness of development and fidelity to the original.[2]

All this seems to be very subtle. What Newman means is that,
normally, in most cases, preservation of type is a characteristic
of true developments, and that alteration usually corrupts the
type; consequently, the exceptions confirm the rule. Newman,
then, in the way he conceived and evaluated this first note, underwent himself a course of development.

In substituting, in the second edition, the word "type" for
"idea", he realized that it was a question more of the external
manifestations of the idea than of the idea itself. The first note,
therefore, no longer relies on the definition of the idea in its essence,
but on the visible form and the attitude which express it. This
presupposes that it is precisely the persistence of the animating
idea that is indicated by the preservation of the type, and this is,
ultimately, what counts. The application of the rule is thereby
greatly facilitated.

The second edition makes no change in the way this criterion
is applied to the Church, and what Newman always had in mind
is made abundantly clear. The Church, in its visible structure
and conduct, has always produced the same typical impression

[1] *Essay.*, p.171.
[2] *Ibid.*, pp.176, 178: "Ideas may remain, when the expression of them is
indefinitely varied. And, in like manner, real perversions and corruptions
are often not so unlike externally to the doctrines to which they belong, as
are changes which are consistent with it and true developments. But this
fact cannot impair the argument which proves substantial identity from
exterior similarity, when the latter subsists. On the contrary, for this very
reason unity of type becomes an even more certain guarantee of the soundness and purity of developments, that it is constantly preserved in spite of
their number and importance".

as the ancient Christian community had on its pagan surroundings. Today, as at its beginning, it gives to the world around it the impression of a hidden superstition, magical and fanatical. Just as in the fourth century, it appears to-day as the *catholica,* well organized, compact and intolerant, among a coalition of heresies more or less numerous, which ceaselessly change and disintegrate. To-day as in the fifth and sixth centuries, it is centred on Rome, confronts great regional schisms, is oppressed in various places by the civil power and is the target of philosophical schools.[1] Newman's meaning is clear enough; it is that the Church's situation and conduct in the world remain unchanged. It always excites the same sympathies and hatreds, gives rise to the same problems and takes up the same attitude to them. This is possible only if the one animating idea persists under all these phenomena, unweakened and incorrupt.

It should now be evident that the normative force of a rule like this one can be appreciated only by considering each phenomenon it applies to, not in isolation, but as an element in a wider whole. The life of an idea is only one aspect of a wider life, that of a single living whole, one and many-sided, the life of a whole community. If the other aspects of this whole persist, that persistence argues to the identity of the idea. We see from this that the norm is not strictly applicable to individual doctrines, but only to Catholic doctrine taken as a whole.

Newman treated the first criterion in such detail because he held it the most important of the seven. He returned to it and underlined its force in his lectures on the Oxford Movement, as the chief motive of his conversion to Catholicism :

He joined the Catholic Church simply because he believed it, and it only, to be the Church of the Fathers . . . because [here he quotes the *Essay*] did St Athanasius and St Ambrose come suddenly to life, it cannot be doubted what communion they would recognize for their own, because all will agree that these Fathers, in spite of whatever differences of opinion, whatever protests, if you will, would find themselves more at home with such men as St Bernard and St Ignatius Loyola, or with the lonely priest in his lodgings, or the holy sisterhood

---

[1] The Church of the first, fourth, then fifth and sixth centuries is described in three sections of the *Essay,* pp. 245-247, 272-273, 321-322.

of mercy, or even with the unlettered crowd before the altar, than with the rulers or the members of any other religious communities.[1]

Further on, Newman recalls with emotion the course followed by his religious convictions, and the same idea occupies the foreground :

> The drama of religion and the combat of truth and error were ever one and the same. The principles and proceedings of the Church now were those of the Church then; the principles and proceedings of heretics then were those of Protestants now. I found it so, almost fearfully; there was an awful similitude, more awful because so silent and unimpassioned, between the dead records of the past and the feverish chronicle of the present. The shadow of the fifth century was on the sixteenth. It was like a spirit rising from the troubled waters of the old world with the shape and lineaments of the new. The Church then as now might be called peremptory and stern, resolute, overbearing and relentless; and heretics were shifting, changeable, reserved and deceitful, ever courting the civil power, and never agreeing together, except by its aid; and the civil power was ever aiming at comprehensions, trying to put the invisible out of view, and to substitute expediency for faith.[2]

Newman was so much impressed by the unity of spirit binding primitive Christianity to the existing Church that even incidental and inexplicable modifications of doctrine could not bring him to doubt the truth of the Catholic Church.

> In the time of the early Roman empire, when Christianity arose, it arose with a definite *ethical* system. . . . Next I have a clear perception, clearer and clearer as my own experience of existing religions increases, that this *ethical* system (*ethos* we used to call it at Oxford), as realized in individuals, is the living principle also of present Catholicism, and not of any form of Protestantism whatever. . . . Outward circumstances, or conditions of its presence may change or not . . . but I say, even supposing there have been changes in doctrine and policy, still the *ethos* of the Catholic Church is what it was of

[1] *Diff. Angl.*, I, pp.367-368. See above, pp.38-39.
[2] *Ibid.*, pp.387-388.

old time, and whatever and whoever quarrels with Catholicism now, quarrels virtually and would have quarrelled, if alive 1800 years ago, with the Christianity of the Apostles and Evangelists.[1]

Second criterion: Continuity of Principles

This second note is as important as the first and is closely connected with it. It concerns the internal aspect of the *ethos,* whereas the first relates to its visible form, its attitude to its surroundings. In a passage we have just quoted, Newman writes "The principles and proceedings of the Church now were those of the Church then; the principles and proceedings of heretics then were those of Protestants now."[2] This sentence joins together the two chief aspects of the *ethos.* We have already shown exhaustively that, ultimately, the *ethos* is determined by first principles, which are pre-suppositions, of which we are mostly unaware, that express the character of an individual society, stimulate their development and determine its course.[3] We have previously summarized the main principles of the theological thought of Christianity,[4] and it will suffice here to set out certain conclusions. Since principles are what determine the nature and direction of development, their identity should be the strongest guarantee of its validity; their stability gives a greater certainty of this than would the invariability of the various doctrines.[5] This observation of Newman's shows, once again, that he attaches greater importance to the justification of the general *ethos* than to that of particular points of teaching.

In this second criterion, Newman distinguishes two elements, the continuity of principles and their degree of influence: "The continuity of these various principles down to this day, and the vigour of their influence, are two distinct guarantees that the

---

[1] Letter to Mozley, published in the *Contemporary Review,* 1898, and quoted in Bremond, *The Mystery of Newman,* p.354.

[2] See above p.266.

[3] See above, pp.141, ff; 171-172

[4] See above, pp.128, ff.

[5] *Essay,* p.181: "A development to be faithful must remain both the doctrine and the principle from which it started; principle is a better test of heresy than doctrine"; p.353: "If it be true that the principles of the later Church are the same as those of the earlier, then, whatever are the variations of belief between the two periods, the earlier in reality agrees more than it differs with the later, for principles are responsible for doctrines".

theological principles to which they are subservient are, in accordance with the divine promise, true developments, and not corruptions, of the Revelation".[1] We notice at once that this rule must be held to apply only to doctrinal thought considered in its totality. For, in Newman's psychology, first principles are, as it were, the instruments which the personality as a whole uses to influence the direction of its thought. No doubt this criterion may be applied to individual doctrines; but the correspondence between an opinion and a certain principle, though it may point to, does not absolutely guarantee, the truth of this opinion. A principle, in fact, may be applied in different ways and in a rigid, one-sided manner.[2] To justify a given doctrine, the whole analogy of the faith must be brought to bear on it;[3] whereas, if the same group of principles continues to operate, that gives a strong reason for affirming that Catholic doctrine, as a whole, has retained its identity throughout history.

Third criterion: Power of assimilation

To assimilate is to incorporate a foreign substance and to transform it organically into one's own. In the case of the Church, it means that, finding in the non-Christian world all kinds of opinions and other expressions of the mind, as well as customs and rites, it adopts and incorporates them, altering their significance in so doing.[4] We have already described how this takes place in showing how an idea develops in a society.[5] The vigour needed for this assimilation may then, according to Newman, serve as a criterion for the fidelity of a particular development. As this is not immediately evident, we shall have to look into the question more closely.

---

[1] *Essay.*, p.353.

[2] *Ibid.*, p.54: "In many cases, *development* simply stands for *exhibition*, as in some of the examples adduced above. Thus, Calvinism and Unitarianism may both be called developments, that is, exhibitions of the principle of private judgment, whereas doctrinally they have nothing in common." cf., also, pp.180-181.

[3] *Newman-Perrone*, p.412.

[4] The application to Christianity is divided into two sections. In the first (pp.357-368), Newman studies the power of assimilation belonging to doctrinal truths; in the second (pp.368-382), that of sacramental grace; in other words, the Church can incorporate pagan rites on condition of purifying them and altering their meaning.

[5] See above, pp.175-176.

Just as the vitality of an idea proves the existence of principles working powerfully for its development, so its power of assimilation indicates that, as it develops, it unifies and concentrates within itself the borrowed elements;[1] for, in any system of thought, the leading idea is what gives it unity.[2] When, therefore, an idea shows great power of assimilation, it thereby demonstrates its independence and ability to preserve its identity. Each particular truth is fully true only in the context of the entire truth. Hence it is that, since error always contains a part of truth, and error in a philosophy consists more often in what it denies than in what it affirms, the truest idea must be the most comprehensive, and one that will be able to assimilate, without losing its identity, all the others in virtue of the truth and value they contain.

A society, just as much as an individual, lives and acts in a wider sphere, and is subject to its various influences. Neither can achieve perfection in isolation. As the intellectual development of the individual, if he is faithful to his true nature, consists in the critical assimilation of contemporary culture in the light of his personal experience,[3] so the true and uniform development of a great idea consists in the acquisition and transformation of the ideas it finds prevalent, while, at the same time, it is always in control of the process, and what it acquires it incorporates in the substance of its own truth. The life of the mind always tends to unity; and what fails to transform the "other" is transformed by it. There is no escape from conflict with the environment. The victor is the one who asserts his own being and self-identity.[4]

From these considerations it follows that the third criterion cannot be used to guarantee the apostolicity of the elements

---

[1] *Ibid.*, p.186: "An attempt at development shows forth the presence of a principle: its success, the presence of an idea. Principles stimulate thought, the idea concentrates it".

[2] See above, p.173.

[3] See above, pp.144-148.

[4] *Essay*, pp.38-39, 40: "And so as regards their existing opinions, principles, measures and institutions, it develops in establishing relations between them and itself, in giving them a meaning, in creating what may be called a jurisdiction over them, in throwing off from itself what is utterly heterogeneous in them. It grows when it incorporates; and its purity consists not in isolation, but in its continuity and sovereignty. It is elicited by trial, and struggles into perfection".

assimilated. Very often, in fact, what is assimilated forms no part of the dogmatic and permanent content of the Church's teaching, but pertains to the non-dogmatic, even fortuitous, products of time and place, which the faith employs as an added strength.[1] Power of assimilation manifests only the independence and vigour of the idea. Once again, what counts is a comprehensive view which, setting the different elements in their place, enables them to be understood. This power is, too, a general criterion guaranteeing that doctrine persists unimpaired in the course of its development. What it does not prove is that this or that contemporary article of faith is reducible to what was given in the beginning.

Fourth criterion: Logical sequence

Growing involves taking in elements from outside and transforming them into oneself, and this applies to the growth of ideas. These, however, also have their own internal source of enrichment, namely reasoning. The two processes are distinct from one another but, often enough, only as two aspects of one and the same operation. What appears from the outside as assimilation is, viewed from within, reasoning. The contribution from without is but the occasion the idea takes to discover its own resources.[2] We have already shown that development consists mainly in a process of reasoning.[3] Logical sequence, therefore, constitutes a fourth criterion of true development. It does not, however, apply primarily to theological deduction, but to the whole living process of growth

---

[1] Most of Newman's examples of assimilation have no doctrinal significance; e.g., the use of Aristotle's philosophy in theology, and the incorporation of pagan rites into the liturgy.

[2] Newman distinguishes clearly between reasoning and assimilation. Cf. *Essay*, p.383: "I use logical sequence in contrast to that process of incorporation which has lately been under review". Still, the distinction is not absolutely rigid, for assimilation follows upon a pre-existing affinity (p.187). Cf., also, *Diff. Angl.*, I, p.54: "Every religion has a life, a spirit, a genius of its own, in which doctrines lie implicit, out of which they are developed, and by which they are attracted into it from without and assimilated to it". Generally, Newman presents development, taken as a whole, as a reasoning, the unfolding of an idea in all its implications, yet, at times, he also describes it as an assimilation, as in the *Essay*, pp.186-187: "So far is such incorporation from implying corruption, as is sometimes supposed, that development is a process of incorporation".

[3] See above, pp.93-96.

that formal reasoning comes to sum up only after the event and in part.[1] If we understand Newman properly, the logical sequence of development shows itself in two ways: first, historically, that is to say true development is seen to be a gradual unfolding of aspects and conclusions, brought to light in a definite natural order. Their sequence makes it seem that the final term is nothing but the natural and logical outcome of the first.[2] Second, logically, which means that the needs of controversy and teaching compel the mind of the Church to pass, on occasion, beyond spontaneous reasoning to the use of logic. When, therefore, these various and independent courses are seen to correspond and harmonize, we find there exists a logical sequence in the spontaneous process of growth which they express.[3] This latter observation shows, once again, Newman's concern for the process as a whole, though here we have a norm which could very well be used as a standard for individual developments.

Fifth criterion: Early anticipation

Since there is a logical bond connecting later developments with the original truth, and logic is always and everywhere the same, it could be expected that doctrines of which the Church reached clear knowledge only later should, from the first, have been expressed in a vague and rudimentary form. Anticipations

[1] *Essay*, p.383: "In my terminology, 'logical sequence' is opposed to that scientific principle which arranges and defends developments after they have happened. Consequently, it includes every advance of the mind from one judgment to another, for example, as by moral fitness, and which it is not always possible to analyse into premise and conclusion".

[2] *Ibid.*, p.195: "There is a continuous process and a determinate way appertaining to the history of a doctrine, a polity or an institution; they both persuade the common sense of mankind that the final result is the outcome of what existed originally".

[3] *Ibid.*, pp.190-191: "External circumstances elicit into formal statement the thoughts which are coming into being in the depths of his mind; and soon he has to begin to defend them; and then again a further process must take place, of analysing his statements and ascertaining their dependence one on another. Yet even then the analysis is not made on a principle, or with a view to its whole course and finished results. Each argument is brought for an immediate purpose. Afterwards this logical character which the whole wears becomes a test that the process has been a true development".

of this kind, therefore, are a fifth test of true development.[1] They prove, at least, that later developments were "in the air" from the beginning, were included, so to speak, in a complex of ideas still more or less unconsciously entertained and destined to take, by degrees, a more and more precise form.[2] We are again concerned with the process as a whole, though this criterion, too, is applicable to separate doctrines.

Sixth criterion: Preservative Additions

In a certain sense, new things may be said to be added to the old, even in cases of true development. The state finally reached is of richer content than the original, though only its fulfilment. The primitive elements are not forfeited by the developed structure, any more than true culture foregoes natural endowments. The initial idea, far from being impaired or obscured by the later, is, in fact, strengthened and clarified, like something that, viewed through binoculars, becomes larger and more definite.[3] Thus, one aspect of the process, namely that of change, is the necessary corollary of another, which is perfection. As an instance of this, Newman points to one of his favourite theological ideas, that the high place given to Our Lady in no wise lessens the honour given to her Son, but rather confirms it and sets it in a stronger light.[4] This conservatism provides a sixth test of development in accord with the original. It is undoubtedly valid for individual doctrines,

[1] *Essay.*, pp.195-196: "Logic being the same in all ages, and developments being, for the most part, but aspects of the original idea—for they are all its natural consequences—the order they take in individual minds is often a matter of chance. It is, then, by no means strange that, here and there, definite specimens of advanced teaching should early occur, which in the historical course are not found till a late day. The fact, then, of such early or recurring intimations, fully realized later, is a sort of evidence that these later and more systematic fulfilments are in accord with the original idea".

[2] *Ibid.*, p.400: "The atmosphere of the Church was, so to speak, charged with them from the beginning, and it delivered itself of them at intervals, in this way or that, in various places and through the agency of various persons, according to the occasion."

[3] *Ibid.*, p.200: "A true development may then be described as one which is conservative of the course of development which went before it, which is that development and something besides; it is an addition which illustrates, not obscures, corroborates, not corrects, the body of thought from which it proceeds; and this is its characteristic as contrasted with a corruption"; cf. also *Apologia*, p.184, and a note of 1871 added in *Ess. Crit. Hist.*, I, p.287; *Essay*, pp.419-420.

[4] *Ibid.*, p.425-436.

but the organic idea of completion, of which change is one of the aspects, brings us back to their interrelation in the whole.

Seventh criterion: Chronic continuance

So long as life continues, development never ceases. If a germ or corruption enters, it too develops according to its nature, and leads, in the end, to division and decay.[1] A state of corruption, by its very nature, can never last. It may have a relative success, if the developing impulse, which is life, comes to a halt, so that the outside form is, more or less artificially, kept in being. This state of endurance without life is called "decadence". Decadent ideas fail to arouse an interior and compelling vitality, but continue as a matter of routine and tradition. A sudden shock may cause their instant disappearance.[2] Continuance in vigour is, then, a proof of growth that is consonant with the nature of the idea. This final test is, obviously, applicable only to the living whole.

Conclusion

We have given, as faithfully as possible, the meaning of the seven criteria of the *Essay,* and in Newman's own order. To show how each applies in detail would take us too far afield. The historical instances given by Newman are not strict analyses but a series of sketches, admirable for the erudition and insight they reveal, but simplified and cursory. Nothing more was called for in an essay, nor, in any case, could he have done more, for scientific exactness in every case would have needed enormous research. Still, they show Newman's remarkable knowledge of theology, and his profound and exact understanding of patristic thought. The century which has elapsed since the *Essay* was published has seen a considerable amount of work on the history of theology and of

---

[1] *Essay.*, p.203: "While ideas live in men's minds, they are ever enlarging into further development; they will not be stationary in their corruption any more than before it, and dissolution is that further state to which corruption tends. Corruption cannot, therefore, be of long standing; and thus *duration* is another test of a faithful development".

[2] *Ibid.*, pp.204-205: "It is true that decay, which is one form of corruption, is slow, but decay is a state in which there is no violent or vigorous action at all. And thus we see opinions, usages, and systems, which are of venerable and imposing aspect, but have no soundness within them, and keep together from a habit of consistency, or from dependence on political institutions. And then at length perhaps they go off suddenly and die out under the first rough influence from without".

the Fathers, but, even so, Newman's knowledge of Patrology still commands respect. If he saw deeper into the problem of development than did the great Catholic theologians of Tubingen, it is, according to A. Minon, because he had a better understanding of the Christian past; it was more exact and objective than theirs.[1]

Of greater importance than his learning are his personal views. For his analysis of development into its essential properties is an important original contribution to a scientific solution of the problem of tradition in apologetics. The analysis itself may seem, at times, hesitant, premature, or over-subtle, but the way he provides examples in abundance for his criteria testifies not only to a wide experience, but, above all, to a rare power of drawing from that experience ideas of the highest significance, not to speak of a balance of judgment which never loses its poise.

In conclusion, we shall attempt a brief and ordered summary of these views of Newman. We have already seen the necessity of setting the seven criteria, arrived at by analysis, in the framework of the single intuition they serve to illumine, and from which he drew his inspiration. Let us look at the way in which the development of tradition within the Church came about. The first thing that strikes us is that this development has its own laws, and they can be expressed, though imperfectly, in logical terms. Looking at each of the doctrines separately, as they succeed one another in time, we see that they are more or less held together by logical cohesion. But it is when we come to view them as a single whole which has come into being, gradually and spontaneously, in the course of centuries that we are forced to conclude that each doctrine is like a stone chiselled on every side with such exactness that they all fit together perfectly to form a single harmonious structure. That gives us the first criterion, *logical sequence*.

Next we take the actual content of doctrine. Here it is evident that, since the time of the apostles, tradition has been enriched by much that is new. Yet the additions are not entirely new. The mind does not perceive, at the outset, all the aspects and corollaries of an idea, but it does divine some of them, however confusedly. It often happens, for instance, that when a conviction finally emerges to our awareness, we have the impression that it was within us all the time, though indistinct and unexpressed. Something of the

[1] A. Minon, *op. cit.*, pp.376-378.

same kind happens in groups of persons. Dogmatic propositions, accepted by the universal Church at a much later date, were obscurely sensed, from the earliest times, by one thinker or another. Doubtless, such presentiments, taken by themselves, are very vague and their real meaning is only brought out in retrospect, by looking at the subsequent course of development. But this later view discovers the new acquisition already intuitively perceived and living in the very first centuries. So the second criterion is *the anticipation of the future in the past.*

As what is new must have been present in the old, so the old is not cancelled by the new. During a later stage, the old will seem, perhaps, very much changed, even, at first sight, hardly recognizable. Yet this will be due, not to any loss or absorption in the new, but to its having found its fulfilment as a living thing. The new form is but the stature of full maturity towards which the original, in its native, imperfect and provisional state, tended by its very essence. So it is that the theology of the present preserves the ancient tenets of the Bible and the Fathers, not like an amorphous pile of stones, but like an embryo subsisting in the adult organism. The third criterion, then, is *conservatism.*

Besides the doctrines with their various developments in the Church, there are the principles which, though they do not themselves develop, inspire and direct the process. They are the expression of the particular character, the personality, the spirit, the atmosphere, the *ethos* of the thinker or the society. If the same principles persist identically, with their vigour unimpaired, that is a sign of fidelity to oneself, to one's own *ethos*, and so of continuous and true development, free from taint of corruption. The fourth criterion of true development is, consequently, *identity of principles.*

The *ethos* is shown not only by the principles governing thought but also in conduct. Our actions are its highest achievement and clearest expression. Our principles themselves are brought to light by our characteristic way of acting. It is our view of life which causes us to react in a certain way to given stimuli, makes our conduct different from that of others in the same circumstances, causes different answers to the same problems. That is how we assert our individuality in the life of society. We make our own characteristic impression on our surroundings, arousing antipathy in some, sympathy in others. It is the same with a society like the

Church. It exhibits a definite moral conduct, which makes a bad impression on the unregenerate world. This conduct manifests openly its hidden principles, the idea which animates it. The fifth criterion of development, then, is the *preservation of type,* a sign of the perseverance of the animating idea, neither enfeebled nor degenerate.

Moreover, social thought, like that of an individual, is bound up with a wider sphere by natural, organic connections. The social environment always tries to shape the individual to its own likeness. This was the experience of Christianity in the actual circumstances in which it was born and grew up. And as the individual keeps his being unchanged only by assimilating, according to his personal decision, the culture of his day, as sustenance for his own *ethos,* so does Christianity remain itself, without corruption, through the course of history, only by its ability to sift, purify and incorporate the religious practices and intellectual values of its contemporary environment. Hence, the sixth criterion of true development is a *sovereign power of assimilation.*

The seventh and last criterion is *chronic vigour;* for corruption leads to death, and so to decomposition, unless the lifeless form is artifically preserved, in which case it subsists in history like a mummy, without living contact with the surrounding culture. The very fact that the Catholic Church still takes part, with youthful vigour, in the most powerful movements at work, testifies to its possession of a life of its own which is impervious to corruption.

We come to distinguish these seven criteria by examining human life in its totality; as applied to the Church they refer much more to the development of tradition, taken as a whole, than to that of individual articles of faith.

These criteria, since they apply to a single concrete idea in its various aspects, are not completely distinct from each other. They are not to be evaluated and used in isolation, but conjointly. Looked at separately, they differ in cogency, independence and range of application; but applied together, each confirming and completing the others, they constitute a powerful demonstration.

Finally, the argument built on them is scientific and polemical. It is most difficult and complicated to use, and depends on the intellectual power and illative sense of the individual. In consequence, it is not so decisive in practice that anyone can depend on it for distinguishing what does, or does not, belong to primitive

Christianity. The seven criteria serve to point out the direction research is to follow, and to solve theoretical difficulties. But, when it comes to finding out what is required of his faith, the believer is not to trust himself with such delicate instruments; what he needs for the purpose is the decision of an authority ever living and actual.

PART IV

Merit and defects of Newman's doctrine :

a critical assessment

INTRODUCTION

WE have tried, to the best of our ability, to work out, on the basis of data scattered throughout his works, a synthesis of Newman's theory of development, and this itself involved a continuous criticism; for it was necessary to bring out the central idea and to arrange accordingly the various parts. In addition, the proper standpoint and method had to be determined, so that the meaning of the subdivisions could be made clear; also difficulties had to be met, what was confused made precise, apparent inconsistencies reconciled. In so doing, we have already, in part, performed the work of criticism.

In some measure, too, we have likewise assessed Newman's psychology and apologetic in their general lines. As occasion required, we have criticized certain particular points or aspects of his theory, and we shall not return to them. The whole purpose of our study was to understand his theory of the development of doctrine; so, in this final part, we shall be chiefly occupied in examining its immediate consequences. As, however, this theory presupposes the whole of his teaching, our assessment will, indirectly, bear also on that.

The judgment passed on a theory of doctrinal development must, of necessity, have a number of different aspects, for the problem is, at the same time, one of theology, history, philosophy and apologetics. As to its historical side, research in Newman's time was not by any means complete; but he knew enough history to state the problem in terms as strict as we in our day require, and that is the important thing. In any case, to understand his views it is not necessary to enter into an estimate of his erudition.

We may, therefore, confine our criticism to the philosophical and apologetic aspects, to his account of the laws and forces which govern the development of doctrine, and to the tests of its essential invariability. These are the two main elements of the problem, and they stand together, since the solution of the first is decisive for that of the second. Were development simply a sequence of syllogisms, formal logic would be enough to test its fidelity to its sources; otherwise, we have to look for other guarantees. We shall, therefore, examine successively the two aspects of Newman's solution. First, we shall try to determine its real nature, to what species it belongs, its place and importance in the whole body of thought on the question. After that, we shall enquire if it is sufficiently coherent, clear and complete, where it is wanting, and what are the subsequent problems it raises.

Chapter I

NEWMAN IN CONTEMPORARY THOUGHT

SECTION A

HIS PSYCHOLOGY OF DEVELOPMENT

A. Logical or biological development?

FIRST of all, let us look at Newman's theory from a philosophical and psychological point of view. Catholic theology, as well as liberal and modernist, was somewhat puzzled, even bewildered, by Newman's psychological theories. They asked if he was speaking of logical or biological development, and failed to obtain a precise answer. Liberals and modernists judged that he allowed logic too much play; Catholic theologians found biological ideas too much in the foreground. We shall explain these two attitudes.

According to Fairbairn and Storr, all development comprises two factors—an organism creating life, and a milieu which determines what form that life takes.[1] According to Fairbairn, Newman failed to see how much the process of growth depends on its surroundings; Storr considers that he lost sight of this dependence in the course of his demonstration.[2] So it was that he separated development from its environment and kept only the dynamism inherent in ideas, that is to say, the logical sequence of development. Storr says that Newman's views in the *Essay* are ambivalent and that, in his later, Catholic, works, he confined himself to the

---

[1] A. M. Fairbairn, *op. cit.*, pp.35-37: "The organism is creative, the seat and source of life; but the environment is formative, determines the shape which the life assumes". Cf. also V. F. Storr, *op. cit.*, p.301.

[2] V. F. Storr, *loc. cit.*: ". . . he tends to lose sight of this biological conception of evolution and to substitute for it a logical conception".

logical aspect.[1] According to him, this was due to the need to make his theory apply to something it did not completely fit, to the Catholic Church, in fact, whose continuing identity throughout history he had taken upon himself to uphold at all costs, and he could do this only by recourse to dialectical subtleties.[2] This easily led him to lose sight of the environment, his view being that its influence was negatived by the exercise of infallible authority, and so the Church of Rome remained unaffected by the general historical laws governing development.[3]

Tyrrell argues on similar lines, but emphasizes another factor. In his view, the question at issue is whether development is to be understood as a gradual building up by the use of materials given in a *past revelation,* or as the unfolding of a melody, which varies according to the culture of each epoch, and which reiterates, in various forms, the theme of an *ever present intuition of faith.* Tyrrell also finds the argument of the *Essay* ambivalent, but attributes this to its attempt to reconcile two different conceptions.[4]

One thing deserves special notice. According to Storr and Tyrrell, Newman conceived Christianity primarily as an idea, that is, not as a *truth once given,* but as a *spiritual force* seeking to become incarnate, exteriorised, by adapting itself to its environment.[5] Tyrrell, therefore, does not hesitate to draw the conclusion that Newman's initial conception was, indeed, that condemned by Pius X in the encyclical *Pascendi*; but he goes on to say that, if a man is to be judged by his prevailing dispositions and sympathies, it would be absurd to call Newman a modernist.[6]

---

[1] *op. cit.,* p.308.

[2] *Ibid.,* pp.302-303: "For the free evolution of the idea and its surroundings is substituted the historical continuity of the Roman Church . . . An institution lends itself to a theory of logical development in a manner which is foreign to an idea interpreted as a spiritual agency or force".

[3] *Ibid.*: "The Roman Church escapes the effects of a true historical development".

[4] See above, p.131.

[5] V. F. Storr, *op. cit.,* p.307: "A vital power or influence, a germ of life which was to find outward embodiment in a polity and a system of doctrine". Cf. also G. Tyrrell, *Christianity at the Crossroads,* p.33: "In this notion of an 'idea' as a spiritual force or impetus, not as an intellectual concept, Newman identifies himself with the modern, and separates himself from the scholastic, mind".

[6] Tyrrell, *op. cit.,* pp.29-30: "If a man is to be judged by what he is fundamentally, and in his dominant aims and sympathies, it is absurd to speak of Newman as a modernist in any degree".

As to Catholic theologians, we have already seen that, for the most part, they find Newman's psychology far too biological. Their attitude to him is, therefore, that of a counsel for the defence, out of regard for his high position; that does not, however, prevent it from being exceedingly wary. He is not a modernist, they chant in chorus, but he somewhat depreciates reason in favour of affective sympathy and moral dispositions; such is the opinion of Père Rousselot.[1] Newman's proneness to consider faith a kind of intuition is pregnant with dangerous possibilities, considers Père de Grandmaison.[2] Gardell, for his part, adds that Newman misunderstood the real nature of the intelligence, and finds himself obliged to point out what is the difference between the life of a plant and that of the mind.[3]

What view should we take? Is it really impossible to find that clear way Tyrrell sought in vain *Through Scylla and Charybdis,* the title of one of his books? Is Newman's theory an assortment of inconsistent opinions, or is it held together as a consistent whole by a dominating principle? We hold that it exhibits a unity and coherence of its own, provided that it is looked at in the light of the original and primary intuition expressed in his psychological descriptions. As we have constantly maintained, the point of view adopted by Newman in his psychology of thought is that of the entire person. We shall now see that this standpoint is not necessarily the same as that adopted in biology.

B. Organic or personal wholeness?

To find a safe passage between Tyrrell's Charybdis and Scylla, between logical development and biological evolution, we must first analyse the idea of wholeness that lies at the base of Newman's psychology of thought. To that end, we can make use of some of the concepts developed in modern psychology and philosophy.

Anyone acquainted with the history of modern psychology is aware that it is characterized by a number of trends which have jointly led to a complete change in standpoint and method. By the beginning of the present century, a science of psychology had

[1] P. Rousselot, "Remarques sur la notion de foi naturelle", *Rech. de Sci. Rel.,* IV (1913), p.28.
[2] L. de Grandmaison, "Le développement du dogme chrétien", *Rev. Prat. d'Apol.,* VI (1908), p.23.
[3] A. Gardeil, *op. cit.,* pp.156-157.

come into being, based, ultimately, on the Cartesian distinction between thinking substance and extended substance.

A radical distinction was drawn between physical facts, known by the external experience of the senses, and psychological facts, known only by the interior experience of consciousness. But, though the two spheres were entirely separate, the methods applied to each had to be as identical as possible. Consequently, the phenomena of consciousness came to be treated in the same way as the natural sciences treat the phenomena of nature. It was assumed that both were cases of complex realities needing to be analysed into simpler ones. As the external world is, for natural science, a collection of physical phenomena, so the soul is, for this scientific psychology, merely a collection of psychical ones.

It is, therefore, possible, by the use of experimental methods, to analyse these and to explain how, starting from simpler elements (sensations, sentiments, etc.), and following definite psychological laws, more complex states of soul come into being and develop.

If, in the view of this "classical psychology", the self, like the physical world, was but the setting for the play of phenomena or the whole group of events, for "modern psychology", on the contrary, the most significant thing about such phenomena is that they belong to a subject, a self, which they affect and from which they proceed. If this standpoint is adopted in earnest, the object, atmosphere and method of psychological research are considerably altered. The object becomes the whole man, the person; the study of his outward behaviour becomes at least as necessary as introspection. Psychological consciousness is but an aspect of a conscious life necessarily involved in a world that affects it in a thousand ways and on which it, in turn, reacts by the whole way it behaves. Consciousness of life is essentially self-consciousness, and signifies a life which is self-possessive, the activity of a self, of a free agent. Hence, the structure of conscious events, even of sense-impressions, cannot by any means be understood by the application of impersonal laws, but solely by the significance each possesses in conduct as a whole, which itself is a manifestation of life freely directing itself to an end, the realization of certain values.

This new psychology developed in close contact with a parallel revolution in biology and it only by degrees emancipated itself from a kind of biologism, becoming more fully in accord with the specific character of its own object. In fact, biology came to adopt quite early a finalist standpoint against neo-Darwinism. According to the upholders of the new biology, the laws of physics and chemistry are insufficient alone to account for the phenomena of life. Though the biological process itself is wholly a matter of physics and chemistry, it shows a directive tendency which is inexplicable by the physical and chemical laws governing inorganic matter. The living being is a whole, whose principle of unity is an active, autonomous tendency, using physical and chemical forces to attain its own end, even in opposition to the tendencies of the inorganic world governed by natural laws alone.

The parallelism of the two tendencies is obvious. In both cases, we have a whole governed by a plan which it aims at realizing and upholding at all costs. The danger, too, of this conception is equally evident. While the old psychology of conscious states threatened to reduce the soul to a kind of psychic mechanism, some of the psychologies of conduct try to reduce man to a creature of instinct alone. It is, indeed, a fact that recent psychology verges, to a great extent, on vitalism and biologism, and so loses sight of the unique character of what is spiritual.

None the less, the psychology of to-day seems to aim at surmounting this biologism; and puts increasing emphasis on the impossibility of reducing what proceeds from human nature to life pure and simple. This results in a more exact idea of man, of a personal whole within whom a freedom, conscious of itself, makes use, while surpassing them, of biological necessities, to realize a plan of which he, not nature, is the author. It is not that, with man, a spirit co-exists with an animal, but that animality itself is taken up, sublimated, transfigured in a noble design. This idea obviously approximates that of the old spiritualist philosophies, and particularly, as we shall see, the Thomist anthropology.

Animality in man is so different from what it is in brutes that it shows clear marks of its transcendent quality. While, in the latter, the body is a complete work of art, a perfect expression of a plan of life drawn up by nature, in man its whole appearance is of something imprecise and unfinished. The morphological structure of the animal suggests an exact idea, worked out by nature in every detail. A competent biologist is able to see this idea in the bodily form, and to describe its dynamic aspect, which is that of life. Man, on the other hand, does not give himself away by his morphology. Nature has inscribed in his outward form only a vague, ambiguous idea. There are present, of course, organs of a highly developed life and their actions show forth the basic tendencies of his life, but his limbs are not endowed with a specialised structure and the response given by the vital tendencies is not fixed by instincts. The idea expressed by the human body, therefore, is only a generic one, capable of being specified in various ways; nature leaves man himself to determine these.

On account of his deficiency in instinct and his indeterminate structure, man is the most fragile of animals. If, in order to live, he were confined to his animal resources, he would very soon have become extinct. But it is his very lack of these that is a sign of far fuller potentialities. The fact that he is incomplete and that his life is not wholly prescribed for him by nature means that he is capable of confronting the world in a manner objective and free. The actuation of his sensory apparatus by impressions from his surroundings results not only in a spontaneous reaction, but in a stirring of his power of thought, in an awareness of objective reality. Behind the very limited world carved out from his surroundings by his own particular needs, the infinite universe of being opens out before him, and is seen to be valuable in its own right. An awareness of objective values, that is, of various aspects of the object which make it desirable for itself, pierces through the apprehension of it as useful biologically. Hence, human consciousness is characterized as being an awareness of a calling to a life higher than the satisfaction of instinct; and this life consists in an absolutely pure and disinterested activity, one of communion with absolute being as the supreme object of our knowledge, admiration, love and generosity. This calling requires us to subordinate the subjective standpoint of animal life to that of the objective values, and to do what reality demands of us. This basic element in human nature is what Newman calls "conscience".

It is evident that this call of conscience can be addressed only to one who is free, or rather that it is what constitutes human freedom. Man is able to evade this call, although he owes his true and distinguishing nature to it. His weaknesses may cause his physical needs and their satisfaction temporarily to dim his consciousness of objective values. He may even succeed in freeing himself from their austere and peremptory demands, on which his freedom is based, by claiming to be himself their creator. That is his pride, his capital sin, to which he is constantly tempted from the time of his expulsion from Paradise.

What constitutes human nature is not a certain kind of structure given at birth, but freedom, and so man is a human being in virtue of his freedom or his conscience. "Conscience", in fact, with Newman, is simply a word to designate freedom as it is found in man, which springs to life at the call of absolute and objective values.

Human nature (in the sense of "quiddity": the answer to the question, what is man?) is distinguished by the absence of a nature (in Aristotle's sense of *phusis,* an organism determined at birth) as the source of specifically human activity. Man has not a nature behind him, but he himself is placed, in virtue of being free, behind nature. As human, he is not determined *a tergo* by his organism, but he possesses it and exhibits its effects as proceeding from his own freedom. He is restricted by it, and it also serves him. Placed, by his body, in the world of nature and man, he is weighed down by it and hindered in many ways. But he is enabled to exert his action on the world, which thus becomes the instrument and the field of his liberty in the creation of culture.

Of itself, the human intellect is nothing but a wax tablet, as Aristotle says, where nothing is written. It is only by contact with things that experience is possible to it and that it is aroused to conscious existence; and only by involvement with the world does it create an interior life it can fashion as it will. This is because man is a free being which, to be able to act or exist, is necessarily dependent on a physical nature, not as a force operating within the free source of his action—which would be contradictory— but as an instrument, an object, a sphere necessary for his own fulfilment. It could, therefore, be said that, in a sense, man has no nature, since the physical nature he owns does not at all determine him *per modum naturae* in the exercise of his specific activity.

Human nature (in the sense of "quiddity") is thus specifically determined by an essential relation, of a unique kind, between a spiritual freedom and a corporeal nature. The character of this relation is exhibited by a dependence, not subjective, but purely objective, of the human act on its bodily concomitant.

Man is "freedom incarnate", freedom "situated in the world", or, what amounts to the same, a substantial union of a natural body and a spiritual soul which, in this very union, transcends the limitations of its material co-principle. Properly understood, these expressions all mean the same.

We are now in a position to grasp the unique and ultimate character of the "whole" that is properly human. It is not an organism, whose principle of unity would be a vital entelechy, but a person, whose principle of unity is freedom. The person, says St. Thomas, is a whole existing in itself, not in the manner of a thing, which is "in itself" purely and simply, and exists only passively, but a "someone", who acts by himself and is a master of his actions. The *dominium sui actus,* or freedom, is what radically constitutes the proper mode of human subsistence or of the person.

It follows from this that the whole which is properly human, or personal, is itself not something given, or born, but is built up in the course of living. Since the principle of this whole is freedom, the human whole must be something that makes itself by means of this same freedom. Man as such, as a person, himself creates his own wholeness by unifying his life under a moral principle. He draws together the scattered powers and untamed forces already at work in the hidden life of his physical organism. He strives to understand them, to become the master of their spontaneous stirrings, not in order to weaken or destroy them—for he needs them for his own free activity—but to integrate them in his life of freedom by the discipline to which he submits them, and by the moral purpose he makes them serve. Thus, the disciplined imagination becomes a kind of subtle and clear-sighted instrument for the intellect which cannot function without it, and the disciplined passions a strong and supple instrument for the will which expresses itself through them and derives its own force from their vigour.

So it is that man is not something ready-made, but something to be achieved by himself. His special dignity and greatness lie in the fact that he is himself the author of his wholeness as a human being and of his personality. He effects this by assembling the uncoordinated powers of his nature in a life that is free, ordered and submissive to the objective values that make their voice heard in his conscience. He fulfils his vocation and achieves his earthly destiny in conquering for himself moral freedom, the freedom proper to a creature, freedom in obedience. He thus takes up and transposes the biological wholeness given at birth into the higher and complete wholeness of the fully developed person.

Likewise, for its proper understanding, the life of thought must be set in the context of the development of the whole person. Human thought is pre-eminently the work of freedom. It springs into being at the call of truth, the objective and absolute rule of its functioning. Truth for man is nothing less than being, absolute being, in which he participates passively by his creation, and which summons him, in his conscience, to a participation which is active, taken up and therefore known and freely accepted. As Newman constantly asseverates, thinking and thinking truly, seeking truth with the whole soul, is the first duty of man, the fundamental act of his obedience.

Thought, therefore, necessarily participates in the freedom of the entire movement of human life, not only in its exercise, but also in its direction. To attain truth, it must be accepted in humility as the objective rule, it must be loved, desired, faithfully followed; we have to purify its mirror, the soul, and make it fully receptive; we must submit to the transcendent quality of truth, to its majesty, its mystery; we must acknowledge the limits to truth set by our weakness and earthly condition, beware of error and hastiness, refrain from doing it violence, adjusting ourselves to it and to all that it demands.

Right thinking, in fact, is not just the result of a proper intellectual formation, but demands a full development of the whole personality. A simple and sincere person naturally grows into the truth by the spontaneous development of his "experimental thought", even though, through want of intellectual training, he may be unable to express clearly his convictions.

Pride, on the other hand, exalting itself above truth as its master and judge, immediately closes up our access to it. It makes us evade a rule beyond ourselves and to substitute for it our own inclination, our desire for power, and the craving for unrestricted liberty. We reject all mystery in advance and set up a clear and strict method as the absolute and exclusive rule of our judgments. Pride makes us strangers to truth, because it begins by alienating us from the truth about ourselves, which is that we are created, and therefore limited, beings. It either leads us along the path of uncontrolled romanticism which takes its imaginings for the inspirations of infallible genius, or it shuts us up in one form or another of rationalism. In either case, we elevate our finite and tainted nature into the creative source and supreme rule of truth.

Our passions, too, when uncontrolled, sully our purity and makes us less amenable to the truth. They constantly threaten to warp our judgment in favour of desires unregulated by that liberty which is the essence of human life.

We may, therefore, draw the conclusion that concrete thought is always a function of the developing personality. It does not take place within four walls, set apart from the turmoil of common life. Since life is its object, it is always involved in it; for it can only be exercised on human experience that precedes reflection, and this itself is an expression of our free, personal participation in life. This "vital" thought which offers itself to our reflection is governed by the moral attitude we adopt towards reality; and, as the instinct of animals is directed by physical needs in sifting the impressions received by sense, so the thought of man is directed by the fundamental choice he makes. In what he experiences, he causes to predominate those impressions and aspects of things that correspond with his own dispositions. If love of truth and obedience to it fail to make his mind purely receptive to it and wholly at its service, it can only be expected that his view of life will be falsified by arbitrariness and partiality.

The person, the spirit, forms a whole, as life is a whole. But "wholeness" is an analogical concept. While the biological whole is driven by a natural tendency in accordance with an immutable plan imprinted on it at birth, the spirit directs itself in quest of a moral end which governs its whole life, of which thought is a part. In a sense, every conception of life is the expression of a moral state.

All this by no means implies relativism, for, of its very nature, moral aspiration can never be a blind impulse. It is a response to the knowledge of being and of absolute value; it is dependent on an idea. At first, this idea is a vague one, a presentiment of a higher reality to which we are subject, a confused awareness of a higher vocation and of an absolute duty to follow it. At this stage, the requisite moral attitude is not clearly outlined. What it does demand is fidelity to the first perceptible glimmer, an openness to transcendent being dimly surmised, a determination to follow, at any cost, the vocation given. It is this attitude of submission, love, desire, surrender, that breaks down the walls of egoism. This moral attitude is, precisely, the primary rectitude of the spirit. One may adopt it or not; and if not, the refusal is accompanied with a warning, an accusation, arising from the depths of the spirit, even if the voice be but faint and fugitive and quickly driven down to the unconscious.

The spirit begins by determining its direction as a responsible person and, in so doing, makes its view of the world more definite. It borrows, for the purpose, from its experience of life and the society in which it moves. As this view becomes clearer, it in turn clarifies the moral aspiration; and the two continue to develop by their interaction.

Thought is, thus, a function of the moral attitude, but this does not affect its objectivity, which is not passively received but actively acquired by thought. Whenever the moral attitude is present, spontaneous thought, growing with the experience of each day, always has considerable objective value. Besides, this personal thought is amenable to control and criticism. The fact that thought, considered psychologically, is personal, is the person thinking, does not rule out the possibility for us to step back and reflect on our spontaneous thought, judging it according to the requirements of sound reason.

These reflections serve to bring out the difference between two ways of conceiving thought as the function of a whole; one, biological, the other, personalist. Newman's conception had absolutely nothing in common with the biological. Historically, it precedes the advent of biologism in psychology. The modernists, on the other hand, were steeped in the dominant atmosphere of biologism. They interpreted, accordingly, the development of ideas and doctrines, and claimed to explain Newman in the same sense. Now that philosophy has succeeded, by the use of its own weapons in driving biologism back on the defensive, we are better able to distinguish his ideas from the modernistic as well as from the traditional.

C. Through Scylla and Charybdis

A theory so original as Newman's could gain acceptance only by degrees, in the light of subsequent findings of psychology. It is not surprising that it was not completely understood either by certain traditional psychologists or by the adherents of biologistic psychology. Newman's own psychology of thought is, as we have just seen, neither logicist, nor biologist, but personalist. Living thought follows other paths than those mapped out by the rules of logic, which apply solely to operations of a very general and abstract nature. Thought, as actually seen at work in the individual, is not an unfolding, by necessary sequence, of concepts in a separated intelligence, but the growing expression of an experience which consists of the whole of human life. It is, therefore, the person, the living human being in the fullness of his life, who expresses himself in his experience and thought.

Newman differs from traditional psychology in his strict differentiation between the real psychological process of thought and its expression in logical terms, without, however, denying their true, but imperfect, agreement; while classical psychology, though admitting, in principle, the normal interaction of the different psychic functions, more or less ignored it in dealing with mental operations in the concrete. The ideal scheme of scientific thought, as worked out in logic, often drew attention away from the real life of thought. The fascination exercised by the clear laws of deductive logic prevented due consideration of the complexities of the actual life of the mind. Hence, when the question arose as to how the Church advances in the knowledge of tradition, theologians, instead of examining the intellectual life of society in its psychological, historical and sociological aspects, were content to study only the logical consistency of theological systems in their completed state.

The attitude Newman took up from the very beginning was the opposite of this; and this accounts for his bewilderment in the presence of an epistemology calling itself psychological, yet abstracting the process of thought from its living, personal context, and claiming to see in it nothing other than a mechanism of universal and necessary propositions.[1] Newman, with his leaning to the concrete, could not but hold thought to be a function of the whole personal life; for him, *genuine* thought, in the case of *real* persons, who are brought by it to *true* conceptions and to firm and *active* convictions, is always that, and cannot be otherwise. Certainly, it can be examined and stated logically, and its very nature makes this desirable; but its logical expression is always incomplete. The

---

[1] This is the basic thesis of the *Grammar*; but Newman does not, consequently, take exception to the traditional psychology, but to the scientism of the day.

deep recesses of real apprehension, the subtle influences of all kinds of contingent circumstances, the decisive force of first principles, cannot be conveyed, assessed and vindicated in a strictly logical treatment. Yet these factors are of supreme importance; it is they which direct real thought, of which they, ordinarily, form a part; and so a critical justification of knowledge has to be able to take account of the effect they normally produce. If, then, we wish to know how real development of an idea comes about, and how its truth is to be guaranteed, we are not to question logic on the point, but the entire process of thought. When we investigate that, we find that our mental procedures are always partly unconscious, or rather implicit, and also too complex, and, in the case of theological questions, too deeply involved in a mystery we never succeed in mastering. So it is generally impossible, in fact, to reproduce adequately, in formal reasoning, the hidden ways implicitly taken by the *fides quaerens intellectum*.

Perhaps we could succeed in doing so in ideal conditions, not to be found in this life; but, so long as our intelligence is in its present state, as we know it, it is not surprising that scientific theology cannot completely deduce, after the event, the conclusions reached by religious thought, and has to leave the evaluation of these to the "illative sense" of living faith and to the judgment pronounced, in virtue of its *charisma,* by living authority. This is not to be taken as a disparagement of theology, which Newman greatly admired and praised, but only as a realistic admission of its limitations.

No doctrinal development can be fully achieved in terms of formal logic; but, for all that, it is not a biological process either. The difference between Newman and biologistic psychology is that he began by a study of the life of the mind in its numerous modes of expression, uninfluenced by any biological philosophy of evolution, whereas modernist psychology came to birth in the atmosphere of such a philosophy.

To see how different they are, it is enough to compare the conclusions of our study of Newman with the criticism, already outlined, of the liberal and modernist theologians. Storr and Tyrrell allege that Newman's primary sense of the word "idea" is not that of knowledge, strictly speaking, but of a spiritual force or impulse. On the meaning adopted it depends whether the psychology of development takes a vitalist or a personalist direction.

If the original idea does not as yet belong to the sphere of knowledge, what is the use of speaking of a final unfolding, a future elucidation, a consistent expression of this idea in an integrated system? The two planes, of real apprehension and of reason, are, thereby, heterogeneous by definition, and, in consequence, we can speak only of an intellectual incarnation in which the original force finds expression. In this supposition, the creative impulse has to draw its intelligible content, its specific properties, not from within itself, but from its environment; and so this content is always dependent on, correlative with, the environment and, therefore, variable. Ultimately, it becomes quite useless to look for a logical expression of development. In other words, we sink wholly into the doctrinal relativism of the modernists, and the essence of religion is, henceforth, no more than religiosity, an irrational sentiment. Tyrrell and Storr, who hold this conception of the idea to be the core of Newman's original theory, are right in concluding that his theory is ultimately equivocal, since they agree that Newman admits a logical factor at work in the process of development.

If, on the other hand, the original idea is, from the beginning, genuine knowledge, though for the most part unconscious, or rather implicit,[1] of *determinate* realities; if, as with Newman, it is a concrete and living interpretation of Scripture and the other sources which make up tradition, then the homogeneity of the two spheres, the intuitive and the rational, is assured in principle. The original idea is able, from its own resources, to give rise to more explicit judgments and these can be a real, if imperfect, expression of that idea. These expressions, therefore, are absolutely and invariably true, though susceptible of being made more perfect. Finally, there remains no opposition between logical sequence and the influence of the environment; for what is under one aspect,

---

[1] As we have already explained, the unconscious idea is not, in the strict sense of the term, unconscious. The very use of the word "idea" would be surprising if we were speaking of a psychic element of which we were totally unaware. Besides, how could an idea that entirely escapes awareness become, as Newman says, an object of analysis and reflection, to be expressed in abstract judgments of rigorous exactness? What Newman calls "unconscious" but also, at times, "implicit", is that all-embracing, intuitive phase of thought which, according to modern psychology, precedes analytic thought and constantly accompanies it. For modern studies of the subject, See G. Dwelshauers, *L'Étude de la pensée* (*Cours et documents de philosophie*) (Paris, n.d.), pp.177-197. See above, pp.99-100.

the assimilation of what is brought from without may, under another aspect, be a true fulfilment of itself, a systematic expression of the original and proper content of inarticulate knowledge.

Here we have two very different interpretations of the development of ideas, each derived logically from its conception of the nature of the original idea. The elements of the first have been taken from Tyrrell and Storr, and they lie at the root of the modernist theory of development; all that goes to make up the second will be found in our exposition of Newman's theory. The difference in standpoint and outlook between this and the vitalist theories of liberals and modernists is clearly to be seen, and we may draw the conclusion that there is no need to accept the incompatibility of logical and biological development. There is no contradiction in saying, with Newman, that the development of thought follows a logical process and is yet a function of the living personality of the thinker, and even of the whole social setting. As he aptly points out, "we think in logic as we speak in prose". Logical cohesion and sequence is the natural way—even in the case of spontaneous thought—in which our judgments are interconnected, just as the dividing of cells is the natural way in which living matter grows and is propagated. Yet it would be a denial of the richness and complexity of thought to try to rule out, in favour of impersonal rules, that "illative sense" which, prior to any formal analysis, already governs the subtle processes of living thought. Besides this, logic can doubtless connect propositions, but it is incapable of interpreting and guaranteeing the general orientation of thought and the synthesis it aims at establishing, any more than the division of cells explains why one kind of flower develops in height, like the tulip or lily, and another in breadth, like the azalea. It is due to our first principles that our view of the world develops in this direction or that, that it is substantially true or false; and these, in turn, depend on our personality, that is, on our moral outlook, on what we, in practice, take to be of vital importance. Ultimately, everything depends on our answer to the question, whether those experiences which all men undergo in the depth of their being,[1] from which our knowledge of objective

---

[1] "These simple and primary thoughts," as Kierkegaard would say (*The Lilies of the Field and the Birds of Heaven*, (Paris, 1935, pp.84-89)) in which man awakes, in astonishment, to his human condition and the nobility of his personal vocation, but which he forgets in the crowd and in worldly cares.

values is derived, are admitted and welcomed, and their implications faithfully pursued.

If we apply this test to revealed religion, it shows that the primary necessity for a true theology is a deep and powerful life of faith, a continuous dwelling of the mind on Christ and his way of salvation, and a scrupulous fidelity to the word of God, that it be not lost. The living hold on this Christian idea is the germ from which the growth of tradition derives its shape and authenticity. Where it is present, the tree of true knowledge will steadily grow and bear abundant fruit for the Church. Where it is wanting, there will grow only poisonous weeds that appear in a single night only to disappear without fruit. "Realizing is the very life of true development"—this is the sum of Newman's theory. The heretic does not differ from the Father of the Church in the logical force of his arguments, but in his lack of faith, that is, of intuition of concrete reality, which is present only when accompanied by humility and submissiveness, with readiness to obey the light from on high. In this sense, therefore, Christian thought is a function of the Christian personality, its value is proportionate to the seriousness of a person's faith; for the first principles of Christian thought are but the expression of the living roots of the Christian attitude to life, and the real possession of these principles, consciously or not, ensures rightness of judgment in matters of faith. Beyond all the elaborations and proofs of logic, however useful they may be, this judgment perceives the truth of faith in the twilight of mystery, in spite of the subtle sophisms of heretics; in the greatest of the Fathers of the Church, their discernment, wholly governed by grace, was resplendent with supernatural genius.

If doctrinal thought is always in vital relation to the thinker's whole personality, it is so, too, with all that surrounds it and with the idea of Christianity as it lives in the Church. The idea lives in the Church, which is a society, and its principles give rise there to a particular atmosphere, a certain spirit. Like the seed spoken of in the Gospel, it is sown throughout the community by education, by the liturgy, and by the living voice of the preacher; it brings forth fruit in those whose hearts, like the good ground, are open to receive it. Thus, the thought of the individual is bound up with the life of the community. Lastly, the wider field of the outside world also has its influence on tradition, not that it determines the form of the idea or of public worship, but as affording material of all kinds for Christian thought to sift, purify and take to itself.

In view of this, the judgment of the liberal theologians we instanced above appears very superficial, in fact irrelevant. Is it true that Newman so detached thought from life as to retain only the logical sequence of propositions? On the contrary, his constant endeavour, all his life, was to determine the exact position occupied by thought in the whole complex setting of actual life, a task brilliantly achieved in the *Grammar of Assent*. At the same time, he did not set out a psychology of thought on biological lines, or jettison logical sequence in the development of doctrine. Nor did he deny the validity of the laws proper to discursive reason. In avoiding both Scylla and Charybdis, in rejecting neither the logical structure of development nor its vital connection with the whole person, he proved most convincingly the balance and force of his genius.

D. *The consistency and the defects of Newman's psychology of development*

Now that Newman's theory has been set out and placed in its context, it only remains to give a summary assessment of its value. We have already seen that the charge of being equivocal is without foundation. It is, in fact, remarkable in its consistency, and forms a part of a general conception in which it is perfectly integrated. If the personalist standpoint be taken as clarifying his whole conception, the unity and coherence of the principal sections is evident; his individual and social psychology of the idea, his research into the criteria of true, homogeneous development, all exhibit one and the same personalist vision of actual, living thought.

None the less, in studying the detail of his theory and its applications, we find certain gaps, and many questions spring to the mind. Newman himself held his greater works to be merely reconnaissances into a mysterious country never yet explored. It would be hard to find a more difficult subject, and it is natural that his analyses, though of a clarity that amounts to genius, should be but provisional and imperfect. Moreover, his way of invoking analogies for everything exposes him to the danger of underestimating the real differences that often exist between things that are alike in part. We have seen, for instance, that the expression "real apprehension" is used for a variety of analogical procedures, and so

hides, to some extent, the essential differences between the knowledge of God by conscience, the knowledge of the world through
the senses, and knowledge by faith considered as a view of supernatural realities. In the Oxford sermon, faith is compared to knowledge through the senses; but he omits to explain what is proper
to knowledge by faith. Still, if we collate this part of the sermon
with other passages from his works, if we bear in mind the partial nature and the particular standpoint of his individual works,
we shall be in no doubt as to his real position.

It might be said of every part of Newman's theory that differences should have been more clearly brought out. How many
different realities are covered by the expression "first principles".
What intellectual processes go to the full development of a social
idea, such as Christianity? If we were to undertake the labour of
gathering together and comparing observations scattered through
his works, we would find, as a rule, all the elements of an answer
to these questions. It is seldom that he gives a full analysis. As
regards the second of these questions, for instance, it is true that
Newman describes five types of development; but we are left
wondering how these five types can find a place in a single process
which is nothing but the unfolding of an original idea in all its
aspects and relations—a formula which seems to Newman to sum
up the whole process of development. How can certain practical
and concrete determinations, for example, sacramental dogmas
and the gradual fixing of the canon of Scripture,—in both of
which history exhibits development most clearly—how can they
have developed as manifold aspects of a single original idea? We
do not say that it is impossible, but, to show the possibility, it was
necessary, first of all, to analyse and define further the various
ways of belonging to an idea, and of inclusion in it.

It follows that Newman's psychology, full and balanced though
it be, calls for more definiteness on many points. The analysis of
its sections and their mutual adaptation is not fully carried out,
and many problems still await solution.

Section B

The Test of True Development

A. Logical or theological?

All agree that, in some sense, there is growth in the Church's knowledge of revealed truth. That it is not a change, strictly speaking, but a true and complete development of the Revelation given by Christ and the apostles, is the firm conviction of the Church, against the Modernists and Protestants. Newman, we have seen, shared this view, and held it to be self-evident. The question is how is the identity of doctrine guaranteed? Catholic theologians and apologists put forward divergent theories on the point and, to complete our judgment on Newman's theory, we have to compare his with theirs.

J. Guitton distinguishes two groups of tendencies. An earlier group, according to him, mainly influenced by Suarez, was dominant in theology until 1860 and viewed development merely as an unfolding, by *purely explicative syllogisms,* of what was already *formally included* in Revelation. A second group, chiefly in vogue in the 19th century, whose greatest representative was the Dominican, Marin-Sola,[1] held development to be a real progress, in which the *virtual* content of Revelation was deduced from what was given originally, by means of progressive reasoning; they emphasized the living and concrete character of Revelation. Guitton considers that Newman belonged to the second group, although, in the variety and fulness of his conceptions, he was far superior to both.[2]

There is an element of truth in this judgment, for, with Newman, development proceeds by a reasoning which is truly progressive and productive. All the same, there is a greater difference between him and Marin-Sola than between the latter and theologians like R. Schultes, O.P.,[3] who see in development no more than a more exact, but equivalent, expression of certain original propositions. Newman, the historian and psychologist of spontaneous thought, would have read with astonishment the bold and naïve attempts of the subtle dialectician, Marin-Sola, to reduce to strict syllogisms particular doctrines like the Immaculate Conception. He admits a certain logical sequence in the course followed by tradition, but would not agree that its whole spontaneous growth was susceptible, after the event, of being com-

[1] See his monumental work, *L'Evolution homogène du dogme catholique* (Fribourg, 1924), 2 vols.

[2] J. Guitton, *op. cit.,* pp.117-118.

[3] R. Schultes, O.P., *Introductio in historiam dogmatum* (Paris, 1922).

pletely expressed in formal syllogisms strictly demonstrable. In particular cases, it could perhaps be done, but not in all; and besides, it is not necessary. Subsequently, it is always possible to detect some sort of logical sequence, but the entire mystery of doctrinal development is incapable of being set out in strict form. The gulf between Newman and people like Marin-Sola is the basic distinction, drawn by Newman and Blondel, between the psychology of concrete, spontaneous knowledge, and the scientific analysis applied to this knowledge afterwards. Hence, we cannot entirely agree with Guitton.

The classification made recently by R. Draguet is, perhaps, more valuable.[1] According to him, contemporary theology provides two chief ways of solving the problem. The first is *mainly dialectical,* and comprises solutions like that of Schultes as well as of Marin-Sola; the second, *mainly theological,* can claim Newman, de la Barre, S.J., Blondel, Simonin, O.P., and Draguet himself.[2] The first group emphasizes logical sequence as the sign of true development and its warrant, but its members differ among themselves as to the nature of the logical connection. The second insists rather on the supernatural character of faith, and on the supernatural organ in charge of doctrine, the teaching authority of the Church; and this solution, too, has its variations, as, for instance, in the part it assigns to reason.

To understand the two positions, we must first, for the sake of clearness, distinguish between two questions. The first is, how does a doctrine, of which the Church only later becomes aware, come to form, explicitly, part of the formal object of faith? The answer, on which all are agreed, is that it happens solely in virtue of a doctrinal definition of the Church or of a general consensus of the ordinary *magisterium.* The second is, where does the Church obtain the guarantee that what it so defines is really part of the original Revelation? Here it is that the ways diverge.

One answer to this question is that the guarantee is to be found in logical sequence, so that it should be possible, dialectically, to refer all the later articles of faith to the primitive belief. The up-

---

[1] R. Draguet, *op. cit.,* pp. 1166-1192.

[2] De la Barre, S.J., *La vie du dogme catholique* (Paris, 1898); M. Blondel, "Histoire et dogme", *Quinzaine,* LVI (1904), pp. 145-167, 349-373, 433-458; H.-D. Simonin, O.P. "'Implicite' et 'explicite' dans le développement du dogme", *Angelicum,* XIV (1937), pp. 126-145; R. Draguet, *op. cit.*

holders of this view certainly insist that the Church's authority guides and controls the formation of dogmatic conclusions, but it acts only from without, in protecting reason from falling into error. The guarantee it provides is, therefore, only an extrinsic and negative one; it does not complete the work of reason in an intrinsic and positive way.

Those who defend the theological solution look to definition by the Church for the required guarantee. The action of reason, certainly, contributes greatly to the elaboration of the faith, but the object of faith cannot be comprehended by reason. Both the definitions of recent times and the original formularies are expressions of a mystery, and what connects the one with the other must undoubtedly share this character of mystery. Reason, therefore, cannot serve as a principle of a complete and final guarantee in questions of doctrinal development. Its action needs to be completed, from time to time, by the Church's supernatural functioning, and in an intrinsic and positive fashion. This function is exercised by the *magisterium* of the Church, where the Holy Ghost, living in the community of the faithful, speaks with authority.[1]

Newman's theory may most suitably be included in the second group, with the understanding that it assigns a positive and considerable part to reason. It is quite possible, in fact, for the theo-

---

[1] De la Barre (*op. cit.*, pp.156-188) finely describes this process and concludes thus: "The work that precedes definition is a work whose result is consecrated; considered in its outcome, and as divinely guaranteed, it constitutes a *transcendent fact*, it is not subject exclusively to the *human laws* of any doctrinal development in general. The *magisterium* intervenes as a higher principle; it is the directive principle, the soul of the doctrine, as the vital principle directs the development of the embryo". Blondel, (*op. cit.*, pp.440, ff.) makes use of his concept of "action" to express the process of development carried out in the community of the faithful under the authority of the Church. He sees in this knowledge by "action" an independent principle of discrimination which does not eliminate, but perfects, the instrumentality of reason. It is Draguet (*op. cit.*, pp.1187-1192) who most strictly put forward and upheld the theological solution. He begins by criticizing the historical or dialectical solution; next, after proving the necessity of a theological solution, he shows how this could be used in apologetics; and concludes by exhibiting it as containing the essentials of a genuine solution. Similar ideas are those of Simonin (*op. cit.*, pp.132-137): "The object of faith is not, in itself, evident to the mind; new definitions, like the old, bear essentially on mysteries, and the passage from one to the other cannot be the effect of perfect evidence which would draw, of itself, the assent of the mind" (p.134).

logical solution to be presented in a too exclusive and exaggerated way. This would be the case if we started from the dilemma opposing the dialectical to the theological solution and proceeded to say that, since the former could not explain the facts, therefore infallible authority alone is the guarantee of true developments. This would give the impression that the function of regulating the growth of tradition is completely removed from reason and ascribed to authority. No one, hitherto, has maintained such an extreme view and, in any case, it is quite foreign to Newman. Development is the work of reason, in its widest sense; it is, therefore, natural that the primary regulating principle should be the judgment of reason. Sometimes, this is capable of the whole task; at other times, not. This is by no means surprising, in view of the disproportion between spontaneous knowledge and logical technique on the one hand, and, on the other, of the fact that Revelation concerns mysteries. It is in these cases that the teaching authority will intervene most decisively. In so doing, it does not totally replace reason, but only supplements it, for reason covers the first part of the ground. Many an individual theologian, led by his deep faith and long experience in such matters, achieves certainty and truth. His "illative sense" does not mislead him, but he is unable to express his conclusions in strictly logical form. The teaching authority, then, under the infallible guidance of the Holy Ghost, guarantees to the whole Church that the conclusion he intimately feels to be true, though he be unable to prove it conclusively, belongs to the original content of the faith. In this case, the deciding factor of the truth of a doctrinal conclusion is not reason, but authority.

Newman's experience led him to assert more and more forcibly the necessity of an infallible authority to guarantee the validity of doctrinal conclusions. This conviction of his is most insisted on in his later works. In addition, his theological solution follows logically from his theory of knowledge. For, if there is a natural disproportion between spontaneous reasoning and scientific argument, particularly in the domain of mystery, it is equally natural that logic should not be able to regulate and assess perfectly the course followed by the Church in the development of tradition. The "illative sense" of the individual, whether theologian or layman, supplementing the work of logic, may suffice for himself personally, but cannot be of universal application. Divine Providence, therefore, having endowed the Church with an infallible authority, has entrusted to it the task of supplying, by its infallible definition, what is lacking, inevitably, in historical and rational theology.

This theory is not only logically self-consistent, but it also provides a very useful starting-point for explaining the actual facts. Some theory is necessary to defend the immutability of doctrine through the course of history. In the present state of historical investigation, it is impossible to reduce the whole doctrinal development in the Church to any kind of clear and irrefutable technical reasoning. A theory such as Newman's may make it possible for all difficulties to be satisfactorily resolved.

B. Critical observations

Before concluding our study of Newman's argument, we have one or two points left to examine. What he was concerned with was to show that what was revealed originally kept its identity unimpaired throughout its development. This meant that he had, first of all, to make a thorough philosophical study of the notion of identity. He was fully aware of this necessity and his whole argument was governed by a very clear perception of what identity involved. We could wish, however, that his general attitude of sound sense on the point had been reinforced by a more rigorous philosophical inquiry.

The notion of identity, considered from an atomistic and superficial standpoint, is different from what it is when viewed in the philosophical aspect of what makes up a whole. The first approach, if consistent, is that of a crude, unphilosophical materialism. Like Democritus, it sees the world only as an enormous factory, where things are made with a certain number of material elements, themselves unchanging. Take away or add one of these, and the thing is no longer identical.

On the other hand, once the whole is thought of as the original reality, irreducible to its parts and itself the essential reality, it is easily understood how changes in the order of the parts in no wise affect the identity of the whole. Further, what looks like change to a superficial and purely analytical view becomes an affirmation of unchanged identity when examined more profoundly. This conception is the only one that can be entertained by a genuine metaphysics. Created being, since it does not possess within itself its own perfection, is defined, metaphysically, as appetite for this perfection. It is this active relation which constitutes created being. Such a being, in its original undeveloped state, is not yet completely itself. Only in its perfect state does it reach its proper identity. Moreover, the embodied spirit cannot tend towards its perfection except by expressing itself in time and place, that is to say, according to the laws and conditions of historical existence. This applies to any spiritual reality that desires to express itself within human history. A divine idea, embodying itself by revelation in human terms, can express itself perfectly and become fully itself only by an uninterrupted historical development. Complete identity, then, is not a material thing to preserve but a spiritual value to conquer, or, rather, the identity of a spiritual reality in the world of history must be dynamic; it can be kept only by active fidelity to itself, by developing according to its nature.

This is, certainly, the metaphysical concept implied in Newman's theory of development, and it governs this theory throughout. Yet Newman failed to express it clearly and to work it out and, in consequence, probably caused some confusion and perplexity in many of his readers.

He might be reproached, too, for not having attached greater importance to the historical element in the historico-religious argument which he considered so conclusive. Doubtless, in this sphere least of all is a pure description of facts in their interconnection possible. Historians investigate facts for the sake of their significance in the human context, and it is possible to establish or detect a meaning in things only as a result of the light we ourselves cast on them. We cannot, therefore, as historians, approach the facts without human, that is to say philosophical, presuppositions. The formal truth of history for us depends on the truth of the pre-existing ideas in the light of which we view the facts. Newman, then, cannot be blamed for giving such emphasis to the reasonable presumptions of conscience and faith. He cannot be denied the right of interpreting the facts in the light of antecedent probability; nor can he be blamed for being ready to pass over incidental difficulties when the general course of the history of doctrine accords well enough with his theological presumption. Yet, seeing that reasoning by convergence draws its special cogency from the independence of the various probabilities that make up the argument, we could wish that he had given the historical part a fuller autonomy and a treatment more exact and detailed.

Obviously, we have to bear in mind the circumstances in which the *Essay on Development* was written. At the same time, it is true that the argument, as set out in the book, does not perfectly meet the requirements of method which were formulated at a later date and with far greater precision in the *Grammar of Assent*.

The seven criteria of true development have already been explained and criticized. As they are set out in the unfinished *Essay*, they manifest a penetrating intuition which, however, is not analysed sufficiently. In our own opinion, they are of the greatest value when applied to doctrine as a single whole, rather than to each dogma in isolation; when their cogency is seen to derive from their convergence; when we do not ask from them more than Newman claimed, that is, not an absolutely conclusive proof, but a reply to an objection brought against a position already established on other grounds. Nor must we forget that the *Essay* remained unfinished, and that there are evident signs of haste and fatigue in the final chapters.

the statement he could wish, that he had given the historical part a fuller autonomy and a treatment were exact and detailed.

Obviously we have to bear in mind the circumstances in which the *Essay on Development* was written. At the same time, it is true that the treatment, as set off in the book, does not portray all the requirements of method which were formulated at a later date and with important precision in the *Grammar of Science*. The ideas entertained of true development have already been explained and criticized. As they are set out in the unpublished paper, they promise a penetrating intuition which, however, is not amplified sufficiently. In our own opinion, they are of the greatest value when applied to doctrine as a single whole, rather than to each dogma in isolation. When their cogency is seen to derive from their convergence, and we do not ask from them that Newton claimed, that is, not an absolutely conclusive proof, but a reply to an objection brought against a position already examined on other grounds. Nor must we forget that the text remained unfinished, and that there are evident signs of haste and fatigue in the final chapters.

Appendix A

BIOGRAPHIES OF NEWMAN

SINCE this book was written, a number of biographies of Newman have appeared. There have been about twelve in the last few years. Most of them are popular accounts, and tell us nothing new; some, however, are important and deserve attention.

We shall consider, first, three studies of him in his Anglican days. *Young Mr. Newman* by Maisie Ward,[1] *Newman's Way* by Sean O'Faòlain,[2] and *Newman at Oxford* by R. D. Middleton.[3]

These three books are the outcome of original research and the copious use of unpublished sources. The first two give valuable information on Newman's childhood, home and relatives. It needed a sensitive and intelligent woman like Maisie Ward to bring out the young Newman in his daily life—a man who kept hid within himself the secret of his soul and genius, and appeared, externally, quite ordinary, healthy, sociable, tender, considerate, one who expressed his affection with simplicity, sincerity and delicacy; cheerful, sometimes abounding in good humour and merriment, gently ironical; active, enterprising, practical, interested in the thousand details of life, appreciative of wine and good cooking, financial adviser to the family ... normal, one would say, absolutely normal. As we read the book, we feel how false is the myth of a Newman estranged, absorbed in his inward vision, divorced from the life of the world. Doubtless, his soul was in

[1] London, 1948.
[2] London, 1952.
[3] London, 1950.

contact with the unseen world, and he considered himself an exile among things of sense; but the presence of the invisible is not an anti-social factor making for strange or extravagant behaviour on the part of the person possessing it, rather it should make him more alive to the real needs of others whose personality, whether they are aware of it or not, is rooted in the same transcendent mystery. So far from upsetting the ordinary forms of social intercourse, it makes it more genuine and saves it from becoming merely formal.

Consequently, there is nothing inconsistent between the young Newman in all his naturalness, as Maisie Ward depicts him, and the extraordinary character of the religious experience he was undergoing. If, at times, the young don seems somewhat pedantic and dominating in his attitude to his younger brothers and sisters, for whose education he felt himself more or less responsible, he never assumed the part of a youthful prophet or saint.

There was nothing forced, no unnatural or puritan restraint, in the family atmosphere, which was simply Christian and devout. The father affected a kind of liberalism, and preached tolerance and openness of mind. From the religious point of view, there was nothing to distinguish the Newmans from the ordinary Anglican family of the period. That does not mean that there was nothing out of the ordinary in them; but they were remarkable, not in their religious atmosphere, but in their characters. Some of their traits are well described by Maisie Ward, but it is to Sean O'Faòlain that we are indebted for a whole gallery of psychological portraits of the Newman family in the course of its history. It was, in fact, to the Newman family history, as a highly individual one, that O'Faòlain was first drawn when looking for a promising subject in psychological biography. As he proceeded, this history seemed so dominated by the genius of John Henry that he became the central figure of the work and the other members entirely subordinate to him. We owe to his original plan many details of the family history—the remote ancestors, the true account of the father's financial misfortunes previously concealed out of respect or misrepresented by filial piety and, finally, the rather disreputable side of the history. He brings to light the various characters of Harriet, Jemima, Mary, Frank, and, particularly, Charles, the black sheep, half genius and half mad, whose relations with the family and with John himself lend themselves well to caustic treatment. The description and assessment of Newman's own personality in this book raise a special problem outside the bounds of biography, and closely concerns this question of development. We shall deal with it in the appendix which follows.

The third book on Newman's Anglican period is that of R. D. Middleton. He had previously published, in 1947, a delightful account[1] of Newman's friendship with Bloxam, his curate at Littlemore from 1837. This friendship, which lasted till the Cardinal's death, and by no means impaired the devotion of each to his own Church, is considered by the author an example of the true ecumenical spirit. It was in this spirit that he conceived the idea of writing Newman's life in the Church of England. Consequently, his first concern was not with the family circle, nor Newman's private life. "The aim of the present volume has been to describe the progress of Newman's thought in so far as possible in his own words during his stay in our Communion" (p.233). This is a plan which many others have attempted to execute, to retrace the journey set out in the *Apologia,* and judge it on the evidence supplied by the documents of the time.

Middleton's study is severely objective. He scrutinises minutely those contemporary documents which reflect the development of Newman's thought. He analyses them with great care, quoting them at length; and in this respect, his work, though the subject is not new, marks a real progress.

We must say a little on the ecumenical spirit of the book. The author, an Anglican, admits that Newman's conversion to Catholicism was entirely justified by the circumstances in which he was placed. His conversion may have been influenced by his emotions but it was itself due, not to them, but to his intellect. Middleton rejects the agreeable suggestion of Dean Church that Newman, a saint in quest of holiness, was converted through realizing that, among Anglicans, sanctity belonged to individuals rather than the Church, and that the Roman Church, as a Church, was nearer to his ideal. "He was no longer able," wrote Dean Church, "to reason in the face of strong emotions. It was a conversion not of intellect, but of emotion." Middleton rightly rejoins that, at the time of his conversion, Newman was hardly acquainted with a single Catholic, and could not have had any experience of actual holiness in the Roman Church; and that it was his experience of

[1] R. D. Middleton, *Newman and Bloxam* (London, 1947).

the personal holiness of so many of his co-religionists that kept him up to that time in the Church of England (p. 238). This opinion will have an important bearing on the discussion which follows.

Middleton's personal view is that the spiritual principles Newman stood for have now so penetrated the Church of England that the reasons that compelled Newman to leave it are no longer valid. While deploring the "great loss" to his communion, he is glad that another part of the Catholic Church was able to profit by Newman's life and teaching. The background to these views of his is expressed in his prayer "that the Church he has left and the Church to which he has gone may, in God's good time, together with the Holy Orthodox Church, become one again in the true fold of the Redeemer which is the Catholic Church, living now as separate Communions their lives apart, yet one in the faith of Christ" (p.241).

Among the biographies dealing with Newman's whole life, we would draw attention to two. One is by Robert Sencourt, *The Life of Newman,* a literary work written in a swift, nervous tempo, with verve and imagination, but its somewhat strident and too confident style makes it rather tiresome to read. The idea of writing a complete life of Newman was suggested to him by Father Tristram, who was undoubtedly better acquainted than anyone with the problems entailed. He himself has published only a certain number of articles and studies of different kinds, all highly competent, on matters of detail; but most of the works on Newman published in the last thirty years or so benefited from his encouragement and help, and, at times, from his corrections. We await impatiently the publication of the rest of his writings.

Sencourt's book has its merits; it makes use of much unpublished material. It is not always accurate in its statements or discriminating in its judgments, but it succeeds in tracing faithfully, in our opinion, the course of Newman's own development. It describes his misfortunes as a Catholic, the Achilli trial, the embroilments with Manning, in bold strokes and, often, throws new light on them. Sencourt excels in descriptions of persons, and creates his principal characters succinctly and vividly. He gives a brief analysis of Newman's principal works, and succeeds in conveying the essentials of each. The *Grammar of Assent* is summarized and assessed in two excellent chapters. The author is alive to all the different aspects of Newman's personality. Yet, perhaps on account of the absence of a dominant standpoint, the impression of Newman that it leaves is rather disjointed. It lacks a centre. We see an imposing personality, a manifold genius, but one who is ultimately mysterious.

Bouyer's work, on the other hand, has the decided merit of seeing Newman's life from a definite point of view, which is expressed in its very title, *Newman, His Life and Spirituality*. Its main concern is neither the influence of his surroundings, nor the development of his convictions, but his spirituality. Nearly all Newman's biographers are misled in taking up the standpoint of the *Apologia*, and following the course Newman himself described. But the *Apologia* is simply a defence of the sincerity of his convictions, his conversion and his faith as a Catholic; it is not an autobiography. Had Newman written one, he would probably have planned it on quite different lines. The important thing is to find a point of view which corresponds with the real centre of his personality; and, on this, we have the unanimous testimony of his friends, his own papers, and his life. He was above all, as Dean Church said, a man eager for holiness. If the pursuit of holiness was his dominant passion, we must undoubtedly conclude that his true history is that of his soul, the development of his spirituality. If we are to look for a model in his own writings, we shall find it in *Callista* rather than the *Apologia*.

This was admirably understood by Père Bouyer, and the biography he has produced is unlike any other. He has used, especially, Newman's sermons, letters, religious poetry, meditations and prayers, journals and intimate reflections. From time to time in his account, he sounds the very depths of Newman's soul, and succeeds thus in disclosing the hidden, continuous movement of a soul seeking God and a purity worthy of Him.

Newman's spirituality could certainly be classified as platonist. The commemorative inscription he composed, *Ex umbris et imaginibus in veritatem,* is a summary of the fundamental movement of his life. The visible world is haunted by the presence of an invisible one, which it both points to and conceals. This presence is felt rather as we are aware of things during the night. Newman's soul finds its way by the feeble glimmer of conscience, "amid the encircling gloom". He does not feel himself borne along on a strong current, but he advances step by step, laboriously in the dark.

His characteristic virtue is constant fidelity day by day, with obedience and blind trust in Providence.

The invisible world is peopled with angels and saints. The dead he had loved are concealed in the surrounding shade, but they are always present, and Newman is always aware of them. Bouyer points this out clearly in regard to the posthumous life of Mary in the spirit of her brother. This presence is not something purely interior. It is projected on to things, which become, in consequence its sacramental sign : "Dear Mary seems embodied in every tree, and hid behind every hill. What a veil and curtain this world of sense is. Beautiful, but still a veil"(pp.140-141). They are all there behind the veil. Newman feels as though he were physically surrounded by their silent presence. One day, he will see them, when

> The night is gone;
> And with the morn those angel faces smile,
> Which I have loved long since, and lost awhile.

But the supreme presence dwelling in the world is that of God. The soul's most deeply rooted desire is for union with Him. Newman sees the present life as fundamentally a deception, though he is fully aware of its attraction. Even apart from sin, which disfigures the veil, and detracts from its value as a sign, life on earth would be worthless, in his eyes, did it not finally issue in a face-to-face presence. "Time is nothing except as the seed of eternity" (p.150).

With Newman, the movement of the soul in regard to the world, as in regard to God, flows in two opposite currents. While he is strongly attracted by God's infinite fullness, fear of the Judge and respect for the divine majesty cause a hidden movement of recoil. This twofold sentiment is conveyed in his immortal poem, *The Dream of Gerontius*. His predominant feeling about the world and life on earth is one of their fragility, their want of substance. It is impossible for him to become attached to them, not only through his convictions, but also by reason of this feeling of his. Yet at the same time he sees in them a splendour and undergoes experiences that give them a hidden attraction—"Beautiful, but still a veil".

This conscious opposition in his deepest feelings is characteristic of Newman alone, and gives to his spirituality a unique personal note. Already in his Anglican days, he had deliberately renounced marriage and any intimacy which would allow another to share the secret of his soul. In this connection, he wrote: "I could not take the interest in the world which marriage requires. I am too disgusted with this world". But, concerning close friendship he adds: "Yet not the less I feel the need of it" (p.195). Later, in the journal of 1859-1876, we see the conflict between two feelings, the desire to please God, and the desire to have his work praised by his superiors and his former co-religionists: "After the supreme judgment of God, I have desired, though in a different order, their praise" (p.365). Hence his double attitude towards the persecutions, the intrigues, the indignities, the calumnies, the misunderstanding of which he felt himself the object. On the one hand, he was deeply wounded by them, and his years of obscurity were so embittered that he compared his journal, not without humour, to the complaints of Job. On the other hand, he bore witness to the profound peace of soul he constantly enjoyed.

In Newman's conscience, there was, in principle, no moral incompatibility between these two orders of feeling. The consolations of friendship, the recognition by others of his integrity and of the usefulness of his work were, for him, real values he had a right to approve and desire. But he was afraid of becoming attached to them, and his conscience was always careful that he did not become too dependent on them. After the success of the *Apologia*, he was glad of the expressions of esteem and gratitude that were sent from all parts; but he did not abandon himself to them: "My temptation at this moment is to value the praise of men too highly, especially of Protestants, and to lose some portion of that sensitiveness towards God's praise which is so elementary a duty" (p.373).

Newman's spirituality is, then, not one of extremes. It is nearer to that of St Thomas and St Francis de Sales than of some of the mystics. The enjoyment of human and earthly values can be harmoniously combined with perfect sanctity. At the same time, he affirms that he ought to be ready to forgo without resentment all that is not God. The circumstances that deprived him of these, that made a void all around him, that threw him back into obscurity and solitude, he accepted as trials that made him turn the more to God, and to seek peace in Him alone.

This peace he possessed; it was a perfect peace, a contentment,

a happiness, he says in the *Apologia*, which he enjoyed uninterruptedly. But it was a peace only in the depths. From his
intimate notes, especially those of a retreat at San Eusebio (1847),
we learn that, from the time of the attacks on him as a result of
Tract 90, he lost that sensible fervour, that "vital impulse of the
heart" he enjoyed in his youth. He suffered from the same dryness
of soul as St Teresa of Lisieux. His way lay through the desert, of
which he gives a harrowing description. He felt he lacked all zest,
vigour and impetus. He drags himself along, unable to rise. The
rhythm of life is, for the most part, slow and sad. His former gaiety
has left him. He always feels tired. He moves slowly and reluctantly
to good works, to prayer, to those exercises, in particular, which
exact minute attention to details. He is listless in the contemplation of divine things. He is subject to scruples in some matters. No
doubt he remains faithful to all his duties, and prays for hours at a
time, but he does everything from a motive of duty, from a sense
of what is right, without heart or inspiration. It all costs him an
effort, a struggle against interior resistance. He feels abandoned,
no longer a useful instrument in the hands of Providence, but a
rejected tool, "dead wood". He even describes his state as one of
despair, "a dark and gloomy state of mind" (p.277). Yet, in the
same place, he acknowledges that the *Deus meus et omnia* is
always on his lips, and that he kept the whole time his "inward
sense of the Divine Presence everywhere", as also "a good conscience and the peace of mind that flows therefrom" (p. 276).

Such a state of soul is not easy to diagnose. Newman himself
recognized the influence on him of the crudeness of treatment he
so often received, which so weighed on his sensitivity, along with
physical fatigue and increasing age. He feared, too, that prolonged
application of the intellect to the things of faith may have stifled
the spontaneous aspiration of the heart. But, over and above these
factors, it is not difficult to perceive one more subtle and of a
deeper significance. God, in fact, was using this means to effect a
passive purification obliging him to prove, by a fidelity void of all
consolation, the sincerity of his will and the genuiness of his choice.

Here again we see Newman's remarkable qualities of absolute
clear-sightedness and sincerity. If at times they lead him to judge
others without allowing for their public position, their implacable
light is focused primarily on himself. He searched all the hidden
places of his spirit to detect sources of illusion, of false attitudes,

of unconscious duplicity, barring the road to God. He unmasked the subtle movements of pride and complacency. This work of analysis it was which formed the staple of his immortal sermons as an Anglican.

It is understandable that some readers feel uneasy about his "egotism", and the introversion implied in this minute self-scrutiny, this way of comparing himself with others, assessing his own qualities and shortcomings, observing the changes in his interior state, analysing his sentiments, recalling in detail his misfortunes, disappointments and sufferings, and estimating their effect on his life. There is, however, no morbid pleasure on his part. He tries to see himself as God sees him, and always finishes by turning to him in entire submission and abandonment.

Newman lays himself open to criticism above all when he ponders his misfortunes and judges his opponents. In his *John H. Newman*[1] a remarkable yet little known work, F. L. Cross puts forward the view that Newman's conversion was chiefly influenced by the resentment caused by the opposition of the Church of England to the publication of Tract 90. He held that Newman was, by nature, "a man of resentment", in the nietzschean sense, and that his conversion was a form of vengeance secretly elaborated for the incurable wound inflicted on him. He admits that, long before Tract 90, Newman's mind had been moving logically in the direction of Rome, and, in this way, the account in the *Apologia* is fairly exact. But, before its publication, the weaknesses he saw in the Anglican position were only intellectual difficulties, and he was the first to admit that ten thousand difficulties do not make a doubt. His personal certitude could be shaken only by a change deep down in his affective attitude to the Church, over and above the movement of his mind; and, from the moment that took place, the intellectual factors took on a quite different significance. The decisive factor in his conversion must then have been emotional, dislike following upon the injury received: "The Church was disgusted with Newman; the only step open to him in retaliation was to disown the Church" (p.143). This judgment, which repeats Wilberforce's accusation in 1864, was endorsed in 1945 by W. E. Houghton in *The Art of Newman's Apologia*.[2]

[1] F. L. Cross, *John Henry Newman: with a set of unpublished letters* (London, 1933).

[2] New Haven, 1945.

We have here a third emotional interpretation of Newman's conversion. Beneath the calm surface of the flow of his thought, perilous and deceptive whirlpools of emotion were seething; "artistic emotion" according to O'Faòlain, before the beguiling image of another world, which is couched in a subtle form of reasoning to harmonize this sublime world with the world of experience in a coherent system;[1] "religious emotion" before the evident holiness of the Catholic Church, says Dean Church; "passionate emotion" before the injury inflicted by the Anglican Church, suggests Cross.

From a psychological point of view, the emotional interpretation suggested by Cross is, *a priori,* the clearest and most acceptable. At what moment and for what reason did difficulties turn into doubt in Newman's mind? This is an obvious question to ask, and it demands an answer. Our reply is that it happened at the moment when the idea of the Church, as he learned it from the Fathers, became, in his view, severed from the Anglican Church of which he was a member. The *Via Media* had attempted to establish that, at this precise moment of history, the Church of England was that which most nearly approximated to the ancient Church. The opposition to Tract 90 made it quite clear that the Anglican Church of the day disclaimed being such as Newman had in mind; it was not averse to Newman, but only to his idea of its Catholicity. The *Via Media,* as he put it, existed only on paper. At that moment, the scales fell from his eyes; and he was obliged, in spite of the pain it caused him, to separate in his mind his idea of the Church from the Anglicanism of the day. We agree, then, that it was at the time of the reaction against Tract 90 that his difficulties turned into doubts; but we hold that his change is perfectly explicable, both logically and psychologically, by the effect on his mind of the events it occasioned, not as wounding him personally, but as rudely shattering his illusions.[2]

The hypothesis of resentment is unnecessary. The psychological explanation of the great turning-point in his life is to be found, not in a "sense of injury", but in his "sense of reality", which, also, some twenty years earlier, had detached him from Calvinism. In notes he made at the time, he had explained that his parochial experience made it quite evident that Calvinism was "unreal":

---

[1] We shall state and comment on this interpretation in Appendix B.

[2] This is, also, the thesis of Middleton's book.

"Calvinism was not a key to the phenomena of human nature as they occur in the world".[1] The fundamental element in Newman's mind is certainly what F. V. Reade calls "realism combined with comprehensiveness".[2] Our explanation, therefore, accords not only with Newman's own account of his conversion, but with the nature of his mind. It is confirmed by the analogy of his previous conversion—the Calvinists had not wronged him in any way; in fact, all through his life he was grateful to them for the religious values they had taught him. It is confirmed, as well, by the letters in which Newman, in the years preceding his conversion to Catholicism, discloses the alarming state of his religious convictions. In the introduction to the correspondence with W. Froude, G. Huntington Harper points out that the development these convictions indicate follows a far more intellectual course than the *Apologia,* whose special charm, in his opinion, derives from a subtle play of emotion in the background of the story.[3] Finally, our interpretation is supported by Newman's Catholic history, of which Bouyer has given, for the first time, an unvarnished account. With his customary clearness and sincerity, Newman criticized what he considered the weak points in the Catholic Church in England. He worked hard to correct them, but in vain. The attitude taken up by his opponents and superiors within that Church was far more personally wounding than that of the Anglican dignitaries during the affair of Tract 90. In the depths of his despondency, he heard the persuasive invitation of friends calling him back to Anglicanism. Yet his reply was as trenchant as could be imagined; the possibility of a return never for a moment entered his mind. Certainly, the "sense of injury" had no effect on his convictions. Newman's life as a Catholic is a perfect confirmation of the intellectual integrity of his conversion. In the Church of England, human considerations were of a nature to keep him there; in the Catholic Church, they were unavailing to make him leave.

Moreover, Newman's attitude to the Church of England after his conversion rebuts the hypothesis of resentment. A resentful person desires to wound, weaken and destroy. But one of the points at issue between Newman and a strong group of his co-religionists

---

[1] *Letters and Correspondence,* I (1891), p.122.

[2] *J. H. Newman, Centenary Essays* (London, 1945), p.146.

[3] Harper, *op. cit.,* pp.60-61.

was, precisely, that Newman wished to do nothing to enfeeble the Church of England, which he regarded as leading him to the Catholic Church, and likely to render the same service to others.

Ultimately, everything depends, of course, on the idea we form of Newman's character. It was highly individual, and comprised various contrasting traits which, interacting freely, made up a delicately balanced system of tensions and harmonies governed by a single basic orientation of the will. We have to approach a character of that sort with the same "realism combined with comprehensiveness" that Reade ascribed to Newman himself. It is only too easy to choose out certain admissions that, in the abstract, are susceptible of one kind of explanation, which, however, cannot be upheld when viewed, concretely, in the unity of the living person. Newman, the "man of resentment", is one example, out of many others, of this kind of interpretation. No doubt he was highly sensitive to the values which go to form the spiritual bond of human society—friendship, esteem, respect, gratitude, loyalty, fidelity, sincerity. When he came up against acts violating these, his moral being was deeply disturbed, and his clear, penetrating insight made him judge them for what they really were. He was equally severe when others were the victims. Moral indignation against injurious conduct is no less virtuous than the anger of God which is, as Guardini says, the attitude of His Sanctity in presence of the evil that offends him.[1] Moral sensibility to injustice is not the same as resentment, nor moral indignation equivalent to pharisaism. In Newman, the moral sensibility that caused him to suffer from unworthy treatment was perfectly combined, in a related tension and harmony, with the aloofness so characteristic of him, that interior, highly conscious detachment from his own feelings and sufferings that enabled him to judge those matters as if they concerned someone else, and to keep undisturbed peace in the depths of his soul, where he made his decisions under the eyes of his Master, regardless of the movements on its surface. Therein lies the root of his sanctity, and Bouyer's book helps us to understand, as far as is possible, the inmost secret of a great Christian.

[1] R. Guardini, *Freiheit, Gnade, Schicksal* (Munich, 1949), p.266.

Appendix B

NEWMAN'S PERSONALITY

A S we observed in the preceding appendix, the interpretation and appreciation of Newman's personality given by Sean O'Faòlain in *Newman's Way* require special consideration. This book, like that by John Holloway, which we shall speak of in Appendix E, gives a modern view of Newman, one which tends to blunt the keen edge of his thought, and to weaken his influence on minds seriously desirous of the truth. This is our primary reason for discussing it at some length; in so doing, we shall be led to the very core of the question of development. Moreover, by this means, our own interpretation of Newman's personality will be set in a clearer light.

There is, indeed, a certain amount of truth in the portrait given by the distinguished Irish writer, and he has brought out very well certain of Newman's characteristics. But, where psychological truth is concerned, the important thing is the view of the whole. I do not say that the author wished to draw a caricature of Newman, or that such was the outcome of his work; but he is, in fact, a caricaturist, and his way of looking at people undoubtedly affected his portrait of Newman. A caricaturist reduces all the varied features of his subject to a single characteristic, by ignoring some lines and exaggerating others. Thus, O'Faòlain's account of Newman sins by omission and by excess, and his method tends to reduce so complex a character to a single basic trait, that of the religious poet. "He is, above all, not a theologian nor a philosopher, but an artist" (p.227). On this point, we might agree; but it remains to be seen what he means by "artist" or "poet".

According to him, Newman lived, from his childhood, under the influence of a poetical and religious experience, a profound impression on the imagination of a mysterious world beyond the visible (pp. 102-103); and it resulted in an extraordinary insensibility and indifference to external and present reality. He saw only those aspects of things which were of significance for his interior world. So it was that, poet and artist though he was, the only thing that interested him in literature was the *ethos,* or moral tendency (p.117); what he said about the arts was nearly always deplorable (p.156); he had no interest in science; "he knew practically nothing about men and women" (p.36); he scarcely seemed aware of the great events of his time; he was unconcerned with the social problems so much in the air (p.173); He "was not really interested in India, or drunkenness, or prisons, or fairs, or wakes, or indeed in human welfare at all" (p.87); in his studies of the Fathers, he was interested only in their doctrines, and not in the persons of the disputants (p.188), etc.

Another effect of this unworldliness was an almost complete lack of worldly wisdom and ambition. "No public personality would ever be of the least importance to this boy, least of all, perhaps, his own public personality. For him the only real personality is the private personality, the anonymous secret, known inadequately even to ourselves, a mind working on a mind, known fully only to the Infinite" (p.41). Newman pursued his course as his interior growth required without a moment's hesitation in sacrificing his renown, regardless of the worldly consequences or the public effects of his actions. Faced with the duty of submission to the Church of Rome, he was anxious, tormented even, only on account of the effects of his change on the minds of his friends and followers.

Newman, however emotional, was yet an intellectual genius; and the visionary showed himself an implacable realist in seeing and judging the world from his dominating religious standpoint. Therein consists, according to O'Faòlain, his real genius. His emotions were translated into logical thought, and so the life of the intellect came to prevail over, and hide, that of the emotions. In his own development he saw, with his clear insight into himself, only the intellectual, dialectical form it took, and the emotional drive at its source. Consequently, the marvellous analyses to be found in the *Apologia,* and in letters and reminiscences, are a kind of *post mortem*; they are sincere, scrupulously exact, but distorted by the intellectual lens which both transmits and conceals the real movement of his life. The *Apologia* is "an absolutely sincere book that yet no biographer could accept unreservedly" (p.224).

All Newman's biographers have taken him too admiringly at his word in these post-mortems, failing to realize that in analysing his own inward crises he always transformed emotion into intellect and that once the experience passed into the refinery of his mind it was, in a sense, falsified. This is what happened, he says, in terms of belief, of opinion, of intermediate or final conclusions; and it is so. But is it *how* it happened? Is it *all* that happened? . . . Most of Newman's intellectualizations are autopsies, or post cogitations. They are quite untrustworthy as complete accounts of what happened (pp. 37-38, cf. also p. 152).

We see, then, a sensitive soul pursuing, in this deceptive world, a shining image, cherished from infancy, ardently desired. The impact experienced between the image and the world raises in him a storm of emotions, which is slowly clarified in the form of thoughts and reasonings. The intellectual side of him, his conscientiousness, his love of the truth, mistrusts emotion. His very passage through an ardent and emotional Calvinism has, besides, convinced him that true religiousness is nourished by mystery, not by emotion (p.107-108). He represses, therefore, into his unconscious mind the movements of emotion that feed his thought, and the most candid scrutiny of his genius for reflection finds, henceforth, only the dialectical versions of them given by the mind.

This subtle dialectic of Newman's is his attempt to harmonize two worlds, the mystical world of his religious experience and the real world of universal experience. He is well aware that reasoning based on this experience of visible reality draws men away from his mystical world. Through his critique of impure reason, he really inveighs against reality (p.238-239). In setting up, on the basis of his poetical and mystical experience, a closely-linked system taking in the whole visible world and explaining it as something more or less unreal and secondary, he aims at reversing the positions, and proving that the intellectuals of the time were not so clever as they thought themselves (pp.153-154, 238). Newman spent his whole life in developing certain ideas possessed from infancy, and stretched them out like an elastic net to make them contain the world as he saw it in his experience of life (p.53). "John Henry Newman had been given by the act of God a nuclear sense of this world as being little more than a symbol or allegory of the only real, eternal world beyond it" (pp. 102-103). With this clay he had to shape a satisfying representation of life here below. For him it was impossible simply to juxtapose the two, or to set them in irreducible opposition, as Savonarola or Cromwell did :

> So sensitive, so civilized, so generous a mind would have to formulate some other and far more delicate balance of vision between this world and eternity. All his adult life will be spent in shaping a vessel to contain and express this synthesis, and he will not come to his maturity until he has shaped or found it, even if it be no more in the end than this flawed imperial image, as full of imperfections as this world of created being must always be. (p.103).

This imperial image is the ancient Church whose continuation he found in Roman Catholicism. Newman's subtle thought is "a courtship between the imagination and his reason, arising to do that which he will later define as the aim of all development in thought—to crown an early impression on the Imagination as a system or Creed in the Reason" (p.228). It is "this blending of intellect and poetry, of brains and imagination" that gives such delight to the author (p.96). Newman is unique! But, properly understood, this delicate use of the intellect has nothing in common with true reason. In Newman, the intellect becomes imagination (p. 112). He analyses thought in such a way that it dissolves at his touch and, in the end, we have the impression that nothing remains of the intellect but a little dust in the hollow of the hand (p. 228).

The whole process takes place so gradually, with such caution and circumspection, that the whole course of his life is taken up with developing the idea of development (p.262).

We are obliged to dwell on this interpretation of Newman, since it challenges his whole theory of development by undermining its foundation, which is Newman's own intellectual growth, used by him as a key to the development of ideas in general and the development of doctrine in the Church. For, if Newman's thought is merely the intellectual form given by reflection to an instinctive and emotional urge; if the starting-point of Newman's development is an emotional experience, a poetical impression on the imagination, and not a real apprehension of religious truth whose rich content is slowly revealed and clarified by reflection, we are dangerously close to the views of Tyrrell and the modernists. If O'Faòlain had touched on the question of modernism, he would, doubtless, have passed on Newman a judgment like that of Tyrrell's: Newman was not, consciously, a modernist, on the contrary he was at the opposite extreme to modernism. Precisely, O'Faòlain would say, because he saw his own development, and so all development, only as intellectually transformed into the terms of a subtle logic; but the real Newman is an unconscious model of modernism, because, in him, we see actually at work the process by which an instinctive, emotional urge becomes clothed in the garb of a logical system. Development, as seen by Newman, was a logical process, but real development was, in fact, a biological process in the sense of the modernists; it was this development he aimed at describing, but which he could perceive only partially.

A discussion of O'Faòlain's views brings us to the very heart of the problem of development. We must begin by doing him justice, for he is an artist whose insight is subtle and acute, as may be seen in a number of instances. His interpretation of Newman, obviously, is closely allied to that given in the first part of this book, where we observed that he was engaged in reconciling the religious experience of his conscience with his experience of the world of history. In a sense, it is true that Newman's experience was turned inwards, withdrawing him into the intimacy between the self and its Creator, and that this movement tended to create a gulf between him and the outside world. On this point, O'Faòlain comments with a great deal of truth, but he is also guilty of much exaggeration.

It is quite true that Newman had no worldly ambition, and that he always went his way regardless of his reputation and the external consequences of his actions. In a sense, he was indifferent to what "they" thought or said of him as an individual. Gossip and calumny drove him to action only when they reached beyond him to the cause for which he sacrificed himself. That was why he wrote the *Apologia*. Middleton, following on many others, brought this out in his recent book.

22

Of greater importance is O'Faòlain's remark about Newman's disregard for the public personality of individuals. It deserves to be emphasized, for it gives, we think, the key to one of Newman's attitudes as a Catholic, brought out by Bouyer. While he accorded his superiors and the dignitaries of the Church unfailing obedience and respect, in his private notes he judged their personal character with astonishing freedom, regardless of their position. He drew a sharp distinction between their place in the hierarchy, which called for his respect and obedience, and their real personality, which left him free to give his admiration and trust according to their individual merit. "The separate members of the Church, my Superiors, though they may claim my obedience, have no claim on my admiration, and offer nothing for my inward trust". (Bouyer, *op. cit.*, p. 443). His truthfulness tolerated no inner falsehood, not even a pious one. He distinguished clearly between the social community with its many duties and that intimate community of confidence and union which is the real domain of the person. His opinions of Cardinals Wiseman, Manning, Barnabo, and even of the Pope as a person were not caused by personal resentment, or a spirit of insubordination or irreverence, but by his uncompromising realism, his truthfulness, and his lively sense that the inner personality and its domain, where "heart speaks to heart", was of its nature, and so in the Church too, something sacred and inviolable. I am not obliged to have any personal confidence in the Pope and to open my heart to him, because he is Pope. Those are things the human person does freely only to other persons he deems worthy of confidence.

Yet, at the same time, O'Faòlain exaggerates Newman's insensibility. The Newman insensible to all that concerned his own position is as fictitious as the man of resentment Cross professed to discern. His moral sensibility to injury and all his ill treatment by others was very keen. We have dealt with this matter in Appendix A, in speaking of the book by Bouyer. Equally keen was his sense of human cultural values. It is not true that he was insensible to beauty in itself, to science, intellectual culture, human character and life. He must, in fact, have been keenly alive to them, but, in the period of his formation, he was on his guard against them in the name of "holiness first", the ideal so strongly impressed on his mind by his reading of Thomas Scott. I would go so far as to say that the bitter tone of some of his sermons is to be ascribed to his defence-mechanism. At any rate, I think that Newman can be understood only in the light of that deep-seated dualism so well brought out by Sobry in *Newman en zijn Idea of a University*,[1] which consists precisely in the simultaneous action of two opposed feelings, one concerned with the invisible world, the other with the evident facts and autonomous values of the human spirit. The child whose mind oscillated between fancy and facts;[2] the adolescent who, reading some impious verses of Voltaire, said to himself, "How dreadful, but how plausible", and who was not above relishing Tom Paine's arguments against Christianity;[3] the youth attracted by liberalism, and so acutely conscious of the transience of the world at the very moment when enjoying most keenly a piece of scenery;[4] the grown man, who, speaking of human nature, caresses it with one hand and castigates it with the other, in the words, "the raw material of human nature, so excellent, so dangerous";[5] such a man is not to be summed up as led entirely by his religious sensibility; the fact is that his personal development was governed by the quest for a harmony and a synthesis which would ensure to one and all of his various sentiments their necessary living space, while assigning each its place in the hierarchy of values.

The most perfect expression of this unstable equilibrium is in the *Idea of a University*. There Newman praises intellectual culture as an end in itself; he rejects the notion of a Catholic literature, and defines letters as the autobiography of the natural man, an autobiography worth reading for its own sake. At the same time, in his Dublin sermons, he sees St Paul's special characteristic as the "virtue of humanity", distinct from charity, though subordinate to it, its object being human nature in itself, its mind, its sentiments, its history.[6] Already he had devoted his leisure, with evident delight, to sketching, in such agreeable fashion, not the teachings, but the characters, of the principal Fathers of the Church; and he had expressed his own preference for St John Chrysostom because, while full of supernatural charity, he had yet

[1] Antwerp, 1935.
[2] Sobry, *op. cit.*, pp.34-36.
[3] *Apologia*, p.31.
[4] *Letters and Correspondence*, I, p.184.
[5] *Apologia*, p.226.
[6] *Occ. Ser.*, pp.108-109.

kept his natural sensibility and keen interest in earthly matters and human nature in all its aspects.[1]

The two worlds Newman wished to harmonize in an inclusive view were not a mystical one and a real one, the first welcomed and desired, the second acknowledged unwillingly, but rather two worlds, of unequal value it is true, but both together and continuously drawing his feelings in opposite directions. Below the surface of that strange, deceptive world formed by sinful humanity he always beheld human nature as it was willed and formed by the Creator, and whose splendour still remained with it under the ravages of original sin, as the ruins of Athens under the destruction of centuries, to the admiration of all who are capable of feeling.

This difference in the appreciation of the two poles between which Newman's thought moves is, of itself, important enough; even more so is the appreciation given by O'Faòlain himself of the poetical and religious experience on which Newman's personality was built up. The problem is whether Newman's religious world was created by his imagination, in the author's sense of the word, or was a real object of apprehension by the imagination in the sense given in the *Grammar of Assent*. When we say that the religious object is taken hold of by the imagination, does this term signify, as with Sartre, "the non-realising function of conscience", or, as we have seen with Newman, "the realising function of conscience", that is, the faculty of communicating with the reality whose impressions we receive in our mind and senses? As we have already explained, Newman often uses the word "imagination" to denote real apprehension, though that term, originally, expressed only one of its aspects—not the instinctive act by which reality is apprehended as existing in itself, but the act which unifies and perpetuates the content of the manifold impressions by which we come to know the nature of this reality. All, therefore, depends on the answer to the question: was Newman conscious of an invisible world through the action of the imagination, a faculty of fantasy, or of the Imagination, a faculty "realising" the spiritual?

If we decide for the first of these, it follows that the emotion in question is, of its nature, antecedent to the intelligence and creates in it the dialectical movement. If for the second, then, as Newman argues in the *Grammar*, the emotion, though

[1] *Historical Sketches*, II, p.284.

accompanying the presence of the reality in time, is yet, of its nature, subsequent to it, being caused by it and manifesting itself in it. In that case, its function is to set free and stir up in the soul, in which the experience of reality holds sway, all its active powers, including that of thought. It accompanies all the procedures of the mind as it seeks an ever deeper understanding and a more explicit and broader perception of reality. Far from disturbing thought, it stimulates and sustains it, and, through its "intentional" character, determined by the very nature of the reality that caused it, it tends to hold the mind close to the reality rather than to loosen its grasp.

We will not venture any further in this matter, which involves a whole philosophy. Whether O'Faòlain was aware of it or not, he was influenced by some very modern ideas that led him to see Newman in what seems a false light, and to give a misleading account of his personality. Positivism, in the form at present in vogue, has given rise, especially in England, to a kind of literary criticism that is extremely methodical and subtle, but highly dangerous. It is a philosophy according to which the terms we use have "significance" only if they express differences that can be established and verified by experience. When, as a result of our awareness of these differences, we express them in definite linguistic symbols, we thereby regulate our conduct in the world correspondingly.

This principle could be granted. It becomes positivist only by virtue of three kinds of reduction, each fallacious, which are the basis of every form of positivism—the reduction of the differences present in our experience of the world to differences in temporal and spatial phenomena of sense, the reduction of all verification to the experimental, the reduction of all behaviour to the pursuit of what is useful or pleasant. It follows that, in life, the choice of ends is left to the hidden operations of instinct, the unconscious, the emotions, or to calculations of expediency, and that "science" is concerned only with the means and techniques to these ends. Differences such as those between beauty and ugliness, good and evil, justice and injustice, are not to be found in our experience of the sensible world, nor are they exactly verifiable. They are merely differences in the emotions we feel in the presence of certain things. Common sense attributes these differences to things (as when I say, this thing is good), but only *per denominationem extrinsecam.* Consequently, moral, aesthetic and religious judgments have no objective meaning or application. They express only differences of subjective emotions which common speech incorrectly projects onto reality. This system of interpretation is only a transference into conceptual language of the emotional life of the subject, and the question of truth does not arise. The system is not concerned with truth and falsity; such a question is, therefore, meaningless.

Heat is a given thing, and cannot simply be reduced to our reaction in terms of expansion, immobility, panting, ventilation, drinking. The positivist would agree that the apprehension of a fact is other than our reaction to it, although the two cannot be separated, and though we take note of the fact only in and through a kind of instinctive reaction shown in behaviour. Yet when Newman says that the apprehension of moral values or of God is other than our emotional reaction to them, though their presence manifests itself in the instinctive, emotional reaction of conscience, the positivist parts company with him, although to an unprejudiced eye the two orders of experience are seen to be analogous. The first, it is true, is of the sensible order, and so is exhibited in a public manner through the senses; the second, being beyond the senses, belongs to an order of "things that can be proved only by obliging everyone to reflect on himself, and so to find the truth of which we are speaking".[1] The language in which the experiences of the first order are expressed is the instrument of a "direct communication"; that which aims at making others discover something belonging to the second order is the more subtle instrument of "indirect communication". In the first, verification is experimental and exact; the facts, the laws, even whole systems, are judged by their correspondence with the results of exact experiment. In the second, the verification is of the philosophical order; particular experiences, general ideas, systems of philosophy, are judged by their relation of intelligibility with a whole in which they have to manifest their significance. The genuineness of an experience beyond the senses is attested by the whole life of the person claiming it, as Bergson so admirably makes clear in *The Two Sources of Morality and Religion.* Just as a fact of the sensible order can be verified, according to Carnap, by certain observable events which follow on it, so the statement of a

[1] B. Pascal, *op. cit.,* p.317.

super-sensible fact can be verified by the visible consequences that
the experience of it will normally bring in the life of the person
involved. This is the way in which, with greater or less probability,
we distinguish, for example, hysterical from mystical phenomena.

The objectivity of the ideas resulting from these super-sensible
phenomena is ascertained by a process of reflection and investigation which shows that the faculty of apprehending these
differences forms a part of human nature, as Newman would say;
or, as we would say now, that the mode of being implied by the
awareness of such distinctions is a part of human existence, and
that, therefore, man, as he is actually seen to be, is absolutely
incomprehensible and absurd if the genuineness of these experiences is denied. This is the way, as we have shown, of verifying
the acts of conscience and of all the other cognitive faculties of
man. C. S. Lewis adds that the content of our moral judgments,
in spite of their proverbial disagreements, shows historically so
much coincidence on fundamentals that we cannot reasonably
doubt the objectivity of the moral order.[1] Obviously, this kind
of verification has to take account of those cases in which conscience appears to be lacking; it needs to explain differences in
moral judgments. But, at bottom, every kind of science, even the
positive sciences, has to face the same difficulty. Each of them
has to confront its difficulties with its own particular resources
and, in the struggle, it advances in depth and range. The exact
sciences probe ever further the secrets of nature by rearranging
their hypotheses, and by sifting their facts of experience so as to
explain exceptions and apparent anomalies in the physical world.
In the same way, the moral sciences try to explain the anomalies
observed in the sphere of values by applying their own tests, those
of the nature and mode of being of the human person. Man being
what he is—not given by nature in a completed state, but, in his
conscious freedom, having, at the instance of the moral values,
to realize himself in the world through the instrumentality of his
body—the necessity of development, the possibility of deviation,
the inevitability of all kinds of deflection from the right way, are
perfectly understandable. We gain a deepening knowledge of
man by studying human anomalies. The exact sciences resolve
their difficulties by their own method, which is a closer examination of the laws of nature. Moral science acts in the same way,

[1] C. S. Lewis, *Broadcast Talks* (London, 1942), pp.9-18.

resolving its problems by penetrating deeper into the knowledge of man as a single whole unique in nature, a person.

Ultimately, a system of philosophy is justified by its ability to comprise the whole field of human experience in the scope of its principles. The more it makes intelligible human experience in its unity as a living whole, excluding no part of it at all, assigning each its due place and significance in the life of man; and the more it acts as a stimulus to thought and extends its scope; the greater its own justification in all its parts. If it remains true that every advance raises fresh problems, more subtle, more elusive, and thereby intensifies our consciousness of the mystery enshrouding all our thought, we must content ourselves with the reflection that the history of positive science tells exactly the same story. Physical nature has never seemed so mysterious as it does in modern science, and yet this science is far from feeling obliged to forego its certainties or the conviction that it is ever approximating more closely to the truth.

The whole question, finally, comes to this—which of the two fundamental views in philosophy is the true one, the common-sense view stated by Aristotle, implied in all the arguments of Aquinas, analysed by Newman in the *Grammar of Assent*; or the artificial, somewhat schizophrenic, position of the positivists who, in violation of informed common sense, are so fascinated by the exact, analytical, impersonal perfection of some kinds of reasoning that they are led to deny all the evidences and factors of experience whose handling requires a more comprehensive, synthetic, personal working of the mind. Newman expressed the common-sense reaction to Locke's theories, and his verdict is equally applicable to modern positivism—"theoretical and unreal".

No reasoning can ever destroy the fundamental insights of common sense, for the fact is that we, literally, "find ourselves" in the world. If we were ourselves the authors of man's situation, we would, perhaps, have arranged it somewhat differently. But, being what it is, the only reasonable thing for us to do is to accept the whole of our experience, use the means nature has given us, follow out completely the way indicated, spontaneously, by experience, take on the whole duty of man with a high sense of responsibility, apply all the means of human life we find on our way to our human perfection, rejecting none that seems less perfect, more

difficult to handle than others, and to approach each problem
with the tools most fitted to deal with it. If human life is not a
joke, we may be sure that each step we take will lead to valuable
discoveries. This is the philosophy of common-sense, and no one
has ever stated it so excellently as Newman; and, though the ultimate ground of his confidence was his faith in Providence, it would
be equally valid philosophically, as he himself observes, if that
faith were wanting.

Appendix C

NEWMAN'S PRACTICAL PSYCHOLOGISM

THERE is some danger in speaking of "practical psychologism" in connection with Newman, since the term "psychologism", according to Lalande, "is never used except to indicate disapproval or rejection".[1] Though Berthelot has tried to divest it of any such implication, it still keeps its pejorative sense. Consequently, our view of Newman has caused certain reactions which seem to be the result of misunderstanding of this vague and ambiguous term. In an excellent thesis for a doctorate on the philosophy of Newman, C. B. Keogh, an Australian, observes with pleasant irony that

> Though Father Walgrave has come nearer than any other writer up to the present to a correct estimate of Newman's theory of knowledge, his work is still capable of being improved upon. Not only has he failed to clear Newman of the charge of conceptualism, but he has unearthed another 'ism' that no one yet, doubtless through oversight, has ever attributed to Newman, namely psychologism.[2]

The first of these two criticisms is certainly mistaken. I have always defended Newman against the accusation of conceptualism.

[1] A. Lalande, *Vocabulaire technique et critique de la philosophie* (5th ed.; Paris, 1947), p.837.

[2] C. B. Keogh, *Introduction to the Philosophy of Cardinal Newman* (thesis presented to the Institut Supérieur de Philosophie à l'Université de Louvain 1950), in typescript, p.195.

In doing so, however, I have taken a new line; I have not thought it necessary to deny that his account of general ideas coincides, for the most part, with that given by the nominalists. It obviously does. What I have done is to explain that this account was made necessary by his conflict with scientism, and that his partial, "economical" description, sufficient for the purpose of the *Grammar of Assent,* is perfectly consistent with a general non-conceptualist view of notional knowledge. To a nominalist, the concept is only a generalised image; to the discerning realist, this image is not everything, but only an element of the whole concept. In Thomistic language, the *phantasma* to which the intellect necessarily turns in conceiving the essence, man, is not the image of Charles or Peter, but a general description of human sensible appearances. The generalized image is, thus, like the body in which the apprehension of the essence is incarnate in order to be able to become an object of explicit thought for an embodied spirit. No doubt, true apprehension by the idea is already felt as present in this act of generalization; whether recognized or not, that is what makes the generalization possible. In all the acts of the embodied spirit, the corporeal element is not simply a datum, but something that the spirit transforms for its own purposes. In man, the work of the imagination is shot through with intellect, and shares in the attributes of the higher form of knowledge. In the formation of concepts, this participation is manifest in the generalized image.

In this way, I think the two accounts Newman gives can be harmonized without forcing either, the one which explains general ideas in the language of nominalism, and the other, highly personal one, which describes apprehension of absolute, necessarily universal, values as a communion of the mind with concrete reality.

There remains the charge of psychologism. In his very interesting book on the personal conquest of truth according to Newman,[1] A. J. Boekraad, while acknowledging the force of our defence of Newman against the accusation of conceptualism, disagrees with our calling his critique of conscience "practical psychologism". Newman, he says, did more than merely show that certain cognitive functions belonged to human nature in general; he also

[1] A. J. Boekraad, *The Personal Conquest of Truth according to J. H. Newman* (Louvain, 1955), pp.255-272.

justified his basic principle by showing that a judgment casting doubt on human nature must, to be a real judgment, assume its own validity in advance, and, consequently, also the justification of the human nature from which such judgment proceeds. The very act by which we question the ontological structure of our mind proceeds from this structure, and has meaning only inasmuch as it cancels its own doubt. We approach thought only through our mind, and thought cannot put in doubt the nature of the mind without destroying itself. Attempting to justify the mind before using it is self-contradictory, and prevents thought taking place at all. Anyone who casts doubt on human nature loses all right to form a judgment, and should content himself, as Aristotle said, with the life of a plant.

That is, undoubtedly, the ultimate basis of Newman's theory. We had already emphasised this in our very first publication,[1] and, lately, we set it out more in detail in a commentary on the central passage in the *Grammar* where Newman justifies the illative sense.[2] Confidence in the powers of our mind, he says, is not a "first principle", that is one of the most general lessons taught by experience, for the mind itself is the ground of experience, and the reliability of our mental equipment, if it needed proof, could be established only by evidence coming from outside experience; but we can never place ourselves outside our experience. Newman concludes from this that it only remains for us to accept our mind as it is, to use it conscientiously, that is conforming as faithfully as possible to the kind of use written into it. By adapting himself to the laws of nature, *homo faber* found his good; by bowing to the laws of his understanding will *homo sapiens* find his.

This is a logical and practical argument, not in the least a metaphysical one. It is, doubtless, sufficient for instructed common-sense, but not for a philosopher. It leaves it quite possible not to trust the mind in its claim to be the organ of truth, but to use it solely in those exact and practical sciences which are not necessarily concerned with ultimate truth, but are useful and significant in the practical ordering of life where they are justified

[1] J.-H. Walgrave, O.P., "Newman's beschrijving en verantwoording van het werkelijk denken", *Tijdschrift voor Philosophie*, I (1939), p.530.

[2] J.-H. Walgrave, O.P. "Newman, Wijsgeer van de zekerheid", *Kultuurleven*, XX (1953), pp.250-263.

by their results. This is, in fact, the attitude of positivists and extreme pragmatists. One can, therefore, escape Newman's dilemma without being forced to live altogether like a plant.

In the last resort, Newman's argument does not logically establish our capability of reaching truth. Its trend is to prove that, for a man engaged in the business of living, the theoretical question is idle and insoluble, that the "motion of confidence" in the government of the mind has no meaning, since there is no alternative. This government is identical with our own being, in so far as we are human, and we have no choice but to be faithful or unfaithful to its natural constitution. The argument of Newman amounts to a proof that, if we wish to live as human beings, we must, in each act of the mind, admit implicitly that it is made for the truth, that it is, therefore, capable of truth, and that it will find truth if it makes judicious use of its possibilities. It aims at impressing on us the practical necessity of an initial human faith in the non-absurdity of our human nature. The ultimate ground of Newman's theory of knowledge is exactly the same as Butler's, who defends the truth of conscience in these memorable words: "Otherwise, the constitution of our mind, from which this judgment proceeds immediately and directly, would be absurd".[1]

All this may serve to an understanding of the meaning of "practical psychologism" as we persist in applying it to Newman's system, though in no pejorative sense. Psychologism, according to Lalande, is a "tendency to make the psychological point of view, in one of the senses already defined, predominate over the specific standpoint of some other branch of study".[2] The psychology to which the psychologist has exclusive recourse can, therefore, be equally a rational or an experimental one. Thus, in the theory of knowledge, where the term is most often used, psychologism consists in justifying knowledge by considering the subject thinking rather than by a critical account of the object thought. The psychologist justifies the validity of knowledge by its root, not by its fruits. In fact, as we have established, extreme psychologism goes with positivistic nominalism; but our whole account is designed to show that other forms of psychologism are possible. Since Newman was not a nominalist, it follows that, if it is

[1] Butler, *The Analogy of Religion*, London, 1848, p.47.

[2] Lalande, *op. cit.*, p.837.

permissible to attribute to him a kind of psychologism, it will not be the nominalist kind.

Theoretical psychologism affirms that some sort of investigation into human nature is the only possible way of solving the problem of knowledge. This is not what Newman says. His object, he says, is practical, not metaphysical. He did not wish to deny that a metaphysical justification was possible; but, in fact, he confined himself to the nature of the mind. It was a method congenial to him, it was sufficient for his purpose, and it was the only one to have any chance of convincing those for whom he wrote the *Grammar*. His point of view was entirely justified.

It is this practical, not theoretical, attitude that we called "practical psychologism". Any discerning person can see that the epithet "practical" rules out any accusation of philosophical psychologism. Newman is, and is not, psychologistic in the same sense in which Blondel's apologetic is, and is not, immanentist. Blondel is far from saying that faith can be justified only by arguments drawn from the inner experience of the subject; but, in practice, he confines himself to developing this dialectic of human experience which should impel man to recognize revelation if he is faithful to his own nature. He holds to the "method of immanence". We could, therefore, speak of "practical immanentism" in connection with him, without implying any censure.

Perhaps nothing could help us more to understand Newman's attitude than to compare his epistomology with that of Blondel. Among the moderns, these two men of genius are the great masters of intellectualism in ethics. They are both equally convinced that we attain truth only by the entire soul, that a moral attitude is indispensable to the quest for truth, and that, in the end, the latter will be granted as a reward. Truth is not an object of proud conquest, but of humble seeking. Man is not the master of truth, but truth the master of man. We must be its servants in order to enjoy its favour and presence.

These two minds are so much alike that it is all the more significant that their attitudes to the problem of knowledge are so utterly different. Blondel's point of view is frankly metaphysical. For him, the intellect is not vindicated as the faculty of truth by a consideration of human nature, but by recourse to the nature of being, in which thought is necessarily contained from the outset. Reflection on thought-consciousness as such should make it clear that the human consciousness is a participation in absolute being, which envelops thought on two sides, that of the subject and of the object; that this being is its source as well as its object; that it prompts as well as invites. The activity of mind starts out from a pre-conscious identity with being. That presence to itself, which is the characteristic of mind, is equally presence to being. All the processes of the mind take place within this encompassing presence; and each of them explores its mysterious immensity in the attempt to apprehend its structure. Thought, therefore, is directed to being, to the reality that surrounds it; and contact with being is contact with reality, and so with truth.

Starting from this general conception, Blondel is able to say with Newman—though in a very different manner—that truth is attainable by us, and that, in each particular sphere, we will attain it provided we observe the laws of the mind, that is, the demands imposed by being on a thought which is ineluctably abstract, piecemeal, and therefore extremely varied in its processes and means of expression.

The difference between the two is evident. While Newman justifies knowledge in general by invoking the nature of the self, the root of the "thought that thinks", Blondel does so by having recourse to being, which envelops and consummates all the "thought that is thought". If we are inclined to call Blondel's method "metaphysicist", as opposed to the "practical psychologism" of Newman, we can do so without implying reproach in either case. Blondel is more philosophical, Newman more practical. Anyone can follow the argument of Aristotle and Newman; they have common-sense on their side; but Blondel will appeal only to the few who have an aptitude for metaphysical thought.

Does this mean that Newman is no philosopher? The question was raised by Fr. Hermans[1] in an article on a thesis by Nédoncelle.[2] I hope that our discussion of Holloway's book will show Newman to have been a true philosopher, and even a great one. But is he a metaphysician? Boekraad and others would like us to think so; but I think their view is based on a misuse of the

[1] F. Hermans, "Newman, est-il un philosophe?", *Nouv. Rev. Théol.*, LXXXI (1949), 162-173.

[2] M. Nédoncelle, *La philosophie religieuse de J. H. Newman* (Sostralib; Strasbourg, 1946); this work is reprinted at the beginning of *Oeuvres philosophiques de Newman* (Paris, n.d.), pp.1-204.

term. Newman always declined the honour of being considered
one. In his last published work, he still insisted that "my form of
mind never led me towards metaphysics";[1] on which Nédoncelle
comments: "Had he possessed a metaphysical mind, he would
have exposed the metaphysicians".[2]

Still, every great system of philosophy must have a basis in
metaphysics; and, if Newman was a real philosopher, metaphysics
must have found a place in his thought. Nédoncelle, perhaps,
points to the solution of the difficulty when he says of Newman
that "he philosophises without being aware of it", and "his standpoints imply a metaphysic".[3] He himself sets out to make clear
exactly what this metaphysic is.

The answer rests on a distinction. Newman's thought is carried
along by his strong feeling for reality. He perceives in the world
the unity and order of being. Over and above the individual
elements he so carefully describes, his intuitive view always takes
in the profound mystery of the oneness of reality as a whole. In all
his descriptions and analyses he remains vividly and acutely aware
of the indivisible richness of reality. As we pointed out in the
introduction, this keen awareness of the one and the "whole" is
the explanation of the slow and painful course of his thought and
the secret of his inimitable style. His metaphysical intuition, therefore, is the highly conscious background of all his intellectual
procedures.

This does not suffice to justify the title of a metaphysician in
the strict sense of the word. His metaphysics always remains in
an implicit state. But the term "metaphysics", in traditional philosophy, indicates a special kind of philosophical reflection; it means
the *prima philosophia*, which explicitly analyses and clarifies what
constitutes the unity of reality and experience. The metaphysician
is one who has proved himself in this particular sphere of philosophy, a sphere into which Newman never ventured. Hence, he
cannot be ranked among the metaphysicians. Wordsworth's
poetry might be said to be penetrated with metaphysics, but to
call him a metaphysician would be an abuse of language. The
ordinary man is not a logician, even though, according to Newman, his thought is perfectly logical; and poetical experience does

[1] *Stray Essays*, p.94.

[2] *Oeuvres philosophiques de Newman*, p.18.

[3] *Ibid.*, pp.18-19.

not make a silent man a poet. In the same way, to be a metaphysician it is not enough to live at a profound metaphysical
level.

Appendix D

THE PHILOSOPHY OF CONSCIENCE

THE philosophy of conscience is, undoubtedly, what underlies Newman's entire thought. All his greater works are ramifications and extensions of what he holds to be the significance of conscience in the life of man. In each of us what is human has its source in conscience. The human person is not a work of nature but the result of his free decisions. This idea, common to so many modern philosophers, could be expressed in Newman's language by saying that man is what he has made of his conscience. The significance of conscience in the life of man is the corner-stone of the whole system of meanings and values which make up Newman's world. We have shown how this applies to the theory of development. His teaching on the subject of conscience gives his whole thought its unity, cohesion and special character.

Since the war, several works have been written on Newman's philosophy of conscience. Most of them, however, deal with it as a part of a wider problem, the philosophy of knowledge, the philosophy of religion or faith. It has to be admitted that the central position of conscience in his thought has been more often stated than demonstrated. Even such excellent works as *Die Glaubensphilosophie Newmans* of A. Karl[1] seem to me not to make clear enough the closeness and depth of the bond between the life of conscience and that of faith which is its continuation. H. Fries's book,[2] on the other hand, brings out very well the fundamental

[1] Bonn, 1941.
[2] H. Fries, *Die Religionsphilosophie Newmans*, Stuttgart, 1948

importance of conscience in the development of religious thought and man's accession to supernatural religion. It underlies the philosophical nature of Newman's views on the question, and clarifies them by a judicious comparison between Newman and Max Scheler.

Another important work is Boekraad's, of which we spoke in Appendix C.[1] Its object is to show that the personal conscience is the main element, not only in Newman's philosophy of religion, but also in his whole theory of knowledge. The conquest of truth is an enterprise in which the whole personality takes part. Thought is, throughout, a free activity for which we bear the responsibility. My very first duty is to be faithful to my potentialities, and to make proper and conscientious use of my faculties of knowledge. Hence, conscience directs the whole life of thought. The moral development of the personality is, as it were, the life-giving environment in which truth develops in the mind. Speaking of moral certitude as the result of informal inference according to Newman, he says :

> He calls it practical or moral, because we do not and we cannot reach the conclusion by means of a series of formal inferences, but only with the help of antecedent judgments, the action of the living mind, and the illative sense, which all act and should act under a sense of duty. In other words, we reach the proper object of the mind, truth, because we take great care to use our mind in the right way, and are thus sure that our mind, rightly used, will be in touch with truth.[2]

This contention of Boekraad's had already been given powerful expression by M. Nédoncelle in the most original book yet written on Newman's philosophy.[3] "It belongs to the moral order to bring philosophy to birth, and, outside that order, its rise is premature and vain",[4] and "a writer cannot be accused of depreciating reason because he subjects it to the moral law, and refuses to dissociate intellectual development from that of the

---

[1] A. J. Boekraad, op. cit.

[2] Ibid., pp.288-289.

[3] M. Nédoncelle, op. cit.

[4] Ibid., p.67.

whole person".[1] Newman's philosophy is one of conscience, or, as Nédoncelle says, a "moral personalism". I am of Boekraad's opinion that Nédoncelle underestimates the value and importance of the general theory of knowledge in Newman's thought.[2]

Nédoncelle admirably shows that, with Newman, conscience is not only what binds the person to a transcendent God, but is also the immanent source of the person himself. He has drawn from the works, especially the sermons, a large number of passages which together make up a striking description of the interior building up of the personality. By this description, in particular, Newman made his very original contribution to the great personalist and existentialist movement of our day:

> The self is always unknowable, for it is always open to further development. . . . It is, in fact, a value in a historical mode; it has to pass through time, and build itself up by degrees. It is not a substance, but it becomes one, and it has to attain to an infinite in order to arrive ultimately at itself by a winding and contingent course.[3]

That is very well said.

The author describes this personalism as consisting of two opposing movements. The first detaches the self from all that is external to it, and, ultimately, compels it to recognize its essential solitude. On the plane of contact with the world through sense— the aesthetic plane, Kierkegaard would say—nothing can rescue man from his isolation, neither the world of sense, nor that of science, nor the crowd with its tyrannical opinions, its impersonal manner of speech and conduct, nor even family or friendship. "The whole world is against us and betrays us . . . the world, that is to say, all that, physically, is ruled by fixed laws and, spiritually, by hearts without law; in short, all that is alien to the inner life of morality and religion".[4]

To the self, thus cut off from the outside world, nothing remains but its interior presence to itself, a void, an unease, but soon a call, a vocation; a self to be built up calls to the self empty and anxious.

[1] op.cit., p.74.

[2] A. J. Boekraad, op. cit., p.26.

[3] M. Nédoncelle, op. cit., p.80.

[4] Ibid., p.54.

The call and its criterion are given in an interior principle. "Conscience is the principle we were looking for; this, and obedience to its law, are what serve to guide the self and bring unity to men".[1] The self goes forward hesitantly, in the dark. If it does what lies in it, the light grows brighter. It becomes aware of a growing consistency; for, to know oneself, one must, first of all, exist, and a man is only what he has made himself. In the peremptory call, a voice makes itself heard, dimly at first, more clearly later, a Person inviting the person, a Master commanding us in the recesses of the heart. Man finds himself, and stands upright before the face of God; the isolation is broken. This intimacy begins the renewal of the bonds with the world, previously broken; other persons are found again "in a union infinitely stronger and deeper, in spite of appearances, than common interests and complicity in evil could possibly effect".[2] Life in the world, and the pursuit of temporal aims once more takes on meaning, for "work in the world is the sole means of building up the self".[3]

To the movement of obedience is opposed that of disobedience and sin : "There exists a rooted evil in the will, bound up with original sin; it is the inclination to do the opposite of what we are ordered".[4] Newman's analyses, so detailed and, at times, despondent, are assembled by Nédoncelle in an ordered account of the development, disintegration, and recovery of the sinning person :

> Two ways lead to the building up of the moral personality, one that of an initial renunciation leading directly to the development of conscience and knowledge, the other that of the world beginning pleasantly enough but ending in bitterness; for evil itself is, in fact, only a stage on the way, and the wounds it inflicts, after a long and cruel experience, help to cast the sinner back towards the good. The world becomes for him, by divine bounty, a sacrament that makes afresh what had been wrecked from infancy".[5]

These passages may be compared with our own account of the

[1] *op. cit.*, p.67.

[2] *Ibid.*, p.85.

[3] *Ibid.*

[4] *Ibid.*, p.71.

[5] *Ibid.*, p.86.

specific psychology of development, and it will then be seen how the two works agree and complete one another.

Nédoncelle observes, comparing Newman with Fichte :

> I believe that conscience is never the sole principle of the synthesis; it does not combine with itself as does the self of Fichte. It combines with other facts, other principles; and it is from this contact that a new development comes into being of which it is the soul and the regulating principle, without being the absolute origin.[1]

The fact is that Newman's dialectic is not, as Fichte's is, an idealist, but an existentialist, dialectic of conscience. There is a real dialogue, a free exchange between the conscience and the non-self, that is, a situation in time made up of manifold contingencies, erected by the agency of human freedom and of sin, worked on by grace, governed, as a whole, by a Providence. On this point reference may be made to our description of the dialectic of conscience.[2]

A final work, on which we shall have to dwell at somewhat greater length, is one by Alfred Läpple,[3] the most learned and technical account, to date, of Newman's thought. The first two hundred and twenty-four pages are taken up with a general introduction; they describe the historical background and attempt to place Newman's life and work in relation to it. This introduction is of great value; it contains a large number of summaries, factual information and technical matters that many will find useful, a chronological table of the life and works, a systematic and descriptive list of biographical sources and writings, a critical summary of twelve different estimates of Newman's personality, an ample bibliography, etc. The rest of the first volume is devoted to the philosophy of conscience.

The special subject of the book is the theology of the individual. In an article, whose title Läpple adopted for his book, K. Rahner issued a warning against a tendency to carry the idea of a mystical

---

[1] *op. cit.*, p.89.

[2] See above, pp.215-228.

[3] A. Läpple, *Der Einzelne in der Kirche, Wesenzüge einer Theologie des Einzelnen nach J. H. Kardinal Newman* (Münchener theologische Studien, II, Systematische Abteilung, 6; Munich, 1952).

community to extremes, and to minimise the value and rights of the individual in society and the Church. We need, he says, to renew the theology of the individual.[1] This is the subject Läpple set out to follow up in the works of the great cardinal, and he chose the right place to look for it. Newman's philosophy of conscience was able to supply him with a solid base for the defence of the individual.

He distinguishes four successive stages in Newman's thought. The first was when, in his early sermons, he inveighed against the philosophical error which, equating conscience with moral refinement of feeling, substitutes an existential monologue for the original dialogue which is the ground of human life. Next, he proceeds to analyse and vindicate, by positive reasons, his "dialogical" and religious interpretation of conscience. After that, he studies the relations between natural conscience and revealed religion; and, finally, endeavours to set out the boundaries of the sacred and inviolable sphere of the individual within the Church. This fourfold division could not be bettered. The last two problems form the subject of the second volume; the first, where the philosophy of conscience is analysed, is the one we are concerned with.

First of all, we shall state the teaching Läpple considers he has found in Newman's works. It is entirely new. Up to now, only two elements of conscience have been discovered in Newman, the moral sense and the sense of duty. Läpple found a third, moral instinct; and so he holds there to be three elements, which are three classes of acts joined together like three stages in the unfolding of moral awareness.

To begin with, there is moral instinct, or "natural conscience", whose act is primary and fundamental. By this act, man, in a given situation, apprehends, antecedently to reflection, and without invoking any moral principle, what actually, *hic et nunc,* is good or bad for him. It is, therefore, a complete act. It is also a natural one; in it man's being is manifested directly. Its production is spontaneous and instinctive. Its object is a particular value apprehended in a concrete situation. It is existential and practical, since it necessarily implies moral and religious involvement.

[1] K. Rahner, "Der Einzelne in der Kirche", *Stimmen der Zeit,* (1946-1947), pp.260-276.

The author compares it to the *Situationsgewissen* of some contemporary systems of ethics.[1]

Moral instinct is the starting-point from which are developed, by a process of abstraction, the moral codes which are the object of the moral sense : "The object of moral instinct is the concrete and particular, that of the moral sense the universal, the moral law in general. The first is concerned with the existential ethics of the situation, the second with the system of morals".[2] The knowledge given by the moral sense is, therefore, not a natural endowment but acquired by cultivation, and is open to variation and development. It is made up of general judgments, and also of recollections of actual situations and previous decisions. The moral sense furnishes us with an intellectual instrument for giving direction to our moral life.

Finally, there is the sense of duty; with Newman, this term "nearly always signifies something that effects a transformation by casuistry".[3] It operates in two ways : by applying a general rule to a particular case, or by comparing a present situation to a similar one in the past. Here the author involves himself in serious difficulties. He has to admit that Newman sometimes uses the term to signify the activity of the moral sense, and, in particular, "that vocation from God which calls me to fulfil the duties of my situation and make my unique and personal decision, and can never be entirely deduced from a general rule".[4] Newman, he says, is neither clear nor consistent in his use of these expressions.

Läpple's interpretation is a surprising distortion of Newman's ideas. First of all, it is quite certain that "natural conscience" never means a moral instinct whose act precedes that of the moral sense and the sense of duty. In fact, the word "conscience" indicates the total entity comprising the moral sense and the sense of duty. The adjective "natural" expresses the fact that conscience belongs to us by nature, and is the source of natural religion.

A close examination shows, beyond the least doubt, that Newman was completely unaware of a moral instinct, as distinct from the moral sense and the sense of duty. He recognized only, as he tells us, these two aspects of the indivisible act of conscience, and

[1] A. Läpple, *op. cit.*, p.278.
[2] *Ibid.*, p.279.
[3] *Ibid.*, p.295.
[4] *Ibid.*

they are both present in the very first act. Conscience perceives in so far as it is rational, it commands with authority, it judges acts and pronounces its decisions; it testifies to the good and approves the deed; it is both the rule and the sanction of good conduct. These are the pairs of expressions by which Newman describes the two aspects of conscience.[1] The moral instinct does not precede the two functions, but is operative in each. In both aspects, as moral sense and as sense of duty, the real conscience grasps its object first in an instinctive way, by real apprehension, and then goes on to make certain generalizations. Newman gives an illuminating account of this in his description of the first principles. It is by instinct that we first apprehend in the individual acts of conscience the commands of a Supreme Lord. From these acts we then infer, by generalization, the existence of a religious universe—an *Umgreifendes,* as Jaspers would say—that we describe in so far as we elaborate a systematic doctrine of God and his relations with the world and with man. Finally, this notional knowledge takes shape in real knowledge whenever it is applied to a particular case, conjoined with a particular experience; as the *varium et mutabile semper femina* conjoined in the mind of Aeneas with his actual experience of Dido's fickleness. Our faith in Providence, the central tenet of natural religion, impressed on us by the intimations of conscience, elaborated into a doctrine by reason, becomes the source of our knowledge of an invisible world, really experienced in being conjoined with the events of each day, interpreted in the light of the divine governance.[2]

In the same way, conscience, in its aspect of moral sense, apprehends in certain experiences of admiration and approval, or of disgust and censure, in connection with particular acts, the immutable difference in the moral quality of our actions. Newman says this apprehension is instinctive. In a single action, we recognize the absolute nature of value, but in a real manner, that is in the experience of the quality of the concrete act. From that, the mind proceeds to a general judgment. It infers a world, a moral "totality", of which the ethical system it constructs is the map. Finally, the mind turns back to the concrete, applying its general principles to particular cases. This application could be purely notional, but in the authentic moral life it is conjoined with a

[1] *Grammar,* pp.105-106.
[2] *Ibid.,* p.402.

repeated experience, always new and original, of the value *in concreto*. The mind unites in a single act practical reasoning and concrete moral experience. So it is that the moral world becomes a real world of experience, and the moral life keeps its truth and vigour.

It is as regards this last phase that Newman's thought invites comparison with the modern situational ethics; for here it passes beyond casuistry to rejoin the *phronesis* of Aristotle and the judgment by connaturality which, according to Aquinas, is the specific act of prudence. Real apprehension of moral quality in an individual act and a determinate situation is what corrects the mere application of practical reasoning, and gives the final decision its eminently personal character. Pages 353 to 359 of the *Grammar* are decisive on this point. Newman there compares his real apprehension with Aristotle's *phronesis*. In both cases (the determination of a factual truth and the decision regarding a particular act) logical reasoning is inadequate. Therefore, just as, in moral judgment, the application of the abstract moral law must be corrected by personal *phronesis*, so, in concrete reasoning, logic must be supplemented by the illative sense. This *phronesis* is "a capacity sufficient for the occasion, of deciding what ought to be done here and now, by this given person, under these given circumstances",[1] and, "as regards conduct the rule for one man is not always the rule for another, though the rule is always one and the same in the abstract, and in its principle and scope. To learn his own duty in his own case, each individual must have recourse to his own rule".[2] Newman adds: "Such is Aristotle's doctrine, and it is undoubtedly true".[3]

The result of our examination is clear and indisputable. Newman does not enumerate three distinct phases in the growth of the moral life called those of moral instinct, moral sense, and the sense of duty. He distinguishes, in fact, two aspects, present from the beginning, in the act of conscience, one of perception, the other injunction. The first is the source of the moral life, the second that of natural religion. Each of them undergoes development in three stages; the first is instinctive, the apprehension of value in the individual instance; the second is one of generalization, the

[1] *Gramar.*, p.355.
[2] *Ibid.*, p.356.
[3] *Ibid.*, p.354.

creation of a notional system of ethics or theology; in the third, the general is applied to the particular, and both the notional and the real are united in a living synthesis.

Two observations are here required. First of all, we must remember that Newman uses the term "instinct", with its derivatives, in a very general sense. It is an analogical term, primarily used of animal instinct; and some acts of the mind are called instinctive on account of their resemblance to that. Every instinctive apprehension has two seemingly opposed qualities. On the one hand, it seems to be mediated, for it apprehends in the concrete instance a particular significance not contained in what is directly presented to sense or intellect.[1] There is, consequently, a *discursus,* a passage from one thing to another; and such a passage is, in Newman's terminology, an act of reason in the widest sense of the word.[2] We may say, with Fries, that here there is a mediate apprehension passing from the impression to its actual cause.[3] On the other hand, this apprehension seems to be immediate, since it reaches its object, the reality, in the subjective impression, without the intervention of a logical middle term. Newman is explicit on this point.[4] Hence, Fries's interpretation is dangerously incomplete. Newman describes what happens, without explaining it. The instinctive apprehension of a reality or an objective value starts from a subjective impression, but also takes place within that impression. It is, therefore, mediate in one respect and immediate in another.

Instinctive apprehension differs from intuition in that its object is concrete reality, while that of intuition is something general, as, for example, the case of Newton apprehending in an instant the law of gravity on seeing the fall of an apple.

Newman's description of how instinctive apprehension takes place is a crucial part of his theory of knowledge. It is by instinct that I apprehend, in the sense-impression, the existence of a real thing, or, in his behaviour, the presence of another person. It is by instinct that I apprehend in my *sentio* (or *cogito,* that is, my conscious existence) the reality of my self. It is by instinct that I recognize in certain irreducible kinds of mental impressions the

[1] Letter to Meynell in Ward, *op. cit.* II, p.259
[2] See above, p.96.
[3] H. Fries, *op. cit.,* p.59.
[4] *Grammar,* p.334, and Ward, *op. cit.,* p.258.

objective values of the good and the beautiful, and in the
intimation of duty the presence of a personal God. An instinct
causes me to apprehend, in an accumulation of independent indications, the concrete truth manifested at their point of convergence. A divine instinct empowers me to enter into communion
with my Redeemer through the words of Scripture,[1] etc. Whatever transcends the subjective impression is reached by an act to
which Newman applies the analogical term, instinct.

The term "instinct", as applied to a mental function, emphasises
its spontaneity and objectivity in relation to the subjective impression. The term "sense", on the other hand, stresses that this apprehension takes place immediately in an impression of a specific
kind and irreducible nature.

"Sense" is applied to a mental function by analogy with the
bodily senses. Newman, in fact, distinguishes between "bodily
senses" and "mental senses";[1] the former receive sensible impressions, the latter mental ones. To each specific class of sensible
impressions corresponds a distinct bodily sense. Hence, a distinct
mental sense ought to correspond to each specific kind of "mental
sensation".[2] The aesthetic sense, for instance, undergoes, in the
presence of things, agreeable or unpleasant impressions of a
specific and irreducible nature, and apprehends in these impressions the beauty or ugliness of the things themselves : "We speak
of it as beautifulness, and henceforth, when we call a thing
beautiful, we mean by the word nothing else than a certain quality
of things which creates in us this special sensation".[3] The "illative
sense" undergoes the impression, *per modum unius,* of a group of
indications, and apprehends in the convergence of their meaning
the concrete fact which explains them. Newman expressly observes
that the word "sense" has the same meaning in "illative sense",
"common sense" and "aesthetic sense".[4] The same is true of the
expressions "moral sense" and "sense of duty". In each case, the
primary object of the sense is a specific kind of impression. In the
presence of certain actions, we feel a specific pleasure or displeasure
in which we apprehend their moral quality; and in these same
acts we experience a number of "intentional" emotions, wherein

[1] *Grammar*, pp.23, 359.
[2] Here again we have a purely descriptive term. The mental senses are
not necessarily distinct faculties in the scholastic sense.
[3] *Ibid.*, pp.64-65.
[4] *Ibid.*, p.345.

is revealed the presence of a supreme personal Being. These two experiences are intimately connected, but irreducible, and so form objects of distinct senses of the human soul. Thus, each mental sense has for its primary object a special class of mental impressions.

The use of the word "sense" should have warned Läpple that the proper object of the "moral sense" could not be an ethical system. The primary object of the moral sense is the specific quality of the impressions in which the mind apprehends the absolute distinction between good and evil. Obviously, since this experience is the source of general ethics and the completed moral judgment, the range of the moral sense includes all kinds of ethical knowledge. The expression "moral sense", then, signifies primarily the faculty of distinguishing between good and evil, as acting spontaneously and instinctively. By extension, it comes to signify ethical knowledge in general, in all its applications. Hence, it is possible to use it in several different ways, by derivation.

Thus, "moral sense" may designate, in particular, that ethical knowledge obtained by deduction from individual experiences of conscience. Newman says so in a letter, whose contents are closely condensed, answering Meynell's request for his verdict on passages dealing with first principles :

> You will find I there consider that the dictate of the conscience is particular—not general—and that from the multiplication of particulars I infer the general—so that the moral sense, as a knowledge generally of the moral law, is a deduction from particulars. Next that this dictate of conscience, which is natural and the voice of God, is a moral instinct. . . .[1]

On this sole passage Läpple bases his interpretation of Newman, that the object of the moral instinct is the individual act, that of the moral sense is ethics in general. If this letter were the only thing Newman wrote, this view of his thought would be reasonable; but in the *Grammar*, especially in the classic sections the letter refers to, Newman expressed himself with perfect clarity. The letter can be explained quite naturally and easily in the light of these parts of the *Grammar*. There Newman says, not that the moral sense is merely a knowledge in general, but that, when viewed in that light—I would say "in its secondary meaning"—

[1] Ward, *op. cit.*, II, pp.256-257.

it is knowledge by deduction. That the construction of an ethical code is not the proper function of the moral sense, is clearly implied by Newman in the way he speaks of it. After distinguishing the two aspects of the indivisible act of conscience, he concludes by saying : "Here I have to speak of conscience in the latter point of view, not as supplying us, by means of its various acts, with the elements of morals, which may be developed by the intellect into an ethical code . . .".[1] Newman distinguishes exactly between the act of conscience which, as moral sense, provides the elements, and the act of the intellect which works these elements into a code.

"Moral sense" may also signify *phronesis,* the virtue which perfects moral judgment. It has this meaning at the end of the passage on the nature of the "illative sense".[2]

The use of the term "moral sense" with these different shades of meaning is nothing out of the ordinary; it is quite in accordance with usual semantic practice. Ethical knowledge has its root in the concrete intuition of value in the instinctive act of conscience. Experiences of the kind become the object of reflection, which expands them into an ethical system. Concrete perception makes use of these general ideas to perfect itself, and so becomes a virtue, a personal guide, clear and certain, for all the circumstances of life. The term "moral sense" is caught up in this process of development, and naturally comes to signify ethical knowledge in general or in one or other of its applications.

We may, therefore, draw the conclusion that ethical science is no more the proper object of the moral sense than the science of aesthetics is that of the sense of the beautiful. The very fact that Newman always treats these two senses as analogous is a final argument in favour of our interpretation.

Lastly, we shall consider another use of the term "moral sense", of a rather pejorative nature, where it means a kind of moral taste dissociated from the sense of duty to become the source of a purely humanist ethic, the code of a gentleman.

This use of the term sets a rather difficult problem. In the most explicit passage of the *Grammar,* Newman says quite clearly that the indivisible act of conscience is seen to have two aspects : in so

[1] *Grammar,* p.106.
[2] *Ibid.,* p.359; cf. also p.345.

far as it perceives, it proceeds from the moral sense, in so far as it commands, it derives from the sense of duty.

Nothing could be clearer. Yet, when Nédoncelle paraphrases it, he does not say, "The act of conscience is indivisible", but "the act of conscience is often undivided";[1] and, one might say, with good reason. For, in fact, Newman at times seems to say that the act of conscience can appear in one or other of its aspects:

> Of course its act is indivisible; still it has these two aspects, distinct from each other, and admitting of a separate consideration. Though I lost my sense of the obligation which I lie under to abstain from acts of dishonesty, I should not in consequence lose my sense that such actions were an outrage offered to my moral nature. Again; though I lost my sense of their moral deformity, I should not therefore lose my sense that they were forbidden to me.[2]

This passage gives rise to a certain difficulty. It is easy enough to understand that the perception can remain when the feeling of obligation is lost, but it is hard to see how the mandatory aspect of conscience can persist in the absence of perception. Hence comes the temptation to ascribe perception to the moral sense and injunction to the sense of duty. Are we to conclude that the perception of the difference between good and evil occurs in two ways, independent of each other but normally both present, namely, in the experience of some acts as morally ugly or beautiful, and in their experience as commanded or forbidden? In this assumption, it is understandable that the sense of duty could subsist in the absence of the moral sense.

This is the supposition that Nédoncelle seems to make. The difference between good and evil is made known both in a purely immanent and man-centred experience and in one that is deeper and more primitive, an "intentional" experience connecting the distinction directly to a divine command promulgated in the conscience. Newman, then, would have combined two theories of very different origin; that of the 18th century ethics of sensibility, whose chief exponent was Shaftesbury, and that of popular religious tradition. The former, the sentimentalist idea of what the Germans call the *Schöne Seele,* would correspond with the moral

[1] M. Nédoncelle, *op. cit.,* p.91.
[2] *Grammar,* pp.105-106.

sense; the second, that of the voice of God, would be retained in the sense of duty.

Newman would be said to have adopted towards Shaftesbury the same attitude as Bergson took later with regard to Ribot and Durkheim. Bergson acknowledged an automatic memory actuated by the brain, but he went on to demonstrate the existence of another, the true memory, that is purely psychological and independent of the brain. He grants to Durkheim a morality originating in the social group, but proves that true morality has a different source. So Newman would have granted Shaftesbury his moral sense, and would then have brought in against him the sense of duty: "For him, too, morality has two sources. He takes hold of, and uses, the first, that is the 18th century sentimentalist view; then he makes bold to demolish it. . . . It is a later, additional idea, invented by a world grown pagan. Good conduct is not a matter of taste, but of obedience to duty, and so to God".[1]

This interpretation is plausible, but presents enormous difficulties. In the *Grammar,* it is quite plain that Newman takes his "moral sense" very seriously, no less than the sense of duty. Conscience, as moral sense, is the source of moral doctrine and life, while the sense of duty is the source of religious doctrine and life. He makes this only too clear. His animadversions are directed, not to the moral sense, but to a conception that eliminates from conscience all but the aspect of moral sense, and, in so doing, reduces this to the level of mere taste.

A different interpretation is called for. We hold that Newman did not hold, unmodified, the profane theory of the moral sense. The moral sense is not an independent factor that can be united with or dissociated from the sense of duty without anything being changed in consequence. It is, in fact, primarily, the discriminating function of conscience. This function has a twofold value, one that is proper to it as such, another that accrues to it by its conjunction with the sense of duty. We experience good and evil as what makes the nobility or the baseness of character; but also, when viewed from the standpoint of duty, as constituting merit and sin. The moral sense and the sense of duty never cease altogether to exist. Even if one or the other seems absent from conscious life, it continues to act unawares, and is always liable to appear once more. Newman states this expressly of conscience

[1] M. Nédoncelle, *op. cit.*, p.96.

considered as the sense of duty,[1] and the same applies to the specific feeling produced by the moral sense. When the sense of duty is in abeyance, the moral sense is no more than a kind of taste. When the moral sense is weakened, it continues to serve the sense of duty by its act of discrimination, but it forfeits its specific sentiment, by which the good or evil act is felt to affect oneself. In that case, I no longer feel wrongdoing as "an affront to my moral nature", but solely as an offence against God. Some who are carried out of themselves by their love of God become insensible to the aspect of sin as a moral defect, but are correspondingly more acutely aware of it as an offence against God. Their moral sense is not absent, but is as if absorbed in the sense of duty, which it continues to serve by distinguishing good from evil.

This, perhaps, is the way the passage quoted ought to be understood; at any rate, unless Newman meant simply that, in the case of the "gentleman" who has lost the sense of duty, the moral sense may be highly cultivated, while, with the ordinary man in whom the inner command inspires a strong feeling of fear, moral discrimination may be very crude. Even this interpretation seems preferable to that which makes his philosophy of conscience a mixture of two scarcely compatible theories. Whatever may have been the influences impelling him to write the *Grammar*, the synthesis it achieved shows no such discordance.

[1] *Occ. Ser.*, pp.64-65.

24

Appendix E

THE PROOF OF THE EXISTENCE
OF GOD FROM CONSCIENCE

WE know that, for Newman himself, the existence of God was as evident as his own. In his inmost experience, the presence of God in conscience was so deeply rooted that the twofold evidence of "myself and my Creator" was absolutely indivisible.

Faith in God was the foundation of his trust in his senses. He expressed this again in 1864, in enumerating the advantages of the proof from conscience.

> It forms the basis for the belief in the senses—for, if there be a God, and I am His creature with a mission, He *means* me to *use* the senses—and I accept what they convey coming from Him whatever be its intellectual and philosophical worth.[1]

What was a philosophical proposition for Descartes, was for Newman a personal experience; for, as we have shown earlier, though philosophically the nature of the mind was his ultimate ground of certainty, personally he always looked beyond the mind to its divine author. It was the Providence of God that had inscribed in the very structure of our mind a mission we had the duty to recognize and carry out. This religious certainty enabled Newman to entrench himself in a state of perfect confidence and assurance.

Newman never worked out his proof of the existence of God.

[1] This passage from an unpublished notebook of Newman's is printed in A. Boekraad, *op. cit.*, p.267 (note). We shall return to it later.

Often, however, he indicates that, were he to do so, he would take as his starting-point the fact of conscience. He has left an outline of such a proof, but its achievement did not come easily to him. He testifies, in the *Apologia,* that he had not succeeded in stating a proof that satisfied his reason.

The proof from conscience is discussed by Flanagan in his book on Newman's teaching on faith.[1] It is a clear and penetrating study mainly designed to defend him against the charge of modernism and semi-modernism; but I think the problem is not very well stated. This is how the author formulates it : "Did Newman hold that we can make an act of faith in a proposition, such as the statement that there are three Persons in God, before we know by *external, objective evidence* that the proposition has been revealed by God?"[2] as if to affirm such a possibility were modernist! The whole patristic tradition, the scholastic tradition up to Duns Scotus, the great thomist tradition, does not hesitate to answer a question of this sort affirmatively. It is true that an almost unanimous tradition in the Church teaches that God has endowed his Church with such an abundance of signs and proofs as to justify it rationally to any reasonable mind that takes the trouble to examine them, and this tradition was ratified by the Vatican Council; but this does not mean that a genuine conversion or personal faith is necessarily dependent on these extrinsic arguments. The Fathers of the Church are unanimous in their commendation of those whose faith is unaided by signs and miracles, and St Thomas does not hesitate to share their view and to affirm that, even were miracles lacking, we would be obliged to believe because the doctrine itself, and, particularly, God's call to us as felt interiorly, would be a sufficient motive.[3] The fact is that the Fathers, the scholastics of the High Middle Ages up to Scotus, and the great commentators on St Thomas, all acknowledge that our certainty of the divine origin of Christianity arises "partly from external testimony, partly, and chiefly, from the light of faith"[4] In the absence of external aid, the interior guide is sufficient, and an instantaneous conversion, without the help of

---

[1] P. Flanagan, *Newman, Faith and the Believer,* London 1946.

[2] *Ibid.,* p.3; the italics are ours.

[3] *Quodlibet,* II, art. 6.

[4] D. Banez, *Commentaire sur la "Somme théologique" IIa IIae, q. I. art.* 4. This doctrine is common to the great commentators on St Thomas.

signs or reasons, like that of Claudel, is theologically unobjection-
able, though, in fact, it is probably rare.

In any case, Flanagan would find nothing in the Vatican decrees
or the encyclical *Pascendi* to support the principle by which he
proposed to settle the question of Newman's modernism.

It is true that Scotus, and, following him, certain nominalists,
e.g. Pierre D'Ailly, opposed the traditional view, defended by the
thomists, that we apprehend the credibility of Christian teaching
by the light of faith. Suarez and his followers, together with the
theologians of Port Royal, adopted the nominalist view; but, as
may be seen from their own words, Suarez and Nicole were driven
into this position by their controversy with the Protestants, who
wished to base faith solely on the interior light of the Holy Spirit.
This is a striking example of how Catholic theology has, at times,
been diminished on the occasion of Protestant controversy. It is
possible that this later theology influenced certain nineteenth century formulas, for instance, those to which the Abbé Bautain had
to subscribe by order of his bishop, or a passage in the encyclical
Qui Pluribus of Pius IX. These formulas, which, in any case, do
not involve the infallibility of the Church, cannot be taken in
support of Flanagan's principle. They state, in general, that reason
precedes faith and leads to faith, that prudent reason ought to
investigate carefully the fact of revelation so as to acquire certainty that God has spoken. They assert, finally, that the fact of
revelation must be proved to unbelievers by external arguments,
and that the controversialist or the preacher has no right to expect
them to believe in the resurrection apart from certain proofs.
These latter requirements, to which Bautain had to subscribe,
relate to the attitude of those in apostolic work. They are far from
implying that the unbeliever himself may not be obliged to accept
the faith without external arguments, and that, in their absence,
he would have the right St Thomas refused him to "resist the
interior call", were this given by the grace of God without the
normal accompaniment of rational motives.

With this reservation, it must be admitted that the author has
given a true analysis of Newman's teaching on the question. He
shows convincingly what Newman meant by ascribing a certain
priority to the individual conscience, and refutes Bremond's interpretation. He devotes particular attention to the proof from conscience, and pronounces it invalid in the form usually attributed

to Newman. He considers that "intentional emotion" is easily accounted for by a religious education and the influence of environment, and that it would be unreasonable to let oneself be guided by emotion if this could not be independently justified by reason. He refashions the argument, starting from conscience, not as the sense of duty, but as a witness to the moral law. The general nature of the argument is the same as that we attributed to Descoqs and de Bruyne,[1] and Flanagan says of it : "I think this was Newman's real proof of God's existence".[2] This, however, is extremely improbable, and the passage quoted says nothing about it. For my part, I agree that the sole absolutely valid proof of the existence of God is the metaphysical one, and that the moral argument, to be strictly conclusive, has to be transformed into the metaphysical one which starts from human contingency, shown specifically in the sphere of morals; but I am certain that this kind of reasoning was foreign to Newman's mentality. For him a certain apprehension of God was among the primary and irreducible facts of conscious existence.[3] From this it follows that a proof of the existence of God amounts to demonstrating, by reflection and analysis, that such indeed is the religious testimony of the spontaneous act of conscience; next, the difficulties in the way of this view must be resolved, namely, the implicit, vague, flexible nature of initial religious apprehension, the influence of environment and education on its birth, the personal character of its consolidation and development, its apparent absence in the case of so many, especially of a certain degree of culture, etc.;[4] finally, this natural act of the mind has to be allotted its place in the general structure of the intellectual process.

Boekraad has lately brought to light a very important passage from Newman, which runs as follows :

> If then our *or* my knowledge of our *or* my existence is brought home to me by my consciousness of thinking, and if thinking includes as one of its modes conscience or the sense of an imperative coercive law, and if such a sense, (when analysed, i.e.) reflected on, involves an inchoative recognition

---

[1] See above, pp.212-213.
[2] P. Flanagan, *op. cit.*, p.20.
[3] See above, pp.149-152, and the whole of Appendix D.
[4] See above, pp. 203-209.

of a Divine Being, it follows that such recognition comes close upon my recognition that I am, and is not only such a clear object of perception as my own existence. . . . It has been my chosen proof of that fundamental doctrine for thirty years past.[1]

To accept God is the same as to accept my own existence, since human existence, that is conscious or thinking existence, implies this confrontation with the divine mystery as a factor in its whole constitution.

This line of argument is very much in the manner of Scheler, as Fries points out,[2] and in accord with contemporary religious philosophy in general. It is not an abstract deduction from metaphysical principles, but a process of reflection on actual existence, on *Dasein,* as Heidegger would say, that is, on this "human existing" apprehended prior to reflection, whose object is to bring into full consciousness. Newman's aim, precisely, is to show that our conscious existence has, as one of its elements, an inner reference to a personal God, and that, in consequence, a complete and true description of it must include the religious factor.

Newman himself points out the advantages of this form of proof. It is not only true, but is also peculiarly fitted to contemporary needs. It is within the reach of all, learned and simple, pagans and Christians. All men, from infancy, bear, in their inmost experience its essential elements. It is, too, of real consequence, being closely bound up with actual life; it is no purely theoretical conclusion of abstract reason, but goes to the very source of religious life and doctrine, and stirs it to action. It both explains and refutes the philosophical error that makes what is the voice of God a mere matter of taste.[3]

We are inclined to restate in this connection what we said in Appendix C on Newman's critique of conscience, of which his proof of the existence of God is an application. This proof, though not absolutely conclusive, has positive value. The kind of reflection of which Newman speaks would be sufficient to lead an upright, unbiased person, of generous disposition and aware that life has some moral purpose, to a religious conviction grounded

---

[1] A. Boekraad, *op. cit.,* p.266 (note).

[2] H. Fries, *op. cit.*

[3] A. Boekraad, *op. cit.,* pp.266-277 (note).

in reason. Newman's argument has, undoubtedly, the advantage of being eminently practical; it is simple, and thoroughly convincing to those who share the experience he describes; at the same time, it brings out clearly the presence of God and our duty towards him. The metaphysical argument, on the other hand, is very difficult to understand perfectly since it presupposes the whole metaphysics of being; its full force is evident only to a metaphysician. Once it is simplified for general use, it becomes more or less defective, and, though it still makes some impression on many, it is not convincing to those versed only in modern methods of philosophy. As it is, experience shows that nowadays there is prevalent a rather unfortunate cast of mind that is not amenable to metaphysical reasoning. In fact, it is this that has led the religious philosophy of our day to prefer Newman's approach.

There is one other remark to be made. We are convinced that all consciousness of God is, ultimately, of a metaphysical nature. The metaphysician, when he shows that the "awareness of being", embodied in our consciousness that we are finite, implies a real dependence of finite beings on an Infinite Being, exhibits, in fact, the essential structure of all awareness of God; but this structure is, normally, hidden within the living body of religious experience. Concrete thought, by which we apprehend the reality of God, clothes in living tissues the skeleton of metaphysical reason, without whose presence the finely-wrought structure of religious experience would fall apart. Surely, it is unnecessary to oppose the classical ways of theodicy to the modern way of reflection on religious experience, apprehended in its totality and spontaneity. The justification of religious thought, as carried out by Newman, may fittingly be combined with a metaphysical proof that exhibits its structure, a proof so clear in itself, yet so difficult to grasp in the abstract. If metaphysical analysis were put forward as the reconstruction of a framework necessary to that natural religious experience whose actual process has first been described, and which has already been justified as integral to the life of the mind, I think the proof of God's existence would thereby be restored to its natural place; in fact, it would acquire additional force, through the bringing out of its full significance for life. In this way, I believe, we would be in the fullest accord with the spirit of Aristotle, who, no less than St Thomas, was Newman's master.

Appendix F

WAS NEWMAN A "SAGE"?

Newman's method

THE method and structure of Newman's apologetics has never yet been examined in detail and as a whole, though Jean Guitton treats of them in a very discerning manner in his *Philosophie de Newman*. Of the two books that deal *ex professo* with his general apologetic, that of Père J. D. Folghera[1] does no more than summarize Newman's principal works of controversy; the second, recently published by Borghild Gundersen,[2] is a study of Newman's historical background and the influences he underwent, and, apart from that, is confined to an analysis, at times very acute, but summary, of his instruments (analogy and probability), the kinds of proof, and the various factors of the psychology of faith. The author's chief concern is to defend Newman's orthodoxy, principally against the charge of modernism.

The present writer has given the main outlines of Newman's apologetic in a small book, *Newman's verantwoording van het geloof in de Kerk*,[3] as has also Canon Aubert, professor at the University of Louvain, in a contribution to the collection *Au Seuil du Christianisme: Newman, une psychologie concrète de la foi et une apologétique existentielle*.[4]

John Holloway's book, *The Victorian Sage*,[5] is a highly

[1] J. D. Folghera, *Newman apologiste* (Editions de la "Revue des Jeunes"; Paris, 1927).

[2] Borghild Gundersen, *Cardinal Newman and Apologetics* (Jacob Dybwad; Oslo, 1952).

[3] Antwerp, 1946.

[4] Brussels, 1952.

[5] J. Holloway, *The Victorian Sage* (Macmillan; London, 1953), pp.158-202.

interesting study of Newman's dialectic seen as a whole. As the title indicates, Newman is classed among the "sages". A sage is a man who has a harmonious conception of the world, of man's place in it, and of the kind of life his condition requires (p.201). It will be noticed that the three questions the sage answers are precisely those with which any philosophy worthy of the name is concerned. What characterizes the sage is that the world into which he desires to lead us is accessible only at a deeper level of experience. To communicate his message an appeal to sense-experience, or to reasoning whether inductive or deductive, is of no avail; for he has to deliver a comprehensive view of reality, a way of seeing things other than everyone can find for himself. The processes he uses do not serve really to prove, but to make us see, the thing in question. It is true he analyses facts, generalizes, defines, distinguishes, reasons, argues; but all these are not designed to set up a rational proof, but to direct attention to a deeper experience of things, one buried beneath the surface of common, daily experience. Hence, his method must be one of "indirect communication", in the words of Kierkegaard. His technique is more germane to that of the poet and artist than of the philosopher and scientist.

> The sage's abstractions, his formal and verbal arguments, his logic-chopping, always can and often do lead on to something realler and richer. His aim is to make his readers see life and the world over again, see it with a more searching, or perhaps a more subtle and sensitive gaze. He utilizes what Pater called "that sort of philosophical expression in which ... the language is inseparable from or essentially a part of the thought". (pp. 296-297).

Hence, Newman's procedure would be rather to persuade by literary devices than to prove by logic. For him, as for all sages, proof consists in making people see. His main object was to bring the reader to "realize" and adopt his point of view. Once that is done, he has only to unfold and describe, in their perfect coherence, the different aspects, the manifold parts, of his view of the world, of man and of life. Reasoning means showing the coherence of individual elements within a fundamental intuition of reality.

Newman's basic idea, as stated by the author in his dry and

succinct fashion, accords strikingly with our analysis of his first
principles of apologetics (pp. 234-238).

> *He believed that reality is a great ordered system with
> the Creator as its apex.* . . . Because of this order, everything
> in the universe has its proper nature and purpose : and the
> natural world, the church, the state, and the human indi-
> vidual, are all created on similar and analogous patterns. . . .
> The world is infinitely complex and varied, but everything
> has its allotted place; it may be bad elsewhere, but there it is
> good. . . . "Every exercise of nature or of art is good in its
> place". This concept of the universe—what in one place he
> calls "the providential system of the world"—is the core of
> Newman's work (p.159).

Providence, the nature of things, analogy . . . we recognize the
triad of first principles that govern the movement of Newman's
thought. This fundamental view, when fully developed in all its
consequences and articulations, becomes, for Newman, the
Catholic system.

Holloway's interpretation of Newman is absolutely right, and
that makes his assessment of him of especial importance. Newman
emerges as the great master of persuasive wisdom. He not only
"proves to have had perhaps the most comprehensive, detailed
and integrated view of things—in the sage's sense—of any English
writer of his century" (p.158), but, in the *Grammar of Assent*,
he has himself analysed and described in masterly fashion, the
course of the thought that wisdom directs (pp. 6-9).

All that Holloway shows us of the techniques of persuasion
used by Newman in his works is equally perceptive. It is not possible to summarize so close an analysis, but we give his conclusion :

> As for the methods themselves, the central point of this
> whole inquiry is that they do not merely state Newman's out-
> look, but they display it. They fuse together to be a picture
> with the qualities that he wants us to see in the world. All the
> time, a variety of techniques—metaphor and analogy, dis-
> cussions of meaning, carefully chosen examples—steadily
> tend to make the controversial non-controversial, so that we
> are not coerced by any 'smart syllogism' into accepting New-
> man's conclusions in the abstract, but brought imperceptibly

to a living understanding of his creed. The continuous texture of his work modifies our receptivity until we find ourselves seeing the world as he sees it. To this end all the parts of his work act in conjunction. Tone, forms of argument, illustration and example, imagery and manipulating senses integrate to make something which has a single unified impact on the reader; and the impact is not that of a formal argument, but in its fullness and vividness more resembles that of a work of art, something which can make the reader find more in his experience, see it with new eyes, because for a while it constitutes his whole experience (p.201).

Holloway's account of Newman's literary and dialectical genius is wonderfully clear, and so persuasive that it might seem impossible to disagree with his estimate. To deal with it thoroughly would require a whole book. The main question concerns his qualification of Newman as a "sage", with all that the word connotes—his opposition of the sage and the poet to the philosopher and scientist, as if the object of these latter were the truth, whereas with the sage and poet, it is open to question 'whether the sense of "true" or "false" relevant in this field of thought is something we fully understand' (p.297).

To answer this, we must first draw attention to Newman's theory of knowledge in general and of conscience in particular. It is based, not on experiences reserved to a privileged few, or on recondite intuitions, but on certain extremely simple and practical principles that anyone would be ready to grant, unless he were misled by some kind of positivist philosophy. Positivists of every kind, logical as well as others, must never forget that their first principles are quite remote from the common-sense of mankind in general, and are the result of reducing the whole of experience to one only of its aspects. It is for them to justify themselves before ordinary, unsophisticated consciousness, the starting-point of all thought, including their own. If anyone makes use of rhetoric to persuade, it is certainly those among the positivists who make out their point of view to be the natural one, and suggest that those who appeal to common-sense rely, in fact, upon a special intuition or subjective feeling. It may be noticed that Holloway does not mention the initial philosophical procedure on which

Newman's whole system depends, and which we have set out in
this book.[1]

Next, we have to examine the distinction between the sage
(and even the poet) and the philosopher. Is it a valid one? No
one has extolled, more than Aristotle, common-sense and experience of life as means of attaining truth—"We must take account
of the unproved assertions and opinions of persons of experience
... just as much as of proofs; for experience has given them a
practised eye, and they see exactly into things".[2] In what concerns living, proofs presuppose common-sense and personal
experience. "The philosopher", as he is called, is, after all, himself
but a sage. The *Nicomachaean Ethics* present the first analysis of
the wisdom in question, and Newman, in the *Grammar,* set out
deliberately to follow Aristotle.

The question, therefore, arises, in what sense is it possible to
distinguish the philosopher from the sage? The starting-point of
philosophy is not some exact finding, and such could not be its
object. In fact, the object of exact science is itself the outcome of
abstraction. The first object of philosophy is much more primitive and comprehensive; it is the conscious presence of a self to
a reality and in it, a reality which manifests itself directly as a
"world", a conscious presence, ever wondering and inquiring as
to the meaning of things and of its own activity. This object, the
starting-point of philosophical reflection, is itself mysterious; it is
the mystery that we are, that constitutes our being, and forms the
background of and envelops all our experience and conscious
activity, even that of our most exact sciences. These are right to
cut out from primitive experience a more abstract object, the
phenomena of sense, and to study the measurable relations that
the world, in that aspect, exhibits. But to refuse the word "true"
to our original, absolute experience, and restrict it to one of its
relative, abstract aspects is as absurd as to deny the presence of
life to a tree, and assert it of one of its branches.

Modern critical philosophy sees, with growing unanimity, that
its task is reflection on the spontaneous life of consciousness; that
is, to explore, elucidate, disclose, evoke, clarify, unfold, make
absolutely conscious, clear and distinct what, prior to reflection,
was already present confusedly, obscurely, indistinctly, implicitly,

---

[1] See also Appendices C and F.
[2] Aristotle, *Nichomachean Ethics*, VI, XI.

in the very activity of conscious life. In a sense, then, to cause to see is to prove. Progress in philosophy does not consist in discovering facts and laws that, previously, formed no part of the life of thought, but in an increasingly complete exhibition of a truth that, before being reflected upon, was already the sustenance of pre-philosophical thought—the spontaneous life of consciousness. In this thought, says Newman, "the whole man moves". The philosopher's reflection finds its object, primitive experience, only in the spontaneous activity of his personal, pre-philosophical thought. If, therefore, he is to succeed in discovering the truth lying at the basis of all our experience, his personal pre-philosophic thought must be in accord with it. This, in turn, depends on a certain moral orientation of the person himself, a certain openness to being, a certain submissiveness to the whole of experience, a candid love of truth. The reflection of the philosopher truly apprehends its object only through the agency of a personal life of both moral and intellectual quality. It is perfectly understandable that the mental apprehension of that original mystery by which we are constituted as conscious beings in this world should be determined and coloured by the personal attitude to reality and life. Since philosophy has for its object, not one that confronts us from outside, but a reality all around us and that constitutes us in our being, it is to be expected that, within the nature and conditions all have in common, differences in basic attitudes freely adopted should involve differences in that "experiential" thought through which reflection meets with its object. The conclusion that follows, says Newman, is not that there is no truth, but "that truth there is and we can attain to it, but that its rays reach us by the intermediary of our moral, as much as our intellectual, being".[1]

It follows that philosophy, to discharge its task fully, must not only convince the intellect, but direct the conscience, judge man's underlying disposition, and emphasise the duty of generosity and purification that reality imposes. Once again, Newman is right, even from the standpoint of philosophy, in saying, as Holloway points out, that he does not care to convince the reason without touching the heart (p.6). The great French metaphysicians of the present, Lavelle, Blondel, Marcel, would agree with Newman absolutely on this point.

[1] *Grammar*, p.311.

All the processes of philosophy taken together constitute a single process of unfolding, in which analogy and analogical description are of the greatest importance. English metaphysicians of today, like Langmead-Casserley and Austin Farrer, make excellent use of these. The latter author's *Finite and Infinite,* one of the most abstruse, technical and difficult works of metaphysical analysis, is wholly based on analogical description, aimed at making clear to the reader the significance of what is contained in the very structure of his conscious life.

We need not go to the extreme of Heidegger and some of his followers, who hold that the poet and the philosopher have exactly the same function, which is to reveal being by means of language; but it is certain they act with the same basic conditions. Hence, the difference between the sage and the philosopher resolves itself into a difference of style. Or rather, taking the term in a narrower sense than usual, the philosopher adds something to the sage; he has to give to his conclusions, after they are formed, a strictly rational form and justification. In that case, we should ascribe to the sphere of the sage many of the intellectual movements—existentialism among them—treated in the history of philosophy.

For a complete discussion of the assessment of Newman by such writers as Holloway or O'Faòlain,[1] we should have to go further and question the difference, which seems so obvious to them, between the epistemological requirements of wisdom and those of the exact sciences. Some English writers today attempt to show that these are identical in all spheres of intellectual activity; we could instance H. A. Hodges, L. Hodgson, and many others. Their fundamental idea may be thus summarized: Experience (with a capital E) is one, but appears to us in several aspects apparently inconsistent with one another. Each of these is exhibited concretely in a series of particular experiences which we call facts, to designate which we invent certain verbal instruments. We attempt to place these facts in a structure that gives them intelligibility and coherent meaning; and, to this end, we have to construct around them an imaginary edifice which, in the physical sciences, becomes increasingly fantastic. Professor Coulson writes:

Physics may have begun with realism, but it has passed

[1] *Newman's Way.*

beyond that stage now; and there is little left of the hard brute facts which we used to think were its sole concern. . . . It almost looks as if what science was doing was the writing of a great fairy-story, in which certain really simple facts were embedded in a fantastic matrix of the mind's imagining.[1]

There is even in all scientific work

a somewhat unexpected personal element, linking Man and Nature in a mutual intimacy. It is almost as if we could describe every scientific observation—the groundwork on which scientific concepts are to be based—as an encounter.[2]

The physical world or Nature is, then, a system made up of a reality observed and a person observing, a system invented by us to give meaning to a particular series of experiences in which our meeting with the real world is embodied.

What physics does for a particular group of experiences, integrated within our total Experience, history, poetry, philosophy, religion do for another group similarly integrated, which convey another aspect of our meeting with the mystery of reality. Each of these creates its own language to communicate to the others the particular experience it has for its object. An expression taken from the language of one may seem to contradict one borrowed from another; but, in fact, the two are no more contradictory than descriptions of the same mountain from different points.

There is no conflict of concepts. Each is valid in its proper context, and wisdom consists in recognizing which context is proper for any given situation. So when the Christian asserts that his will is free, and that this freedom—to do good or to sin—is God-given, it is no answer to propound however brilliant an account of history as determined.[3]

We may, therefore, conclude that there exist certain models of intelligibility other than that of exact science,

equally good at coordinating experiences, and, in certain circumstances, more satisfying. . . . They are equally true. For

[1] C. A. Coulson, *Christianity in an Age of Science* (London, 1953), p.12.
[2] *Ibid.*, p.18.
[3] *Ibid.*, p.24.

the Christian, these specific models are the concept of a personal God, an interpretation of the life and death of Our Lord, and the activity of the Holy Spirit. If you say: 'These help me to relate together many of my most precious experiences and feelings', you have started where the scientist starts when he tries to develop a scientific theory.[1]

There is no need to endorse completely these highly original views; we will observe only that they express, in scientific language, ideas very similar to Newman's. Under Aristotle's influence, Newman always insisted that mental processes are of many different kinds, that each corresponds to a particular aspect of that one fundamental reality that is the object of our common Experience; that each is adequate to convey its own truth if it submits to the demands of its own special object, and if used with care and conscientiousness; and that, in general, apparent contradictions are explained by differences in standpoint, and may be reconciled, by mature investigation, in a higher and wider order that comprises the entire hierarchy of reality.

[1] *Ibid.*, p.25.

BIBLIOGRAPHY

I. The Works of Newman[1]

1. Parochial and Plain Sermons, *8 vols., 1834-1843*, (Rivington, London, 1882).

2. Fifteen Sermons preached before the University of Oxford, *1843*, (Longmans, London, 1898).

3. The Arians of the Fourth Century, *1833*, (Longmans, London, 1897).

4. The Via Media of the Anglican Church, *2 vols., 1837 and 1891*, (Longmans, London, 1891).

5. An Essay on the Development of Christian Doctrine, *1875*, (2nd edition, J. Toovey, London, 1846; 15th impression (modified edition of 1878), (Longmans, London, 1914).

6. Essays Critical and Historical, *2 vols., 1871*, (Pickering, London, 1871).

7. Discussions and Arguments, *1872*, (Longmans, London, 1897).

8. Loss and Gain, *1848*, (Burns and Lambert, London, 1858).

9. De Catholici Dogmatis Evolutione (*The Newman-Perrone Paper on Development*, ed. Rev. T. Lynch, in Gregorianum, vol. XVI, *1935*, pp. 403-444).

10. Discourses addressed to Mixed Congregations, *1849*, (Longmans, London, 1919).

11. Certain Difficulties felt by Anglicans in Catholic Teaching:
    Vol. I, *1850* : twelve lectures, (London, 1888).
    Vol. II, *1875* : Letter to the Rev. E. B. Pusey on his *Eirenicon;* letter to the Duke of Norfolk, on the occasion of Mr. Gladstone's recent expostulation. (London, 1888).

12. Lectures on the Present Position of Catholics in England, *1851*, (J. Duffy, Dublin, 1857).

13. The Idea of a University, *1852*, (Longmans, London, 1931).

14. Sermons preached on various Occasions, *1857*, (Longmans, London, 1913).

15. Callista, *1856*, (Burns & Oates, London, 1876).

---

[1] In this list, I have confined myself to those works that I have consulted. A more complete bibliography will be found in J. Guitton, *La Philosophie de Newman*, pp. 196-212, or in H. Tristam and F. Bacchus: *Newman*, in the *Dictionnaire de Théologie catholique*, vol. XI, col. 353-397 (this article analyses almost all the works and minor writings of Newman).

16. Ueber das Zeugnis der Laien in Fragen des Glaubens (on Consulting the Faithful in Matters of Doctrine) *1859*, in *Ausgewählte Werke* (Matthias Laros, Vol. III, pp. 198-239). This article, which appeared in the *Rambler* of July, 1859, has not been reprinted among Newman's works. Only one extract from it appears at the end of the later editions of *The Arians*. The complete article is readily accessible only in the German translation, and I have made use of this.

17. Apologia Pro Vita Sua, *1864* (Everyman's Library, London, 1934).

18. An Essay in Aid of a Grammar of Assent (1st edition, Burns and Oates, London, 1870; new edition, modified in places, Longmans, London, 1906).

19. Tracts Theological and Ecclesiastical, *1871*, (Longmans, London, 1899).

20. Stray Essays, *1890* (out of print).

21. Letters and Correspondence of John Henry Newman during his Life in the Anglican Church (ed. Anne Mozley, 2 vols., Longmans, London, 1891).

22. Cardinal Newman and William Froude, *Correspondence* (Gordon Huntington Harper, Baltimore, 1933).

23. Ward, Wilfrid: *The Life of John Henry Cardinal Newman based on his Private Journals and Correspondence,* (2 vols., London 1912). In this book, Ward publishes a great deal of matter from Newman's Catholic journals, notebooks and letters.

24. Addresses to Cardinal Newman with his Replies (ed. W. P. Neville, London, 1905).

25. Tristram, H.: *Cardinal Newman's Theses de fide and his proposed Introduction to the French Translation of the University Sermons,* in Gregorianum, vol. XVIII, 1937, pp. 219-260.

II. Works about Newman[1]

(A) *Biography*

1. Tristram, H. and Bacchus, F.: Newman, in *Dictionnaire de théologie catholique,* vol. II, 1931, col. 326-354.

2. Ward, Wilfrid: The Life of John Henry Cardinal Newman, (2 vols., London, 1912).

3. Bouyer, Louis: Newman, his Life and Spirituality (London, 1958).

4. Cross, F.L.: John Henry Newman: with a set of unpublished letters (London, 1933).

---

[1] Here again, I make mention only of works that I have actually used. A more detailed, but still far from complete, bibliography will be found in Guitton, *op. cit*, pp. 212-230, or in Gunning, *op. cit.* pp. 733-747.

5. Ward, Maisie: Young Mr. Newman (London, 1948).

6. O'Faòlain, Sean : Newman's Way (London, 1952).

7. Sencourt, Robert: The Life of Newman (Westminster, 1948).

8. Thureau-Dangin, P. : La Renaissance catholique en Angleterre (3 vols., 3rd edition, Paris, 1927).

9. Gunning, J. H.: John Henry Kardinaal Newman (Amsterdam, 1933).

(B) *On the Oxford Movement*

1. Church, R. W.: The Oxford Movement (3rd Edition, London, 1892).

2. Evans A.W.: Tract Ninety (London, 1933). This book contains the text of Tract 90, together with an historical commentary.

3. Janssens A.: De beweging van Oxford (Davidsfonds, 1930).

(C) *On Newman's Theory of Development*[1]

1. Bremond, H.: Newman: Le développement du dogme chrétien. (4th edition, Paris 1906).

2. Byrne, James J. : The Notion of Doctrinal Development in the Anglican Writings of J. H. Newman, in *Ephemerides Theologicae Lovanienses,* vol. XIV, 1937, pp. 230-286.

3. Chevalier, J.: Trois conférences d'Oxford, III, *Newman et la notion de développement* (2nd edition, Paris, 1933, pp. 81-118).

4. de Grandmaison, Léonce, S.J.: Le développement du dogme chrétien, Part II, Les théories du Développement au XIX siècle, par. 2, *La Notion newmanienne du Développement,* in Revue pratique d'Apologétique, (vol. VI, 1908, pp. 18-33).

5. de Groot, J. V. : Denkers van onzen tijd (2nd edition, Bussum, 1918). This book contains a criticism of Newman's theory of development.

6. Dublanchy E.: *Dogme,* in Dictionnaire de théologie catholique (Vacant-Mangenot, vol. IV, Paris, 1911). See col. 1630-1636.

7. Fairbairn, A. M.: The Place of Christ in Modern Theology (London, New York, 1893). See pp. 25-44.

8. Gore, C.: The Holy Spirit and the Church (London, 1924). See pp. 208-228.

9. Guitton, J.: La Philosophie de Newman, Essai sur l'idée de Développement (Paris, 1933).

---

[1] Under this heading are listed only those works which deal specifically with Newman's theory of development, or else with this theory in a broader, not merely doctrinal, aspect. Works that discuss doctrinal development in general, or in authors other than Newman, are listed under Section E. Most of these contain a more or less developed and explicit consideration of Newman's theory.

10. Haecker, T.: Christentum und Kultur (Munich, 1929). See pp. 160-180, which is the Preface to his translation of the *Essay*.

11. Hayot, M. : *Bremond et Newman*, II. *La Question du Dogme*. In Revue Apologetique, (vol. LXVII, pp. 449-460, 1938).

12. Janssens A.: Inleiding tot de theologie (Brussells, 1934). See pp. 111-124.

13. Loisy, A. : *Le développement chrétien d'après le Cardinal Newman*, in Revue du Clergé français, (vol. XVII, 1899, pp. 5-20).

14. Storr, Vernon F.: The Development of English Theology in the Nineteenth Century (London, 1913). See pp. 283-287 and 294-316.

15. Tristram, H. and Bacchus, F.: *Newman* in Dictionnaire de théologie catholique, (vol. XI, Paris, 1931). See col. 358-384 on the *Essay*.

16. Tristram, H.: *A. Moehler et J. H. Newman*, in Revue des Sciences philosophiques et théologiques (vol. XXVII, 1938, pp. 184-204).

17. Tyrrell, G.: Through Scylla and Charybdis or the Old and the New Theology, (London, 1907). See pp. 139-154.

18. Tyrrell, G.: Christianity at the Cross-Roads, (London, 1909). See pp. 29-34.

19. Van Ginneken, J, S. J.: Voordrachten over het Katholicisme voor niet-Katholieken (Bruges, Rotterdam). See pp. 142-159.

(D) *On other aspects of Newman's work*

1. Bremond, H.: The Mystery of Newman (London, 1907).

2. Ellis Baker, J. : The Novel and the Oxford Movement (Princeton, 1932). This book has an interesting critical study of Newman's two novels.

3. Folghera, J. D., O.P.: Newman Apologiste (Paris, 1927). This is an introduction to the Newman controversy.

4. Janssens, A.: Newman, Inleiding tot zijn geest en zijn werk (Brussells, 1937).

5. Juergens, Sylvester : Newman on the Psychology of Faith in the Individual (London, 1928). A good introduction to the *Grammar of Assent*.

6. Karl, A.: *Die Glaubensphilosophie Newmans* in Grenzfragen zwischen Theologie und Philosophie, XX (Bonn, 1941).

7. Przywara, Erich, S. J. : Einführung in Newman's Wesen und Werk (Freiburg, 1922). This constitutes vol. 4 of *J. H. Newman, Christentum, ein Aufbau*; the seven other volumes go to make up a synthetic anthology of Newman's work, translated by Otto Karrer and published also in English, under the title *A Newman Synthesis* (London, 1930). H. Tristram gave a very good criticism of this

attempt in *A Newman Synthesis* in The Clergy Review, February 1937 (vol. I, pp. 126-142).

8. Sobry, P. : Newman en zijn Idea of a University (Brussels, 1935).

9. Tardivel, F.: La personnalité de Newman (Paris, 1937).

10. Tristram, H.: Newman and his Friends (London, 1933). A very interesting study devoted to those to whom Newman dedicated his works.

11. Van de Pol. W.: De Kerk in het leven en denken van Newman (Nijkerk, 1936).

12. Willebrands, J. G. M.: *Het christelijk platonisme van kardinaal Newman,* in Studia Catholica (vol. XVII, 1941, pp. 373-388).

13. Willebrands, J. G. M. : *Kardinaal Newman : de persoonlijke aard van het denken,* in Studia Catholica (vol. XVII, 1941, pp. 425-444). This is a very sound study of the first principles of Newman's psychology.

14. Zeno, Dr., O. F. M. Cap : Newman's leer over het menschelijk denken (Utrecht and Nijmegen, 1943).

(E) *On the Development of Doctrine*

1. Bainvel, J. V.: De Magisterio vivo et de traditione (Paris, 1905).

2. Blondel, M. : *Histoire et dogme. Les lacunes philosophiques de l'exégése moderne,* in La Quinzaine, (vol. LVI, 1904, pp. 145-167; 349-373; 433-458). The last article is on the development of doctrine.

3. de Grandmaison, L. : Le dogme chrétien. Sa nature—ses formules—son développement (Paris, 1928).

4. de la Barre, S. J. : La vie du dogme catholique. Autorité—Évolution (Paris, 1898). This work comes very close to Newman's position.

5. Draguet, R. : *Évolution des dogmes,* in Apologétique (Paris, 1937, pp. 1166-1192).

6. Gardeil, A., O.P. : Le donné révélé et la théologie (Paris, 1910). See pp. 151-186.

7. Marin-Sola, F., O.P.; L'Évolution homogène du dogme catholique (2 vols., 2nd edition, Fribourg, 1924).

8. Minon, A. : *L'Attitude du Jean-Adam Moehler (1796-1838) dans la question du développement du dogme,* in Ephemerides Theologiae Lovanienses, (vol. XVI, 1939, pp. 248-291).

9. McKenna, P., O.P.: The Theology of Faith (Dublin, 1914). See pp. 248-291.

10. O'Doherty, E.: Doctrinal Progress and Its Laws (Dublin, 1924).

11. Oxenham, H. N. : Le principe des développements théologiques (Paris, 1909).

12. Pinard, H. : *Dogme*, in Dictionnaire Apologétique de la foi Catholique (Paris, 1910) col. 1151-1182.

13. Prunier : Évolution et immutabilité de la doctrine religieuse de l'Église (Paris, Bloud, 1898).

14. Simonin, H.D. : *Théologie thomiste et développement du dogme*, in Revue thomiste (vol. XVIII, 1935, pp. 537-556).

15. Simonin, H. D. : *"Implicite"* et *"explicite"* dans le développement du dogme, in Angelicum (vol. XIV, 1937, pp. 126-145).

16. Schultes R., O.P.: Introductio in historiam dogmatum (Paris, 1922).

17. Tuyaerts M., O.P.: L'évolution du dogme (Louvain, 1919).